D1095023

Flowers-by-Wire

Flowers-by-Wire

The Story of the

FLORISTS' TELEGRAPH DELIVERY ASSOCIATION

by

MARC WILLIAMS

MERCURY HOUSE
Detroit

COPYRIGHT 1960
MERCURY HOUSE

Library of Congress Catalog Card
Number 60-11565

PRINTED IN UNITED STATES OF AMERICA

Introduction

FTD is many things to many people. To its eleven thousand and more members it is a peculiar mixture of fraternity and essential business service. To the floricultural industry, it is a powerful, cohesive group of retail florists who take the lead in the solution of problems that beset the industry. To the business analyst, it is a modern-day giant in the commercial world. To its world-wide public, because of the familiar emblem—winged Mercury with a bouquet of flowers—FTD is the somewhat mysterious force that propels flowers-by-wire just about anywhere man goes—and guarantees that they will get there. To me, it is my life.

I suppose that is why I have been asked to acquaint the reader with the contents of this book. How I would have embraced this remarkable publication just a little more than four years ago! When informed that I was being considered for the position of Executive Secretary and General Manager of FTD, I was residing in the nation's capital. Frantically, I sought a source of information about my would-be employer. In the Library of Congress I discovered a complete file of the Association's monthly magazine, the FTD NEWS. For weeks I pored over those old volumes, learning the hard way the information and history that is so conveniently set down for you in this book.

That was my beginning with FTD. Most of you preceded me into the Association, but I know you will be as thrilled as I was when you review the proud story of your FTD through the pages of FLOWERS-BY-WIRE. With remarkable insight and objectivity, author Marc Williams introduces you to an intrepid group of florists who pioneered the flowers-by-wire concept to a waiting world. From a faltering beginning, bulwarked only by vision and a certain characteristic stubbornness, one sees the emergence of a new, distinctive force — a power to make the glory and loveliness of flowers available to 20th century man throughout the world.

I don't think this book will mean much to a reader who has not been a part of the flower industry in America. I am not so sure it will be too meaningful to the reader who has never been a member or an employee in an FTD shop. But, if you have been "FTD," settle back for a solid treat that will touch every emotional fiber in your body. Although a relative newcomer to FTD circles, I felt the early pains endured by the founders; I thrilled to the emergence and hearty public acceptance of a new idea in sending flowers over great distances literally in minutes.

There is all of the excitement of a Pier Nine brawl over such issues as the Clearing House, the service charge, and elections of national officers — with the charm of gentlemen who accept the verdict, clap the other fellow on the back and, with renewed admiration forged from serious combat, go forward together to new achievements, new satisfactions.

You're not "FTD" if you don't get a big lump in your throat as the founding order gives way to the new — the old giants stepping aside in favor of young, vigorous leadership that accepts with pride the responsibility of carrying the elite florists of the United States and Canada to untold heights in business accreditation and economic success.

This is something of the spirit and feeling that grew in me during those first days in Washington when I talked to Granville Gude and his lovely sister, Amelia Gude Thomas, in the back of their store on "F" street. "Oh," as Eddie McCarthy would say, "the book's a grand yarn." And there are still a lot of you around who've lived it. There's no question that it's going to make you the proudest member of your community.

For those of us who have come recently to the FTD scene, I suppose we might feel cheated, save for the stirring saga recorded in the pages to follow. There aren't many new ideas in the world, and there hardly seems time, much less fifty years, in which to run up so proud a record. But, we can doff our hats to the likes of the Andersons, the Bertermanns, Baum, Brietmeyer, the Gude family, Gammage, Grakelow, Knoble, Lang, Luke, Penn, the Pochelons, Rock, Sceery, Schling, Valentine and an almost endless list of great florists who stand as pillars of strength and wisdom along the upward path of FTD. We can know them all through the pages of this book and be so much richer for having met them here.

JOHN L. BODETTE

Detroit, Michigan
June 1, 1960

Author's Preface

SELDOM is a writer afforded the pleasure that has been mine in preparing and writing this story. Through this work I have been introduced to fifty years of the life of an association of men and women who are of a type I have never before encountered. Florists are different: they are at once stubborn and sentimental, frugal and generous, independent and closely associated. Their trade organization, the Florists' Telegraph Delivery Association, has had fifty years of remarkable and exciting growth. Among nonprofit associations it is a phenomenon.

Starting in 1910 with fifteen members, it has developed through the dedication and vision of its members into a world-wide organization of some 25,000 florists, closely linked by telegraph, telephone, and other communication services, through which a customer in any city can, within a few hours, have fresh flowers delivered to an address in any one of 188 countries.

The path of FTD to its present prominence has not been unfailingly smooth and pleasant. The exigencies of wars, the cutbacks of depression periods, and the natural fluctuations of business cycles have had their effects. In the hands of less skillful management, the organization might have faltered or failed, but its almost unvarying upward course points to the thorough dedication and hard work of its members and their elected representatives. They have willingly sacrificed self for the good of the whole and the result shows in the strength and reputation of the Florists' Telegraph Delivery Association.

Research for this story has been conducted through the verbatim minutes of the many conventions, Board meetings, committee reports, correspondence and clippings available in the Detroit offices. I am also indebted to the memories of the many members I have interviewed for their word-pictures of the early organizers and the many exciting events in the life and growth of the Association. The office staffs at FTD Headquarters and at the Society of American Florists have given generously in time and material to help me clear up vague and incompletely documented points. To all of them, I extend my heartfelt thanks.

This book does not purport to be a complete history of the Florists' Telegraph Delivery Association, but the story of its founding and development to its present importance. I shall be very happy if your enjoyment in reading it approaches that which I have had in writing it.

Marc Williams

Detroit, Michigan
May 15, 1960

Contents

CHAPTER ONE

Toward a Wider Horizon

I T WAS TO widen their sphere of service, that the florists of America years ago began to search for a way to transmit their products over the whole country and supply people, wherever they might be, with fresh flowers.

They were faced with two problems: limited transportation facilities and the perishable nature of their commodity. Although some success had been achieved by packing flowers in ice and shipping them by express, it was a hit-or-miss method, frequently a failure. It was vital to the development of the trade that a practical method of transmission be devised.

What enterprising florist first thought of telegraphing his colleague in the next town and asking him to deliver flowers from his own stock is not known. Whoever he was, he had hit upon the only way of delivering fresh flowers over great distances. He had opened up the whole world to an important service. He had laid the first tile in the groundwork of the Florists' Telegraph Delivery Association.

The year 1884 was not favorable to the launching of new enterprises. The expansion of business which followed the Civil War was beginning to abate. Banks, over-extended in the first flush of Northern victory, were tottering. By all the signs, the country stood on the brink of a severe industrial depression.

But even in the face of impending business collapse, the fact of American progress was apparent. Employment was

11

still high. For the first time since Columbus, the urban
population exceeded the rural. Inventions, designed to benefit all branches of industry, were being patented daily. Edison
was beginning his career. Westinghouse, Eastman, Burbank
and Bell were becoming familiar household names.

It was then that the Society of American Florists and
Ornamental Horticulturists was organized.

Being obviously to the benefit of every single member of
the floricultural profession, the Society was warmly welcomed. It gained a representative membership almost immediately. National conventions were well attended. Problems
common to all florists were considered by the best brains
in the business. Much valuable advice was made available to
all members.

Enthusiasm for SAF continued to grow. But it was soon
realized by some of the members that there was a divergence
of interests, inseparable from an organization so widely
based. The problems of the grower and wholesaler were not
necessarily those of the retailer. In some instances, those
interests were opposed, even competitive. The grower was
concerned with the culture and production of flowers; the
wholesaler with a limited distribution. But the retailer, who
was the true, professional florist, was faced by the buying
public. It was he who must appraise the public demand,
must educate the populace in the acceptance of flowers as
suitable gifts, must please the fickle purchaser not only with
fresh and lovely flowers, but with prompt delivery, attractive
packaging, plus all the counsels and services peculiar to the
retail trade.

These differences plainly existed. But no mention of an
organization, devoted exclusively to the retail trade, was
heard in the councils of SAF. The problem confronting
the retailers was the broadening of their range of service.
How were they to expand their business unless they could
increase the territory over which they might distribute?

How might they rush flowers everywhere in fresh-cut condition on arrival?

Telegraphing flower orders had already been attempted on a limited scale. Florists well-known to each other, whose credit and reputation for payment could be trusted, had done some experimenting. Some such arrangements had long existed, not without success. Mindful of these private transactions, an organization was proposed within SAF to enlist all members in a flowers-by-wire plan.

In 1892, at the SAF convention in Washington, D.C., a tentative plan was drawn up, looking to the delivery of flowers by telegraph order. But there was no constitutional provision made, or any procedure established, able to guarantee the payment of bills rendered by delivering florists. Defaults developed. So, the arrangement died of its own imperfections. Other similar plans were undertaken over several years. They, too, were unsuccessful.

The need for such an arrangement was pressing. There were many men in SAF, with profitable businesses in their own cities, who had risen both financially and politically, and realized that their only areas of expansion lay in other cities. Two objections were apparent to this: expense and the loss of direct supervision. A workable long distance arrangement was imperative.

Some effort had been made toward separate retailers' meetings at the annual SAF conventions. But in most cases these were found to conflict with the general meetings and little benefit came of them.

The SAF convention was held in Cincinnati in November, 1909. J. A. Valentine, of Denver, was president. He was also much interested in the welfare of the retailers, although himself a grower. Since 1898 he had been general manager of the vast Park Floral Company enterprises in Denver, a grower-wholesaler-retailer combine. In his capacity as president, he called a separate meeting of retailers and, according to the minutes of the meeting, "read a carefully prepared address discussing trade conditions, the need for a florists' delivery association, and suggesting in a general way methods in which the organization might be formed."

Twenty members of SAF attended the meeting. Valentine had circulated letters to all retailers informing them of his plans and several replies from those unable to attend were read to the assembly. The sentiment of all was in favor of the proposed organization. Irwin Bertermann of Indianapolis, who was serving as chairman of the meeting while Valentine presented his paper, was instructed to appoint a committee of not less than four members, with Valentine as chairman, to "take such steps as may be necessary to prepare a program and have it put in force at the Rochester convention in 1910."

Bertermann appointed the following to the committee: J. A. Valentine, chairman; William F. Gude, Washington; Philip Breitmeyer, Detroit; W. J. Palmer, Buffalo; Ernst Wienhoeber, Chicago; John Bertermann, Indianapolis; and W. L. Rock, Kansas City; with W. N. Rudd, Morgan Park, Ill., to serve as secretary. These men represented the best business analysts in the floral industry, as did the other members at the meeting. Each of them was a successful, operating florist.

So, for the first time in history, an attempt to form a telegraph-delivery arrangement was made under the official sanction of the SAF. The presence of President Valentine and his penetrating discussion of the retailers' problems had lent this meeting a status not achieved before. The urgent need manifested with increasing force since the earlier haphazard efforts at organization sent members away from the meeting aware of the dawning of the year of decision. The events to come in the next twelve months would, they knew, determine whether the florists' trade was to be restricted to local operation, or to face the future with no limit on its expansion.

J. A. Valentine was not a man to expect his committee to do all the work. He was peculiarly equipped to direct the

formation of the new organization. He was of more than average size, with broad shoulders. He was a deliberate man, not much given to humor. His forehead was high and his slightly greying hair, parted on the side, was combed loosely back in an erratic wave. His steady, penetrating eyes looked out through small, steel-rimmed spectacles. His sweeping mustache covered a generous mouth.

He was a graduate of the University of Iowa, subsequently entering a law office to read for the bar. Not satisfied in that field, he embarked on the railroad construction business, both of which endeavors seem to have developed his organizational ability. Moving to Denver, he succeeded A. B. Seaman as owner and general manager of the Park Floral interests. Soon he had this operation running so smoothly and his employees so well trained that he was able to leave the active supervision for weeks at a time.

It was this fortunate state of affairs that so notably benefited FTD in its early years. After the 1909 convention, Valentine went back to Denver resolved to complete the organization of FTD before the next convention in Rochester.

He traveled widely, interviewing florists in many cities for ideas and suggestions looking to a successful telegraph delivery system. He analyzed their doubts and misgivings. He devised a practical billing method. And he was meanwhile estimating the degree of supervision and control to which the average florist, a businessman of independent mind, would submit. Back in Denver, he collated all this information and began his study.

Later that year, at the Chicago Flower Show, Valentine spoke with retailers from the East and Midwest, testing his theories and ideas about the association and noting their reactions to his suggestions.

On January 27, 1910, at a meeting of the Carnation Society in Pittsburgh, a group of interested retailers met to discuss the telegraph delivery idea. Said Valentine later, "I think

not over six or eight were there altogether, and we organized in a preliminary sort of way."

This resulted in the election of temporary officers, after which an adjournment was made, subject to the call of the president. Officers elected at this first meeting, to serve until the regular election in Rochester, were: J. A. Valentine, president; W. J. Palmer, vice-president; H. B. Dorner, secretary; and W. L. Rock, treasurer. Nine directors, in groups of three each, were elected. The first group consisted of A. B. Cartledge, Philadelphia; William F. Gude, Washington; and Fred H. Meinhardt, St. Louis, and was to serve for one year. Elected to serve for two years were Philip Breitmeyer, Detroit; Ernst Wienhoeber, Chicago; and George Asmus, Chicago. The three year group was composed of W. L. Rock, Kansas City; Irwin Bertermann, Indianapolis; and John Bertermann, Indianapolis. This arrangement provided for a directorate in which members would serve staggered three-year terms, beginning in 1913.

No further business was conducted. All were content to wait until the SAF convention met in Rochester later in the year, in the hope that a larger group, more representative of the retail branch, would be present to discuss and examine the entire question.

Valentine went back to Denver and began to draw up the Constitution and Bylaws of Florists' Telegraph Delivery.

CHAPTER TWO

The First Meeting

THE MONTHS preceding the 1910 Rochester convention of SAF had some remarkable features. Halley's Comet flamed in the sky, a visitor from outer space which some thought to herald the end of the world, believing that when the earth passed "through the tail of the comet," it would be burned in compliance with Biblical prophecy.

Ty Cobb won the batting championship of the American League for the first time. Christy Mathewson, the immortal pitcher of the Giants, was almost unbeatable in the other circuit.

Women minced along the streets in narrow hobble skirts and loose blouses featuring wide kimono sleeves.

The population of the United States passed 90,000,000 and scientific and industrial progress was at its peak. Synthetic rubber came into use. There was a new product called rayon. Completely automatic breadmaking machinery came into limited commercial importance. The first decade of the century drew to a close, with the automobile industry reaching the foremost rank. The airplane began to loom as a possible competitor.

There was an air of expectancy apparent in the small group of florists that met in a parlor on the second floor of the Hotel Seneca in Rochester during a recess of SAF. President Valentine of Florists' Telegraph Delivery had issued the call for the meeting to be held at 10 a.m. Thursday,

August 18, 1910, and a single room would have easily accommodated those who attended. Present were: Valentine, Vice-President W. J. Palmer, Secretary H. B. Dorner (who was also secretary of the SAF), John and Irwin Bertermann, Alfred T. Bunyard, William C. Gloeckner, I. L. Pillsbury, J. F. Ammann, George Asmus, Fred H. Meinhardt, J. T. Temple and Homer Wiegand — all members of SAF. Also attending were two representatives of the trade press, H. B. Howard of the FLORISTS' REVIEW and W. J. Stewart of HORTICULTURE. Sitting on the fringe of the group was another man, M. H. Elvidge, who had come on a matter of much importance to himself.

President Valentine must have felt disappointment at the handful of interested retailers who gathered at his call. He and others of the Pittsburgh group had been in correspondence with American florists everywhere regarding this meeting, ever since the temporary organization at Pittsburgh. They were urged to attend the Rochester convention and to realize the importance of the proposals to be considered. But, the SAF was a grower-dominated organization. The retailers who attended were, in most instances, also growers. Valentine had specifically said, both in 1909 and at Pittsburgh, that one of his prime interests in the retail organization was to get more retailers into SAF.

He repeated that thought, as he called the meeting to order. He said, "When I was elected temporary president, I was also president of SAF and I was looking around to find out the reasons why our membership in SAF was not larger. I found that the proportion of retailers in that organization was very small, and it seemed to me as though we could, through some incentive as this, induce more retail florists to join the parent organization."

That is not to say that he was not deeply interested in the organization and promotion of FTD. But it is doubtful that even he, with his fine business mind, even vaguely foresaw the importance of the proposed telegraph delivery project. In the time since the Pittsburgh meeting, he had drawn up a proposed Constitution and Bylaws for FTD. In this, his foresight was evident. The two documents anticipated many of the problems that would arise, and provided means for dealing with them. He had had folders printed, setting forth the Constitution and Bylaws and outlining a form of clearing house and trust-fund arrangement, which was entirely original and surprisingly workable, even today. He had placed these folders in the hands of some before the meeting. He now distributed copies to all present.

Valentine ended his opening remarks by saying, "I would like to have some of you give your views now as to what you think we ought to do and how we should proceed further; whether you are interested enough to go ahead along active lines, and whether it is possible to go ahead and get members on the lines laid down in this little folder."

The Clearing House plan outlined in the folder called for three kinds of payment by members. First, there was a $5 membership fee to be charged each florist who chose to join. This was not a dues payment, but accompanied the application for membership. Next, and most important, was a payment into what Valentine termed a "trust fund and a guarantee fund." The amount of this was determined by the population of the city where the florist had his business, at approximately twenty cents per 1,000 persons, with a minimum payment of $5. Thus a florist in a city of 25,000 or less would pay $5, a man in a city of 100,000 would be charged $20, etc. This would make the trust payment for a florist in New York City, which then had a population of 3,500,000, come to $700.

William Gloeckner held up the folder. "I have not had time to study it out very well," he said, "but I would like to know what this money is to be used for, this trustee fund? I would like a little more explanation."

"I will be glad to explain," said Valentine. "In the first place, that $700 is an estimate of the amount to be paid by

New York, and the first member who comes in will pay that amount. If some other New Yorker comes in he will pay one-half of that, to be refunded to the first man that came in. If a third man comes in, he will pay one-third and a proportional refund will be made to the other two men, so that each fellow will have the same amount on deposit and the total deposit for the city will remain constant at all times."

"May I ask whether the intention is to put so much on deposit and then reserve a certain amount for running expenses?"

"Yes, you will have your regular dues in addition to that deposit," Valentine replied. He explained that, under his plan, each member would pay as annual dues an amount equal to 10 per cent of the amount he had on deposit. For instance, if only one man in New York was a member and paid the entire deposit of $700, his annual dues would be $70.

Valentine went through all the provisions of the folder. The others listened, with an occasional question. The President carefully answered each. It was evident that he had spent much time and thought on his plan.

"If we perfect this organization," asked Gloeckner, "as fast as we get in new members, will the older members be notified that such new members have been elected?"

"Most assuredly," said Valentine emphatically. "This organization is going to be strong enough to publish our membership as a standing advertisement in each trade paper in the country. The more retail florists seeing this list published, the more will realize it is to their benefit to join."

"We could probably make arrangements with the trade papers for an alphabetically arranged list in a special department by itself," suggested W. J. Palmer. "I believe we would find that that page would bring more members to our Association." Mr. Palmer visualized one page of a trade publication as sufficient space to carry the names of all the members of FTD.

W. B. Howard of the FLORISTS' REVIEW assured the meeting, "It can be easily arranged whenever you get ready."

Pillsbury said, "I suppose that until it is thoroughly worked up, three-fourths of the orders would have to go to florists who are not members of the organization. But some arrangement could be made to notify our members that their bills were not paid. They can be advertised with the rest of the members."

Valentine was quick to see the danger in this procedure. "I'm afraid in that case you might be up against the blacklist proposition," he cautioned. "We should not create a situation that will compel any one of our members to give his order to any other. You are going to benefit greatly from fellow members. But it would be poor policy to require a man to do all the business in your town with you, exclusively. I saw that thing worked out in the old Association, in which there was one concern that said, 'These orders *have* to come to us,' so they filled them in a slovenly manner."

Valentine here put his finger on one of the reasons for the earlier failures. Efforts had been made to reserve exclusive rights to telegraph business to just one man in each town. It was to avoid that pitfall that he spent so much time and effort. He had been a florist manager since 1898, handling a large operation in a large city, and realized that open competition was essential.

W. J. Palmer took the floor. "I would like to ask," he said, "what effect it would have on the Association if a man were to receive an order for a casket blanket from a man located in a city of 150,000, his initiation dues being $30. We all know that a casket blanket cannot be made for $30. I refer to this because I received such an order one time and I immediately wired back stipulating a certain price. I received an answer, 'Go ahead and make it as fine as you can.' Now, it happened that when this man got his bill, the amount was higher than he expected and I had to wait several years before I got my money. In such a case how is this Association going to pay my bill to an amount greater than that deposited by the party?"

"That is easily answered," replied Valentine, "because it provides here," indicating the folder, "that it shall be taken out of the general guarantee fund which is made up of the fees from each member."

Valentine pictured the Association as vital enough to the florist business that pressure brought by the group on any individual would force him to maintain his credit standing in preference to being dropped.

J. F. Ammann next suggested, "I believe that, among the men in small communities, it would be unusual for such expensive orders to be sent in."

Valentine was cautious. "That is probably true. Still there are people with luxurious tastes in small towns."

"The average order would not exceed the amount of the deposit," continued Ammann. "Anything above $25 or $30 is rare, especially when the order is sent away."

"At any rate," said Valentine, "Mr. Palmer would be in a better position in our organization than outside it. If he were a member, he would not be taking any chance. The chance would be the Association's, spread over the entire membership."

The discussion then turned to M. H. Elvidge of New York, who was in the act of forming the "International Floral Service," which had for its purpose the establishment of a wire service for florists, similar to that proposed by Valentine. Elvidge was a businessman and salesman. He favored a corporation which would limit its membership to one florist in each city, who would command all the city's telegraph business. In return, the florist would pay to Elvidge an amount much in excess of what Valentine thought adequate. Elvidge's plan was the direct opposite of what Valentine thought best for the florist business. Valentine believed that any profit realized by such an organization should be for the benefit of the florist members. He did not approve of only one florist in each city being eligible. He thought that free competition would promote better service and that exclusiveness would cause the service to deteriorate.

Elvidge had explained his plan to Valentine, and had been in correspondence with other florists. He had come to the convention with his plans. Apparently he had not attempted to place them before SAF on the convention floor.

Although Valentine did not agree with any aspect of Elvidge's proposal, he felt it should be placed before the meeting. He introduced Elvidge, saying, "I have told Mr. Elvidge that, at the proper time, we would be glad to have him tell his side. I know nothing of his financial standing, or that of the concern which he represents. He is ready to have you look into the matter and is willing to refer you to the commercial organizations. Some of the trade papers have already investigated his standing."

Valentine then went on to state his position. "I cannot quite see," he said, "how we can carry out our ideas by co-operating with Mr. Elvidge. It seems to me that his ideas and ours are in conflict. I had quite a long talk with him, trying to reach some common ground. I could not find it. But I am not going to decide for you gentlemen. If Mr. Elvidge can show you a better scheme than ours, or that his can be allied with ours, I am not going to stand in his way."

Elvidge was now in a position where he must present his plan to the group. It was apparent that Valentine had maneuvered him into this position and he would have to explain a plan which was not too firmly set in his own mind.

As Elvidge talked it became plain that he had not sufficiently investigated the business possibilities of his organization. His speech was rambling. He promised that he would spend "a great deal of money in a publicity campaign." He was not sure of the amount that each member-florist would have to pay. "But," he said, "I judge for a city like this (Rochester) it would be $75 to $100."

Elvidge concluded by saying, "I don't know that I can

explain more thoroughly, except that my strongest point will be a publicity campaign."

This was not a convincing description of a thoroughly planned business organization in comparison with Valentine's completely conceived plan.

Valentine now took up the question of comparative costs. Under the Valentine plan, the deposit required from the city of Rochester, with approximately 200,000 population, was only $40, on the basis of 20 cents per 1,000. He said to Elvidge, "As I understand it, you were speaking of $70 for a city of this size. Did you mean that as a specific charge?"

"I had not estimated the exact amount," said Elvidge, "but I judge it would be around $50 to $75. In other words, it would be a yearly charge, similar to Dun and Bradstreet, or cable service, or anything of that kind."

Irwin Bertermann, who had listened silently, then came to Elvidge's defense. "I feel that Mr. Elvidge's plan is going to do us some good," he said. "Any agitation of the floral business will do good, whether we co-operate with him or not. He has begun the plan at a time when there is a need, a need for some proper association of this kind. Whether we join with him or not, the country is large and there may be room for two organizations. Any movement of this kind helps the floral business."

George Asmus was dubious. "While Mr. Elvidge's plan would seem favorable, if we did not have our own movement on foot," he said, "I for one believe in home insurance. I believe that having the retailers pay their bills through our medium is better than trusting to one man who is making a business out of it. I would like to see the Association formed on the lines first proposed through the SAF, because I believe in the Society and its retail aspect. I believe we are more capable, as a body, of doing this than is any individual whose principal project is to derive a profit."

Elvidge was on his feet immediately. "I wish to refer to one statement made by the gentleman," he said. "He thinks that an organization is in a better position to handle this than an individual. I cannot agree, for this reason: If I needed an engine repaired I would not hire a carpenter. We must conduct this enterprise on a plain business basis. I have made arrangements to put up at least $15,000 as a beginning to promote interstate membership through salesmen traveling from town to town. This will require some months. It should not be a question of my making money out of it, but whether I am going to benefit the florists. And I believe, after showing Mr. Valentine, your president, what we propose, that he will not hesitate to take on the agency for Denver and pay $50 for it. I would be glad to pay $50 the first year and every year thereafter."

Elvidge was capable in an argument. He insisted, however, that he had not come to the convention to present his plan. It was his plan to button-hole the members privately, sounding them out on their attitude toward such an organization. He seems not to have known that Valentine had been working for a year on the rules by which FTD was to operate.

Homer Wiegand now entered the discussion. He found two elements of Elvidge's plan to be objectionable. "His idea may be good," said Wiegand, "but his one man in a city doesn't strike me. That may be all right for that one man. But where are the rest of our members going to come in? And also that advertising scheme — if you pay $50 for your city now, that $50 is not going to pay for much advertising. I would like to hear from him on that."

"As I said a while ago," Elvidge began, "my plan involves one man in a smaller city. In the larger cities, it might be two or three. I have not yet perfected those details."

This admission was damaging to the Elvidge cause. It strengthens the belief that Valentine, knowing why Elvidge had come to the meeting, had forced him to expose the weakness of his preparation. This, of course, would make Valentine's completely organized plan more attractive to the members. It is evident that Valentine had no thought of advantage for himself. He simply believed that the florists should be the ones to organize and direct their own telegraph delivery system.

Irwin Bertermann, a strong force in SAF as he later became in FTD, still advised consideration for Elvidge's plan. "I feel that a plan of this kind should not be abruptly cast aside," he said. "I have always believed that competition is the life of trade. Mr. Valentine, with many of our members, has worked this out and given it much thought. It is for us to put it in working condition. If we find, in a year's time, that Elvidge has a better organization and, if our directors feel that our business is not what it might be, then I will be willing to leave it in their hands to take whatever steps they decide upon."

Bertermann's insistence of fairness toward Elvidge's proposition should not be interpreted as opposition, either to Valentine personally or to his plan. Valentine was the immediate past-president of SAF, well-known in that organization, as he was in the industry. Bertermann was a young man, both in the floral business and SAF. His star was destined to rise and he himself to be president of SAF in 1922-23. He was not in a position to oppose Valentine politically at this time. Bertermann was one of the great believers in publicity for the florist industry. He was convinced that, if two organizations were formed, the competition for members would bring sharply to the attention of both florists and the public the existence of a system of flowers-by-wire. More florists would join and more customers would seek the service. This attention to publicity, which was a part of Bertermann's sense of business, was to become a significant factor in the ultimate development of FTD.

Bertermann's remarks brought the morning meeting to a close. H. B. Dorner announced that the SAF meeting was waiting for them to join it, and he asked permission to take the stenographer with him.

Valentine closed the morning session by announcing,

"There is a great deal still to come before this meeting. We have only started. It is a help to us to have this stenographer present and to have these notes, so that they can be published in the report of SAF. We want our proceedings to go in with yours."

A stenographer's note is appended to the transcript of the meeting, stating that the members mentioned as present were those that were there when the meeting opened. He notes that "one or two gentlemen may have come in later whose names were not secured. At the afternoon session, positively all those present were noted."

And so the first organizational meeting of FTD ended without the formal organization being perfected. It was evident, however, that nothing stood in the way of the plan. Only details were left for discussion. Had Elvidge had his plan more developed, perhaps his presentation would have had more effect. Valentine's opposition was counteracted somewhat by Bertermann's willingness to endorse it. But George Asmus, the incoming president of SAF, no doubt expressed the will of the majority in desiring that such an organization be formed within SAF. Later developments bore this out.

The afternoon meeting was called to order by Valentine. J. T. Temple and Homer Wiegand did not attend, but five members came who were not at the morning meeting: E. P. Tracey, Albany; DeForest W. Ludwig, Pittsburgh; George M. Geraghty, Toronto; Fred C. Weber, St. Louis and H. E. Smith, Danville, Ill. Fifteen florists were at the second session.

Elvidge was present, and it is evident that he had been busy during the recess interviewing leading members of SAF, including William Gude of Washington and Thomas F. Galvin of Boston. Galvin had consented to become a member of the board of Elvidge's proposed corporation.

Valentine said to the meeting, "We must decide how much, if any, more time we will give to this proposition of Mr. Elvidge's. It is my impression that we have given about

as much time as we can afford. Mr. Elvidge has asked for a
moment to state his position finally. I think we can give him
that, and then decide whether we wish to proceed with other
things, or to proceed with him."

Elvidge made his final presentation. He quoted George
Asmus, the incoming president of SAF, making the suggestion that the group appoint a committee to confer with
Elvidge; and that a report from the committee be ready for
the Boston meeting of SAF in March.

Valentine called for a motion either to appoint the committee or lay the matter on the table. John Bertermann
moved that the matter be tabled. The motion carried. Thus
Elvidge left the meeting and his plans faded from the FTD
scene.

Irwin Bertermann now moved that the Constitution and
Bylaws drafted by Valentine be adopted, including the name
of the organization — "The Florists' Telegraph Delivery."

The matter of the name provoked one of Valentine's rare
excursions into humor. Several members thought that the
word, "Retail," should be included in the title. Valentine
was a man who liked his own way. He had given much
thought, not only to the rules and procedure of the organization, but also to the name. He was not to be swayed easily.
Various suggestions were put forward by the members.
Valentine listened to them all and then said, "All you gentlemen are going to use the title in your advertising, to show
that you are members. The briefer the name is, the more
convenient. I am reminded of an organization that was
started out in our town. They organized what was called the
Denver and Lookout Mountain Resort, Land, Transit and
Improvement Company. It took a man half a day to sign
a check."

It was not hard, during the laughter that followed, to get
the motion carried that established the name suggested by
Valentine.

The attention now turned to the election of officers and

directors. Pillsbury moved that the same officers and directors who had been elected at the preliminary meeting in Pittsburgh be confirmed for the first year of the Association.

"The Board of Directors, as I understand it, are elected for varying terms," said Ammann. "You might elect the officers and then take up the directors afterwards."

"I second the motion as to the president, vice-president and secretary, and the directors that are on here for one year," said Gloeckner, indicating the list mentioned in Valentine's folder.

Valentine demurred. "Gentlemen," he said, "if you will allow me I would like to put that in a different way. I do not wish to serve as president of this organization another year. I have put in almost a year's work, talking, working and boosting. I would like to have somebody else continue that. While I am enthusiastic, I am beginning to get a little tired. It is much better to have your executive officer from some central point than from way out in the Rocky Mountains."

"For that very reason, you should be the president," said Pillsbury.

"It is your pet scheme," said Gloeckner, "and I think you ought to serve as president for another year, until you get us on our feet."

Valentine gave in. "I always try to be a good soldier," he said, "and I want you to understand that in that spirit I take it." There was a genuine and hearty round of applause. "As I understand it, the motion was to confirm the election of the officers whose names are set down here for the respective terms for which they are designated," continued the president. "There appears to be an oversight there in not designating which were to serve for what length of term. I do not know certainly which of these directors were elected for how long. Do any of you know?"

"I do not," said Rock. "I did not make a memorandum of it at the time."

"I have a little notebook that I kept notes in," said Valentine. "It shows that the directors elected at that time at Pittsburgh for three years were W. L. Rock and John Bertermann; for two years, Ernst Wienhoeber and Philip Breitmeyer; for one year, A. B. Cartledge and W. F. Gude. The motion is then that the officers as stated here and the directors for these terms, shall be confirmed and continued for another year, or until our next annual meeting." The motion carried.

Valentine was mistaken. At the Pittsburgh meeting, in addition to the directors mentioned, Meinhardt had been elected to serve the one-year term, Asmus for two years and Irwin Bertermann for three years. But as will be seen, the result was the same.

"We should elect three more directors," announced Valentine. "I think nominations will be in order."

"I nominate Irwin Bertermann for a three-year term," said Rock.

"Isn't one Bertermann enough?" asked John Bertermann.

"No," stated Rock, "I think we could use the whole Bertermann family."

"I nominate George Asmus for director for two years," said Ammann.

"I would like to see Mr. Ammann on that board," John Bertermann said.

"I am only a little country florist," protested Ammann, who came from Edwardsville, Illinois. "I would rather see the cities represented. I would nominate F. H. Meinhardt as a director for one year."

Valentine announced the nominations and, in doing so, disregarded John Bertermann's nomination of Ammann. It is not possible to say, at this late date, whether this was an intentional oversight. Valentine was a strong-willed man. It could be that he agreed with Ammann that the cities should be represented, because he saw a great opportunity for the expansion of the membership in the cities. It is also

FTD PRESIDENTS

J. A. VALENTINE
Denver, Colorado
1910-1912

IRWIN BERTERMANN
Indianapolis, Indiana
1912-1916

WILLIAM F. GUDE
Washington, D. C.
1916-1919

PHILIP BREITMEYER
Detroit, Michigan
1919-1922

EDWARD SCEERY
Paterson, New Jersey
1922-1924

CHARLES H. BROWN
New York, New York
1924-1926

FTD PRESIDENTS

WILLIAM J. SMYTH
Chicago, Illinois
1926-1928

CHARLES H. GRAKELOW
Philadelphia, Pennsylvania
1928-1930

THOMAS C. LUKE
Portland, Oregon
1930-1932

FRANK J. BAKER
Utica, New York
1932-1934

OTTO LANG
Dallas, Texas
1934-1936

ERNEST S. SIMMONS
Toronto, Ontario
1936-1938

FTD PRESIDENTS

WILLARD CRAIN
Cincinnati, Ohio
1938-1940

WILLIAM E. JOY
Columbus, Georgia
1940-1946

EDWARD J. McCARTHY
Brooklyn, New York
1946-1948

H. ROLLO MUELLER
Columbia, Missouri
1948-1950

GRANVILLE GUDE
Washington, D. C.
1950-1952

JAMES LAWRIE
Toronto, Ontario
1952-1954

FTD PRESIDENTS

ED LUDWIG
Pittsburgh, Pennsylvania
1954-1955

VICTOR STEIN
San Francisco, California
1955-1956

MRS. MARION FISHER
Syracuse, New York
1956-1957

EUGENE R. DAUDELIN
Chicago, Illinois
1957-1958

STANLEY C. MINSHALL
St. Petersburg, Florida
1958-1959

IRVING ALLEN
Bremerton, Washington
1959-1960

possible that, in the general discussion, he did not hear Bertermann's nomination of Ammann.

Irwin Bertermann was elected for the three-year term, George Asmus for two years and Fred H. Meinhardt for the one-year term. This is exactly the result that the election in Pittsburgh had produced. So, Valentine's mistake had rectified itself.

Now once again the thorny question of fees and dues came up, and there seemed to be a reluctance to discuss it.

Bunyard, of New York City, said, "It will be a brave man, who puts up $700 and waits for someone to take the burden off his shoulders. I would like to be that man myself, but it looks pretty big to me."

"I think that New York City should not be represented by more than three or four," suggested Palmer.

"I think that any good florist who is doing any kind of a business now, would not want to be outside this organization," continued Bunyard.

Rock was doubtful. "You would be surprised," he said, "how they talk about that. I spoke to some of the leading florists in New York. They say they do not want to go into it. That looks funny to me."

The talk now drifted away from the question of fees. Valentine verified Rock's doubt. He told them that he had written to the florists in New York whom he knew and had received a reply from only one — "a very evasive sort of answer," he called it. Two or three replies had come in from Philadelphia, and one prominent florist there frankly said that he did not want to join the organization.

Geraghty now asked if the advantages of FTD would extend into Canada, and Valentine assured him that they would.

Valentine brought the discussion back to the point with: "What disposition will you make in regard to this question of the fees to be paid?"

"I think we could safely leave that in the hands of our

Board of Directors, or whatever you might call them,"
suggested Gloeckner.

"Will you put that in the form of a motion?" Valentine
asked him.

"Yes, sir."

Before the motion was put to the meeting, Geraghty broke
in, "You take Toronto, for instance, having a population of
300,000 people. That would make it $60 for the first man to
join. Now, would there be $60 profit coming from tele-
graphic orders, so that he could come out even in the year?
I doubt it."

"I'm afraid that Mr. Geraghty is under a wrong impression
about that $60," Valentine said quickly. "If so, let me set
him right. It is not an annual fee, like that proposed to us
this morning by Mr. Elvidge. It is a deposit, in what I call
our deposit fund. If, after a while, you choose to leave the
Association, it will be returned to you, after the expiration
of the time in which bills can be filed with the secretary of
the Association. Bills are guaranteed absolutely to members."

"That is a good thing," agreed Geraghty, "because I have
several bills that I would like to collect. I hope they will all
go into it."

"There is no disposition on our part to make it ex post
facto," warned Valentine.

Valentine now put the motion to refer the matter of dues
and fees to the Board of Directors. The motion carried.

"I would like to ask a question about membership," said
Ammann. "I think there are some of us here who have not
signed up for membership. Can we sign up now and pay our
initiation fee?"

"I do not think we are in a position to do that," Valentine
replied. "The Board of Directors has not yet fixed the basis
upon which we can come in. But you can rest assured that
they are not going to lose much time in asking for your
money."

This was the last statement of the meeting and the group

adjourned without setting a day for a future meeting.

It was not a dramatic occasion. Valentine had skillfully steered the meeting in the way he thought it should go and had accomplished most of his aims. He had avoided the threat of Elvidge's competing organization and had overseen the election of a Board of Directors, interested in the movement and of substance in the florist business in America. He knew that their names would recommend the new FTD to other florists and help assure its future.

Thus, Florists' Telegraph Delivery was organized. There was still much to be done. There were disappointments and lean years ahead. But the motion was started and the ball was rolling. The mists of the future hid the story of success or failure.

CHAPTER THREE

The Early Days

*T*HE NEXT MEETING of the new Florists' Telegraph Delivery again coincided with a meeting of the Society of American Florists. The date was March, 1911, in Boston. Since the original meeting in the preceding August, the retail florists of the country had shown minimum enthusiasm. Despite the obvious need for such an association and all the promotional work done by Valentine and others, only 40 members of SAF had joined.

One of the reasons for this lukewarm attitude of the retailers was the failure of the Board of Directors, elected the year before, to set the amount of dues and guarantees to be assessed against the members. Inquiries of interested retailers went unanswered.

President Valentine called the meeting to order on Wednesday, March 29, 1911, and explained the situation, admitting that little had been accomplished.

H. B. Dorner, pleading the press of his duties as secretary of SAF, submitted his resignation as secretary of the new Association. It was accepted and Irwin Bertermann was elected secretary.

Settlement of the problem of dues was recognized as vital. Valentine therefore appointed a committee, consisting of W. J. Palmer, W. J. Smyth and Will Rock, to work with the president and secretary, with the aim of creating a schedule of dues and guarantees. The discussion occupied the entire morning. When the group adjourned for lunch, no decision had been reached.

At the afternoon session, the consideration was resumed and finally the following rates of guarantee deposits were established:

Cities less than 5,000 . . . . . . $ 1.00

5,000 to 25,000 . . . . 2.50

25,000 to 50,000 . . . . 5.00

50,000 to 100,000 . . . . 10.00

100,000 to 150,000 . . . . 15.00

Cities over 150,000 to be charged $1.00

per 10,000 population up to 500,000.

William F. Gude moved that $50 be the maximum guarantee deposit, regardless of the population above 500,000. The motion carried. Thus the first guarantee fund called for in the Bylaws was established.

Valentine's proposal based upon an approximate payment of 20 cents per 1,000 population was apparently unacceptable. The rates established were reasonable, under current conditions, and probably contributed to the growth of the Association. This was especially true among the smaller operators in the smaller communities.

The annual dues, as distinguished from the guarantee deposit, were set at $1 for cities of less than 5,000; $2 for cities between 5,000 and 200,000; and $5 for cities in excess of 200,000. Eleven new members were secured for FTD at this meeting.

Present at the morning meeting were V. A. Cogill, Fred Meinhardt, Albert Pochelon, W. J. Vesey, Jr., W. L. Rock, E. W. Wienhoeber, W. J. Palmer, W. J. Smyth, S. A. Anderson, G. M. Geraghty, J. A. Valentine, Irwin Bertermann, H. B. Dorner and representatives of the press. In addition, J. Schultz, J. F. Ammann, A. Herr, George Asmus, William F. Gude, W. F. Kasting, Sidney Hoffman, Sr. and H. Penn are listed by Secretary Bertermann as attending the afternoon meeting.

The Association was now ready to solicit membership. Bertermann lost little time. On May 25, 1911, he circularized the retail florists with the following letter:

"Much effort has been put forth to perfect the details of the Florists' Telegraph Delivery so that it may be of much service to all retailers becoming members. The cost has been made most reasonable and the various benefits derived from the Association should more than repay you for becoming a member. We are enjoying the hearty support and cooperation of a large percentage of the prominent retailers of the country so that the complete success of the organization is now assured.

"For your own sake and for ours we would like very much to have you as one of the members. If you are with us in this effort to enlarge our business and to eliminate some of its uncertainties, kindly sign the enclosed card and return with a check for the amount indicated, at an early date, so that your firm may be given the proper amount of publicity.

"If you are not already a member of the S.A.F. it will be necessary to add $5.00 to the amount stated on the card.

Very truly yours,
Irwin Bertermann,
Secretary

"P.S.

Please note that membership fee and deposit in guarantee fund are to be made only once. The annual dues are the only annual expense.

I.B."

It is not known where Bertermann obtained his mailing list or how many names it contained. The letter had little effect in securing members.

When FTD met at the Baltimore convention of SAF, on August 17, 1911, only six members were present. Neither

President Valentine nor Treasurer Rock was there. Those attending were S. A. Anderson, F. H. Meinhardt, Jacob Schultz, August R. Baumer, I. L. Pillsbury and Irwin Bertermann. Meinhardt was named chairman.

Bertermann reported that the organization "was in a prosperous condition; that some forty members had joined since the Rochester meeting and that everything indicated that enough would join to assure a successful organization."

Rock sent his treasurer's report by mail. It showed that the Association had to its credit $1,142; which included the guarantee fund, the annual dues payments and the membership fees.

But Bertermann was optimistic. He reported that "it seemed to be the sense of the meeting that the retailers, while not attending meetings in numbers, were more than willing to become members and to see the organization flourish."

A representative of Western Union addressed the meeting. He asked that his organization be designated the official telegraph company for FTD. He is quoted in the minutes as promising that "his company would be willing to call on all members of the Florists' Telegraph Delivery and urge upon them the many advantages of their service." The meaning of that statement remains obscure. If the Western Union man was promising that representatives would call on retail florists, explaining the advantages of belonging to FTD, he was promising something destined to be the subject of debate among the members of FTD for years. If this was really his meaning, no young and struggling organization could afford to decline the services of a world-wide sales organization, attempting to increase FTD membership. But, if he was only undertaking to sell Western Union service to the present FTD members, then he was offering small consideration for an exclusive right to the business.

Jacob Schultz moved that the proposition be submitted to the officers and the motion carried. This ended the matter for the time. Later on, the possibility of having Western

Union representatives take over the recruiting of FTD members in return for FTD business was a plan that was thoroughly considered.

Because of the small attendance, no election of officers was held in Baltimore. The members instructed Secretary Bertermann to keep them advised of new members, so that their lists of corresponding florists could be kept current. They then adjourned until the following August in Chicago.

Through an oversight, the meeting of FTD was not included in the program of the SAF convention in Chicago, so it could not be called to order until 9:10 p.m. on Wednesday, August 21, 1912, following two sessions of the regular SAF meeting. Consequently, it was a short meeting, but some of its actions are vital in the history of the organization.

The significance of these actions was not apparent at the time. There was little cause for gladness in Secretary Bertermann's report. The membership numbered only 57 retailers, a gain of 17 since the meeting of the year before. And the treasurer's report gave the 16 members present small reason for elation. The treasury showed $1,156.96, a gain of less than $16 for the year. Everybody recognized the vast potential membership. All expressed faith in the future, but those sentiments bore a strong resemblance to whistling past the graveyard.

John Valentine was tired, as he admitted. But the members had enormous affection and respect for the veteran organizer and the efforts he had made. He was nominated for re-election, but he was not to be swayed. Valentine had reluctantly accepted the office at the last election. He now refused to serve, declaring that the office required the talents of a younger and stronger man, and that it was now necessary to conserve his own health. He stated his belief that the SAF secretary was the proper administrative officer for FTD. This view might have caused differences between him and the more independent retail members of FTD.

No one doubted that his experience and advice would continue to be available. His nomination was reluctantly withdrawn.

Irwin Bertermann, upon hearing Valentine's valedictory, said, "Mr. Valentine thinks that the secretary's office might well be merged with that of the secretary of SAF. I do not coincide in this view, but I do agree that we ought to have a new secretary. For that reason I will not again serve another term."

This might imply that Valentine and Bertermann had differed about the conduct of the secretary's office. No evidence of that appears. Valentine merely thought the two organizations could be more closely administered through a common secretary. Bertermann, through his experience, knew how much labor the secretary's office entailed. He believed that the successful promotion of a strong membership for the floundering FTD would require the full time and effort of all the officers, particularly of the secretary.

It was natural, he felt, that the larger and stronger SAF would demand the lion's share of a combined secretary's time. This was not to FTD's advantage. One other thing might have influenced him. Dorner, with whom he was well acquainted as secretary of SAF, had been replaced by John Young. Young was fated to become an excellent secretary, with years of devoted service to SAF. But he was at this time an unknown quantity.

William Rock arose. "I want to say that I will not serve again," he announced. "I think it is too severe a load to take care of your money."

A revolt was growing. The meeting was late at night, following two long days of SAF meetings, the first day having seen three sessions and the second day two, including the election of officers. Everybody was fatigued and tempers had worn thin. The only officer who did not refuse to serve another term was Vice-President W. J. Palmer, who did not attend the convention.

So the demonstrated indifference of retailers to having their own organization and the disagreement over the administration of the young FTD might well have caused abandonment of the enterprise and marked another failure in the efforts to form a flowers-by-wire service.

It was Philip Breitmeyer, well accustomed to such public displays through his experience as mayor of Detroit, who brought order back to the meeting. He was an impressive speaker, tall and distinguished in aspect and manner. He had the faculty of presenting a problem against its background. He rose and waited for attention.

"There is an opportunity for an organization of this kind to do a great deal of work and a great deal of good," he said. "We realize Mr. Valentine's position. We realize that in every position of this kind, which is accepted as an honor, the labor is not always easy. The membership of this Association ought to be greatly increased. Our firm has on its books over 600 florists all over the country, who for the past 10 or 15 years have served us as the members of the Florists' Telegraph Delivery serve each other. We have interchanged orders throughout the United States and Canada. Why the Florists' Telegraph Delivery membership is only about 60, which is 10 per cent of the number we have on our books as correspondents, I cannot understand. As President Valentine has said, there is much work to be done, and if Mr. Valentine does not feel inclined to serve, he should not be forced to, and we should find another good man for the position."

Each listener knew that Breitmeyer was speaking the truth. If his firm had 600 corresponding florists, then there was a potential of 600 listings for each man present, through membership in a strong FTD. With only 57 members in two years, the Association was pitifully short of its possibilities. The baby was sick. Perhaps a transfusion was indicated.

Breitmeyer went on. "I sympathize with Mr. Valentine, because I have often been in a like position. I have been called upon to do much public work. I have offered my services so widely that I feel need of rest. For that reason, I would move that the present secretary, Mr. Bertermann, be elected president of this organization. He is a young man and in the midst of a busy center of the florist business. I believe he could fill the position well. Mr. Valentine has said that he does not want a re-election, and I therefore nominate Mr. Bertermann as president of this organization for the ensuing year."

William Gude immediately seconded the nomination.

Bertermann demurred. "I think perhaps we might do better and get an entire change of officers," he said.

William Rock then moved that the nominations be closed and the motion carried unanimously. In a dramatic turn of events, the man who had refused to serve as secretary found himself president.

Fatigue fell away from the members. They knew that something was happening to the new Association; something of which they wished to be a part.

Nominations were opened for vice-president. The group seemed to turn unconsciously to Breitmeyer. This time he did not rise, but spoke matter-of-factly from his seat, "Since Mr. Gude is away down at the other end of the country, I suggest that we nominate him as vice-president."

The suggestion was seconded and the nominations closed. Breitmeyer, it turned out, was far from through. His next move had probably been planned for some time, but, like a shrewd politician, he knew that he would have to await the proper time to initiate it. Valentine's refusal to accept another term had given Breitmeyer his first opening. Now he must see what course the meeting would take.

Valentine had shown his skill in maneuver, when he had disposed of Elvidge's threat of a rival organization, at Rochester in 1910. He had not forgotten the techniques, and a secretary was still to be chosen. He moved his forces quietly into line.

"I am going to suggest," Valentine said, "that someone

make a motion to cast a unanimous ballot for the remaining officers. You might just as well do it all at once. What Mr. Bertermann has said about my views as to the office of secretary is true. There are reasons why the secretary of SAF might also serve us well, as secretary of this organization. A prime reason for this is that the first question which arises with an application for membership in this organization, is whether the applicant is a member in good standing of SAF. It is a prerequisite for membership in this body that the applicant have previous membership in SAF. Mr. Bertermann has found it necessary to make inquiry of the secretary of SAF, on the matter of eligibility, before he could accept applications. Therefore I think it a good plan to have the secretary of SAF also secretary of this Association. That is a suggestion only. Nominations are now in order."

"It will be hard to elect the secretary of SAF as our secretary here, without his consent," suggested Rock.

"I have discussed that with Mr. Young," replied Valentine. "He is willing to do anything to further our cause."

Gude asked, "Must all our members be members of SAF?"

"That is in our Constitution," said Valentine. "This body was organized as a section of SAF."

That provokes the question whether Valentine foresaw a time when the total of retail florists, who did none of their own growing, and hence could not properly belong to SAF, might actually exceed its membership. He had long been a prominent member of SAF and the Carnation Society, serving as president of each. While he must have recognized the value of FTD to the industry, he may have feared the time when the child outgrew the parent.

"Then I think," said Gude, "that it is well and proper that the SAF secretary should assume that work."

A voice inquired: "Is Mr. Young in business?"

"Mr. Young is not now in business," replied Valentine. "His business is being secretary of SAF. He has no private business at present. Our Bylaws do not require the secretary to be a member of the organization."

Each point which Valentine made in favor of John Young strengthened his position. It was nearing the time when someone, as Valentine had suggested, would rise to nominate the SAF secretary.

If Breitmeyer had a plan, this was the time to propose it, although the circumstances were not so favorable as when he nominated Bertermann. He rose to his impressive height and waited until all eyes had turned toward him. "In view of the fact," he began slowly, as if meditating on a thought that had just occurred to him, "that this organization requires a degree of hustling and work, outside of what the present officers might have done, or would do, would it not be best, this time at least, to select a man other than the present secretary of the SAF?"

He paused, and looked about him, as though expecting an answer. Then, raising his voice, he continued.

"I believe this is an organization that requires a great deal of push on the part of the man selected. I have in mind a young man who I think has the push in him, Mr. Pochelon of Detroit. He is young and energetic, a man who will jump in and work for the interest of the organization. I would like to place in nomination Mr. Albert Pochelon, of Detroit, Michigan!"

Someone seconded the nomination and a motion that the nominations close quickly carried. The issue was settled. The FTD had a secretary of its own, one who could devote full time to the job. Albert Pochelon, whose slogan was "Push along with Pochelon," was ready to begin pushing.

Valentine gave no indication of his disappointment. He waited for the group's attention and then announced: "Next in order is nominations for treasurer."

Breitmeyer rose again. "I move that we all rise," he said, "and ask the man who did the work last year to do it again." The members came to their feet; all but Rock. The group broke into hearty, affectionate applause. After a long moment, Rock's face broke into a slow grin and he shrugged his shoulders in a gesture of resigned acceptance. Gude moved the formality of casting the ballot. Some minutes later, the entire Board of Directors was re-elected by acclamation, and the meeting adjourned.

The importance to FTD of this election cannot be over-emphasized.

Irwin Bertermann had grown up in the florist business in an area which produced, commercially and experimentally, the greatest number of flowers sold in the Midwest.

In William Gude, FTD had secured a champion in the nation's capital who was destined, unofficially, to reach high station in that city. He became the friend of presidents and florist to the White House. He had the ear of high officials and in troublesome times he was a tireless and dedicated worker for the interests of his profession.

Rock was a meticulous record-keeper and careful investor. Under his care, the money entrusted to him was profitably placed. Any small investments which did not produce income for the Association were because of circumstances which no one could foresee or control.

Albert Pochelon was born in Zurich, Switzerland and grew up in Stuttgart, Germany. He had come to the United States at the age of seventeen. He was devoted to the florist industry and to the American concept of business, in which a young man's efforts were the only limitations on his advancement. He brought to each task an enthusiasm which infected all about him with a desire for its successful completion. His ideas ranged far ahead of the present, so that when one goal had been reached, he foresaw the next.

Philip Breitmeyer, wise advisor and a source of strength and vision, was dedicated to the principle of FTD.

As a body, they were a happy blending of the characters and personalities necessary to the future fortune of FTD.

Albert Pochelon lost no time beginning the promotion of the Association among the retail florists. With the concurrence of the other officers and directors, he embarked on an aggressive publicity campaign, to bring the advantages of membership in FTD to every retailer in the country. Letters went out from his floral company to 1,400 florists, urging them to join. Knowing the value of shop talk and gossip, carried from florist to florist by supply salesmen, he enlisted as many of those as possible to preach the gospel of FTD throughout their territories. They agreed to help and the results were apparent almost weekly in increased interest among the retailers.

The secretary sent a roster of FTD florists to every retailer on his list, over the objections of some members who thought those lists should be distributed to members only. Pochelon saw greater good from wider circulation, reasoning that each list was both a bid for business for FTD members and a solicitation to join the Association.

Western Union managers, through their general superintendent, had been delegated to supply Pochelon with lists of florists in their respective towns and also to solicit FTD business and, in so doing, spread the word of the benefits of belonging. A list of foreign florists was in preparation, but the secretary was not yet ready to release it, because it was incomplete. However, he was ready to supply the names of florists in foreign cities upon request.

The success of this campaign was apparent at the next convention of SAF in Minneapolis. The meeting was called to order by President Bertermann on Wednesday afternoon, August 20, 1913. There were only 19 members of FTD present when the meeting began, but others came in later.

In his address, the president stressed the progress that had been made during the year. Membership had increased from 57 florists in 47 towns to 125 members in 95 towns, an increase of more than 100 per cent, and the greatest growth the Association had ever attained in one year. In the matter of finances, the guarantee fund had reached $2,600, from the $1,310 of the year before, and the income from annual dues had risen from $203 to $396, again almost double.

Treasurer Rock's report showed the expenditure of $670.40 for FTD advertising in trade papers. There were four principal florists' journals at that time. The money was about evenly divided among them, with the FLORISTS' EXCHANGE having some advantage.

Pochelon was constantly demanding more publicity in those papers for FTD. At one point in his report to the meeting he said, "The trade papers, who ought to do everything in their power to increase the florist trade, have done, with one exception, very little. It is surprising how little they have done for us. And what a lot of stuff you see in these papers for the benefit of the grower and every other branch but the retailer! And it is the retailer who has to see where the money comes from, to keep the rest going."

This evoked a spirited answer from H. B. Howard of FLORISTS' REVIEW. He pointed out that the papers had done a great deal to publicize FTD, but insisted that publicity should have news value and not become mere editorial advertising. Pochelon was not abashed. He had a great appreciation of the value of publicity and strove continually for editorial space in the national journals and in local and regional papers as well.

It had been a gratifying year for the officers and members of the young Association. From a shaky start and an early history that came near duplicating the former failures, it now appeared that growing interest among retailers and the public in the flowers-by-wire idea, plus an efficient and energetic official corps, had made the success of Florists' Telegraph Delivery much more probable.

At the election of officers, all the incumbents were re-elected, although President Bertermann declared that his office should be given to another. John Bertermann and William Rock, directors whose terms were expiring, were re-elected. Irwin Bertermann immediately resigned as director and Henry Penn, of Boston, was appointed in his place.

I. L. Pillsbury seemed to express the thought of the membership when he said: "It seems to me, since our organization is new and is getting in good shape, that the men at the helm should be retained for the next year." And so it was.

The fifth annual meeting of FTD was August 19, 1914, and was the shortest convention in the history of the Association, lasting one hour. The members came together at 9 a.m. in Paul Revere Hall, in Boston, before the yearly convention of SAF was scheduled to meet in the same room at 10 a.m.

At this time, there was no provision for deducting a commission from orders wired to European florists. Max Schling, of New York, took the floor to tell of the care these orders required and to suggest that the sending florist ought to be compensated for his time. He had contacted his correspondents in Paris, Rome and London and they had agreed readily to permit him to take fifteen per cent for his trouble. President Bertermann insisted that the discount should be twenty per cent, but no action was taken at this time.

Upon the motion of S. A. Anderson, of Buffalo, the group agreed to double the yearly dues. There might have been more discussion of this motion, but already members of SAF were standing in the doorways, waiting to begin their convention. There was necessary haste in the FTD proceedings.

All incumbent officers were re-elected by acclamation for the ensuing year. These were President Irwin Bertermann, Vice-President William F. Gude, Secretary Albert Pochelon and Treasurer William Rock. Rock did not attend. The three Directors elected were Harry Papworth, of New Orleans; G. E. M. Stumpp, of New York City; and O. J. Olson, of St. Paul.

Both Papworth and Pochelon spoke briefly on the necessity for the good of the organization of spreading the officers and directors over a larger territory in order to further the enlistment of more members. More than 200 florists had enrolled by this time, enough to show that the Association had a great attraction for far-seeing retailers wishing to expand their contacts and their business.

Rock's report, mailed to Pochelon, showed that the guarantee fund now stood at $3,581.50, while the amount of the annual dues had reached $995.

The members voted to pay $500 a year for full-time clerical help for Secretary Pochelon in his membership drive. He asked nothing for his time. The vote was unanimous.

As the gavel sounded for adjournment, the members of SAF were taking their seats to begin their meeting.

At the semi-annual meeting of the Executive Board of SAF in March, 1915, there were enough members of FTD present to take up unofficially some of the matters which caused concern in the retail organization. Principal among these was the question of amendments to the FTD Bylaws in cases where experience was showing that some of the requirements were, as William F. Gude put it, "a little too drastic."

The Bylaws of that period required that regardless of the amount of the order, "whether 50 cents or $100," the delivering florist must bill the sending florist within 10 days and, if a remittance was not forthcoming within 30 days, the delinquent member must be reported to the FTD secretary.

"Of course, none of us does that," said Gude. "It is like our automobile regulations, requiring a speed limit of 12 miles an hour while most of us go 20. Everybody is breaking the law and, until somebody complains, we go ahead until we run into a stumbling block." There were other weaknesses.

Of course, nothing could be done at this meeting which would affect the FTD Constitution or Bylaws. But the incident indicates that the growth of the Association was causing the members and officers to realize that revision was needed in several areas.

These were straws in the wind, the wind of growth and progress. Changes were imminent. The sleeves of the jacket were becoming too short. The shanks of the young organization were protruding below its trousers cuffs. New clothes were needed.

The August 4, 1915, business meeting of FTD was held in San Francisco in conjunction, as usual, with the SAF convention. Because of the distance and the press of business, William F. Gude was the only one of the officers to make the trip, although this was a great year for San Francisco. Fully recovered from the 1906 disaster, the city wished everyone to see its "new look."

The Panama-Pacific International Exposition, held in 1915 in San Francisco, attracted thousands of tourists. As a feature of that exposition, Alexander Graham Bell himself opened the first transcontinental telephone line from New York by again calling T. A. Watson, this time in San Francisco. Elsewhere in the country, business men were not too happy.

The absence of Bertermann, Pochelon and Rock handicapped the organization's opportunity to transact FTD business. But it did give some of the members a chance to express themselves on certain topics which were assuming importance. Chief of these were the matters of delinquent florists and changes in the Bylaws.

Both Rock and Pochelon had sent written reports to the convention in the care of John Young, the SAF secretary. These were read to the meeting by Vice-President Gude. Pochelon, as usual, had written a strongly worded message in which he said, among other things, "It is almost beyond my understanding that there are not more retail florists around the country who have enough sense of business to grasp the idea of the FTD and how many towns we have sent orders to, where we did not know whether the town had a good retailer or not, and simply had to chance it with the telegraph company to turn these orders to the best and nearest florist.

"I hope through your kind efforts at San Francisco we will

be able to enlist a few more members in the Far West and especially a few more towns. I wish that FTD was represented in every town of the U. S. and Canada. A membership in FTD is the best and cheapest investment in the publicity line any good retailer can make, and I can almost guarantee that after joining our Association for one year, no one will ever think of withdrawing. In fact, no one would want to give their membership up if the cost was double, triple, or five times as much."

Observed Gude, "Please bear in mind that, while Mr. Pochelon seems to be a little aggressive, we owe him a debt of gratitude for what he has done for us all. That man has done more than all the rest of us put together, and I would like to see him have due credit for it. Really this thing appeals to me, because in my own firm I know we must have on our books 500 new names on account of the FTD."

Pochelon was slightly in error, however, when he predicted that no one would ever want to withdraw. In the treasurer's report there is the record of repayment of guarantee funds to two resigning florists.

Apparently these men had run into financial difficulties and had been forced to make assignment of their businesses. This is the first instance on record of the loss of an FTD member. But 1915 was not a prosperous year in many fields. The minutes show that a number of florists over the country were behind in their accounts and were being carried by their creditors.

Gude, in his opening remarks, said: "The reason that we have to revise these Bylaws is, as you know, that at least two of our members have failed during the year and they owed some of our members money. Under the Bylaws, if their creditors did not send in their bill within 10 days, and if they did not receive their pay within 30 days or otherwise make a report to the secretary, they have no claim on us. For that reason, our Bylaws should be revised, and the Executive Committee has it in charge."

It is not surprising that changes were in order. The original Constitution and Bylaws drafted by Valentine in 1909 and adopted at the Rochester meeting the following year, had done admirable service. They were created out of the experience of one man for an organization without prior life and therefore with unknown needs. Only the hard work and dedication of its members had held the organization together in its early, faltering days. It was faltering still, but it had shown enough strength and value to justify the work invested in it. If a drastic revision of its rules was necessary for its future health, this was the time to make it.

There was ample time to discuss the proposed changes at San Francisco, and it was so utilized. The small group present did not have authority for the revision. But out of this meeting came many ideas that would be useful when a new Constitution was written.

All the incumbents were re-elected for another year, and I. L. Pillsbury expressed the opinion of the members present by saying, "I move a vote of thanks to the officers for their efficient efforts during the past year, particularly Mr. Albert Pochelon, whose work stands out prominently."

The terms of three directors, Philip Breitmeyer, Ernst Wienhoeber and George Asmus, expired with this meeting, and, to fill their positions, Frank Pelicano, of San Francisco; August Lange, of Chicago; and Frank X. Stuppy, of St. Joseph, were elected.

Various methods of predetermining the responsibility of new members were suggested: bank references, business references, investigation by other retailers in the same town, and a vote of five members before a new application could be accepted. It is not recorded how Pochelon might have reacted to these restrictions on his recruitment program. Finally, a motion was drafted and passed "that any member against whom any complaint whatsoever has been filed for non-payment of bills for any reason whatsoever, be immediately stricken from membership, if in accordance with our

Constitution and until proper restitution to all parties concerned has been made, and that notice be sent at once to every member." The constitutionality of that move at that time is doubtful.

The meeting adjourned sine die.

At a florist trade fair, held in Cleveland, November 11 of the same year, another FTD meeting was called by President Bertermann to discuss the problem, now increasingly disturbing, of the failure of florists to remit for telegraph orders sent by them to delivering florists.

There were two aspects to this problem. The year 1915 had been a bad one. Many businesses, not only florists, had been forced into circumstances which prevented promptness in settling accounts. There was also the thought, expressed by several FTD members, that the organization had been permitted to grow too rapidly through the indiscriminate acceptance of retailers about whom there was too little credit information.

The Bylaws provided that all such bills should be paid within 30 days. But, when they were not paid within that time, there was little that could be done except to turn the bill over to the secretary and let him bring moral pressure to bear upon the delinquent. Pochelon had, until lately, been singularly successful in collecting past-due accounts. Generally, when he got the bill within a reasonable time, he was able to bring the account to book. But with depressed business conditions, the better florists were inclined to be lenient with their late payers. Consequently, the bill sometimes ran for six or eight months before it came to the secretary's office. This increased the difficulty in reaching a settlement. Pochelon insisted that bills be sent in promptly.

There was talk of raising the guarantee fund payment. But most of the larger members were afraid of this, because of the effect it might have on the recruiting of smaller florists. They still realized that broad representation, especially in the smaller towns where large deposits would be the most harmful, was the goal to be reached for the most efficient functioning of the FTD service.

Two important suggestions came out of this short meeting and they were to be important in the future business affairs of the Association.

William C. Gloeckner, of Albany, suggested that when a member went beyond 60 days without paying his bill, he lose his 20 per cent commission. Said Pochelon: "Mr. Gloeckner makes the best suggestion. If the bill is not paid within 60 days, the 20 per cent discount is lost. Then you will get your men to pay their bills."

Pochelon saw in such a provision more persuasive power in the collection letters he was sending the members. It is hard to see how it would be easier to get a man to pay 100 per cent than to cause him to remit the 80 per cent called for in the Bylaws.

Valentine suggested a Membership Committee to pass on all new applicants. Pochelon argued that, if he had to wait for a mail report from five investigating committeemen, weeks might elapse before he would be able to tell the applicant whether he had been accepted.

"This is not a committee which will restrict the powers of the secretary," said Valentine, "but if you have an applicant about whom there is any doubt, and you want the assistance of the committee, you can ask the committee to report on the applicant. Otherwise, you can admit the applicant without consulting the committee."

"In other words," said Pochelon, "you want to put more power on me."

"We cannot change the power of the secretary at present," Valentine assured him. "You admit anybody that comes if you want to."

"I have too much responsibility," objected the secretary.

"You won't have to make use of the committee if you don't want to," said Valentine. "If you want to admit the members without consulting them, all well and good."

"I want it put on the record," Pochelon told the stenographer, "that every time a member makes an application, the secretary will write five letters to this committee, and the five of them must reply to him."

This was moved and carried.

These two innovations — the loss of the 20 per cent commission to florists who became delinquent to the sending member and the appointment of a Membership Committee to supervise the admission of new members — were later to become important in the affairs of FTD.

Between this meeting and the regular SAF convention at Houston, Texas, in August, 1916, there was a brisk correspondence among the officers, directors and those members who took close interest in the conduct of the Association's affairs. The meetings of the past year and the serious business questions which had plagued the officers were thoroughly explored. It was increasingly clear that the short meetings, amounting actually to time taken out of the regular SAF meetings, did not give leisure to the members of FTD to work out problems and situations peculiar to the retailers' trade.

At the Houston convention, a short meeting was held. William F. Gude was elected president; George Asmus, of Chicago, vice-president; and Rock and Pochelon were re-elected. As directors, Karl P. Baum, of Knoxville; Logan D. Thomson, of Atlanta; and T. J. Wolfe, of Waco, Texas, were installed with terms to expire in 1919.

Following the elections, one of the most momentous decisions in the history of the florist industry was submitted to the convention and carried almost unanimously. It was decided that, henceforth, FTD would hold its own annual business meeting, separate from the SAF convention.

This did not indicate a divorce. Instead, it emphasized growth and progress. No one doubted that the time had arrived when it was impossible to hold annual meetings of two such important organizations simultaneously, when all members belonged to both associations. The separation was inevitable. It was accomplished with utmost friendliness and good wishes from each to each. The years have proved the wisdom of the decision.

CHAPTER FOUR

FTD On Its Own

*A*s HAD BEEN agreed the year before, FTD met in convention at the Hotel LaSalle in Chicago, October 11 and 12, 1916. This was the first meeting devoted solely to the affairs of the retail members of SAF, who composed the Florists' Telegraph Delivery. It was felt by the retailers that there were enough matters of singular interest to their business to justify a separate meeting. There was no thought of withdrawing from SAF. On the contrary, it was insisted that the first requisite for membership in FTD was an active, paid-up membership in the parent organization.

The meeting was called to order at "sixty minutes past eight o'clock" in the convention room of the hotel by President William F. Gude. Seventy-nine members were present. Secretary Pochelon, bouncily enthusiastic as ever, announced that the Association on that date consisted of 328 members.

Most of those present were acquainted with each other through their SAF affiliation. Gude quickly put them at ease with his geniality and personal allusions. At his suggestion, each man rose and introduced himself and his firm — "the Rotarian procedure," said Gude.

He was a big man, 6 feet tall and weighing about 250 pounds. Although his voice was soft, it had great carrying power. His manner was jovial. He reminded the members that there was much to be done and many topics to be discussed. He hoped, he said, that they would be attentive and enter fully into any discussions with whatever questions or comments that they might have.

In his address, the president re-emphasized that the suggestion for separate FTD meetings arose only because business matters, exclusively affecting the retailers, could not be properly discussed at SAF conventions with full consideration for both groups.

The most pressing business of this meeting, he told them, was the adoption of a new Constitution and Bylaws. It had been realized for some years that a new set of rules was needed. The president had appointed three groups, consisting of Pochelon, Rock and some of the other "wheelhorses," to draft three sets of Constitutions and Bylaws. The evening before the opening of the meeting, these groups had met to compare and harmonize their ideas of what the new rules should cover. It was a late hour when complete accord was reached.

Gude then read the revised Constitution and Bylaws to the assembly. The new Articles were longer. "FTD" officially became "FTDA." The general office was established at the home of the secretary or wherever he should establish his office. There were important additions to the key objectives of the Association; viz., to educate members, to give publicity to the service, to encourage the exchange of ideas between members and to promote co-operation. Active, foreign and associate memberships were defined. There were definite rules concerning membership. Annual dues and guarantee fund requirements were carefully worked out. The duties of the officers were drawn up in full. The rights and duties of members were developed with equal care. The new Constitution marked the arrival of big-association thinking, covered many more contingencies, and gave FTD a firm basis for growth.

As the president concluded the presentation of the new Constitution and Bylaws, conversation filled the room. Midway down the center aisle, a bulky figure rose, with lifted hand. "Mr. President, may I have the floor for a moment now?" he asked.

"Yes, Mr. Valentine." As Gude's voice carried over the room, the conversation subsided. Everyone turned to look toward the man who stood in the center aisle. There was universal respect and admiration for the founder.

"I do want at this time to express my appreciation of the enormous amount of painstaking work, obviously given by this committee to the preparation of this proposed Constitution and Bylaws," Mr. Valentine said slowly. Although his health had failed considerably in the past year, his voice was clear. "Those of you who have never undertaken work of this kind perhaps cannot appreciate the labor and detail in the preparation of a Constitution and Bylaws, to be complete and consistent.

"I do not want to be understood as passing an opinion on all these Articles. But, considered as a whole, it seems to me that they represent a mighty successful effort to furnish us with a new suit of clothes. Before anybody attempts to modify any of these Articles submitted by the committee, he should carefully consider whether he has anything better to offer!"

As Valentine sat down, the silence showed that his statement had hit home. There was no use in meaningless discussion of the questions presented.

Albert Pochelon took the speaker's stand to pay tribute to Valentine and his successor, Irwin Bertermann. A rising vote of thanks was tendered each.

In many ways the new Constitution was revolutionary. It was not in character for the members to accept without question such drastic changes. But Valentine's admonition not to speak, except to suggest improvements, had placed a responsibility on all who had heard the Constitution for the first time for which they were not prepared. Gude had a sense of drama and suspense. Wisely, he did not at that time call for a discussion. Instead, he recognized William L. Rock, who had probably written most of the new rules.

Rock presented a logical explanation of the changes in the Constitution and Bylaws. When he had finished, Philip Breitmeyer moved that they be adopted. He was seconded by William C. Gloeckner, and the resolution was formally framed.

Max Schling, of New York, was the first speaker to discuss the questions. He suggested only one change: that instead of the suggested guarantee payments, which had been raised to $5 for a florist in a town of less than 25,000 and up to $50 for a city of over half a million, each florist be bonded in amounts from $25 up, according to population. He pointed out that the small $5 payment would not protect the Association members from delinquent florists.

Pochelon agreed with this in principle but showed Schling that, during the past year, of all properly submitted bills, only $6 remained uncollected by the secretary's clearing house methods. Schling seemed satisfied. He was a wise and friendly man and his opinions were always the result of expert business analysis. But, aware of Pochelon's ability, he was content to state his position and then bow to the will of the majority.

Several minor points were raised by other members. These were carefully explained by the various officers. Then cries of, "Question! Question!" began to be heard from the floor. President Gude put the question of the adoption of the revised Constitution and Bylaws. It carried unanimously.

There were four major areas of change in the new Constitution.

First, the dues and guarantee fund payments were increased. Annual dues ran from a minimum of $5 a year to a maximum of $30 for cities over 150,000 population. The guarantee fund payments ranged from $5 for a city under 25,000 to $50 for a city above 500,000. These were substantial raises, amounting to 400 per cent in the case of a town of less than 5,000 population, which had formerly been assessed at one dollar. But, on a dollar basis, they were not exorbitant.

The guarantee fund payments were raised comparably.

Second, the new Constitution officially provided for an Arbitration Committee to handle disputes between members. This lent constitutional sanction to a committee which the president had already appointed unofficially.

Third, the president was authorized to appoint a corps of district representatives. In the words of the Constitution: "The representatives shall be geographically districted." There was no certain territorial division of the country for this purpose. Each representative was supposed to cover the area around his home city, as far as his influence could extend. His duties were set out in the Constitution. They consisted primarily of soliciting members, offering advice to the secretary on local conditions, and generally publicizing the flowers-by-wire idea in the district. There was no provision for investigation or recommendation of applicants.

The most drastic innovation was a fourth article concerning the rights and duties of members. In this provision the authors sought to cure, or at least ameliorate, a great many of the hardships which had beset the Association through lack of control over the methods of its members. The article contained 12 sections, each aimed at a single undesirable practice.

Members were advised to use the utmost care in the transmission and filling of orders. The price differential between geographical areas was to be carefully explained to the customer. The 20 per cent discount was made standard. No orders were to be submitted to any but members of the retail trade. Any violation of this section was a matter for the Arbitration Committee. The delivering florist was to bill the sender within 10 days and remittance was to be made within 45 days, under penalty of losing the discount. After 45 days without payment, the sending florist was to submit his bill to the secretary, and if it was still unpaid after notice from the secretary's office, the bill was to be paid from the guarantee fund. If the delinquent did not reimburse the fund within

10 days, he was subject to expulsion. This article also empowered the secretary to use his influence to collect bills from non-members.

The unqualified acceptance of these rules was of more significance than appeared on the surface. They were not mere amendments. They established a new way of life for the organization. They supplied the basis for strength and discipline. Although the growth of the Association would require many changes, the new Constitution and Bylaws were products of test and experience, of trial and error. The organization moved out of its childhood into a robust and enthusiastic adolescence. It faced the future with vigor and confidence.

The importance which FTD was beginning to assume in the business world was shown by four national advertising agencies asking permission to present plans for national campaigns to the meeting. These agencies were Gundlach Advertising Agency, Hilmer V. Swenson Company, Doubleday, Page & Company, all of Chicago; and Campbell-Ewald of Detroit.

Each of these presented a similar plan, calling for advertising in magazines with large circulations and involving an expenditure of approximately $5,000 per year. This was not within the scope of the Association at this time, so all the plans were rejected. However, a resolution was passed authorizing Pochelon to seek voluntary contributions to a publicity fund, which he would administer, with two other members, for the purpose of promoting FTD among florists and increasing its membership. The contribution amounted to approximately $1,800. It shows the appreciation which florists of that time felt for the value of promotion and publicity.

Also authorized at this meeting was a directory of florists, to be compiled by Secretary Pochelon. This was something toward which he had long been working. He already had in his Detroit files extensive lists of florists, assembled from information obtained by letter, from Western Union and Postal Telegraph, and in other ways, which composed his mailing list for FTD publicity. It would be easy to convert those lists into a reference book for telegraph flower orders.

At the suggestion of Karl P. Baum, of Knoxville, a contest was announced for an FTD emblem, suitable to use on letterheads, store fronts, and delivery automobiles to replace the 1914 Mercury design. Reports were to be made on the contest at the next annual meeting.

Smaller matters were disposed of and much discussion held regarding the florist business in general. The convention drew to a close with the feeling among the members that they had, as the Florists' Telegraph Delivery Association, become a solid and important business organization.

J. A. Valentine made the closing remarks of the meeting, thanking the local organizations for their hospitality and concluding, "Ever since we were children we have heard how good a thing it is to help our fellow man and be kind to him. It seems to me that the way we have been conducting our deliberations exemplifies that principle."

It was the grand old organizer's last appearance at an FTD annual meeting. He died before the next convention.

The first annual meeting held exclusively by FTD had ended with much accomplished. Possibly of the greatest importance was the realization that much remained to be done. Changing times revealed the shadows of approaching difficulties. The members left Chicago with these problems in their minds.

Detroit was chosen as the next meeting place for the following October. Before that, much work impended. Hidden in the future were drastic historical changes which would vitally affect the new Association.

Albert Pochelon with a new project was like a cat with a catnip-mouse. He couldn't wait to pounce on it. By November of 1916, he was ready to issue the first *Directory of Retail Florists*. This was a well-arranged book, larger than its 4,200

"I RECOGNIZE THE TRUST PLACED IN ME . . ."

(From the FTD Member's Creed)

WILLIAM L. ROCK
Kansas City, Missouri
Treasurer 1910-1949
Treasurer Emeritus
 1949-1954
A florist since 1897, William L. Rock was named treasurer of FTD at its original meeting in Rochester, New York, in 1910. He remained in the post until his resignation in 1949, at which time he was named treasurer emeritus. He served in that capacity until his death in 1954, having given 44 years of devoted service to FTD.

ALBERT POCHELON
Detroit, Michigan
Secretary 1912-1924
Executive Secretary
 1924-1929
Elected secretary of FTD in 1912 when membership numbered 57, Pochelon began a recruitment drive that saw enrollment reach 1,200 in less than four years. His penchant for publicity and his constant efforts to promote the cause of FTD were major factors in the early success of the Association. He was made executive secretary in 1924 and retired in 1929.

FTD SECRETARIES
AND GENERAL MANAGERS

H. B. DORNER
Urbana, Illinois
Secretary of SAF at the time FTD was founded, Dorner served as secretary of the young Association during its first year.

◄ **IRWIN BERTERMANN**
Indianapolis, Indiana
Replacing Dorner, this strong and dedicated member served as secretary until the election of Albert Pochelon in 1912.

JOHN BESEMER
Detroit, Michigan
From his position as manager of the FTD Clearing House, Besemer moved into the office of Executive Secretary and General Manager in 1941, replacing Barber. He was the first man to hold the combined post.

AL BARBER
Detroit, Michigan
Upon the retirement of Albert Pochelon, Barber became executive secretary in 1929 and served until poor health forced his resignation in February, 1941.

PHILIP W. JONES
Detroit, Michigan
Experienced in industrial management and public relations on a national scale, Jones served as executive secretary and general manager from 1949 to 1953.

J. PAUL OSTRANDER
Detroit, Michigan
Executive secretary and general manager from June, 1953, to April, 1954.

JOHN L. BODETTE
Detroit, Michigan
Executive secretary and general manager since 1956, Bodette has supervised a complete Headquarters reorganization and has seen the establishment of numerous modern member service facilities in FTD. ▼

HAROLD R. HEWEY
◀ *Detroit, Michigan*
From his position as manager of the Sales and Advertising Department, Hewey was twice called upon to step into the top Headquarters spot. He served as acting executive secretary from January to June, 1953, and as secretary from April, 1954, to his retirement in November, 1955.

MORRIS R. LILES ▶
Detroit, Michigan
Originally called to FTD as an expert management consultant, Liles acted as general manager from 1954 to April, 1956.

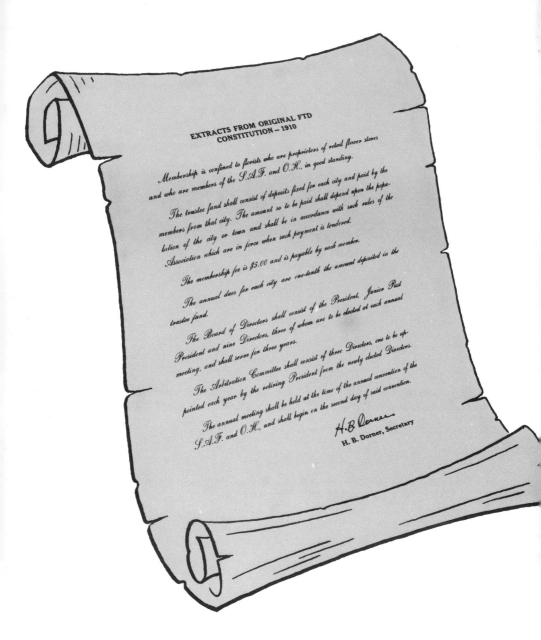

EXTRACTS FROM ORIGINAL FTD
CONSTITUTION – 1910

Membership is confined to florists who are proprietors of retail flower stores and who are members of the S.A.F. and O.H., in good standing.

The trustee fund shall consist of deposits fixed for each city and paid by the members from that city. The amount so to be paid shall depend upon the population of the city or town and shall be in accordance with such rules of the Association which are in force when such payment is tendered.

The membership fee is $5.00 and is payable by each member.

The annual dues for each city are one-tenth the amount deposited in the trustee fund.

The Board of Directors shall consist of the President, Junior Past President and nine Directors, three of whom are to be elected at each annual meeting, and shall serve for three years.

The Arbitration Committee shall consist of three Directors, one to be appointed each year by the retiring President from the newly elected Directors.

The annual meeting shall be held at the time of the annual convention of the S.A.F. and O.H., and shall begin on the second day of said convention.

H.B. Dorner

H. B. Dorner, Secretary

No complete copy of the Constitution and Bylaws adopted at the Rochester meeting in 1910 exists, but the above extracts, taken from the files of SAF, are known to have been included in the first rules drawn up by John A. Valentine for the conduct of the Association. Not all of these provisions were accepted in the final draft of the revised Constitution and Bylaws under which FTD began its operation.

listings really required. But Pochelon was looking to the future. The volume was large (9½ x 12¼ inches), bound in heavy grey stock, with the title, sub-title and Mercury emblem printed in dark green. Inside was a foreword from Pochelon outlining use of the book, the new Constitution and Bylaws, a roster of the officers and directors, and the first public listing of the district representatives.

Then followed 56 pages, of three columns each, the center column carrying the names and addresses of Canadian and American florists. The right and left hand columns were blank. The right was headed "Remarks and Corrections." The left was for "Orders Received and Orders Sent To—."

Each member received two copies of the directory, with instructions to make corrections of any erroneous names and addresses contained, to add the names of any florists originally omitted, and, at the end of the year, to return the corrected copy to Pochelon. Eight full-page ads of suppliers in the back of the book helped defray the cost of publication.

The directory was received with enthusiasm. There was some criticism of the inclusion of the names of non-members, but Pochelon justified this by insisting that the only way to get new members was to show them the advantage of receiving wire orders from present members.

The general world situation, with a war in Europe from which the United States believed it could stay aloof, was acute by the time FTD met in Detroit, October 2 and 3, 1917.

Germany's unrestricted submarine warfare and the torpedoing of civilian passenger ships had focused the sentiment of the Americans overwhelmingly toward England and France and against the Kaiser. Woodrow Wilson, who had been re-elected president on the slogan, "He kept us out of the war," now saw our entry as inevitable. William Jennings Bryan resigned as Secretary of State, rather than serve a war administration. There was a powerful bloc of citizens of German extraction which tried to keep the country neutral.

But it had been proved that the German Embassy in Washington was directing espionage in the United States, not only against its European enemies, but also against this country, and was endeavoring to stir up unrest in Mexico to keep America busy on this continent. These deterrents were not successful and on April 6, 1917, the United States declared that a state of war existed with the German empire.

The first American troops embarked for France on June 19, 1917. The desire of servicemen to remember mother on her "Day," with floral gifts and the wish of parents to comfort their homesick or wounded sons with the fresh and fragrant beauty of flowers, tended to establish the practicality of the international aspect of the flowers-by-wire idea.

There was another war-created development. Rail transportation in the United States and Canada was overburdened with men and materials for the war effort. It was impossible to ship fresh flowers by express, as both wholesalers and retailers had been doing, and feel any certainty about their condition at the destination. So, in March of that year, President Gude, Philip Breitmeyer and Max Schling visited the heads of the three principal express companies in New York City to discuss this situation. This was before all express companies were combined into a single service by the railroads. They were received with great consideration, but it was explained that there was nothing possible under the double strain of war-time emergencies and a threatened strike by express company employees. Said Gude, "I was very favorably impressed with the managers of the three companies. My colleagues who were with me will bear me out in that statement."

It was imperative that florists, both wholesale and retail, find a dependable way to deliver flowers at a distance. Flowers-by-wire was actually the only answer. Pochelon made this a main point in his report to the convention. He also added some cheer to a gloomy situation by announcing that, since the meeting the previous year in Chicago, 58 more florists had joined FTD.

In the treasurer's report, W. L. Rock informed the meeting that annual dues now amounted to $5,755.90 per year and that the guarantee fund stood at $7,155.09. Investments of $6,721.36 were accounted for, paying interest during the year of $326.38. There is some irony in the fact that $2,000 of this fund was invested in Imperial Russian Bonds! Cash on hand amounted to $5,799.90 in the guarantee fund and $435.73 in the general fund from the annual dues. This was the best financial report the members had yet heard.

In the formative years of the Association, almost every yearly meeting produced a feature which might be called the high point of the convention. This is not to say that each meeting was fashioned about a single theme. It is to show, rather, that the growth of the organization was in a series of definite steps, each unique, but each leading forward to a more efficient business association.

The main feature of the 1917 Detroit convention was an analysis of the retail florist business by Herman Knoble of Cleveland. Knoble had long been a strong member of FTD. He was a grower, wholesaler and retailer, as many of the members were. But he kept his three activities absolutely separate. He kept different books, by different systems, and had the faculty of considering each activity in its proper light. He was a statistician and business analyst and, as head of a committee consisting of himself, S. A. Anderson, of Buffalo; and George Asmus, of Chicago; he had been instructed by President Gude to compose a financial picture of the retail florist business, for the enlightenment of the average florist.

Outside the large operators, who had to maintain efficient bookkeeping methods, most of the florists then operated on the "pocket principle." When they sold flowers they put the money in their pockets and when they needed supplies, they took it out. What remained in the "pocket" was profit.

Knoble sought to change this by drawing up an analysis of his own business as a model for other florists. No such report had ever been attempted by FTD. Following is the expense break-down submitted by Knoble in his report:

Overhead expense 45.1%

Mdse. of every description, except
    baskets, ribbons & chiffons . . . 37.0%

Baskets, ribbons & chiffons 4.3%

FTD out-of-city a/c 3.6%

Profit & Loss Account 10.0%

Further analyzing the overhead, Knoble offered these statistics:

Cost of advertising	6%	Rent to gross	2% to
Salaries	21%		25%
Delivery expense	9%	Av. value of orders	$4.01 ea.
Cost per delivery	$ .40 ea.	Amt. bills rec. av.	
Cost per mile with		entire yr. per mo.	18.4%
White Trucks	$ .204 ea.	Cash business	32.3%
Cost per mile with		Charge business	67.7%
Ford Trucks	$ .115 ea.		

Although Knoble advocated a three-for-one mark-up on raw stock — that is, flowers costing $1 should be sold for $3 — his figures showed that he was not realizing that. This he could not understand. The cost of his stock remained almost constant at 37 per cent, no matter how he figured it. He found that if he bought stock for $1 and sold it for $3 he was only getting a mark-up of 2.7 for one. This troubled him. He knew what he wanted and what he ought to do. But he was not doing it.

His report stated: "It is our judgment that plants purchased for resale should be figured on a basis of 3 for 1. In other words, if a plant costs $1 it should be sold for $3. If this plant is placed in a basket, the basket should be figured on a basis of 2 for 1, in addition. If this plant was placed in a basket costing 50 cents, the complete article should sell for $4.

"Cut flowers bought for resale should be figured on a basis of 2½ for 1, and preferably 3 for 1. That is, carnations costing $4 per hundred should sell for $1.50 per dozen. Roses costing $8 per hundred should sell for $3 per dozen. In figuring made-up work, we believe that the maximum to be allowed for the cost of raw stock should not exceed 33-1/3% of the retail price of the finished article, deducting the selling price of the basket that the flowers are arranged in. As an illustration, where you aim to make a $5 basket, if this basket costs you 50 cents, according to the previous figure it would sell for $1 without any flowers. You will then have to deduct a dollar from $5, leaving the balance of $4, and the cost of the flowers in this basket should be 1/3 of the $4, or $1.33, this to include flowers and greens. This illustration is figured on a maximum allowance, and you should, whenever possible, aim to make that even less than 1/3. Thirty per cent would be much better. Of course, your ability to buy will be a feature that will govern this situation more or less in detail."

S. A. Anderson of Buffalo reviewed Knoble's figures and suggested that he add 20 per cent of the cost of his raw stock to cover broken, wilted and otherwise unusable stock. Knoble did this and refigured his mark-up on that basis. He found that in order to sell his flowers at 3-for-1, he could not afford to pay more than about $.833 for an order for which he received $3. He incorporated Anderson's suggestion into his report to demonstrate to the listening florists the intangible items which sometimes had a serious effect on their profits.

Based on modern accounting practices, Knoble's figures left many unanswered questions. They were founded on a series of rules-of-thumb which the present-day accountant would have difficulty in accepting as proper premises upon which to build an analysis. Knoble, a shrewd business man, had arrived at a schedule of costs and prices that earned him a profit of approximately 10 per cent. That it cannot be

explained in terms of modern methods is beside the point.
The fact is that it worked.

The report was a bombshell to the meeting. The membership was electrified. Never before had they seen their
business so exposed to view. Every bone and muscle of it
could be intimately examined. Those who had not kept
accurate records of their operations were able to compare
the authoritative report of Knoble with their own books and
see where they had departed from successful procedures.
With Knoble's formula, they were able to evaluate their own
businesses and, by applying his yardstick, to correct their
own operations in emulation of one of the most profitable
florist businesses in the country.

J. J. Windler, of St. Louis, moved the acceptance of the
report. He was seconded by Breitmeyer. President Gude said,
"I hope, before putting the motion, I may be pardoned if I
say that in all my experience in the Society of American
Florists and the Florists' Telegraph Delivery Association, I
have never heard a more complete, practical and concise
report than the one submitted by Mr. Knoble."

Applause rocked the room. Gude let the excitement continue for a brief moment, and then opened the question to
discussion. The ensuing comments fill 20 pages of the convention minutes.

This report was the high point of the 1917 convention. But
it was not the only important action taken by the Association.

William F. Gude was unanimously re-elected president.
Philip Breitmeyer was elected vice-president. Albert Pochelon was retained as secretary. W. L. Rock was re-appointed
treasurer. H. G. Dillemuth, of Toronto, was the first Canadian elected to the directorate. Herman P. Knoble, of
Cleveland, and Edward Sceery, of Paterson, N. J., were
named to the Board to serve for three years, and W. J.
Smyth, of Chicago, was elected to serve the unexpired term
of Logan D. Thomson.

Three thousand dollars was appropriated for the SAF

advertising fund. A "pledge of our unswerving loyalty and undying fealty," along with a floral remembrance, was dispatched to President Woodrow Wilson.

In the high jinks which ended the convention, an oil painting donated by Poehlman Brothers of Chicago was auctioned off and went to Breitmeyer for $150. Every unsuccessful bidder donated the amount of his bid to the FTD publicity fund. Breitmeyer rented the painting to a series of florists, to be displayed in their shops at $25 per month, the money going into the publicity fund.

Secretary Pochelon had somewhere obtained a toy goat, covered with real Angora hair, and able to emit a plaintive "Baa-a-a-a" when squeezed. He kept it on the desk before him throughout the convention, defying anyone to "get his goat." He now raffled it off, and Herman Knoble was the successful bidder at $50.

"Baa-a-a-a!" said G. E. M. Stumpp, when his bid failed.

Pochelon's goat was always returned to him after each meeting and remained a feature of the FTD conventions for years. It is still cherished by members of his family.

Before FTD's next convention in Cleveland, on October 8 and 9, 1918, the reality of World War I had been driven home to the people of the United States in its starkest terms. War headlines and casualty lists were daily features of the newspapers. The government had assumed complete control of all American railroads January 1. Wheatless, meatless and fuelless days were enforced. Few homes were without a man "over there." The revolutionary Russian government surrendered to the German army and signed the Brest-Litovsk treaty, freeing hundreds of German regiments to strengthen the pressure against the Allies on the Western Front. The battle of the Meuse-Argonne was at the height of its fury, and the fate of the war hung upon its outcome, when the members of FTD assembled in the ballroom of the Hotel Hollenden for their opening meeting.

Due to the urgencies of the times, the 87 members who

registered as present (the stenographer notes that there were a few who attended without registering) knew that this year's convention was strictly a business meeting.

There was generous applause as President Gude rose to open the meeting. The entire company rose with him. The organ sounded an opening chord and the group broke into "The Star Spangled Banner." As the first words of the anthem rang out, Mrs. Frank Friedley and Mrs. Herman Knoble entered the hall from opposite sides, one bearing the Stars and Stripes and the other the Canadian banner and, advancing to the platform, they presented the colors to the president, who planted them on the stage. The audience remained standing for the presentation and joined in singing "God Save The King."

Gude stood silent for a long moment. "Ladies and gentlemen," he finally said, "this will not be a time for long-winded speeches. All of us here are busy men, and doubly so at this time, or we would not be here now. Consequently, we are going to start in this morning on a strictly business proposition."

This was not the old Gude, the genial, jovial president who put everyone at ease with his pleasant personality, his quips and personal allusions. There were no Rotarian-type introductions, no easy-going banter. Here was a serious business man, purposeful almost to the point of grimness. Those who studied his face saw a tired tightness to his features which told of long hours of work and worry, not only over his own affairs but those of the entire membership under the stringencies of the war time.

The fact that Gude occupied the president's chair during this time was a singularly fortunate thing. He had a personal relationship with President and Mrs. Wilson and supplied the flowers for the White House. Many of the most influential men in Washington were his friends and, while he could not strictly be called a "lobbyist," he had many effective opportunities to explain the plight of the florists and to impress important people with the value of flowers to a nation at war. When the industry was in danger of being declared non-essential, and so denied fuel necessary for the greenhouses, it was largely through his efforts that restrictions were eased and the production of flowers allowed to continue on a limited basis.

To open the convention, Gude read a prepared speech which was a model of concise and cogent statement. He pointed out the need for more efficient business methods among the members of the Association, in view of the 100 per cent increase in business during the preceding year. There was, he declared, too much carelessness in the keeping of accounts and in acknowledging telegraph orders. He noted that some members, in defiance of the Bylaws, were using unethical practices and he decried this as unworthy and unbecoming an honest business.

He touched upon the need for flowers in wartime. "Are flowers non-essential?" he asked. "I should answer positively, No! Because flowers signify life itself and we know that without flowers there would be no fruit of any kind. So flowers are used to cheer the human race everywhere from childhood to old age and are used to express our sympathies when loved ones finally pass over to that great beyond of a higher life. There are no words in our language that have expressed thoughts, sympathies, kindly feelings and good cheer like flowers can and have."

There was reason for Gude's concern. The unparalleled influenza epidemic had alarmed the nation. Cancellation of the convention had been seriously considered. It was only because the disease had not reached the Midwest in the degree which had affected the Eastern Seaboard, that plans for the meeting went forward. Government restrictions on gatherings had been put into effect. In the East, stores were not permitted to open until 10 a.m. Theatres, churches, schools and other gathering places were closed. The more timorous of the citizens wore surgical masks on the streets.

Fear of infection approached mass hysteria. A public sneezer was avoided as though he had given the Biblical cry, "Unclean!" Baggage cars were filled with caskets.

Added to this was the effect of the ferocious struggle in the woods and fields of France, where the desperate German armies fought out their vicious, hopeless days.

As Gude went from topic to topic, the pressure under which he had been working became apparent to the audience. His grimness was communicated to the members and set the tone of the entire convention. It was, as he had announced, purely a business meeting.

Gude, in the gravity of the occasion, had not lost his sense of showmanship. At the end of each paragraph of his speech, he lifted his eyes from the manuscript and, as if punctuating the statement just concluded, brought his great fist down upon the speaker's stand and cried, "SAY IT WITH FLOWERS AND BUY MORE LIBERTY BONDS!"

This was the first use of the now famous flower slogan before an FTD convention and it became the watchword of the meeting.

Treasurer William L. Rock was not at this Cleveland meeting. As a member of the Missouri militia he had been called into federal service and was in training camp. He had, however, submitted a printed report covering the period up to July 31, 1918, and had augmented that with a written report to October 8, 1918. Pochelon read both reports to the convention.

Receipts for the past year totaled $4,438.75, including $81.25 interest on investments. Balance on hand amounted to $12,989.87. This consisted of investments in private bonds, $5,719.36; United States Liberty Bonds, first and second issues, $1,500; and cash on deposit, $5,770.51. The guarantee fund was in excess of $9,000. Pochelon explained Rock's absence by saying, "He feels terribly about it because he figured so long on coming here, and really I could almost see the tear-drops on the letter I got from him just before I left on Sunday."

On his own part, perhaps inspired by the analysis submitted the year before by Herman Knoble, Pochelon had concerned himself principally with the circulation of a questionnaire to the members during the past year. He appeared at the Cleveland convention with an enormous sheaf of letters and forms, of which Gude said, "I think there are not over 400 or 500 pages of it, and it will not take over 10 hours to get through with it."

The secretary had sent out 600 letters containing the questions to which he desired answers. This figure indicates that the membership had increased by about 35 per cent since the preceding convention, although Pochelon did not announce the exact number of members, as he had at other conventions. Pochelon chose to discuss four of the questions as pertinent to the meeting and to the welfare of the members.

Two of these inquiries, No. 9 and No. 10, were similar. They were: "Have you increased your out-of-town business since becoming a member; and to what amount?" and, "How many orders do you send out, and what amount, approximately, during one year's business? How many orders do you receive, and what amount, approximately, during one year's time?"

The answers to these questions confirmed the conclusion that Knoble had reached the year before: viz., that florists did not keep good records and that few of them knew at any time the state of their business. Even Henry Penn, of Boston, one of the most successful florists in New England, admitted that he did not have the information necessary for authoritative answers to the questions. He moved that the secretary's office devise a simple bookkeeping method, available to all the members, so that they might keep in closer touch with their own results and better supply Pochelon with the information he desired. Many felt the need of such a system, but none actually developed until years later. It was in tentative form only, supplanted by a more detailed and workable system in 1957.

The number of American soldiers in Europe had caused the question of European members to assume new importance. There had been no organized drive for foreign members, but William Leighton of Glasgow (now Jack Dobson's shop) had been a member since 1916 and 15 applications had been received from France and England. There was substantial business on Mother's Day and at Christmas between army camps in Europe and the United States. No fee or dues had been established for foreign members. Pochelon's next question was: "What shall be the annual dues for members in foreign countries?"

This did not apply to Canadian members, who were enlisted under the original plan. In view of the amount of business which faced the meeting, Acting President Breitmeyer limited the discussion of this question and, when Pochelon suggested a $5 dues and no payment into the guarantee fund, the motion was quickly adopted. This was the first official recognition of foreign members. It set the stage for the international expansion of the Association.

Pochelon now propounded his favorite question: "What do you think of establishing a system in our FTD clearing house of past due bills, whereby a bill that is past due and sent to the secretary can be immediately paid by him, less the mutual 20 per cent discount, the member owing the bill to reimburse the clearing house for the full amount of the bill by return mail?"

This was the first mention of a mandatory clearing house procedure, a matter which was to plague the Association for years, until finally adopted. Pochelon favored this arrangement. But there was considerable opposition. Even Gude said, "We cannot undertake to go into the banking business."

Many members resented the idea of the mandatory clearing house, considering it a direct interference in their business methods. As Knoble put it, "If I should choose to let every florist in the United States owe me anywhere from three to 10 months, I do not think it at all concerns the rest of the men here."

All admitted the weakness of the collection method as it stood in the Bylaws. But none favored having the secretary's office dictate when they must pay their bills. George Asmus moved that the question be submitted to the Board with power to act. His motion carried. This was far from the end of the matter. It was to come before the convention many more times. Probably no single question caused such acrimony and division among members of FTD as the mandatory clearing house suggestion. Its eventual solution, to the satisfaction of all, demonstrates the good sense of the members and the strength of the Association.

For some years the conventions had pondered the question of admitting traveling men, who called upon florists, as associate members; an effort to prompt these "drummers" to promote membership in FTD.

Differences of opinion existed on the subject. Some considered these men the logical ones to recruit members. Others argued that no one should be accepted into any sort of membership, unless actively engaged in the retailing of flowers. This question now arose again. As before, the discussion tended to get out of hand. It was finally moved and carried that the matter be referred to the Board of Directors for decision.

There is no doubt that, at this time, some members of FTD and some florists who were not members had been guilty of unethical practices toward other florists and the public. What is now called "curtailment" was easy to practice and hard to detect. But there had been some detection. Reports of discrepancies had been relayed to the secretary, sometimes by the recipient, and sometimes by the sender. It was plain that these practices would damage the reputation of the legitimate members of FTD and there was an effort among the leading florists to eliminate such methods. F. C. W. Brown of Cleveland moved the establishment of a "Better Business Commission." His motion was quickly seconded and passed. For a time this Commission handled all matters concerned with business ethics, as well as publicity. It later developed, through several transitions including Sales and Advertising Services, into the present Marketing Division, which covers marketing, advertising and public relations activities of the Association.

In the election of officers, which brought the business of the convention to a close, the incumbents were continued in office with the exception of the directors whose terms were expiring. To complete the Board, W. J. Palmer, of Buffalo; A. F. Borden, of Los Angeles; and C. H. Grakelow, of Philadelphia, were named for the regular term of three years.

As before, the meeting ended in a flurry of free-will contributions. But this time it was not for publicity but for Liberty Bonds. No contribution was for less than $50 and others ran to $100, $500, and even $1,000. In less than 15 minutes, the members had subscribed $8,800 to be invested in the war effort.

Philip Breitmeyer, acting for President Gude who had to leave on an early train, announced the adjournment of the convention, to meet the following year in Buffalo.

Admittedly, little was accomplished at the Cleveland meeting. It was a time of war and uncertainty. There were problems of manpower, prices, supplies, reduced inventories and other shortages, as well as the indecision inseparable from times of international strife.

Perhaps if the membership had known that November 11, 1918, would see the end of the war, with Germany and her allies defeated decisively, the decisions made at the Cleveland convention would have been more progressive. But it is not given men to see the future. The expansion plans, which had been uppermost in the minds of the members, would have to wait until another year. It remained to be seen what effect the end of the war would have.

CHAPTER FIVE

Facing the Postwar Problems

*T*HIRTY-THREE days after the adjournment of the Cleveland convention, the German armies capitulated. The armistice ending the first World War was signed November 11, 1918.

The wild elation which followed the end of the war could not absorb the energy built up for the war effort. A tremendous force ebbs slowly. But if it might be turned into productive channels, the incentive for production might equate that intended for destruction. In the Florists' Telegraph Delivery Association, this strength was directed toward increased membership recruiting.

L. F. Darnell, who had been manager of the Gasser interests in Cleveland and was thoroughly acquainted with the florist industry, was engaged by FTD as a membership organizer, February 1, 1919. He went on the road to sell the idea of FTD to those florists who had been hesitant about joining. This was one of the greatest bargains FTD ever acquired. Darnell's salary was $2,400 a year, plus expenses. From the time he began until the 1919 convention in Buffalo in October, which was eight and a half months, he signed 278 new members.

His missionary work may have benefited from the fact that, sometime in the spring of 1919, the Board of the Society of American Florists met in Detroit with the Board of FTD to discuss the clause in the FTD Bylaws which made membership in the SAF a prerequisite for joining the FTD. Some confusion had existed; FTD members believing it an

SAF rule, and SAF members attributing it, correctly, to the FTD Bylaws.

As had been mentioned, and as Pochelon frequently laid before the membership, this was one of the rules which caused retailers to hesitate about joining FTD. In many localities, the growers and wholesalers, the original members of SAF, were also in the retail business. This placed them in competition with the strict retailers who must rely on these competitors for stock, which had not led to perfect harmony between the groups. The constant question was, "Why should I have to belong to SAF in order to belong to FTD?" There was no satisfactory answer.

At the Detroit meeting, it was amicably agreed between the two Boards that this requirement could be eliminated without misunderstanding. This was done. President J. F. Ammann, of SAF, later said: ". . . the best thing you could do was to wipe out the compulsory clause in your Constitution making men belong to the SAF in order to belong to FTD, because you had grown up to a full-grown man; you were no longer an infant and you did not need a guardian. But you know that the father of this society was the SAF, and all I ask from you in behalf of that great old organization is that you stand by it as loyally as you have in the past and help us now to go out and create more new children."

Such rapid growth in membership brought a corresponding increase in matters to be considered by the annual business meeting. Long before the Buffalo convention, it was realized that much pre-planning would be necessary to place before the two-day assembly all the items of importance. It was decided that the officers, Executive Committee and certain key members would meet in Buffalo the day before the convention, to plan an agenda which would streamline the conduct of the meeting. This was the first instance of such a meeting and there was some apprehension that the membership might interpret it as an attempt to bypass democratic procedures. This proved not to be so. But one of the matters decided was who would be nominated for the elective posts for the following year. This, of course, did not bar nominations from the floor.

It was decided that Philip Breitmeyer would be presented for president and Irwin Bertermann for vice-president. To be nominated for director, three to be elected, were W. J. Smyth and Karl P. Baum for re-election, Max Schling, George M. Stumpp, J. W. Grandy, Jr., Olaf J. Olson, George Schultz, F. C. Weber and Vincent Gorly. Pochelon and Rock were to be re-appointed. It was also decided that Indianapolis would be the city of the next meeting. Admittedly, this was a kind of "smoke-filled room" procedure. But the men making the decisions were the most active and influential in the Association. They had its interests deeply at heart. They were not attempting "Tammany tactics," but were sincerely working for the general good. It was in this light that the general membership accepted the pre-arranged agenda.

During the framing of the agenda, a discussion arose between Karl Baum and Max Schling about the price differential among different regions of the country. Schling suggested that FTD ought to have a trade paper of its own, which would keep the members informed of such differences and enable them to predict with fair confidence the cost of flowers to be delivered at a distance. Pochelon declared that several such papers had issued from his office, some of them carrying news, but that they had been abandoned for lack of interest. Baum and Schling thought such a paper could be developed into a genuine benefit to the members. This was the first mention of what later became the FTD NEWS. The prediction of its value to the members was destined to be fulfilled with emphasis.

At the opening of the business meeting on the following day, October 14, 1919, President Gude delivered a speech, of which Breitmeyer said: "I feel that this address today is one of the best ever written. There is so much food for thought in it that if we should leave this room at this moment we could go home and thank God for having had men in our midst who could give us this spirit of thought that has been given to us this morning."

This was the Gude of better times and, although he had lately passed through a serious illness, the relief from the strain of wartime worries allowed his jovial, expansive personality to reappear, to the delight and admiration of his listeners. But his address was a forward-looking examination of the florist industry, as related to FTD, with sound and searching suggestions for the post-war consideration of matters of membership, business, publicity, ethics and expansion into foreign countries.

William Rock, in his treasurer's report, astonished the audience by announcing that the $14,473.48 collected as annual dues during the past year exceeded the total amount of dues paid during the eight years preceding. Also, $6,209 had been added to the guarantee fund by new members, with only one member retiring and withdrawing his $10 payment. As evidence of Pochelon's collection efficiency, only $9.21 had been paid out of the guarantee fund during the life of the organization. Receipts from all sources had increased 254 per cent over the year before. Expenses had risen only 146 per cent. Rock's report was not given in a detailed breakdown. He had mailed a printed auditor's report to all members before the convention. There was now in the general fund $5,337.14. The guarantee fund amounted to $14,607.94. The total was $19,945.08. The growth of the Association from its shaky start of nine years before was called amazing by everybody.

Secretary Pochelon, while amusing the members with many stories and quips, conveyed the solid information that the Association now consisted of 1,206 members, representing 829 towns in the United States, Canada and Great Britain.

He then broached his favorite subjects of the Clearing House and publicity. Another questionnaire had gone out from his office to 1,200 members and 217 answers had been received. The important question: "How much FTD business did you do in the past year?" was answered by 133 of the members. The total, as compiled by Michael Bloy, Pochelon's newly-engaged assistant, was an impressive $465,000, an average of over $3,400 for each answering member. Six hundred of the members, according to the secretary, had not been in the Association long enough to answer the question.

As FTD was beginning its tenth year in 1920, its tin anniversary, Pochelon had brought to the meeting an assortment of tinware decorated with flowers. This he called the "tinth" anniversary bouquet. One of the items was a large four-sided grater. Showing it to the audience, and indicating its different sides, he said, "Look at this: the four stages of FTD life. This is rough and this is smoother and this is smoother still, and one of these days there will be no roughness at all."

As usual, Pochelon had a motive in his apparent frivolity. One of the articles was a large dishpan with a cover. Calling to Grakelow, Rock and Gammage, he handed the pan to them and told them to go through the audience and get it filled with greenbacks for the publicity fund. Grakelow thought a one-armed man should have the job, but Pochelon assured him that three policemen were standing at the door. The pan was passed and returned to the secretary with the cover in place. When Pochelon removed the cover, the pan was seen filled to the brim with bills of every denomination. The crowd roared. The secretary, however, would not accept appearances at their face value. Plunging his hand into the pile of bills, he drew out a large derby hat which had taken up most of the space. But a rough check showed that $660.10 had been added to the publicity fund.

Before the election of officers, Karl P. Baum offered a resolution that all past presidents become ex officio members of the Board of Directors, along with the incumbent president and vice-president. It was carried unanimously.

As had been planned at the pre-convention meeting, Breitmeyer was elected president. Irwin Bertermann was nominated vice-president and unanimously elected. Rock and Pochelon were re-appointed.

In the election of directors, Karl P. Baum, of Knoxville, and W. J. Smyth, of Chicago, were again named to the Board and were joined by a new member, W. W. Gammage, of London, Ontario.

One of the vital topics discussed at the Buffalo convention was fated to assume greater proportions in the business life of the members. This was the matter of shorter work hours for employees and the problem of Sunday closing. It is true that beneficial results sometimes follow the senseless evil of war and this could be said of the first World War. The beginning of automation was fostered by the introduction of mechanical advances in many lines, resulting in more production per hour. The effect of shorter factory hours was beginning to find reflection in other fields. None but the unseeing would deny that the 8-hour day was coming and, although nobody yet foresaw the 5-day week, there was a vigorous movement in favor of Sunday closing.

One other significant move was made. Pochelon was voted a yearly salary of $2,000 and Rock of $500; not only in recognition of the work these two had done, but as a realization that FTD had become a sound and virile Association and that the work entailed in handling its affairs was no longer in the part-time category. It had become a business association to be reckoned with. The meeting adjourned to meet the following year in Indianapolis.

Before the next convention, a new member appeared in the FTD family. The suggestion of Baum and Schling and others had been acted upon. The FTD NEWS appeared, beginning with the August, 1920, issue.

At the SAF convention in Cleveland, August 18, 1920, the officers of FTD, joined by Gude, Palmer, Grakelow, Gammage and Bloy, held an informal meeting at the Hollenden Hotel. Both Bertermann and Breitmeyer praised the new FTD NEWS, seeing in it a splendid opportunity to get information to the membership. But perhaps the most significant point made at the short meeting was Treasurer Rock's discussion of the Canadian clearing house operation.

In March, 1920, because of the difference in the rate of exchange between United States and Canadian money, it had been decided by Rock and Pochelon to establish a Canadian bank account, out of which remittances to Canadian florists could be made in payment for orders telegraphed into Canada by American florists.

This account had been built up with checks from Canadian retailers sent to American florists in payment of orders telegraphed from Canada. Pochelon insisted that the American florists send the Canadian checks to him, for deposit in Canada to the credit of FTD, and he would then remit an FTD check for the same amount in American money. In this way the Canadian florists received payment in their national currency, as did the Americans, the latter losing nothing in exchange discount.

Rock reported that not enough American florists took advantage of this arrangement, seeming to prefer depositing Canadian checks in their own accounts and taking the exchange disadvantage.

Said Rock to the meeting: "I think somebody ought to recognize the fact that the florists should pay their commission bills at the FTD office. They are building up a tremendous amount of money over there in Canada." His suggestion was seconded by Pochelon. "Let us have your American checks," the secretary told the group. "Let us pay your Canadian bills for you, the same as we are paying your Canadian checks, in full value."

This plan later became the standard procedure for international exchange between the two countries and the success of the operation did much to smooth the way, if such a rocky road could be said to have had any smooth stretches, toward the establishment of the FTD mandatory clearing house process, now in use.

By the time FTD met in Indianapolis for its annual business meeting in 1920, the membership had risen to almost 1,700 florists, and the guarantee fund stood at $21,000, $10,000 of which was uninvested and which Treasurer Rock announced would be invested, with the advice of the Board of Directors, before the convention adjourned. This was a pleasant contrast to the situation of 10 years before, when thirteen men had met to organize the Association.

Election of officers and directors was held on the first afternoon of the meeting. Breitmeyer was re-elected president by standing acclamation. For vice-president, Karl Baum nominated H. G. Dillemuth, of Toronto. The nominations were immediately closed and the chairman, Irwin Bertermann, ordered the secretary to cast a unanimous vote for the Canadian, who had been a director. For the post of director, three to be elected, Gude nominated Max Schling, of New York City; Herman Knoble, of Cleveland; and Edward Sceery, of Paterson, N. J. Said Geraghty, "I second that nomination. You have got the cream. You cannot skim the milk and get any more cream." They were unanimously elected.

In the selection of a convention city for the following year, and as further recognition of the Canadian membership, Toronto was unopposed. It was also decided that the next meeting would run for three days instead of the usual two.

The first day's meeting ended with a minstrel show performed by members of FTD. Apparently some of them were more than surprised at being called to the stage and handed a script. But the show, designed by Pochelon to illustrate by jokes, sayings and situations, some of the common failings in the florist industry and in the retailer's relations with his customers and the public, was a huge success.

One of the important moves taken at the Indianapolis

meeting was the amendment of the Bylaws of the Association, to provide for associate membership and foreign membership. As to foreign florists, there had existed a working agreement which somewhat resembled membership. There was no provision in the Constitution, however, for the admittance of those retailers. The year before, in Buffalo, this had been discussed by the Board of Directors and the amendment offered by Treasurer Rock embodied suggestions put forth at that time.

The same was true of associate members. This was an old question. Pochelon had long advocated admitting florist-supply salesmen as associate members, to obtain their good offices in the promotion of memberships. Nothing had been done about it until the decision was taken in Buffalo to consider the admittance of suppliers, wholesalers, growers and other allied trades to a restricted membership. Members of these divisions could not hold office or be elected to the Board of Directors. The wisdom of this amendment has been proved over the years. The Foreign and Associate Divisions have been potent forces in the growth and success of FTD.

Before the convention adjourned for the year, Pochelon conducted his inevitable campaign for contributions to the publicity fund. This time he had a wooden tub passed through the audience. It came back containing $1,719.

Retiring Vice-President Bertermann was presented with a service of sterling silver. Charles Grakelow, who was delegated to purchase the set, had enlisted Bertermann's aid in buying it by telling him it was to be a present for Breitmeyer. Bertermann even insisted on contributing five dollars to the fund. As the silver was presented to him there was prolonged applause and cries of, "Speech! Speech!"

Grakelow held up his hand. "Now, before he says anything, and so he will have an opportunity to catch his breath, I want to say that Mr. Bertermann exemplified what I have said about him by his kindness to co-operate when I went to him this morning and said, 'Irwin, we are going to take up a collection to get Philip Breitmeyer something,' and he said, 'What do you want me to give?' I said, 'A five-spot.' " Here, Grakelow returned the bill to Bertermann amid laughter. "Then I said to him, 'We want to patronize a man who is a friend of yours or a customer of yours; a man who, when we leave town, will feel that you have done something for him and that what we did in making the purchase was appreciated.' So he chose the place where it was to be bought.

"Then I said to him," went on Grakelow, 'What do you think Phil would like to have?' He said, 'Why not buy him a ring?' I said, 'The average fellow does not particularly care for jewelry.' He said, 'No, I'm not particularly fond of it myself.' I said, 'What do you think of giving him some silver, that his good wife and he may enjoy, and which she may feel is a partial payment for the many hours of his company which she has lost while he was laboring for us.' He said, 'That is a beautiful idea. If I were you I would get something in a silver service.' So I will close my remarks by saying that he also chose his own present."

The delighted crowd gave Bertermann an ovation. He was much affected. Holding up the set of silver, he said, "Beautiful as it is, it means little aside from the real, true friendship expressed by it. And as I get older, although I am not an old man yet, I will always possess and carry with me this expression of your regard. I thank you." Once again the audience showed its affection for the man who had worked so faithfully in the early days to found the solid Association whose benefits they now enjoyed. It was some minutes before President Breitmeyer could bring them to order, not that he tried very hard.

One more resolution was adopted before adjournment: one favoring Sunday closing. This had been a suggestion of Baum and others for some time. It was unanimously adopted. With the concluding formalities, the 1920 meeting of FTD passed into history.

The year 1921 was marked by widespread unemployment,

business failures and strikes. But FTD was able to announce that "the time has come when FTD is acknowledged to be the best and strongest organization for retail florists. European trade papers have lately written a great deal about our organization and have studied our Bylaws and Constitution." Membership passed the 2,200 mark. The guarantee fund approached $27,000. There was considerable interest growing in the work of 850 German and Austrian florists who had an association similar in some respects to FTD.

At the beginning of the year, the British Florists Federation heard a member offer a resolution: "Many of you have, no doubt, heard of the Florists' Telegraph Delivery Association of the United States and Canada. It would lead too far to attempt here and now to describe its working and expound its merits. Suffice it to say that it is a most powerful combination of about 2,000 florists who are anxious to make this Association international and desire our cooperation. I therefore beg you to move the following resolution: that a committee be appointed to consider the advisability of co-operation with FTD." The resolution was unanimously adopted. Up to this time only a few florists in Great Britain had taken advantage of the new amendment providing for foreign members in FTD, but the FTD story was well known in Europe and its expansion into that area was not far in the future.

The Board of Directors met April 11 and 12, 1921, at the Association Headquarters in Detroit to consider the coming convention at Toronto and other pressing questions. This was the most fruitful meeting that the Board had yet held.

A temporary Finance Committee, consisting of Karl P. Baum, Chairman; H. P. Knoble; and W. J. Smyth, had been appointed to investigate and analyze the financial structure of the Association and suggest methods of accounting and auditing that would give the officers and directors a more realistic picture of the economic standing of FTD. Karl Baum delivered the report of the committee. It was recommended that more business-like accounting practices be introduced, so that a yearly budget for the operation of FTD might be compiled, and that accounts be immediately readjusted so that the executive office could have all the facts of the Association's financial status. It was suggested that the committee be made permanent, with members to serve staggered terms as the directors did. The report was accepted by the Board and the committee made permanent, with Knoble to serve one year, Baum two years, and Smyth the three year term.

Baum called upon John M. Besemer, a certified public accountant who had recently joined the FTD staff, to outline his ideas on an accounting system for the Association. He was given authority to establish it.

It was also decided to invite representatives of the industry from Great Britain and Europe to the Toronto convention, as an acquaintance gesture and perhaps looking to further expansion of FTD service.

L. F. Darnell, notably successful in adding members to the FTD roster, was hired for three more months.

The FTD NEWS provoked a thorough discussion, with Bloy and Swenson present to hear the suggestions and to offer, out of their experience, ideas for the promotion of the magazine. Bloy, Pochelon's assistant, had undertaken to edit the magazine while Swenson, a Chicago advertising man specializing in florist accounts, took the position of advertising manager. There was some question of the advertising rates and the subscription price. Board members generally wished both raised, that the magazine might begin to show a profit. Bloy and Swenson held out for the prevailing rates, insisting that the present objective was to increase circulation. They felt that increased prices would hamper this effort. They pointed out that circulation figures were the biggest selling point to advertisers.

From its initial issue of 1,200 copies, the circulation of the FTD NEWS had risen to 3,303 and was growing. The adver-

tising income was rising. The month of March showed
$4,435.70 collected from advertisers, bringing the total
income for the life of the magazine to $23,668.20. But there
was a current operating deficit of $1,112.29. Bloy and Swen-
son felt that if they could increase the circulation by making
the FTD NEWS available to a larger audience, the increasing readership would attract more advertisers and thus
eliminate the deficit.

Regardless of the wishes of Bloy and Swenson, the Board
decided that the publication was exclusively in the interest
of members. It was so restricted. This provision still prevails.

The question of a new Handy Book, to replace the one
distributed in 1917, was brought before the Board. The
Handy Book was a directory of most of the towns in the
United States and Canada and showed the FTD member-
town which could best serve the smaller towns nearby, which
had no members. The first one had been compiled by Pochelon and his office force chiefly from reports of members and
from research in a standard atlas. It contained many errors.
Many of the mileage designations were incorrect, some of
them far off, especially in the West. There was a certain
usefulness in the book, but it had not been a complete success. It was planned to issue a new directory of the same kind,
based on accurate information. The main problem was the
cost of a new edition, estimated at $3,500. Also, business
conditions were in a slump, with a rapid turnover of florists,
as in other businesses. The rate of obsolescence of the listings
was another factor.

Several plans were suggested. A looseleaf system was urged.
It was thought by some that replacement pages could be
printed in the FTD NEWS, to be inserted into the main
edition to correct errors and add members. It was finally left
to the staff of the NEWS to arrive at the best plan. It was
decided, upon resolution, that the book would be delivered
at printing cost to the membership.

So it appears that a new, serious note had been sounded in

the Association. It had been popular to say at yearly meetings that FTD was now "grown up"; that the time for big-association thinking had arrived. This had not always been true; but now the note was in tune. Projects like the FTD NEWS and the new accounting system were adding maturity and responsibility to the operation. The head office was handling an impressive amount of money and investment of these funds required closer supervision, not from fear of laxity or dishonesty, but to know at any moment the precise status of the Association's financial affairs.

There were also serious considerations for the future. A time of unprecedented business expansion was imminent. This could not be divined by the members of the Board, but they were laying a solid base, from which they could take advantage of a rising economy.

A motion to invest $2,000 in Canadian bonds and $5,000 in short term American certificates was carried; also, a suggestion to allow 10 cents per mile and $5 per diem to officers and directors for attending meetings.

Another resolution was passed before adjournment, which might not have had the wholehearted support of Secretary Pochelon. It was decided to discontinue the free-will contribution to the publicity fund at future conventions. The thought was that this feature might cause certain smaller members not to attend. The meeting adjourned pending the annual convention in Toronto.

The florists of the Canadian city went "all out" for the annual meeting, October 11, 12 and 13, 1921. The King Edward Hotel, the scene of the meeting, was lavishly decorated with flowers, ferns, palms and other greenery. Two large billboards bearing the slogan, "Say It With Flowers," had been placed before the City Hall, further decorated with the intertwined colors of the two nations. Above the space between the billboards an imposing arch carried the legend, "Welcome FTD." All Toronto's luncheon clubs had been alterted and, since most of them met at the King Edward

Hotel, invitations were issued to visiting members of Kiwanis, Rotary and other clubs to join the Toronto members at their weekly luncheons. Entertainment was arranged for the visiting ladies during the business meetings and, as this was to be the first three-day meeting, there was time for sightseeing by the members themselves.

At the directors' meeting, held the day preceding the meeting, President Breitmeyer announced that, during the time since the last directors' meeting in Detroit, matters had been going so smoothly that he had no recommendations to present.

Perhaps the most important subject mentioned at the directors' meeting was the matter of the Clearing House. The word, "mandatory," had never been used in this connection since Gude, some years before, had warned, "We cannot undertake to go into the banking business." But now Hilmer Swenson and Harvey Larsen, supported by statistics from John M. Besemer which showed that the Canadian Clearing House had successfully handled $40,000 in the first 17 months of its existence, concluded their report with these words: "The new proposed extension of this feature to embrace all clearings of balances between members should receive your careful thought and consideration. With the Canadian Exchange Department we only go part of the way, but this could be extended to take in the operations of the entire Association, and each member benefited thereby. Of course, the details have to be perfected . . ."

There is no doubt that this report was first cleared with Pochelon and almost certainly with Breitmeyer, also, the latter remaining in close contact with the affairs at the head office through frequent visits and his almost daily luncheon meetings with the secretary. Although the two men were business competitors, with establishments only a short distance apart, they were fast friends. Where FTD was concerned, they almost always saw eye-to-eye.

The business meeting opened with the recitation of the

FTD pledge, a statement of FTD ethics written by Michael Bloy. It had been printed and distributed to all the seats in the hall. The Mayor of Toronto welcomed the florists to the city. He was thanked by Charles Grakelow. Flowers were wired to both President Harding and King George.

President Breitmeyer's opening address expressed his optimism in the face of a slack business year and extolled the progress made. He had reason to be optimistic, and proud as well. The report of Treasurer Rock, who was not able to attend the meeting, showed that the Association now had $40,000 on hand. The expense of conducting the affairs of the Association for the past year had approximated $18,000. This was the most successful report to date. Membership was estimated at almost 2,300 florists.

Michael Bloy reported that the FTD NEWS had begun to show a profit. This magazine had been one of the phenomena of the publishing field. Since its first issue, it had climbed steadily in advertising and in circulation. It had grown from 64 pages to 128 pages in the issue just distributed. Max Schling and others took the floor to praise both the magazine and the staff, calling it one of the most significant steps in the history of the Association.

Although Breitmeyer had arranged an agenda for the meeting, he did not adhere to it. Instead, he contrived a system of questions from the floor, on the theory that many less vocal members attended the meetings without opportunity to ask questions or obtain information. This he called the "Question Box." Questions submitted by the members were answered from the floor by florists experienced in the field concerned. This proved a popular and informative feature and occupied most of one day's meeting.

Some barbed humor was provoked by a question which the president undertook to treat facetiously. Someone asked, "Why is it that the women are never placed on the committees of FTD or asked to take any active part in the business?" The query received a solid round of applause.

Breitmeyer said, "What are you doing here, anyway, if you are not taking active part? Isn't that a silly question to ask? If you had sat in the meeting of the Board of Directors last night, you would have been choked with smoke, as I was. Why should you women want to be in all those things? Today we had our committee on window decorations. We selected two ladies and found that the weather was not just right to send out the ladies to judge those windows. So we eliminated the ladies. I think Mrs. Getz asked that question, so I will call on her."

Instantly on her feet was Hester A. Getz, of Cleveland, her eyes flashing. "No, I did not," she declared emphatically, "but the trouble is, you want to think for us. How did you know we didn't want to go out in the rain?"

She was stopped by prolonged applause. When she could speak again, she continued: "You would not like someone to say to you, 'You don't want to do that.' Give us a chance. We are no longer, in the United States, classed as imbeciles and drunkards and so forth, as we have been until woman suffrage came into effect. Please get out of your mind the fact that women want to usurp the place of men. They do not. Only for about 200 years have women been anything but chattels of men; you have owned us, and that is what we object to. We do not want to take your place. We want to be ourselves!"

By the time Miss Getz sat down to a crashing round of hand-clapping, Mrs. Helen M. Schluraff of Erie, Pennsylvania, was on her feet, frantically trying to attract the chair's attention. When she could be heard, she seconded Miss Getz's attitude: "I think the time has come, in the business development of our country when women should be regarded only on the basis of whether they are capable florists. It does not make a bit of difference in a business proposition. It is a question of whether you are a good business florist."

To the delight of the audience, President Breitmeyer beat a hasty retreat. Holding up his hand, he backed away from

ORIGINAL FTD LEDGER
KEPT BY ALBERT POCHELON

These pages from the original FTD ledger kept by Albert Pochelon after he became secretary of the Association in 1912 show the names of several members who became prominent in the affairs of FTD in later years. The L. Bemb Floral Company, shown upper left, was Pochelon's own firm. Breitmeyer, Rock, Wienhoeber, Palmer, Sceery, Bertermann and Smyth are other well-known names. The ledger is 7¾ by 5 inches.

The Clearing House began operation on an optional basis following the Baltimore convention of 1922. By 1923 (above), a system of handling member reports was well established and the Clearing House became a separate department of Headquarters.

Use of the Clearing House by all FTD members was made mandatory at the St. Louis convention of 1923, to begin January 1, 1924. By 1925 (below), it had become necessary to increase the size of the staff and install new systems of accounting and indexing.

By 1926 (below), the Clearing House was using electrical machinery for the processing of members' accounts. The increased efficiency of handling and reporting the clearings had fully demonstrated the value of the Clearing House system to FTD members.

.. AND NOW

A corner of the modern Clearing House, showing part of a battery of key-punch and verifier machines. These electronic machines, in the hands of their highly skilled operators, process each month more than 700,000 IBM cards with ten operations per card.

A part of the "heavy electronic equipment" in the FTD Clearing House. From left to right are collator, sorter and interpreter. In the foreground is a tabulator. This 2,000-pound machine translates IBM cards into the typewritten reports received by FTD members.

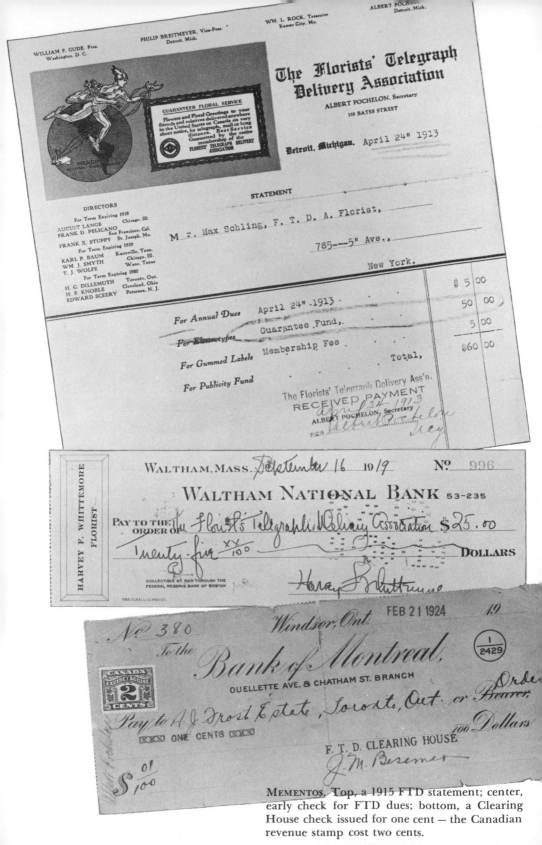

MEMENTOS. Top, a 1915 FTD statement; center, early check for FTD dues; bottom, a Clearing House check issued for one cent — the Canadian revenue stamp cost two cents.

the speaker's stand in mock fright, expressing his capitulation, "I am willing that Mrs. (she was really Miss) Getz be
elected president of the organization. Now what do you
ladies want?"

"We want to be treated just the same as men," she told
him.

But when Breitmeyer offered her the chair, she refused,
and the incident ended in a laugh.

Introduced at this meeting was the slogan, "Faith, Truth
and Determination," built on the letters "FTD" by Secretary Pochelon, who explained that the slogan represented
the history of FTD: 25 per cent Faith, 25 per cent Truth
and 50 per cent Determination.

Miss Helen Wick was called to the platform to read a
report on the operation of the Canadian Clearing House, and
once again the discussion of a like system for the American
florists came up. There had been steady progress toward
some sort of centralized collection system since the first days
of the Association. But lately, against the objections of some
of the stronger members, talk was beginning about the
feasibility of immediately turning over to the secretary's
office the collection of all accounts. There was opposition to
this idea, but also argument in its favor.

Breitmeyer brought the issue out into the open by
stating, "A clearing house such as we will have some day
means a force of 20 or 30 people. We are going to have a
banking institution. FTD will have its own bank and do all
the clearing of all the bills that has to be done." President
Breitmeyer's prediction was correct. But before its realization, there were to be strong words and adamant attitudes,
both for and against.

The first day's meeting closed with one of Pochelon's
minstrel shows entitled, "Flowers of Paradise." According
to Breitmeyer's announcement it was to be "the cream of
all we are going to have."

The question box idea continued into the second day. The

most spirited discussion of the entire meeting concerned the
Sunday closing problem. At the directors' meeting preceding
the business meeting, Ammann had moved that the question
be decided on the floor. It was opened. It had been suggested that, in the next printing of the official list of
members, those shops which closed on Sunday be designated
by stars. Many objected, maintaining that it discriminated
against them. There were two attitudes on this point: one
that it shifted business away from the marked shops, and the
other that it was a mark of distinction to be closed for the
Sabbath. The argument waxed hot. Miss Getz accused the
Association of changing its attitude since the Buffalo meeting, which favored Sunday closing. This the president
vehemently denied, insisting that Sunday closing was a
matter of individual decision and not one for dictation by
FTD.

"Well," said Miss Getz, "the attitude is so different from
what it was at Buffalo that I wanted to know what caused
the change. The sentiment then was that you would rather
give the man and woman who would not close on Sunday
the cold shoulder. I wondered why the change of heart."

Breitmeyer called on Bertermann to explain the attitude
of FTD on this question. But Bertermann skirted the
question. Instead of answering, he sided with Miss Getz
against the star designating the Sunday closers. Ammann
now took the floor, and upheld the star designation as
informing brother florists that there were certain retailers
to whom it would not be wise to send orders for Sunday
delivery.

He said, "It is not a mark of disgrace to have a star in
front of your name, simply because you are closed on
Sunday. I think it is the finest thing we can have, and I am
glad that the Board of Directors decided yesterday on that.
The star will not be put in front of anybody's name unless
by request. I think it is a mark of honor."

Grakelow explained that his city had many Seventh Day

Adventists and Jewish customers who held marriage ceremonies in the principal hotels on Sundays. He could not, he
said, afford to close on Sunday, because he would be denying
service to a substantial number of his customers. He tried to
reduce the tension by saying, "I will say that we cannot
have a star, and if any of you come to Philadelphia and see
a chap walking along the street singing, 'Will There Be Any
Stars In My Crown?' that's me."

But the laughter and applause that followed did not stop
the argument. Max Schling advocated staying open to serve
the working man, and Bertermann rose again to observe, "I
am afraid if we put a star in front of these names it will put
a premium on keeping open on Sunday."

Pochelon said, "Let the FTD Association go on record,
anyway. Do not take any FTD orders for Sunday delivery.
I never have been to the workshop on Sunday yet."

"Can we make an order today that we are going to close
up everybody on Sunday?" asked Breitmeyer. There were
cries from the floor of "No! No!" Continued the president,
"Now, we wanted, of course, to have your advice in the
matter; and I can see that we are no further ahead than we
were in the meeting of the Board of Directors, because there
is a difference of opinion. And I dare say that out of our
membership of 2,000 you will not find 25 who will have a
star. If they wish to close their shops, they are at liberty to
do it."

Carl Reck, of Bridgeport, Connecticut, now rose to say,
"I would like to say that it is absolutely illegal in New
England to keep your store open for business, and you can
be put in jail for it. A store should not be kept open on
Sunday and there should be no FTD order sent on Sunday
or delivered on Sunday."

"Do we want to go on record?" Breitmeyer asked again.
This time there were cries of "Yes!" from the floor.

Reck was still standing. "I make a motion at this time
that there shall be no FTD orders sent by any member of

FTD to an FTD member for delivery on Sunday." The motion was seconded.

Grakelow rose to a point of order, insisting that he was breaking Philadelphia's Sunday closing law at the insistence of the clergy, the judges and the makers of the law, "and as long as they insist on our breaking it, we will break it rather than lose such a wonderful clientele."

Breitmeyer had had enough. "I am going to close this argument without any vote," he declared.

"Question on the motion," shouted Reck.

"No, we will not vote on it," repeated Breitmeyer to the applause of the audience. "I do not know anything about parliamentary rules, but we will not vote on it."

"I rise to a point of order," insisted Reck. "I would like to know your authority."

"I am just resigning the chair for somebody else to take it," said Breitmeyer, and throwing up his hands he retired to the back of the platform and sat down, leaving the speaker's stand vacant.

"There is a motion before the house," called Ammann from the floor.

Now Reck relented. He said, "As the discussion seems to have been taken so much to heart, with your permission I will withdraw my motion." This statement was greeted with applause.

Said Ammann, "I was going to offer an amendment to that motion, but since the maker has withdrawn it, I will make this motion: that this organization give those members who want to be recognized as closing on Sunday the privilege of having a star in front of their names." The motion was seconded.

This brought Herman Knoble to his feet. "That is equally bad, to place a premium upon those who care to remain open on Sunday. I do not want a star in front of my name, indicating to Charlie Grakelow, who remains open on Sunday, that he cannot send me an order, because I might get that order telegraphed to my home, or to the manager's home or to my sister's home, and if it is necessary for the order to be delivered on Sunday, it is delivered. If not, we deliver it on Monday morning. Now, forget about the star and withdraw your motion." There was more applause for this statement. Knoble was much respected as a good businessman and a straight thinker. It is also possible that he had stated the position of the majority.

"Mr. President," pleaded Grakelow, "I appeal to you to declare this entire discussion out of order."

Ammann was still on the floor. "As the maker of that motion," he stated, "I stand here before you, simply placing before this audience an action that was taken yesterday by the Board of Directors of this organization, without any discussion in that body. Since the members of the Board have got on the floor of this house today and created this dissension, or helped to create it, I withdraw my motion." There was more applause.

"The thing is all closed," declared the President. Heaving a deep sigh of relief, he said, "If we had all of our 2,000 members here, what would we do?"

The answer to Breitmeyer's question is that things would be pretty much as they were at Toronto. FTD has never deserted the principles of democratic discussion of important issues. They are the same in 1960 as they were in 1921. Only the issues have changed — not the procedure.

At Toronto, the members heard the first discussion of mechanical refrigeration ever offered to FTD. Herman D. Schiller, of Chicago, had made a study of the new cooling method and prepared a report. This was some years before mechanical refrigeration became common in the home. The industrial use of electrical refrigeration was still beset by problems and "bugs."

But Schiller foresaw the eventual application of the system to the display cases and storage rooms of florists, with ice used only for small package shipments. He envisioned large shipments of flowers from coast to coast in refrigerated railroad cars, with the country-wide distribution of cut flowers serving to standardize prices and make a greater variety of stock available to the average florist. This in turn would benefit the FTD florist by permitting the sending florist to assume that any kind of flowers he specified would be in the receiver's stock.

As with all predictions based on the fact of industrial revolution, part of that vision has not materialized. But he was right in most of the report.

There was much discussion of industry problems, merchandising ideas, ethics and publicity. In the election of officers for the ensuing year, Brietmeyer was re-elected president, and Grakelow, Borden and Palmer re-elected to the Board. The election of a vice-president was deferred until after the selection of a convention city for the next meeting. It had become the custom to elect a man from such city as vice-president.

There was a spirited competition between St. Louis and Baltimore for the 1922 meeting. The St. Louis representatives had come heavily prepared for a convincing campaign. Baltimore boosters were also well prepared.

But the speech that turned the tide in favor of the Maryland city was made by young Robert L. Graham who, speaking for his home town, said, "I am sure that every man here today had a father. Away down in Baltimore I have a real, good, genuine father, and before I left for Toronto, father said to me, 'Now, kid, go to Toronto and bring the boys to Baltimore in 1922.' I have always found that the best way to keep in with Dad was to do what Dad said. For your business meetings we have already engaged a suitable hotel. For your rest, refreshment and enjoyment, we have good old Chesapeake Bay oysters and crabs and fishing, and dandy pillows on which to lay your heads. So come to Baltimore for your spiritual good and for the good of your business. Come to Baltimore for rest and refreshment, and to help me keep in good with Dad."

The young man's humor and boyish personality immediately swung the meeting to his side and, backed by Feast and Grakelow, he was able to secure the 1922 meeting for his home city. The vote was Baltimore 110, St. Louis 49. Then Charles Feast, of Baltimore, was elected vice-president. Rock and Pochelon were re-appointed treasurer and secretary. At the mention of Pochelon's name, he was accorded a rising ovation. Thus was adjourned one of the most successful meetings of the now burgeoning Florists' Telegraph Delivery Association.

A directors' meeting was held in Detroit in May, 1922, at which several suggestions were offered, to be of significant influence on the future stability of FTD. The report that Karl Baum had made on the district representatives had shown the directors that perhaps they were not in sufficiently close touch with the general membership of the Association. Only a small percentage of the members attended the annual meetings. In the hinterlands, there were hundreds of smaller florists, enthusiastic and hard-working supporters of FTD, who were unable to take advantage of the conventions, but were strong boosters in their own territories.

J. F. Ammann, field man for SAF, attended the meeting and echoed Karl Baum's suggestion for a better organization of the districts. He told of his work for SAF and the creation of a district organization for that society. It was evident that he knew what he was talking about and that he had the ability to do the same for FTD. At the suggestion of the president, a committee consisting of Bertermann, Feast, and Schling was appointed to confer with Ammann.

Also considered was the intrusion of politics into the election of the Association's officers. It was brought to the attention of the Board that undercover letters were being written between prominent florists, advocating certain men for office. This was an effort to by-pass the recommendations of the directors. Although the Board did not criticize the writers of these letters, recognizing their democratic right to express their views, it appointed a Nominating Committee, to agree on recommendations of officers. Previously this had been done in informal discussion.

A supplement to the latest Handy Book was authorized. Bloy reported that the last issue of the Handy Book made a profit of $3,500.

In the matter of new members, it was mentioned that several of the older members had objected to the enlisting of younger florists in their territories, some of them even refusing to recommend them for membership. Baum suggested that new members be subjected to a period of probation, until the stability of their operations could be determined. It was his thought that the Association could afford to be more particular, since it was now in the position of having membership sought by florists, instead of seeking members. This was true. With a membership, expected to exceed 3,000 before the end of the year, FTD had reached a place where its importance in the industry was established. Many young men, who had learned the business under the older firms, were branching out for themselves and seeking membership. Action on Baum's plan was deferred.

It was also decided to invite Carl Engleman of London to attend the Baltimore meeting at the expense of FTD. There was wisdom behind this invitation. Engleman was a prominent British florist and had evinced an interest in the international aspect of FTD. The directors realized that Europe presented a fertile field for expansion. They were looking about for someone familiar with the European situation, to travel about Europe, making contact with these florists as Darnell had done in this country. If they could bring Engleman to Baltimore, they could assess his qualities for this job and perhaps prevail upon him to undertake it.

John Besemer, the accountant, presented a plan for a clearing house operation, proposing a collection of 2½ per cent as a collection charge of bills cleared. Some of the directors and Rock, the treasurer, thought this commission too high and likely to keep members out of the clearing house. In the end it was decided to appoint a Clearing House Committee, to consider the problem for presentation before the annual business meeting at Baltimore. The committee consisted of Rock, chairman, Borden and Knoble.

There were several other proposals at this meeting. The question of women directors arose. Apparently Miss Getz's rebuke at Toronto had not gone entirely unheeded. The decision was made to offer the district representatives a $5 per diem expense account to help them attend the annual meetings. Karl Baum, considered the authority on the district organization plans, was empowered to notify the district representatives of the Board's decision and to secure the attendance of as many as possible for the Baltimore meeting.

The Board met once more before convening at Baltimore. That was in conjunction with the SAF convention in Kansas City on August 17, 1922. It was a short meeting, sandwiched in between the regular meetings of the society, but two important reports were received by the Board. The first was from J. F. Ammann, who had been on the road since the previous May, setting up district organizations through Kentucky, Indiana, Ohio, Michigan, Wisconsin, Illinois, Iowa, Kansas, Oklahoma and Texas. He reported that the florists in these states were enthusiastic over the new plan. His trip had been a morale booster, as well as tending to solidify and integrate the interior structure of the Association. He had cleared his plan with Pochelon, who could not attend this meeting and, although the Bylaws had no provision for this fanning out of authority, he was encouraging the district representatives to establish unit organizations in their territories.

This harmonized with a tentative suggestion made at the Detroit meeting, a result of Karl Baum's suggestion that the United States and Canada be divided into 12 territories of five districts each, each territory to elect a director. With one representative from each district and a director from each five districts, it was thought that all members would be more democratically represented in the national council.

Pochelon had also briefed Ammann on the proposed rules of the Clearing House Plan which had been devised by John Besemer, in consultation with the secretary, in the Detroit office. President Breitmeyer adjourned the meeting in deference to the SAF conferences, but plans were made to meet the following day at the home of William Rock to consider the unit organization and the Clearing House Plan. This meeting was not reported, but it is known that important decisions regarding the matters to be presented at the Baltimore meeting were made.

CHAPTER SIX

The Big Decision

HE 1922 annual meeting in Baltimore saw the fulfillment of young Graham's promise of hospitality. His offer of luscious Chesapeake Bay oysters and other of the city's famous seafood was carried out with such enthusiasm that several members were not able to answer the roll call at the meeting on the second morning. One of these was Herman Knoble, of Cleveland, scheduled to read a paper on business methods in the operation of a florist shop. A basket of flowers was sent to his room.

Baltimore also saw the first formal meeting of district representatives. It was conducted by Karl Baum as temporary chairman; Fred Weber, temporary secretary; and J. Fred Ammann, FTD field manager. A resolution was framed for presentation to the general meeting, stating the aims, duties and rules of the district representatives' organization, which is still the basic pattern of the present organization. The temporary officers were made permanent and, when the resolution was read upon the floor of the business meeting, it was unanimously adopted, marking the formal inauguration of the district representative system which had been informally in effect since 1916.

Ammann, in his report to the meeting, suggested the division of the United States and Canada into 12 self-governing regions. But this refinement was reserved until later. It was recognized that since the district representative plan could not be applied in all parts of the two countries because of

105

the scarcity of members in some areas, it would be better to delay the final districting of the areas until Ammann had visited all the localities and outlined the plan to the individual florists. However, enough was accomplished at Baltimore to provide the basis of the solid organization that exists today.

One of the representatives present at Baltimore was Carl Engleman, from London. He presented a paper on the European situation, of which Gude said: "There are a number of valuable suggestions there and I move that it be referred to a committee of three, to go over and report recommendations tomorrow."

The district representatives also had framed the resolution setting up the Clearing House. This was the next order of business. The resolution was read and the floor thrown open for discussion of the proposed plan.

Since the Toronto meeting, at which the Clearing House Plan, printed in a special edition of the FTD NEWS, had been distributed to the general membership, the members had been studying the proposed Clearing House arrangement and forming their opinions, for or against. The discussion consumed the remainder of the first day's meeting. It is surprising that no more acrimony was actually generated, perhaps because the FTD NEWS had kept the issue before the members between the two meetings, with opinions expressed by leading members of FTD. All present had come to Baltimore prepared for the question. Some of these opinions were completely reversed at the meeting.

Breitmeyer called on Herman Knoble to explain the plan. Knoble had expected to have Rock's notes, but Rock had remained in Kansas City and had not sent the notes to Knoble. But the Clevelander was never at a loss in the explanation of accounting practices. He made a concise presentation extemporaneously, explaining that through investing a part of the guarantee fund as part of the plan, a sizeable yearly return could be realized for the Association by the operation of a Clearing House.

Karl Baum then read the resolution drawn up by the district representatives, which called for the initiation of the plan effective January 1, 1923. Dillemuth, F. E. Palmer, Gude, Neil, and McCarthy either spoke on the plan or asked questions for clarification of certain points. These were answered by Knoble, Besemer, and Pochelon.

Finally, Max Schling was recognized. "To tell you the truth," he said, "absolutely the truth, in my innermost heart I was against it at first, but since our friend, Herman Knoble, said that we are going to get a dividend, I am for it."

Schling then expanded on the Clearing House idea, showing that it would be not only a fool-proof collection plan, but a direct money-saving operation for every florist. Although he had been opposed to the plan, he had nevertheless carefully considered it.

He now astounded the membership by announcing: "I am right now prepared to offer you $250,000 for the first five years (operation of the Clearing House) and $500,000 for the second five years, and I would be a millionaire in 10 years." Schling's offer was not merely a dramatic gesture. He had discussed this offer with a New York banker and his offer was bona fide.

The chair said, "Inasmuch as this is a very important subject and it is now getting late, we will let you talk on this subject the first thing tomorrow morning." He adjourned the meeting.

Frank Schramm, of Toledo, objected. "I don't see why we should waste any more time on this and bring it up in the morning, when the same men are going to handle our Clearing House that have handled the Association; and I would make a motion that we put it to a vote." Nevertheless, the adjournment stood.

That night, wherever a knot of florists could be found in the lobby of the hotel, in the dining room or on the sidewalk before the hotel, it was a good bet that the topic of their conversation was the Clearing House. The officers and leading members of the Association were besieged with questions. Far into the soft October night, the plan was dissected and examined, reassembled and discussed, and without doubt it intruded upon the dreams of many an FTD florist in Baltimore, disturbing his sleep more than had the oysters of the night before.

At the meeting the following morning, President Breitmeyer opened the discussion with a short statement of the billing procedure which the plan involved. Then he called upon Ira C. Harper, who summarized the opinions of the men who had spoken in favor of the plan. When he had finished, Gude moved the adoption of the resolution. The reporter read the resolution to the members again, and the question was called for. The resolution carried unanimously by a rising vote. The Clearing House, which Pochelon had envisioned for years, was now an established fact.

In a way, the vote was an anticlimax. Much more fireworks had been expected. There had been for years a violent disapproval by some important members of any form of enforced collection. It was considered by many an invasion of the private enterprise of the individual. Both Knoble and Gude had opposed the plan at first. Now they supported it.

This change of view can be explained, in great part, by the manner in which the plan was presented to the members. Instead of offering it to them at one of the annual meetings, without giving them a chance to mull it over in private and study it in detail, the opposite approach had been used. It had been tentatively presented to the Toronto meeting, without a vote or even an opinion being requested. Following the Canadian meeting, at which a printed explanation of the plan had been distributed, the question had been kept alive through the columns of the FTD NEWS. The members were urged to study and consider it. And the urging had been heeded. Members *had* examined and discussed the Clearing House with their brother florists. Solid opinions had been formed. And although there had been some last minute shifts of position, no one could say that the Clearing House Plan had not had the full consideration of the members.

It was accepted on the basis of its value and promise. Its unanimous approval by the members indicated that all were satisfied that it would be a step forward in the growth and progress of the Association.

It would be pleasant to report that the acceptance of the plan ended all misgivings. But the truth is that no single move by the membership led to so much bitterness and hard feelings. Nothing so shook the foundation of FTD as the acrimony engendered in the early days of the Clearing House operation. Basically it was a sound plan, but many rough stretches lay in its path ahead before it could find a smooth roadway upward and forward.

Breitmeyer, although nominated to succeed himself, refused to ask for a vote. Edward Sceery, of Paterson, New Jersey, was nominated for president and, being the only candidate presented, was unanimously elected. St. Louis was chosen as the convention city for the next year and accordingly, Fred C. Weber of that city was elected vice-president. Rock and Pochelon were re-appointed. Baum, Gammage and Smyth were re-elected directors and the meeting was adjourned.

It is hard to estimate the importance of the Baltimore meeting. Great forward strides had been taken. In a sense, an era had ended: an era of individualism in the florist industry. The strength and power of the Association had been so demonstrated that retail florists, always the most individual of businessmen, had been willing to surrender a part of their business operation to the Association.

Into its hands they had placed the supervision of their credit system. They had done this willingly and with full knowledge of the facts. The regrets, if any, were to come later.

CHAPTER SEVEN

The Clearing House Story

HE YEARS 1923 and 1924 constituted one of the gravest periods FTD had encountered. The establishment of the Clearing House, voted unanimously by the membership at the Baltimore meeting, seriously divided the membership. Although no member had voted against it at Baltimore, many refused to co-operate with it; some through apathy but many from open condemnation of the system. Two of those who did not enter into the Clearing House operation were members of the Board, a fact which became known to the rank and file. This dissension among the directors was reflected in the general membership.

Edward Sceery, the new president, had promised the members that he would spend his time traveling in the interest of FTD affairs. He kept his word, and it was well for the future of the Clearing House that he did. He joined Ammann in the field manager's travels, visiting and talking to organized units, stressing co-operation with the Clearing House, explaining its operation and showing how complete membership acceptance of the plan would benefit the entire Association.

Ammann also performed valuable service in his organization work with new units. These two men on the road, with Pochelon and Breitmeyer in Detroit, exerted every effort to get the new plan off to a good start. Breitmeyer wrote a letter to every member who was not using the Clearing House, urging him to do so. Pochelon continued his flow of letters of explanation and pleas for confidence in the plan.

The FTD NEWS carried almost every sort of article which the editors could prepare, detailing the rules of the Clearing House, publishing letters from co-operating members and seeking by the printed word to supplement the talks and letters of the members. This propaganda may have been beneficial. The first reports of the Clearing House at the end of January showed only slightly over 50 per cent of the membership participating. The statement indicated that 1,281 reports had been filed, totalling $105,793.85 and representing 21,186 transactions. It was not a heartening situation.

There were 1,650 reports in February, the second month of operation, and, after four months, it was estimated that 65 per cent of the members were co-operating.

The semi-annual meeting of the Board of Directors was held in the Association offices in Detroit, April 30 and May 1, 1923. The principal topic was the Clearing House. To replace President Sceery on the Board, Henry Penn, of Boston, had been elected by a mail vote of the directors. This procedure was authorized by the Bylaws and it was regularly conducted. But Pochelon objected strenuously to Penn, though not for personal reasons.

At the meeting, there were harsh words between Sceery and Pochelon, the latter contending that a director from either Missouri or Oklahoma should have been chosen to make the Board represent a wider area. This situation was soon smoothed over and the meeting proceeded to the main question: the operational and financial difficulties of the Clearing House.

The first clearings had not been smooth. There were several reasons for this. The operation was strange to the office personnel. Mistakes were made in the remittances, which caused the members affected to wonder if they had been wise in espousing the plan. Many reports from members were improperly filled out, illegible, lacking addresses or otherwise insufficient, necessitating correspondence between office and member to render a true statement of his account. This situation consistently improved, however, and it could be told that the plan would work eventually, with the big "if" of wholehearted co-operation from the entire membership.

This was verified by an auditor from the First National Bank in Detroit. John Besemer, Clearing House manager, explained to him that, when a customer wished to order flowers delivered in a distant city, he went to his local FTD florist who accepted the order and the payment. The florist then wired the order to his FTD correspondent in the distant city, specifying the sort of floral gift desired and the amount paid. The receiving florist made up and delivered the order, sending his bill direct to the Clearing House, instead of to the sending florist. The Clearing House deducted a 2 per cent handling charge and credited the receiving florist's account with the net amount of the order, less 20 per cent, which it credited to the account of the sending florist.

Accounts were balanced monthly, each member receiving a bill or a check, as his account showed debit or credit. The auditor was impressed with the simplicity of the system, likening it to the plan used by banks in carrying on the financial business of the nation.

With this assurance, the Board went into the financial situation. This was not so promising. The success of the operation depended upon each co-operating member making his report by the tenth of the month following the transaction. This had not been general procedure in the industry, where accounts were paid when most convenient, some florists letting the accounts drag out 45 to 60 days, a practice condoned by most of the receiving shops.

From the tenth of the month following the transaction, the Clearing House then had until the twentieth of the month to process the reports and make payment to the credit members or bill the debit members. This not only caused a work concentration for 10 days, but seriously strained the financial structure of the Clearing House for the same period. Slow payments by members, who had ordered more flowers than they had delivered, caused the remittances to members with a credit balance to create a deficit in the Clearing House operating fund. This fund was not too healthy in the first place, consisting of $14,000 borrowed from the FTD general fund and $12,000 borrowed from the FTD NEWS fund.

Besemer, in his report to the meeting, stated that at that time the Clearing House would need $60,000 to $70,000 per month, to clear successfully the accounts expected. It was plain that some financial rearrangement would have to be made. Pochelon himself had signed notes at the bank for enough money to complete the clearings of the former months. Bertermann suggested that the plan be reversed, so that each member, when he sent in his monthly report, would also send his check to cover all charges he owed filling florists. Besemer objected strenuously to this arrangement as destroying the Clearing House idea altogether. He was supported by John H. Hart, vice-president of the First National Bank in Detroit, brought into the meeting by Breitmeyer to review the Clearing House Plan and to give financial advice.

After a detailed explanation of the plan to Hart by Besemer and Pochelon, and some pointed questions by the banker, Hart said, "I really think your financial troubles are mostly imaginary." He made a suggestion. If they would pass a resolution, he said, authorizing the officers to borrow needed funds and then submit the resolution, a copy of the Bylaws, a statement of accounts receivable and of the amount of the guarantee fund, the bank would honor the necessary note. With this Hart left, the thanks of the entire Board going with him.

This interview had solved the most pressing problem facing the Clearing House. Said Pochelon: "I think what Mr. Hart said was wonderful. He had more confidence in the

florists than the florists have in themselves." The necessary
resolution was quickly passed and the meeting turned to
other matters, shortly adjourning to meet next at the annual
business meeting in St. Louis. One obstacle had been
successfully surmounted. But there lay ahead at St. Louis
the problem of the adamant opposition of a strong section
of the membership. Forceful measures were necessary to
overcome the antagonism.

Before the October meeting at St. Louis, Sceery continued
his travels, preaching the gospel of FTD. A strong move was
started for 1,000 new members before the year's end. This
campaign was surprisingly successful, in view of the clouds
that were darkening on the horizon. The Clearing House
continued in operation, with both the clearings and the
procedures improving. This was greatly due to the intense
work of the manager, John Besemer. He was a man after
Pochelon's own heart, for he, too, knew no quitting time
when there was work to be done.

Despite all the criticism of the Clearing House plan, its
clearings slowly increased. But there was a solid minority of
members who refused to co-operate. Some members of the
directorate remained in this group. This may seem surprising, after the unanimous vote at Baltimore, when the
Clearing House was authorized by the membership. This
reticence is hard to explain unless it is acknowledged that,
being in the minority, they considered the discretion of wise
silence the better part of business valor.

The meeting at St. Louis was the largest gathering of
florists that had ever been held. Registrations showed that
721 members had arrived, ready for the fireworks. They
brought with them enough non-members to swell the convention visitors to 1,000. There were two reasons for this.
The campaign for members was progressing and the fortunate central location of the convention city enabled many
to attend who never had before. Probably the main attrac-

tion was the impending Clearing House debate.

During the year, since the authorization of the optional Clearing House for a year's experimentation, the pro and con elements had been feverishly at work, lining up support for their views in the larger middle ground of the membership. The situation was so unsettled that a dramatic presentation from the floor of the meeting could have swung the issue either way. This middle ground held some of the most important men in the Association. It could be said that some of them wore two hats, one pro, the other con. This was the danger which the Clearing House faced. A stampede, provoked by a skillful speaker, could have wrecked the operation forever. This was known to the Headquarters staff. It is perhaps fortunate that they understood the actual situation better than the opposition did.

Early on the first day of the meeting, following the long directors' meeting of the day before, President Sceery was stopped on the stairs leading to the hotel coffee shop by a large group of Midwestern florists, in St. Louis to oppose the Clearing House. "Here he is," cried their spokesman, motioning to his fellows who gathered about the president. Then, addressing the president, he said, "Will you allow us to have a secret ballot on the Clearing House?"

Sceery studied the group. He knew them all. "Are you asking me a question you will ask me from the floor?"

"Yes."

"I will overrule it," declared Sceery, "and if you do not like it, appeal from my decision."

"Why won't you do it?" the man insisted. He was a leading florist.

"If you don't like my decision," repeated the president, "appeal from it. I am in a hurry. The meeting starts in 10 minutes and I haven't had breakfast." And Sceery hurried away.

This indicates the tension over the issue, building already. A secret ballot would have revealed the strength of each side, which the proponents of the plan would rather not have the membership know at this early stage.

It is a documented fact that President Sceery himself had come to the meeting to oppose the Clearing House. But at the directors' meeting, the fervency with which Pochelon, Breitmeyer, Gude and others advocated retaining it on a mandatory basis had influenced him to change his mind. He had gone to his room after the meeting and altered his official address, so as to espouse the Clearing House cause in its fullest application — an indication of how tensely the matter was poised to move in either direction.

After the formalities of the opening of the meeting on October 9, 1923, the president delivered his official address.

He was personally known, through his travels, to more florists than any previous chief officer. He was an imposing figure, of more than medium height and somewhat grey, with his hair parted high on the left side and combed upward into a long "sausage roll" along each side of his head. As he progressed through the speech, each recommendation was greeted with hearty applause. He was a skillful speaker, able to convey great sincerity.

He saved the Clearing House matter until the end, knowing it to be the most important consideration of the meeting. As he concluded his recommendation that the Clearing House be made a mandatory function of FTD membership, he paused and looked out over the audience. There was silence for a long moment. Then it broke. As the cheering began and continued, it built in intensity until Charles Grakelow advanced to the front of the platform and held up his hand. When quiet had resumed, he moved that a committee be appointed to consider the recommendations made, "and that a rising vote of thanks be given you for the most able paper, I feel safe in saying, that any president has ever given to the body he represented."

As the audience rose, applauding, a number of members hurriedly left the hall.

"I will appoint on that committee," announced Sceery, as the applause faded, "Mr. Charles H. Grakelow, of Philadelphia; George Asmus, of Chicago; Charles H. Brown, of New York; Tom Joy, of Nashville; and James Smith from my own home place, East Orange." Turning to the audience, he said, "I say to you again that the success of this convention is very largely in your hands. This is your convention. The responsibility is on your shoulders." The president resumed his seat and, after a few remarks from Vice-President Weber, the meeting recessed for lunch.

Many a member missed his lunch that noon. There were hurried caucuses by both factions. Knots of florists gathered in the lobby, in members' rooms, around luncheon tables. Pro whips and con whips hurried from group to group, soliciting support for the side they represented. Prominent men of the profession became rallying points for rank and file members, worriedly seeking advice and enlightenment. No political convention was ever more intensely concentrated on the principal issue of the meeting. It could be felt in the air. It could be seen in the hushed hurrying about of the members.

Well might anxiety fill the air. FTD was at the crossroads. Success for the mandatory Clearing House meant a strong, solvent and centralized Association. Defeat would see a retreat to lackadaisical methods, delinquent accounts, loose control and gradual deterioration. It had happened to similar organizations.

In the early afternoon the meeting reconvened. Several committee reports were read. It is doubtful whether they were heard. Then came the report of the Committee on the President's Address, given by Charles H. Grakelow. It is noteworthy that President Sceery, although he remained critical of the Clearing House and its operation for a long time, seemed at this time completely committed to the idea. That is obviously why he chose Grakelow to give the report which contained the resolution calling for the mandatory

Clearing House. Grakelow had appeared many times at these meetings. He was known and respected as a brilliant speaker, witty, convincing, even inspiring. He, more than any other man present, could have swung the balance either way; although Breitmeyer, Gude, Bertermann and Sceery himself were speakers of the first rank. Also, Grakelow, like Bertermann, was not enthusiastic in his support of the plan. If he had been moved by the opposition and induced to present their case, the result would perhaps have been different.

Grakelow moved through the resolutions of the Board regarding the recommendations of the president, presenting each for a vote, cultivating as much drama from the occasion as possible, heightening the suspense by the moment. Finally he said, "The last motion, Mr. President, is this." He paused and, seeming to look each member on the floor directly in the face, he said, "Your committee in accordance with your recommendations, moves you now, sir, on the matter of the Clearing House. And I may say that this action was unanimous, not a dissenting expression; the vote was unanimous and the committee was a harmonious 100 per cent on this. So I move you, sir, following the line of your suggestion, that the Clearing House be recognized as a permanent feature in our growth; that it be considered a fact in existence and, to make it workable, practicable and satisfactory, we recommend that it be made mandatory as of January first, 1924."

There was no hesitation this time. Instantly the applause swept over the room, solid and assuring.

As Robert L. Graham came to his feet to second the motion, others did the same. Soon the entire audience was standing and continuing to applaud. Grakelow held up his hand for silence and the applause dwindled away as the members resumed their seats.

"The chair recognizes Mr. Graham as seconding the motion," announced Sceery. "You have heard the motion made and seconded. Are there any remarks?"

Now was the time for the opposition to present its case. A member was on his feet. Without waiting to be recognized, he blurted, "I would like to ask if the Clearing House is now in our Constitution and Bylaws?"

"It will be by the time this goes into effect, the first day of January," replied Sceery calmly.

"I asked a question," the man persisted.

"I am answering your question," said the president.

"I asked you if it was in there now!" continued the defiant questioner.

"It is a part of our law, yes, adopted in Baltimore last year." By this time Sceery was somewhat nettled.

"According to that," the man shook his finger at the president, "you will have to notify every member in writing before you can take a vote on that!"

Grakelow stepped forward again. "May I say, Mr. President, that the Board of Directors empowered two of the Board yesterday to confer with a corporation counsel, of the city of St. Louis, and in accordance with his decision rendered yesterday, we, your committee, feel that we are absolutely within our rights in presenting this motion. I, therefore, ask for a question on the motion!"

Applause began again, and there were cries of "Question! Question!" throughout the hall.

Sceery raised his hand. "The question has been called for. As many as favor the motion say 'Aye'." There was no mistaking the shattering response. "Contrary, 'No'." Dead silence, a tense watch-tick of anxious silence, then bedlam broke loose. Over the roar of the crowd, Sceery shouted, "It is unanimously carried and so ordered!"

The president permitted the celebration to continue a little longer and then asked the members to resume their seats. "I want to thank this committee," he said, "for the attention they have given this report. I have spent a great deal of time in the preparation of the report and I thank you from the bottom of my heart."

What resembled the beginning of a parade to the mourner's bench commenced when Herman Schiller, of Chicago, stood up, red faced, to confess: "Mr. President, it was my most painful duty to represent the unit opposed to the Clearing House. In Chicago, there have been a great many of us who have continuously cleared. Others have not. I now want to bring the message and assurance to you, Mr. President, and to the entire Board of Directors and officers of the FTD — that the Chicago and vicinity unit will cooperate 100 per cent with the FTD Clearing House!"

The entire delegation from Chicago, between 30 and 40 members, came to their feet, cheering. There was prolonged applause and cries of, "Three cheers for Chicago!" Mike Bloy, from the platform, shouted, "What has become of the Chicago banner?"

"The Chicago banner has gone to the train that is going to carry us to Chicago," shouted Schiller, over the hubbub, "where you are to spend Friday!"

Cried Mrs. Norman Stuart, with a hint of hysteria in her voice, "We will name Friday, in Chicago, Victory Day for the Clearing House!" More applause. From the other side of the house, a Mr. Cooper stood up to announce, "I am 100 per cent for the Clearing House. I would like to make a motion that, from now until the time this thing becomes mandatory, every one of our members support this organization and pay no bill to any man direct, except through the Clearing House!" The president did not think this was necessary.

Now it was Grakelow's time, and he, too, confessed that he had not been co-operating. "I think," he said, "when a man makes a mistake, he should acknowledge that he made a mistake. I want to say to you that we declined clearing in February. We have not cleared since then. But when I got around the Board yesterday, with the directors, and learned how the thing functioned, and that we were supposed to send the checks of the individuals on to Detroit, instead of keeping them ourselves, which with me is a weakness; it is a failing . . ."

Laughter stopped him for a moment. But he went on to promise full co-operation and to make the sound suggestion that John Besemer take the speaker's stand to answer any questions, or make any explanations, that the members might desire.

This was an excellent move. John Besemer had developed the Clearing House plan, knew it thoroughly, and his aptitude in accounting was famous. A native of Kalamazoo, Michigan, he had gone to work before finishing high school, but had studied accounting at night. Later, he was able to finish his studies in Chicago, where, at the age of 21, he had passed the state board examinations for Certified Public Accountants. He practiced his profession in New York for a time and then came to Detroit. Since no reciprocity agreement existed between Illinois and Michigan in the matter of his accountant's license, it was necessary for him to qualify before the State Board of Michigan, which he did easily. Pochelon had been impressed by him and had engaged him as an accountant in the FTD offices, where he was engaged when it became necessary to plan the accounting procedures for the Clearing House. These had been largely Besemer's work.

As he took the speaker's stand, ready for all questions, John Besemer looked much like a high school boy, preparing to deliver his commencement address. But any doubt of his capabilities vanished in his assurance and sincerity. His answers were ready and complete. There is no doubt that a great many of the dissidents were reassured by what he told them.

One man, George Wienhoeber, a prominent Chicago florist, defied the will of the majority. In his favor it is recorded that, in the early days of the Clearing House operation, he had had a disproportionate share of the early mistakes in his accounts. So he had ceased to use the Clearing

House and had gone on a completely cash basis.

"I cannot figure out how anybody would object to taking cash with their order," he argued from the floor, "and I cannot figure out how an Association can compel a man to do business in any other way than that in which he wishes to do business."

President Sceery stepped to the front of the platform. "Let me answer you," he said quietly, "by saying that this organization has decided, this afternoon, that beginning the first of January we are going to have 100 per cent co-operation. Let us not side-step the issue. This is what we are going to do. If you will co-operate, you will send your check to the Clearing House. Otherwise, if you are not going to give us co-operation, we will have to lose your membership." The audience showed its approbation by applause.

Wienhoeber did not hesitate. "All right, gentlemen," he said, "I will withdraw from the FTD Association at the present time."

That was the day's only resignation. Out of 3,000 members, the casualties were light. During the next year, 108 members were dropped by FTD for failing to live up to the Clearing House rules, principally for non-payment. Eight of these were reinstated during the year. Approximately 250 resigned rather than accept the Clearing House Plan.

This does not mean that the Clearing House path was wide and smooth. Any new machine or system contains "bugs" and the Clearing House had its share. But at its head it had Pochelon and Besemer, dogged, determined, hard-working. After a time, through experimentation, trial and error, the system began to function. But, more important, the membership began to realize that most of their money worries were being taken over by the head office in Detroit; that the 2 per cent collection charge which they were paying to the Clearing House was actually saving them substantial amounts in bookkeeping, postage and lost accounts. With this realization, there came more confidence and trust in the florist industry, more pride and loyalty for the Florists' Telegraph Delivery Association.

The first full year of mandatory operation closed January 1, 1925. The Clearing House had handled 659,621 orders, for a gross of $3,881,817. The next year it cleared more than $5,000,000 and continued its remarkable climb, without regression, until the great depression of the '30s. The 1933 clearings were slightly above the 1925 amount, but the climb then resumed. From 1941 to 1943 it more than doubled, and again from 1942 to 1944. The postwar period affected the gross amounts of the clearings very little, dropping only about $2,000,000 for 1947 and 1948 (from $30,000,000 to $28,000,000) with a recovery in 1949, which came barely short of picking up the total lost in the two previous years. There has been no regression since.

At the beginning of the Clearing House operation, the concept of special business forms for special purposes was just beginning to be introduced to the business world. The first FTD reports came in on the members' own forms. The untangling and standardizing of the reports was a principal reason for the early mistakes.

By 1926, John Besemer had a standard form developed for the operation. This was distributed to the members, with the request that it be used to lighten the load of the Clearing House. Even the simplest description of the procedure of reporting at that time seems detailed and difficult. Members received pads of "Orders Filled Forms" printed in triplicate — white, pink, and yellow. These sheets were perforated into six sections. The top section contained the reporting member's name and city. This same information appeared on each of the perforated sections, which were called "tips." There were blank spaces on the tips, for listing the recipient's name and the amount of the order and another space for entering the name of the florist to be charged.

In making his report, the filling florist entered the proper information in the blank spaces and returned the white and pink copies to the Clearing House, retaining the yellow copy for his records. In the Clearing House, the pink copies were kept intact, but the white slips were separated at the perforations and sorted.

At first this sorting was done by hand, but later a machine called a "sortergraph" was used, to mechanize the operation and reduce the margin of error. The sorted tips were posted, item by item, to the Clearing House account of the member charged. The pink copy was used in crediting the filling member's account. The ledgers were balanced and cards containing all the information listed in the members' statements were retained in the Clearing House files. The 2 per cent collection charge was deducted from the amount of orders. A statement was mailed to each member, showing either a debit or credit balance. This was a laborious process.

As soon as they could be procured, the latest Underwood accounting machines were installed. With them came a special Underwood representative to train the personnel in the use of the machines and to stay at the FTD offices as long as supervision was necessary. At this time, the FTD offices were on the sixth floor of the Pochelon Building, at 815 Bates Street, in downtown Detroit.

With the business expansion of the '20s, printing companies and firms specializing in business forms introduced "engineered" material for office paper work. Efficiency experts lent their talents to developing new methods of routing work loads in offices and industries. Following this trend, the FTD Clearing House adopted an increasingly efficient set of forms for members and for inter-office use.

When it was apparent, in 1948, that electronic equipment had reached a practicable point of development, the FTD Clearing House installed complete IBM equipment. This increased the efficiency of the operation with less personnel, a saving to the membership in both instances. As these machines were improved and new models developed, offering increased efficiency per unit of floor space, they were installed until, at present, there is little manual operation. New electronic devices are constantly added to the equipment, as their utility and accuracy are demonstrated. All this has been necessary to keep up with the growth of the industry and the FTD Clearing House Plan.

Under the present procedure, each member reports to the Clearing House weekly the number of orders for flowers that he has filled upon request by wire, telephone and mail. This report, made on a special form and sent to FTD Headquarters in a distinctive envelope, goes direct to the Clearing House, now a beehive of electronically clicking machinery, activated by the nimble fingers of dozens of specially trained girls, the IBM keypunch operators. A card is punched for each order, translating the order into machine language at the rate of 500 per hour. These orders are verified by a recently developed electronic device. Keypunching is one of the few remaining manual operations.

From the keypunch machines, the verified card goes to the electronic sorting machine, where a battery of sorters is handling cards at the rate of 1,000 per minute. Then the card goes to the collator, where it is automatically determined whether all orders being processed are for members actively affiliated with FTD. Next, the card travels to the heavy equipment section, which is the printing department for all Clearing House reports. This completes the card's trip through the 10 electronic phases of the Clearing House operation.

Considering that the average number of orders processed each month exceeds 600,000, more than 6,000,000 card operations are handled by this department monthly. This figure should stagger the imagination of even so enthusiastic a visionary as Albert Pochelon.

In 1959, the Clearing House processed 7,896,337 individual orders for flowers, with a dollar volume of $60,129,653.

Three FTD employees saw the Clearing House develop

from the early, laborious hand operation to the mechanical and electronic marvel of today. Jennie Prendergast came to work at FTD as a bookkeeper in 1924 and retired in 1957. She recently passed away. Still active are Laura Dennis, who joined the FTD staff in March of 1926 and now works in the Membership Fulfillment Division; Isabel Elsbernd, who came to work in the Clearing House in April, 1926, and now works in the Publications Division; and Dorothy Smith, a member of the Clearing House staff for 21 years.

The Clearing House has been called the heart of FTD. But to say that it is the vital organ of the Association is like saying that the heart is the most important detail of the body. No one organ of so complex an organization is of prime importance. Each is subordinate to the whole that nourishes it.

It is true that the present international scope of FTD and the large volume of its domestic and Canadian business could not have been realized without the efficient reporting system which the Clearing House bestows upon the industry.

Those early members who saw in the Association the possible, eventual means of transporting such a perishable commodity as fresh cut flowers over half the world, were the spiritual kindred of those who prophesied a city lighted by the press of a button, a voice and an image appearing out of the air, a journey to the moon and back. The objectives were different. But the method was the same; visions, plans, and everlasting work, against adversity and disbelief.

FTD ADVERTISING

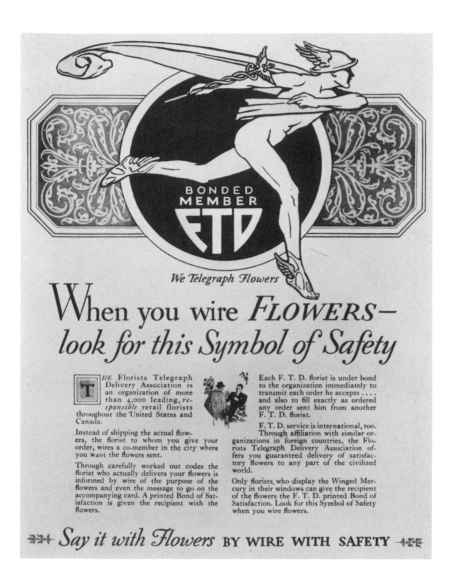

FTD's first national magazine advertisement. This was a full-page, two-color display in the February 11, 1928, issue of LIBERTY MAGAZINE. It was run simultaneously in the February, 1928, issue of the FTD NEWS for the information of members. This was the first appearance in print of the newly adopted Mercury emblem which replaced the one that had been in use since 1914. Two suppliers advertising in the FTD NEWS used the new emblem in the same issue.

FTD had become a substantial national advertiser by 1937. The Board of Directors appropriated $150,000 for a four-color magazine advertising campaign during that year, marking the first time the advertising allocation had exceeded $100,000. Above is the four-color Christmas ad that ran as a full-page display in the December 20, 1937, issue of the SATURDAY EVENING POST. Note the Mercury emblem design at that time.

FLOWERS-BY-WIRE

Say it much better...

Our Deepest Sympathy

• Upon the death of a friend or dear one, it is a very natural impulse of kindness to convey one's heart-felt sympathy. At such a time, flowers can often express sympathy more simply and more beautifully than words.

• If you wish to order flowers by wire, any official F.T.D. florist who displays the Winged Mercury Seal, will most graciously handle all details of the order. And you can be happy in knowing that lovely fresh flowers with your personal message of sympathy, will be delivered to any city specified in the U. S., Canada or Overseas . . . in a matter of a few hours.

FLORISTS' TELEGRAPH DELIVERY INTERNATIONAL
484 East Grand Boulevard, Detroit, Michigan

"Saying it much better" meant a continuation of four-color half-page magazine ads in 1947. A more personalized approach was used, calling attention to the fact that for every occasion, flowers convey a natural and expressive message of sincerity. A simpler ad format replaced the vogue of ten years before.

Transplant your love overseas

In 4 Hours

You can *actually* transplant your thoughts of love, of congratulations, or of remembrance for any occasion, through beautiful Flowers by Wire. Your loved ones, relatives or acquaintances on the European Continent and in the British Isles — receive them by speedy F.T.D. International Service, in only 4 hours.

• Your order will be handled quickly and inexpensively by any official F.T.D. florist, located in all U. S. and Canadian cities. Look for the Winged Mercury Seal displayed on their windows. Simply give him your flower order — if you want advice, you'll get it cheerfully. He'll handle the details. Your lovely flowers and personal message will then be delivered Overseas, easily and speedily.

• May we suggest that for Birthdays, Holidays, Anniversaries, for Business or . . .
IN ANY EVENT — WIRE FLOWERS.

FLORISTS' TELEGRAPH DELIVERY INTERNATIONAL
484 East Grand Blvd., Detroit 7, Michigan

This ad ran in November, 1946, and shows that FTD was aware of the number of Americans stationed overseas following the close of World War II and desired to keep this thought before the flower-buying public. Note that the Mercury emblem has been changed again.

An Important Message

By Dr. Frederick Brown Harris

Chaplain of the United States Senate

"Please Omit Flowers" is a request often issued when arrangements are announced for what is usually called a funeral service.

In life's darkest hours, when hearts are torn by poignant grief, when it seems as a dear one goes from our sight and side that life has tumbled in, a strange new directive puts a taboo on the Creator's petaled masterpieces which can say nameless things that no human lips can utter.

Whence comes this incongruous suggestion? Omit flowers — in the Valley of the Shadow, when every yearning impulse is struggling vainly to express feelings that are too deep for words!

Then it is that flowers offer wings to affection, appreciation and consolation, to wistful memories and assurances of sympathy.

In "Say it with Flowers" there stretch enchanting vistas of sacramental beauty like the glory of a garden or the shimmer of moonlight on a silvery sea.

Indeed, your floral gift can say things of exquisite delicacy and tender meaning for the expression of which a dictionary leaves you impotent. Heart meanings conveyed by flowers become prismatic, whose white light breaks into a perfect shower of crimson, violet and gold.

How bleak and bare the "last rites" can be when there is no loft from which comes the solace of a multicolored, surpliced flower choir in the chapel of death.

Reprinted from Dr. Frederick Brown Harris' syndicated newspaper column "Spires of the Spirit".

FLORISTS' TELEGRAPH DELIVERY ASSOCIATION

In an intensified drive against a resurgent "Please Omit" problem in 1956, FTD augmented its regular advertising program with the above full-page ad placed in READER'S DIGEST, CORONET and eleven of the nation's great newspapers. This opinion of a highly respected clergyman on the subject of funeral flowers was so widely quoted that it had a far-reaching effect.

For six months in 1958, FTD sponsored the Edward R. Murrow PERSON TO PERSON show over 124 television stations in the United States and Canada. The estimated audience for each broadcast was 20 million persons, more than 11 per cent of the combined populations of the two countries.

Something warm and human and wonderful happens when you send flowers-by-wire

FLORISTS' TELEGRAPH DELIVERY

This Emblem Guarantees
Quality and Delivery
—or your money back

To find your FTD florist,
see phone book Yellow Pages:
"Florists–Retail–FTD"
World-Wide Delivery

Featured in FTD magazine advertising for 1958, 1959 and 1960 is one of the great advertising photographs of all time, shown in the four-color ad above. The impact of this art on the flower-buying public has been tremendous, and the accompanying slogan effectively interprets a woman's joy at receiving nature's most perfect and welcome gift.

CHAPTER EIGHT

The Marketing Story

*A*LTHOUGH THE WORLD may beat a path to the proverbial woodland home of the man who builds a better mousetrap, that man would have few visitors if he kept the news of his invention to himself. The most important phase of any commercial production activity is distribution, which consists of three phases: availability, awareness and incentive. In this, flowers are no different than mousetraps.

Flowers must be made available to the public. The public must be aware that they are available and it must be given the incentive to purchase them. The method by which these three essentials are accomplished is simply the never-ending application of advertising, sales aids, public relations and community project promotion. These activities are the special province of the FTD Marketing Division.

It was perhaps fortunate that the early organizers of FTD were believers in the value of publicity. Although there was then no organized activity along that line by the Association, the members had often undertaken to bring the fact of flowers to public attention in various ways.

Soon after the formation of FTD, a group of members attending the National Flower Show at Philadelphia conceived the idea of telegraphing flowers to the mayor of each town represented by a member present. This spontaneous stunt resulted in front-page articles in every town to which the bouquets were sent.

As early as 1914, the Cleveland Florists Club employed

Ella Grant Wilson, a public relations counsel of that city, to conduct a series of campaigns, acquainting the public with various uses to which flowers were particularly suited. Some of her promotions gained them national publicity.

But most of these promotions had a hit-or-miss quality, conducted privately and not directly relating to FTD. Most members did some local advertising, but there was still no concerted action by the Association. Working for SAF, which was then also the voice of FTD in matters of national advertising and publicity, Major B. F. O'Keefe, who conducted an advertising agency in Boston, had developed the slogan, "Say It With Flowers."

That is one of the great advertising slogans of all times. It belongs officially to SAF but it is still enthusiastically used by the entire industry.

On the subject of marketing, Herman Knoble's analysis at the 1917 meeting had not been superseded, although each annual meeting featured talks and demonstrations of marketing ideas and sales promotion, among them Pochelon's minstrels and skits.

With the beginning of the FTD NEWS, each issue carried articles by prominent florists on marketing, advertising, publicity and retailer education. Henry Penn, of Boston, was recognized in the Association as one of the abler publicists in the flower business. President Gude appointed him chairman of an informal Publicity Committee, to give the benefit of his experience to the membership.

It was not until 1923, at the famous St. Louis meeting which saw the establishment of the mandatory Clearing House, that a formal Publicity Committee was named. Penn was made its chairman. For the first time, the promotion of publicity, also involving sales aids and education, was made a function of the Headquarters staff. H. V. Swenson assumed this duty, in addition to those of advertising manager of the FTD NEWS. He was called upon by President Sceery to read a paper to the meeting on the work being performed by the publicity department of the Headquarters. At the end of the paper, Sceery remarked, "Well, Mr. Swenson, that is surely a well gotten-up paper; but it seems to me that all you men want to do is take our money away from us. I think there should be a little conservation of the money that we tried to get together. There is always some scheme to take it away from us." But, he did nothing to interfere with Swenson's plan.

Although the sales promotion plan was kept in operation for some time, it never became popular with the members. In 1927, it was decided to concentrate on publicity and a bureau under the direction of Gwen J. Dew was organized. Its duties consisted in sending out newspaper releases and bulletins, and furnishing the membership with promotion ideas to be used locally. Some sales aids were distributed. Later in the year a "Better Business Service" was developed in the form of a kit of merchandising information and marketing aids. This kit was supplied to the members by Headquarters and was replenished regularly with new material.

As in many efforts of this kind, the local florists often neglected to use these supplies. Local publicity and merchandising were found to be a two-way street. It did no good for the Headquarters staff to make plans and ideas for marketing and promotion, to supply the material for the plan and otherwise offer aid to the florist, if the merchant himself did not enter wholeheartedly into the scheme. This was what befell the Better Business Service. Too many florists placed the material in their desk drawers and forgot it.

To encourage application of the aids supplied by the Publicity Bureau, it was consolidated with the Field Department in 1928 and the combined services renamed the Educational Department. It then became the duty of the field men to instruct the local florists in the proper use of the material sent by Headquarters. Included in the kits were suggestions on how to get local publicity in newspapers, before luncheon clubs and other gatherings, how to make the public aware of the desirability of flowers for certain occasions, and how to establish good will between the florist and his public. Also, the field men offered advice on the attractiveness of the shops and on the basic principles of salesmanship and customer contact. Cost analysis and sound merchandising practices were also stressed.

A new Mercury emblem was adopted in 1928 to replace that in use since 1914. It was the central theme of the first national advertisement ever run by FTD. This was a full page, two-color display in the February 11 issue of LIBERTY MAGAZINE.

Meanwhile, a new advertising and publicity medium was coming of age. Radio, which had been chiefly regarded as a scientific toy, began to exert enormous impact upon the public by 1930. Better programming and mechanical improvements in both sending and receiving sets, had impelled radio forward more swiftly than any other medium. FTD was quick to take advantage of this. Recorded talks on flowers were sent to more than 500 radio stations every month.

The success of the radio programming was such that the decision was made for a concentrated advertising program. To finance that plan, the membership voted an advance of 1 per cent on all incoming FTD orders and the same on outgoing.

FTD went on the radio for the first time in 1931, with a special Easter program featuring a string ensemble from the Philadelphia Orchestra. Electrical transcriptions were sent to 125 United States and Canadian stations. The popularity of this one-shot program with both the public and the members was such that the matter of radio advertising was pursued with renewed vigor. A national Advertising Committee, appointed by President Thomas Luke and consisting of himself, Charles Grakelow, Arthur Leidiger and William Rock, appropriated $62,000 for a program to be broadcast weekly over a 33-station National Broadcasting Company network. To handle the arrangements, Brooke, Smith & French, a Detroit advertising agency, was engaged.

The talent chosen for the first FTD network show was an orchestra and soprano, under the direction of Rudolf Friml, the famous light opera composer. The program was broadcast "live" and recorded at the same time, so that transcriptions could be sent to stations not served by the network, if a local florist wished to sponsor it over his home-town station.

The depression period, then at its lowest point, made all businesses suffer. But, as observed before, great economic crises do not affect the florist business as severely as they do other enterprises. FTD was riding out the faltering economy. Clearings dropped only about $2,000,000 per year. But, in the face of this loss, it was decided by the Board of Directors, through advertising and service committees, to concentrate on publicity and service.

The depression was not the only factor that began to affect the florist business. A movement referred to as "Please Omit Flowers" began to concern members of the Association. This was a plan to induce mourners and friends of deceased persons to contribute to a charity in the name of the deceased, instead of expressing condolences through the universal language of flowers at the bier.

The florists, of course, recognized anyone's right to suggest a charitable gift. But they were concerned with the practice of many newspapers to include the term, "Please omit flowers," in obituary notices. This was a direct attack on the florist industry, a gratuitous affront to a business that was spending more money every year on advertising in newspapers, magazines and radio which, without doubt, the newspapers would be glad to see continued.

Frank J. Baker, of Utica, New York, occupied the president's chair during this period. He was a strong advocate of publicity and advertising and it was under his

administration that the first International FTD School was
held in Detroit in 1932. This school attracted 1,056 entrants
from 40 states and 2 provinces. It was not restricted to FTD
members, but was open to all professional florists. The idea,
as expressed by President Baker, was "Not more florists, but
better florists."

So successful was this concentrated 2-day course in
design and merchandising, that it was decided to make it
available to a greater number. In 1933, four schools in
different parts of the United States were held. Again, the
turnout more than justified the effort. Also in this year,
radio advertising was again included in the advertising
budget and, at the suggestion of the advertising agency,
through their public relations department, a National Flower
Shut-in Day was organized.

This program was budgeted at $10,000, half of which went
to sponsor the Walter Winchell Program. Winchell was then
one of radio's great figures. With his machine-gun delivery
and the intimacy of the news content of his programs, he
had replaced the fabled Floyd Gibbons as the highest-rated
commentator. Winchell also had the faculty of inducing the
public to back the various special days and charities he
promoted. He did an outstanding job for FTD on National
Shut-in Day. An estimated 167,000 shut-ins received flowers
from friends on that day.

Speaking before the annual business meeting, Charles
Grakelow said that the publicity received from that promotion was worth $160,000 to FTD.

But not all the advertising and publicity appropriation
for the year before had been spent. A balance of $26,637.05
remained and this, added to the $62,000 to be realized from
the "1% and 1%" assessment, gave the committee $88,637.05
for the next year's campaigns. Also, it was decided that the
$15,000 allocated to the annual business meetings and
subtracted from the publicity appropriation, should thereafter be made an item of the general budget. Thus, the

advertising and service promotions for the next year had a healthy allocation for their use.

The National Shut-in Day was continued in 1934 and 1935, increasing good will and improving public relations. Kate Smith, an enormously popular singer, joined Winchell in promoting the idea. Newspapers in 37 cities participated in Winchell's "Orchids to Heroes" feature, the "heroes" being men and women who performed outstanding public services during the depression.

In March of 1934, a national advertising program was launched in the SATURDAY EVENING POST, COLLIER'S, TIME and the LITERARY DIGEST. In the following year, a news photo service was established to draw attention to the florists' windows. Naturally, the picture stressed the national use of flowers and their popularity with prominent figures of the day.

In 1936, the advertising and publicity budget was raised to $91,500, with the publicity item not to exceed $10,000 of the announced budget. The wisdom of this expanded allocation was shown in the report to the 1937 convention in Philadelphia. With general business down 29 per cent below normal, FTD wire orders reached the highest volume ever recorded in a fiscal year, a 23 per cent advance, with a total of 1,801,960 orders for a gross dollar volume of $6,986,374.

This rise had two significances: the effectiveness of the advertising and publicity program and the beginning of a return to normal business following the depression. Ernest S. Simmons was president at this time and he wisely advocated the continued expansion of the public relations efforts. The membership rolls reached a new high of 7,151. The enthusiasm engendered by better business conditions and the conviction that the promotions on a national scale were major aids in the recovery of depression-ridden shops, injected new spirit and determination into the membership.

President Simmons supported the programs of advertising and publicity by advising members to maintain attractive shops, display merchandise of strong eye appeal, maintain trained personnel, study flower styling, manage their firms carefully, institute stock control, attend FTD schools and apply interpretative salesmanship. The Board appropriated $150,000 for a four-color advertising campaign in leading American magazines, and advised continued emphasis on public relations.

To promote the association of flowers and fashions, FTD engaged the services of Mrs. Charlotte Lindholm, a fashion consultant of New York, who wrote under the name of "Felicia Adams." FTD acquired the exclusive rights to articles written under this name. Mrs. Lindholm had extensive contacts with fashion illustrators, fiction illustrators, advertising art directors, department store stylists and window dressers. This enabled her to make flowers conspicuous in fashion illustrations in magazines, advertising copy and store windows.

The publicity program was continued, with releases of photographs and carefully composed sales suggestions. Also, it was decided that the Publicity Department work more closely with unit publicity committees, helping local groups to plant stories and photographs, containing (1) the name of the Association and (2) suggestions for the use of flowers-by-wire service by the public.

One of the stimulants developed was the slogan, "It's Fun to Wire Flowers." This struck instant approval with both the public and the industry. "Stunt" publicity was eliminated and only what was dignified and of definite value to florists was advocated. Said Mr. Luke in his report, "It is well for all of us to bear in mind that in the light of the advanced or more prominent position of FTD in the style and fashion world, all publicity must be in keeping with that position. The mantle of dignity will impress editors and writers and make all of our releases better received by them."

During the fiscal year of 1937-38, a curious circumstance affected the business of the FTD membership. It is not easily explained. Perhaps it cannot be explained at all. The United States and Canada experienced a marked decline in their death rate. It was estimated that there were 75,000 fewer funerals than normal over a 12-month period. That certainly produced at least 150,000 less funeral orders. But a substantial increase in sales, in the face of this decline, indicated that the advertising campaign must have developed many new customers for flowers-by-wire. Or, perhaps it had increased the frequency with which old customers used the service. It was decided in the 1938 convention in Portland, in view of the increase noted in business, "that our Association go forward with its advertising program, consistently following the sound principles which have proved so profitable in the past, and that full-page, four-color advertisements characterize our advertising for the future." The activities of the Publicity Committee were also approved, as were those of the Service Committee.

In "going forward with its advertising program," drastic changes were decided upon. It was the opinion of Ernest S. Simmons, chairman of the national Advertising Committee, that the agency which had been handling the FTD advertising for six years had not grasped the basic advertising needs of FTD.

There was not enough merchandising of the flowers-by-wire idea. There was a lack of definite tie-up between the individual shops and the buying public. It was the consensus that the advertising had been too institutional and esoteric.

Consequently, the Advertising Committee had invited presentations from other agencies. The ideas and suggestions of Young & Rubicam, of New York City, pleased the committee greatly, and it was decided to turn the national advertising campaign over to that firm, through their office in Detroit.

Young & Rubicam informed the committee that 90 per cent of the flowers-by-wire business was done for citizens in the upper income brackets. It recommended that FTD advertising be directed to this group, through media and along lines that had special appeal for that part of the public. Another fact uncovered by the agency was that the average age of an FTD customer was between 40 and 50. This, too, indicated the approach to be taken. Some customers made only one purchase a year. It was desirable that such customers, who already understood the value and appeal of flowers, should be attracted more often, with an objective of six or eight times a year.

A plan for revamping this entire program of FTD was presented by Young & Rubicam. It was suggested that the three committees be combined into one Sales and Advertising Committee so that a more definite co-operation among the committees might be attained and the energies of the whole promotional program more easily directed toward a definite end. A sales manager was suggested, to work from Headquarters through traveling field men, supplied with suitable sales material.

A recommendation, approved by the Executive Committee, was put to the Board of Directors at the January 27, 1939, meeting, President Willard Crain presiding. It was as follows:

> "That the new FTDA sales plan be adopted and
> that a committee be set up, to be known as the Sales
> and Advertising Committee, on a rotating basis, to
> have charge of these activities."

Mr. Grakelow inquired whether this new committee contemplated taking over the work of the Service Committee. President Crain was of the opinion that the Service Committee would eventually be absorbed by it to unify the entire promotional program, including the schools and other public relations activities.

To this Grakelow objected, reminding the Board that FTD had reached its present pre-eminent position through the diversification of committees. He urged utmost caution before so drastic a step was taken. Herbert M. Sauber, chairman of the Associate Division, expressed the belief that such a move would be the most important step since the adoption of the Clearing House. Most of the Board agreed.

In view of the opposing opinions, a secret ballot was taken. Seventeen votes were cast, 15 for the consolidation and two against. This was the beginning of the unified Sales and Advertising Department, directed by a specialist in sales promotion from national Headquarters. When Frank Baker, chairman of the Service Committee, heard of the acceptance of the recommendation, he said that he was glad to retire as chairman of that committee in favor of "this plan (which) was the first business proposition he had seen yet in connection with FTD advertising."

In November of 1939, Paul C. Kimball was engaged as sales director of FTD. The choice of Kimball, who had been with Macy's department store in New York, was made jointly by the Sales and Advertising Committee and Young & Rubicam. At their suggestion, he had gone to New York, Philadelphia, Boston and Washington to study the promotional methods in use among the florists of those cities in furthering the approaching Christmas business. Later he visited Cincinnati and wound up the trip with a visit to Frank Schramm, a prominent florist of Toledo, who later became a director of FTD.

When the Board of Directors met in Detroit, January 25, 1940, Kimball was asked to outline whatever plans he had for the promotion of the sale of flowers. He informed the Board that the Association was now obtaining, free of charge, releases on 280 radio stations; that the Sales and Advertising Committee had clippings from over 2,000 newspapers; that advertising counsel had a record of 103 million impressions, based on a Gallup survey; that since the committee had earmarked $10,000 for this work, 500 million readers would be reached; and that many of the releases told the FTD story and often suggested that the reader specify an FTD shop when he wanted to wire flowers.

Other material had been sent directly to the members. Broadsides had been prepared containing sales talks and attractive sentences to be used in referring to flowers. These were known as "sales sentences." It was urged that clerks memorize these sentences and make use of them.

Shops in nine cities had been selected as tests and, soon after St. Valentine's Day, a concentrated sales plan was to be introduced and tested in those shops until the middle of June. The plan would then be evaluated. A color film had been prepared for the use of schools and flower shows.

As a result of all this, said Kimball, sales were up six per cent in the number of orders, and five per cent in dollar volume.

The new sales director also advocated better bookkeeping by member florists. In this he was facing the same stumbling block that Knoble, Schling and others had encountered.

He also suggested that florists streamline their stock, to make easier the customer's task of selection. "If you show a customer six things," he said, "it is harder to sell him than if you show him only three."

All in all, it appeared that Kimball knew his business and was ready to offer solid merchandising and promotional assistance to the members in the operation of their shops.

Speaking before the meeting of the Board of Directors preceding the annual meeting at Cincinnati in September, 1940, Chairman Simmons of the Sales and Advertising Committee, praised the new program and the Sales and Advertising Department, calling it the most progressive step that the Association had yet taken, not only for the organization itself, but for the individual members.

On display at the convention was an exhibit, acquainting the individual shop owner with all the steps necessary to the preparation of a national advertisement, from start to finish. There was also on view a complete documentation on the free newspaper publicity and radio notices for the past year, and likewise a color movie showing the uses and advantages of flowers for decorations. Members were urged to arrange showings of this film in their own communities.

A series of regional 2-day conventions was planned to enable the Headquarters representatives to come closer to the membership; to carry the results of the national meeting to members who were unable, for reasons of finances or press of business, to attend the conventions. These regional meetings were to be featured by talks and demonstrations on arranging and designing, salesmanship, traffic and delivery problems; an ambitious program of much merit but, most important of all, the application of big business methods to an industry long conducted chiefly on a local basis.

The sales and advertising budget for the fiscal year 1940-41 was placed at $216,410, to be spent exclusively for advertising and sales promotion, eliminating contributions for flower shows, exhibits and other local activities, except the regional conventions.

The effectiveness of the new approach became evident in two ways. Business rose 11.9 per cent, which was more than double the increase for the preceding two years; and FTD won the gold medal award from ADVERTISING AND SELLING MAGAZINE presented for outstanding advertising and sales promotion by an association. A survey showed that the FTD advertisement which ran in the September 2 issue of LIFE MAGAZINE, under the headline, "Have You Ever Sent Your Wife 'Just Because' Flowers?" was read by more men than any in the issue, with one exception. Publicity during the year was placed in 18,000 issues of publications with a total circulation of over 175 million, and 300 radio stations requested and received talks on flowers, highlighting the flowers-by-wire idea. Newspapers also gave excellent co-operation in running publicity feature articles.

On the sales promotion side, four field men were then employed. The military draft, induced by Hitler's successes in Europe, made the recruitment of competent field men difficult. Two of these representatives worked throughout the Christmas season in florist shops to gain a thorough grasp of the business. Regional conventions were held in Philadelphia, Kansas City and Dallas. Meetings were scheduled for Atlanta and Chicago. Kimball attended these to acquaint the membership with the plans of the Sales and Advertising Department. A test promotion for Thanksgiving was conducted in certain shops by direct mail, window and interior displays, and sales instruction for sales people.

Kimball left FTD in the autumn of 1941, and was replaced by Harold Hewey, who had studied accounting at the University of Toledo. After practicing for some time, he had opened his own florist shop in Buffalo, serving as unit chairman and district representative of FTD. He knew the business well and, in 1923, had written an authoritative cost study of retail shop operation.

Drastic changes were contemplated in sales and advertising. Then came Pearl Harbor, whose effects could not be foreseen. Many members, still active, remembered the hardships endured by florists in the first World War. There came an attitude of watchful waiting. Sales of flowers had much declined in Canada, on the entry of the British Empire into the war in 1939. But the industry in the Dominion had made a rapid recovery. By 1942 it was almost in its pre-war condition.

Although sales promotion had not been so successful as before, the sales and design clinics had been well attended. As many as 2,200 florists came to the clinics in the more populous areas. Out of the $237,836.49 budget for the year, only $14,900 had been expended for publicity. Added to this amount was the 15 per cent agency commission, which brought the cost of publicity for the year to almost $17,500.

The committee thought that all such activities could be handled from the Detroit office more effectively for the money than by Young & Rubicam. It was decided to divorce the publicity aspect of advertising from the agency and make Detroit Headquarters responsible. It may have been in the minds of the committee to establish their own publicity department. This was not done, however. In September, the public relations firm of John Clements Co., Inc., of New York, was engaged to handle this work. They sent a representative, Paul Thomas, to Detroit. He established himself in the Headquarters office and worked directly with that staff.

It was decided to retain Young & Rubicam for another year and an advertising budget of $274,488.20 was approved in July, 1942.

Due to war conditions, the annual business meeting scheduled for New York in 1942 was canceled. The Sales and Advertising Committee met in that city, with the representatives of Young & Rubicam, to plan campaigns for the year. It was decided that all advertisements for the next year should be in color, each to carry a line urging the buying of war stamps and war bonds. The $20,000 that would have been spent on the convention was donated to the USO, resulting in favorable publicity across the nation.

Also in New York, conferences were held with the John Clements Co. regarding the spectre of "Please Omit," which again, under the mistaken idea of aiding the war effort, was beginning to stir. Plans were made to start a campaign to combat this evil.

During the following year, the Clements Company made an excellent record in public relations, obtaining mention on national radio networks on the programs of Al Jolson, Kate Smith and "Truth or Consequences." There was some objection to the meagerness of the $15,000 appropriation for this work.

The committee agreed with John Clements that he had done well on the $1,200 a month allotted him. In conjunction with GOOD HOUSEKEEPING MAGAZINE, a club study program had been organized to promote the study and use of floral arrangements. There had been 13,800 requests for the study kit from women's clubs across the country, 800 from the city of Chicago alone. More than 200 original poems were received from members of the study clubs. These were turned over to Young & Rubicam, for any ideas on promotion which they might contain.

The agency had continued its excellent work in the quality publications, according to the committee report of that year.

In the matter of sales promotion through field men, the war had made some changes. Hewey found it advisable to take men off their regular promotion work and send them into the field to organize delivery pools as a result of gasoline rationing. In 39 days, reported Hewey, they had organized 40 such pools in cities containing five or more FTD florists, and, by using the mails, had arranged pools in 127 more cities in the same period. Under Horace Head, chief artist, the schools and clinics were continuing. Head managed them without help from the field men. There had been a 15 per cent decrease in attendance in the 28 schools held during the year. But this was considered encouraging in view of the manpower shortage and gasoline rationing.

The contract with Young & Rubicam expired in July, 1943, and the Grant Advertising Agency was engaged to direct the advertising efforts of the Association, beginning in July. War conditions were causing growing concern among the members. But the advertising program was continued.

There was, however, a drastic change in the sales promotion and publicity aspects of the Sales and Advertising Committee's work. Over 1,000 delivery pools had been established by the field men, working directly in the towns where the pools were deemed necessary. This allowed one delivery truck to serve several florists.

The unit schools and clinics also changed their emphasis. Where before they had sought to teach florists new designs and methods, it was now decided to focus the attention of those clinics on training of inexperienced shop help, with which the florists had been obliged to implement their staffs, due to the war's drain on manpower. There was a pressing need for this training, and not only for the period of the war. Many foresaw the post-war years when, it was realized, many men and women who had worked in florist shops might not return. Horace Head, who conducted the clinics, was given two months in which to prepare material for this new series. In the meantime, plans were made in 30 centers for similar schools.

Some regional conventions were continued and were proving successful, uniting the members in the Association as never before. Their only contact with their fellows had previously been through the annual business meetings.

Because the conduct of war put increased amounts of money into circulation, business continued to gain. At the first business session of the Board of Directors in 1944, it was announced that clearings for the preceding eight months had approximated 10 million dollars, representing a business gain of 55 per cent, with an increase in the number of orders of 26 per cent. Foreign military orders amounted to $750,000.

These increases enabled the Sales and Advertising Committee to expand the national advertising, public relations and service programs.

But a new anxiety had arisen among the members. What effect, it was asked, would the war and the world-wide distribution of so much of the country's population in military service have on the buying tastes of the public after the coming of peace? To investigate this and to plan for those developments, a Post-War Committee was appointed by President Joy and an appropriation of $5,000 made for its expenses of research and instruction. This was to begin with the circulation of a pamphlet, discussing post-war prospects and asking for suggestions from the members.

The John Clements Company, in facing the problem, went to Adela Rogers St. John, the celebrated short story writer, and asked her to compose a story which would emphasize the comfort conveyed by flowers at funerals. Mrs.

St. John demurred, calling the subject too morbid for popular fiction, especially in time of war, with its widespread effect on American homes.

Soon after this talk with Mrs. St. John, she received word that her son, Flying Officer William St. John of the Royal Air Force, had been killed in a crash in England. Many flower orders were cabled from America for his funeral. And then Mrs. St. John received, from English friends, a half dozen roses, taken from the young man's grave.

She immediately telephoned Mr. Clements that she would write the story.

This was the origin of "Flowers at Sunset," a dramatic tale of a young boy who had lost a friend. At the meeting of the Board of Directors in March, 1944, Clements played a recording of the story for the members. They were greatly impressed with its simple dignity and emotional appeal. Clements presented bound copies to the directors and told them that the agency was having 450,000 copies printed, including a description of flower customs and a statement of the aims of FTD.

This was to cost $37,500, plus the agency fee. It was to be distributed to American Legion posts, cemetery managers, clergymen, newspapers and magazines, radio stations, service club officials, and to a list of teachers in colleges, high schools and normal schools. Copies were also to go to funeral directors, women's clubs and one to each member of FTD.

It would also be distributed gratuitously, as announced in certain advertisements of FTD.

Director John H. Claus inquired if the records of the story were available. They were. He suggested that pressings be made available to radio stations. It ran 11½ minutes, exactly proper for a 15-minute program. This turned out to be one of the greatest benefits which the Sales and Advertising Department ever received.

Beginning in 1945, the public relations account of sales and advertising was transferred to the Grant Advertising

Agency, for closer co-operation and looking to the integration of the entire marketing program. The Sales and Advertising Committee was still under the direction of Ernest Simmons. Projects previously developed were continued, with emphasis on newspaper, radio and magazines under the direction of Herb Devins of the Grant Agency. The end of the fiscal period showed an all-time high gross of $31,834,130 in FTD clearings.

The arrival of V-J Day was a happy event for the Western World. For the florists it was also a time for stock-taking; for estimating and planning their place in a post-war society that would exhibit many fundamental changes. New problems and new opportunities were before them. There was a new need for international planning in the air age which had just dawned upon the world. Members could foresee another chapter in their remarkable history.

With the close of the conflict and despite apprehensions of some who remembered the first World War, most of the contemplated difficulties did not materialize. Instead of a depression, the country entered one of the greatest times of economic expansion it had ever known. Thanks to preparation by the solidly established Sales and Advertising Committee, FTD was able to take full advantage of this economic climate.

Publicity kept constantly before the public the name of the Association and the idea of flowers-by-wire. Advertising provoked the buying incentive. The service phase of the committee integrated all efforts of the program and helped to apply the program at the local level. This accomplished two things. It increased the member's business and, at the same time, convinced him, by business growth, that his contributions were not an expense but an investment.

One significant straw in the wind was demonstrated to the Board at its Detroit meeting in June, 1949. George F. Rentschler of Madison, Wisconsin, replaced Ernest Simmons as Sales and Advertising chairman. He, like his predeces-

sor, realized the value of the work done by the Sales and
Advertising Department. He was an acute statistician. On the
basis of his investigations over the preceding five years, he
recommended that he be permitted to lay before the
membership at the forthcoming convention the project of
raising the advertising budget from 1 per cent and 1 per cent
to 2 per cent and 2 per cent. The expression "1 per cent and
1 per cent" meant that the sales and advertising budget
depended on an advance from each member of 1 per cent
of each incoming FTD order, and also 1 per cent of each
out-going order. In support of this he cited some advertising
expenditures for gift items that competed with flowers-by-
wire: jewelry, $11,640,000, or 6 per cent of total sales;
perfume, cosmetics and toilet goods, $88,300,000, or 13 per
cent; candy, $22,500,000, or 7 per cent; fancy leather goods,
$76,800,000, or 12 per cent; and FTD, $500,000, or 2
per cent.

Said Rentschler: "Our competitors have built huge sales
volume with adequate national advertising. FTD is competing for the same consumer dollar with a sub-normal ratio
of advertising power.

"We must recognize that the gift item field is big business.
We must get more consumer dollars away from our competitors and into the flowers-by-wire orders. To win our share,
we must meet competition on more even terms. We must
provide a more normal ratio of advertising support. For
example, by increasing our advertising budget from 1 per
cent and 1 per cent to 2 per cent and 2 per cent on each
order, we can double our selling power."

He went on to cite Parker Pen Company, Kraft Foods,
Whitman Chocolates, California Fruit Growers Exchange,
Mars Candy Company, Folgers Coffee, and Old Dutch
Cleanser as companies that had increased their sales from
40 per cent to 100 per cent in a few years by doubling their
advertising appropriations.

He concluded: "The committee believes that our present

successful advertising pattern should remain undisturbed, and that any advertising done beyond that be considered in the light of employing new techniques and media. It is the studied opinion of the Sales and Advertising Committee that this more normal ratio of advertising support (2 per cent and 2 per cent) will produce a larger volume of FTD business much faster each year."

But Rentschler and the Sales and Advertising Department were to encounter a legal technicality, which defeated the 2 per cent and 2 per cent move at the Montreal convention.

The proposal to raise this contribution was presented to the convention and, after a short discussion, adopted. At the meeting next morning, President Rollo Mueller announced, "At this time it is my duty to advise you on proceedings that we took yesterday in our convention activities that were illegal. I want to assure all of you that it was purely accidental that the presentation was made improperly. I am referring to the sales and advertising report, the recommendation that we increase our sales and advertising from 1 per cent and 1 per cent to 2 per cent and 2 per cent. It has developed that, through error, this amendment was not advertised to the membership in proper order. It could not be considered as an amendment and it does require an amendment to make legal the 2 per cent and 2 per cent. If there was any possible way to go ahead with our decision yesterday with a 2 per cent and 2 per cent program, as you folks in majority approved, I certainly would stand pat on the proposition, but in my office here I have to adhere to what is legal."

Thus Mueller regretfully held that the matter could not be introduced at the Montreal convention. Of this ruling, Grakelow said, "Mr. President, I have always held you in very high esteem, but I say to the membership now, Rollo Mueller has risen to a height that confirms our high inventory of him when we elected him originally."

Even with this disappointment, there was sunshine among

the clouds. The decade ended with national income down by 2 per cent. As to competing gift items, jewelry was down 7.3 per cent; luggage, 3.2 per cent; liquor sales, 6 per cent; disposable income per person, 1 per cent. In the face of this decline, clearings of FTD members were up 6.8 per cent. So ended the post-war period.

The mid-century coincided with another war crisis. By the middle of June, the Korean struggle was joined. This was not a declared war of the United States but prosecuted under the banner of the United Nations. But it was everywhere realized that the principal support for the effort would be furnished, both in men and material, by this country. Apprehension over this was reflected in business analyses. But no serious slump materialized. Although the FTD sales and advertising budget was reduced by $6,500 in expectation of business reverses, actually the gross dollar volume of orders rose $100,004.

During the year following the Montreal convention, both the advocates of the 2 per cent and 2 per cent provision and its opponents kept interest alive in the amendment. Before the 1950 convention in San Francisco, the matter had been properly presented, as required by the Bylaws. It was ready for consideration on the floor of the meeting. Opposing it was a proposal to leave the 1 per cent and 1 per cent in effect and, in order to raise more money, to place a service charge of 25 cents on each wire order, this to be collected from the customer.

With the introduction of the recommended amendment, a spirited contest developed on the convention floor. There had been in effect before this, a member's service charge of 4 cents per order, in addition to the 1 per cent and 1 per cent. But this had not supplied the needed increase in the advertising budget. The floor fight became a three-way affair: those who favored 2 per cent and 2 per cent, those who wanted to retain the 1 per cent and 1 per cent plus 4 cents, and the members who advocated the 25-cent service charge in addition to the 1 per cent and 1 per cent. Tommy Luke headed this last group. Upon the introduction of the Sales and Advertising Committee's recommendation, Luke offered his plan as an amendment to the amendment and made a short talk in support of it. He then called on another member, Jerry Anderson, of Buffalo, to explain the economics of the plan.

This move had been carefully arranged. When Anderson took the floor he produced two baskets, one twice the size of the other, and explained that the membership of 8,500, under the present plan, was now required to fill the smaller basket, and if the 2 per cent and 2 per cent plan went into effect, members would be required to fill a basket twice as large, out of their own pockets. This was a telling argument.

But, he argued, if the customer paid the 25-cent service charge on each order, then FTD would realize over a million dollars per year at no cost to the members. Moreover, Anderson supported his statements by citing three surveys taken in three recent years, which showed that 80 per cent, 75.5 per cent and 78.3 per cent of the public interviewed believed that the 25-cent charge was reasonable.

Ray Williams, of Shreveport, spoke for the original amendment. He showed the members a card which had been sent to a number of members not in attendance. How many were mailed and who mailed them is not known. They were dated August 28, 1950, the convention being called for September 4, 1950, and they contained the message: "Should FTD tax you $250 next year for every $100 this year? That is what they propose to do in San Francisco without legal notice to you. This is your FTD. Suggest you wire your regional director care of the Palace Hotel."

The card was unsigned. It also carried two misstatements. It implied that the change to 2 per cent and 2 per cent from the 1 per cent and 1 per cent plus 4 cents would increase the member's contribution by 250 per cent, and that the plan was an illegal attempt to change the Bylaws. But the amendment had been legally advertised. After the fiasco of the year before, the committee made doubly sure of the legality of the move.

Williams disposed of the postcard with definite figures. Indicating a lady in the front row, he said, "Supposing this lady here sends me a $5 order. Under our present plan we place 5 cents for advertising, which is one per cent. She pays 4 cents for a service to members. If our 2 per cent is adopted, she will pay 2 per cent, which is 10 cents. Under our present plan she pays 9 cents. Is that two and a half times?

"On an incoming order, we now pay 5 cents. Under the plan that we recommend, we would pay 10 cents on the complete transaction between Mrs. Watson and me. There would accrue to the sales and advertising and members' service program 20 cents, instead of 14 cents. This postcard, which I hope was honestly sent but is certainly misleading, said the percentage of increase would be two and one-half times. It isn't. It is 44 per cent. Forty-four per cent is not two and one-half times. I would like to hear from the gentleman, or any gentleman, who is a proponent of this service charge where, in the name of all that's good and holy, did they get that 250 over 100?"

Williams was on sure ground. The postcard was misleading and designed to excite the membership against the increase. From the flood of telegrams that poured into the regional directors, it had that effect. Others spoke, but the most telling argument against the service charge was presented by Victor Stein, of San Francisco, who was aware of strong competition for flowers-by-wire business on the West Coast.

Taking the floor, he said, "I have only one thought in mind and that is the competition that we must consider within our own industry. That subject has not been mentioned. I think it is one that is most vital to us in the consideration of this proposed service charge. We have got to meet competition. We do not like it when the fellow around the corner has a 79 cent a dozen sign in his window for gladiolas. Because we are ethical, we sell them at a proper price. How would we like it if any competing organization to ours would have a large sign in their window saying, 'No service charge here. We are here to serve you at no extra cost. Wire flowers'."

This brought applause. "Do we," he asked, "know what proportion of that dollar it costs us to make that sale? The sale is readily made for us. They come into our shop ready to buy, with one thought in mind, that they want to wire flowers to some other city. The sale has been made. The payment is guaranteed to the person who receives the order. Why shouldn't he then be willing to share with the man who assumes the credit at the other end in the selling by making it equitable at 2 per cent and 2 per cent instead of 9 per cent and 4 per cent, or 9 per cent and 5 per cent? If we pass this service charge, we not only have the competition from other luxury items but we have competition within our own industry and down we will go, and it won't take long."

Sentiment seemed divided between the 2 per cent and 2 per cent plan and the service charge. But Stein had caused serious consideration by his mention of rival organizations. When the vote was called for, 24 members supported Luke's plan. The contrary was asked for. Said President Mueller of the vote against the service charge, "I do not think it will be necessary for the teller to take an actual count. The amendment is lost. We now revert back to the amendment, that we have the 2 per cent and 2 per cent. Mr. Luke, do you wish to speak on that amendment?"

"I move you, Mr. President," said Luke, "to make it a happy family that we make it unanimous for the 2 per cent and 2 per cent, and let us all go out of here all pulling for a bigger and better FTD!"

One member stood his ground and voted against the motion. It lacked only that one vote of passing unanimously.

One other amendment was passed at the San Francisco

convention, directly affecting the Sales and Advertising Department. A Member Service Committee was formed to take over the field service division of sales and advertising. The thought behind this innovation was that, since the advertising and public relations budget had been increased by the adoption of the 2 per cent and 2 per cent amendment, more work would be transferred to the responsibility of that department and that the field service could better be handled separately. The new committee was to advise Philip Jones, the general manager. The field service men were to report directly to Jones, who was to have charge of the personnel and the direction of their activities.

The new budget for sales and advertising was tentatively set at $900,000, with $50,000 of this earmarked for public relations.

Both the Grant Agency and the Sales and Advertising Committee quickly took advantage of the increased power given by the new appropriation. Results came rapidly. For the first time in history, the budget recommended for the fiscal year of 1951-52 exceeded a million dollars. The amount was estimated at $1,116,452.

The advertising schedule, under the new budget, continued with 66 magazine advertisements appearing in 15 leading periodicals. Added to this, through the new appropriation, there was a schedule of 224 newspapers in 144 cities. Due to increased collections and increased FTD business, it was later possible to increase this to 311 papers in 183 cities. This meant a total circulation of 32,206,792 per issue and a projected total impression figure of 700 million for the 1951-52 year.

Public relations promotions included tie-ins with Twentieth Century Fox on the picture, "Bird of Paradise," and many localized promotions, resulting in more than 1 million lines of free newspaper space in the United States, Canada and foreign countries, FTD flower credits and stories in 11 national magazines and the participation of FTD officials and public relations representatives in more than 30 radio programs.

A survey of the growth of FTD business between the years 1941-1950 was presented to the Board of Directors in September, 1951. In that time, clearings had increased from $9 million per year to more than $31 million. It was also shown that, with only 22 per cent of the public aware of how to send flowers-by-wire at the beginning of the survey period, 50 per cent were acquainted with the flowers-by-wire method by 1950.

At the January, 1952, Board of Directors' meeting, it was announced by the Sales and Advertising Committee that, in the last six months of 1951, clearings had increased by 15.5 per cent and that the number of orders was up 11.2 per cent, with the average order hitting an all-time high of $7.53. This was the first reflection of the increased advertising budget made possible by the increase to 2 per cent and 2 per cent. In the words of the committee report: "Already there are certain indications that this advertising is beginning to 'snow-ball'." If the "snow-balling" continued as indicated there was reason to believe that the fiscal year would end with total clearings of between $36 million and $40 million, much ahead of the originally estimated $35 million.

Such a rosy outlook, however, may be modified by inscrutable fate. There arose, early in 1952, an unexpected contingency that threatened, at least temporarily, the very existence of FTD.

Shortly before Easter, Western Union and Bell Telephone employees announced the breakdown of their salary negotiations with their employers and the unions' decision to call a strike.

This came like a bomb blast to the FTD florists. They were innocent bystanders. They were caught in the middle. Reaction came fast and furious. Losses of more than a million dollars were predicted, immediate cut-backs in advertising funds were recommended, operating budgets were to be curtailed. A meeting of the Finance Committee was hastily summoned.

Had these forebodings materialized, the business of two of the most important days for florists — Easter and Mother's Day — would have been seriously crippled. The momentum of the developing promotion programs would have slowed down. The rising trend of clearings would have been obliterated. Months, perhaps years, might have been required to regain such a favorable position.

The Sales and Advertising Committee refused to accept this attitude. Confident of the ability of the Association and of the co-operation of the florists, the committee accepted the challenge and intensified its advertising, merchandising and publicity campaigns.

Newspaper advertising copy was immediately changed, urging the customer to get his orders in early. New advertisements were substituted in a matter of hours. Publicity releases to all media received wide coverage. The results were more than gratifying. The public responded. Easter business held up well.

But the strikes were extended through Mother's Day, and the public became aware of the work-stoppages in industries essential to flowers-by-wire. However, the Sales and Advertising Department had more time to plan for this event. All June newspaper advertising was canceled, those funds increasing the coverage for the first part of May.

For the first time, FTD decided to use the new medium, television. For five days preceding Mother's Day, the FTD sales messages were carried over NBC-TV's network of 28 stations, with Dave Garroway himself presenting the story on the new TV show, "TODAY." In non-TV areas the size and frequency of newspaper advertisements were increased, again pointing out that FTD would guarantee delivery.

The highlight of the week was a demonstration of FTD in action. A flowers-by-wire order, sent from New York to Chicago, was delivered in 40 minutes. President Granville

Gude, Clarence Muelleman and Andrew Grupp appeared on the show and Garroway interviewed Gude for 15 minutes, during which the president described the workings of the organization and its foreign counterpart, Interflora. An order was sent to London through FTD Interflora. On the last day of the week the English recipient, interviewed on the air, gave an enthusiastic report on the arrival of the flowers and said that he would send an order to his mother in the United States.

Members were sent large window posters, supporting the show and the newspaper campaign. During this time the greatest magazine campaign in FTD history was at work. The story of FTD was carried by 16 magazines for Easter and Mother's Day, to an audience of more than 50 million.

As a result of this concentrated advertising, FTD members were able to go through their best season with an increase in business, despite the strikes.

Beginning in January, trade papers were entered, with advertising directed at business men, funeral directors and hospital personnel.

Public relations efforts were increased and the staff of the department enlarged, to take care of the accelerated promotional campaign. As proof of the profit of this, the leading magazine in the publicity field named the FTD campaign the most successful trade association program in America. Every three weeks during the year, a national magazine had carried a story on FTD.

Despite strikes in industries most necessary to the transmission of flowers-by-wire, plus the rising inflation that was becoming the concern of the government, FTD ended the fiscal year with a dollar volume increase in clearings of 10.3 per cent, and with the number of orders raised by 5.1 per cent.

In view of such satisfactory business, the Sales and Advertising Committee decided to allocate $15,000 to match a like amount by Interflora, for public relations promotions for the international organization, thus placing the program on an international basis.

In the matter of financing the increased advertising, it was decided in a joint meeting of the Finance Committee and the Sales and Advertising Committee that a different method of funding was needed. Advertising designed to run for the Christmas trade must be paid for in November. But, since the Christmas advertisements are charged against the December collections, a reserve fund was found necessary to provide for these payments. The Board of Directors, following some misunderstanding about the advertising fund, had decreed that a reserve of $250,000 must be accumulated by January 1, 1953. This had caused some disruption of the advertising schedule. Edward Goeppner, of the Sales and Advertising Committee, had asked for the joint meeting to consider the situation.

A budget for the Sales and Advertising Committee was submitted, which allowed the accumulation of a reserve fund of $256,744.34 as of December 31, 1952. This was predicated on a total anticipated collection of $471,716.63 and a carry-over of $122,379.78 for a total available fund of $594,096.41, less advertising and administrative expenses of $337,352.07. This was a conservative estimate.

At the beginning of the new decade a slogan had been proposed, unofficially. It was never used in advertising or became more than an unwritten vow among the members themselves. It concerned the Clearing House and its growth. The slogan was "50 in the '50s," meaning that the goal of the Clearing House was to reach clearings of $50 million during the 1950s. At the convention in Houston in 1953, the clearings for the fiscal period, ending June 30, 1953, had reached $40,781,024. This was a gain of almost $4 million over the last fiscal year. It seemed that the aim of the slogan was to be realized.

However, the committee was not carried away by the increase in business. The budget for the fiscal year 1953-54 was founded on a gross business of $41 million. The figure was explained thus: "In our opinion, it is sounder thinking to budget conservatively and take any volume increases in stride and to have these as a buffer for discretionary spending as might be mandated by the Board or the convention."

The last four months of 1953 showed that a total of 56 advertisements were carried in 18 national magazines, with a total of 143,746,377 impressions — a new four-month high for magazine ads alone. In addition, the public was informed of the "test order" program in an advertisement which explained how FTD worked; i.e., the careful consideration given to each order and why the customer could believe the statement "Guaranteed Delivery." For the first time in years, a full page in color was run in October and November. This advertisement, entitled, "It's All-Ways Better to Say It With Flowers-By-Wire," covered in copy and illustration all the consumer advantages of FTD: speed, guaranteed delivery, world-wide service, low price and convenience. Both of these important advertisements were merchandised on the member store level. A counter-card copy was mailed to each member for display during the running of the advertisements. Each card bore the prominent legend, "We Are Your FTD Florist."

Advertising in the business press was intensified under the two strong themes, "Flowers Are Beautiful Business Builders," and, "There's a Place for a Plant in Every Man's Office." Another advertisement quoted a testimonial from M. A. Spayd, president of the Standard Register Company of Dayton, Ohio, and was headlined, "$500,000 Payoff to this Flowers-By-Wire Promotion." The nurse-and-hospital campaign was continued, also the newspaper campaign through 428 papers in 266 cities, an increase of 50 papers in 40 additional localities.

Public relations exposures included a story in READER'S DIGEST. Five other national magazines carried FTD stories, for a circulation figure of more than 20 million.

Radio and television exposures included more than 60 mentions on such programs as Jackie Gleason, Robert Q. Lewis, Inner Sanctum, Studio One, Kraft Theatre and the Kate Smith Show.

This effort continued into the first half of 1954 and, although the "recession" had set in and business was generally down by an average of 12 per cent, FTD business had actually risen by 1.1 per cent, not an impressive figure under ordinary circumstances, but emphasizing the value of promotional advertising and public relations in a time of business decline.

This points up one of the eternal contentions of advertising consultants; viz., that the time to increase advertising and promotion is in periods of decline, that the last expenditure to be cut back in a falling business curve should be advertising. The FTDA has had opportunity to demonstrate the accuracy of this through 50 years of wars, depressions, recessions, and periods of adjustment. The Association is considered in advertising circles to be one of the wisest users of promotional effort as a way of maintaining business across the valleys of the economic cycle.

In the light of business conditions which existed everywhere in the nation, the budget for sales and advertising was not increased for 1954-55, but was based upon estimated clearings of $41 million.

Rising costs of advertising, coupled with this static budget, caused a readjustment of advertising plans. The important program directed at hospital management and nursing staffs was continued. The soaring popularity of television made practical the production of a TV movie, HOW TO DO IT WITH FLOWERS. By January 1, 1955, 60 stations across the country had requested and shown the film, demonstrating the role that flowers play in all phases of good living. In a shift of emphasis more local newspapers in the United States and Canada carried FTD advertisements and publicity.

On the public relations side of the promotion picture,

FTD CRASHES FRONT PAGE!

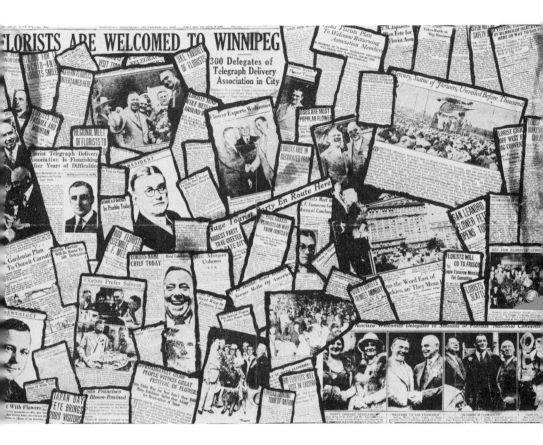

One of FTD's publicity triumphs was the great San Francisco Convention Tour, conceived by President Charles H. Grakelow. Trains from Philadelphia, New York and Chicago, loaded with FTD members, headed west from the Windy City over the southern route to Denver, Los Angeles and the 1930 convention in San Francisco. Committee and Board meetings were held enroute; side trips furnished relaxation and special cars were available for dining, dancing and entertainment. Return was made over the northern route from Vancouver to Chicago. Newspapers in more than 111 cities heralded the trip with feature stories, devoting more than 60 columns of space to the tour, not including more than ten columns of picture coverage. Civic welcoming committees met the trains at all stops. Twelve hundred persons made the journey at an average cost to each of $625. The resultant publicity and good will could only be estimated in the millions.

When Congress decided in 1959 to consider the question of designating a national flower, FTD volunteered to conduct an opinion poll through its member shops to determine America's favorite blossom. Special ballot boxes were distributed to FTD members along with printed ballots listing 20 of the most popular flowers and plants, with space for write-in votes. Americans by the millions cast their ballots. Above is one newspaper-size page of clippings of the campaign. Enough clippings to fill thousands of such pages were received. This was probably FTD's most successful public relations effort.

increased use was made of the Hollywood office of the Grant Advertising Agency, concentrating on publicity films. Excellent exposure was also secured on important television programs. For the first time, FTD sponsored a flower float in the Tournament of Roses Parade in Pasadena. The entry was entitled, "Deep in My Heart," and it coincided with the release of an MGM picture of the same name. Syndicated columnists, TV, radio and national mat services were utilized to spread the news of this float. President Edward Ludwig was on hand at the Parade to act as "flower spotter" for the network TV broadcast. He literally "stole the show."

So it will be seen that the adjustments to the advertising schedule, while putting a double load on the shoulders of the Sales and Advertising Committee and the Grant Agency, produced the desired results. As the fiscal year ended, FTD was able to announce that clearings had set an all-time high of $44,692,166, totaling 6,114,659 flowers-by-wire orders. With such an increase, it was decided to enlarge the budget of sales and advertising for the 1955-56 fiscal year, and $1,401,220 was allocated for the promotion of flower sales, an over-all increase of 8.9 per cent.

Still out of reach, however, was the elusive "50 in the '50s." It became now a point of pride, although unofficially. Everyone realized that the possibility was present. It remained for the proper advertising and publicity to bring it to pass.

Early in 1956, an important administrative change took place. Harold R. Hewey, who had been serving as general manager, left the Association in the fall of 1955. M. R. Liles, a business and management consultant who had been called in to make a study of the operation of the Association, assumed temporary management of the Detroit offices. In the meantime, a search went on for an experienced administrator who could take over the position of secretary and general manager. In May of 1956, John L. Bodette was selected as the man whose business background and experience best qualified him for the position.

The new general manager took hold of his duties with a firm hand. After a study of the Association structure and the relationship between the Detroit Headquarters and the membership, he was able, at the meeting of the Board and the committees in July of that year, to present recommendations for reorganization of the activities along much more efficient lines.

His recommendations somewhat involved the Sales and Advertising Committee. He suggested that those activities handled by the Member Service Committee, and principally concerning merchandising and public relations, be channeled through a new organization to be known as the Sales and Advertising Services Committee. This was accepted by the members at the 1956 Boston convention, and the new designation and duties were applied to what had been the Sales and Advertising Committee. Alfred Bloomingdale, who had been head of the Member Service Department, was installed as director of the combined departments.

The combination of these two committees, merging the two departments, brought into one fund the operating budgets of both and formed a much broader financial structure. It also afforded a closer co-ordination between the activities of each, opening to full exploitation a shadowed area which had existed between the separate committees.

With the new financial potential, new media were considered. At the suggestion of the general manager, $150,000 of the advertising budget for the year 1956-57 was allocated for the entry of FTD into the Yellow Pages of the telephone directory. This proved to be one of the best investments in advertising that the Association ever made. More than 99 per cent of FTD florists are now listed in those pages in their cities. At present the FTD Yellow Pages contract is the largest "closed heading trademark contract" in the world.

Member sales training programs were intensified under the new consolidated arrangement. With the addition to the amount available for this service of $55,000 from the combined fund, a recorded sales education program entitled, SOUND SELLING SERIES, was included in the members' training program. The entry into traditional media was broadened.

Publicity efforts were concentrated on securing free exposure on TV and, as a result, mentions were noted on the Bob Hope Show, the NBC Spectacular, "Twentieth Century," twice on the Will Rogers Show, four times on "Today," four times on the NBC "Home" show, and also on "Ozzie and Harriet," "Matinee," "Stand Up and Be Counted," and the Lawrence Welk Show.

Magazine and newspaper publicity and advertising were increased as the enlarged budget allowed. The committee report, presented to the Board of Directors by Al Simon, reflected its satisfaction with the results accomplished. The accomplishment was that the Clearing House was able to report a substantial rise in the amount of FTD business for the calendar year 1956. This report made the realization of the $50 million figure anticlimactic. The 1956 figure was $49,804,913, an amount so little short of the goal that there was no doubt of its fulfillment.

With the goal in sight, the Board decided to make assurance doubly sure. It added approximately $200,000 to the budget for 1956-57, bringing the amount appropriated for sales and advertising service to $1,599,072. This, it was believed, would put the clearings over the fifty million mark. As will be seen, an astonishing surprise was in store.

Publicity for the year included another prize-winning float in the Tournament of Roses Parade, sponsorship shared by FTD with Minute-Maid. Other TV sponsorship was deferred until more financially feasible.

Magazine and newspaper advertising was continued, with attention to the national magazines as before. In the newspaper advertising, Bodette had advised that the base of the coverage area be broadened to take in not only the centers of population, where FTD already enjoyed recognition, but regions of less concentrated population. This, he urged, would educate more people to use the flowers-by-wire service and introduce more new customers to the use of FTD facilities.

Alfred Bloomingdale resigned his position with FTD in September, and Gordon Conn, who had joined FTD as advertising manager in January of 1957, succeeded to the directorship of the department.

In March, 1957, Dr. Ian Stuart, a charming and cultured Dublin Irishman who had acquired American citizenship, joined the staff of FTD as community relations director. Dr. Stuart is a gifted and stirring speaker. His duties consist of visiting 75 to 80 cities each year, giving more than 200 talks to luncheon clubs, garden clubs, chambers of commerce and kindred organizations. He delivers inspirational messages on the foundation, growth and current events in the United States and Canada as well as talks on the power, beauty and meaning of flowers for all occasions. For his excellent work in selling America to Americans through his inspirational talks, he was honored with a Special Freedoms Leadership Award in 1960, through the Freedoms Foundation at Valley Forge.

Dr. Stuart's visits support the national marketing program by carrying the message of flowers-by-wire into communities not always reached by advertising and public relations. His geniality and warmth of personality cause him to be invited frequently to appear on radio and television, and it is on these broadcasts that he is able to tell the real story of FTD, its inner workings, its ethics and prestige and the service advantages it offers in the transmission of fresh flowers to 188 countries.

This goodwill ambassador of FTD travels more than 150,000 miles every year carrying the FTD message through Canada and the United States.

The quest for a suitable television program continued, and in December, when the Edward R. Murrow PERSON

TO PERSON show suddenly became available, it was decided that this program, on the basis of its ratings and popularity, offered the best combination of qualities for the exploitation of the flowers-by-wire idea. The program was signed for 26 weeks, beginning March 21, 1958. The program was to be broadcast over 124 stations in the United States and Canada. It was estimated that it would be seen in 10,526,000 homes. This meant that more than 20 million persons would watch the once-a-week telecast.

But, before the FTD television show took to the airways, there was the review of the calendar year of 1957 to consider. Here the membership had reason to enjoy a Merry Christmas and Happy New Year. For, when the figures were in, it was found that the elusive goal of "50 in the '50s" had been exceeded by more than $5,250,000! The total clearings had been $55,664,754, the largest FTD business increase in any year.

This remarkable rise reflected several things: the broader base of the advertising coverage, which secured penetration into areas not before fully acquainted with the advantages of FTD service; the continued publicity exposures on top television programs and the growing TV coverage; closer supervision of advertising copy and art, with concentration on months not characterized by special flower days; and the over-all tightening up of the entire FTD operation, for more efficient exploitation of the Association's services to the consumer public.

The latter months of 1957 and the first part of 1958 were characterized by a business recession of some depth. But FTD sales stood up better than the national business average. To bolster the sales and income of the members, a plan to include candy in the FTD telegraph plan was advanced by Sales and Advertising. This caused considerable difference of opinion among the members of the committee and the membership, too. The plan was not accepted by the general membership.

Before the end of 1957, Sales and Advertising conducted a national survey on the "Please Omit" problem, which covered all the newspapers, radio and television stations in the United States. It was found, after evaluating the results of questionnaires sent to these facilities, that the problem was not of major consequence in radio and television. But between 75 per cent and 85 per cent of the country's newspapers accepted such obituary notices. Another surprising fact unearthed by the survey was that florists themselves had either not been aware of this business detriment in their areas or that they were remiss in making their objections to it known to publishers of their newspapers. Less than 16 per cent of the papers reported that local florists had complained and 27.9 per cent reported that they had received only occasional objections.

Another fact uncovered by the survey was that 92 per cent of the death notices published in newspapers are given to the paper by funeral directors.

This information was turned over to the Florists' Information Committee of the Society of American Florists. Up to this point FTD had contributed $105,000 to the operating expenses of FIC. With this help, FIC was able to send its field men into the affected areas, to hold meetings with the advertising departments of the papers and also with the funeral directors, in an effort to arrive at a solution, fair both to the funeral directors and the florists. This survey is being continued.

Since it was decided that the contract with the Grant Advertising Agency should expire in 1958, it became the concern of the Sales and Advertising Services Committee, and likewise of the department, to consider a successor. There was no lack of applicants. The FTD account had assumed major proportions. Fifty national agencies vied for the privilege of being its representative. The choice was narrowed to five agencies and, from the five, Keyes, Madden and Jones, of Chicago, was finally selected.

It was believed by both the committee and management that better publicity and public relations exploitation could be obtained by entrusting this phase of the program to a separate agency. This was communicated to the profession. After presentations by some outstanding public relations firms, Edward Gottlieb and Associates of New York was given the contract to handle the publicity affairs of FTD on a national basis. The intra-Association publicity and public relations were retained under the Sales and Advertising Services Department.

The budget for the fiscal year 1958-59 was set at $2,220,000, the largest appropriation yet made for sales and advertising. With this allocation and two new agencies with which to deal, Sales and Advertising could see many long hours of thought and consultation ahead.

The television show, Edward R. Murrow's PERSON TO PERSON, which FTD had been sponsoring on alternate weeks, with LIFE MAGAZINE holding the weeks between, was replaced during the summer of 1958 by a dramatic show called, PERSONAL APPEARANCE, featuring Hollywood stars. FTD picked up one broadcast of Murrow in September when he returned to the air. But it was decided not to continue the TV program, in view of a general decline in business which prevented a sales increase large enough to underwrite continuation of network television.

The new agency developed a slogan which had particular appeal, and which was used on billboards, in 15 to 30 radio spots in 150 top FTD markets, and in 10 full-minute TV spots per campaign in 25 FTD markets. Full color advertisements were run in LIFE and the NEW YORKER. The slogan was "Something Warm and Human and Wonderful Happens When You Send Flowers by Wire." It was attractively presented with a glamorous young woman holding a bunch of red roses, her face expressing joy at the gift. Promotion was supported with counter-cards, featuring the national advertisements. Special flower days were emphasized.

Widespread newspaper coverage was resumed to help combat the "Please Omit" problem. The new schedule included a series of 85-line advertisements on the obituary pages of 70 newspapers.

Headquarters public relations had booked Dr. Stuart into 73 cities to address 201 groups, with a total audience of 67,861 persons. He appeared on radio and television 112 times, for a total of 1,474 minutes, reaching an estimated 13,750,000 listeners and viewers. Newspaper coverage of Stuart's appearances, estimated from circulation figures, reached more than 12,500,000 readers.

On the financial side, the end of 1958 showed that, despite the business decline in other fields, FTD members had again increased their total business, although there was some effect from prevailing economic conditions. The total dollar volume for the year including Interflora was $56,962,883, a gain of $1,298,129 or a little more than 2.25 per cent.

As 1959 dawned, there was an optimistic feeling among the members and the staff at Headquarters that the old goal of "50 in the '50s," which had already been much exceeded, was an under-estimation of the "power of flowers" in a recovering market. The goal should, it was urged, now be set at a $60 million year in the mid-century decade. The early months confirmed that optimism. March, April and May together showed sales up 14.4 per cent over the same period of the year before.

In co-operation with Keyes, Madden and Jones, Sales and Advertising realigned the newspaper, radio and other advertising outlets. Newspaper coverage was expanded to over 400 papers. Additional radio and TV markets were contracted for. This schedule of advertisements and spots was arranged to give the utmost penetration into areas where the potential for business existed. It was designed with a broader base than had ever been used before.

Where a zoning system had dictated that only cities with a population of 50,000 would be considered for newspaper advertising, it was decided to include "metropolitan marketing areas" of 100,000. For the first time, this allowed newspaper advertising in cities below 50,000, where there was large suburban coverage. In addition, it was planned to use papers in at least two cities in each state, despite the population figure.

Another device to broaden the "anti-Please Omit" advertising, was to reduce the lineage of the advertisements from 85 to 50, permitting the use of more newspapers. Magazine exploitation was scheduled in a varied list of class publications aimed at upper income families. Religious magazines were continued, business publications were renewed and, for obvious reasons, AMERICAN FUNERAL DIRECTOR was listed for six insertions. Outdoor advertising was intensified and rescheduled. A series of stuffers, calendars and other local advertising and sales aids were planned. So was a float entry in the coming Rose Bowl Parade.

On the publicity and public relations side of the ledger, several unprecedented "beats" could be listed. A short-short story, "Nine Roses for the Commissar," by Oscar Schisgall, appeared in THIS WEEK MAGAZINE, with a circulation of 13,500,000, through the Sunday papers of 42 major market areas. This story was built around the FTD-Interflora world-wide flowers-by-wire plan. It was read by perhaps 25 million persons. To many of FTD, this brought memories of the story, "Flowers at Sunset," written by Mrs. St. John. It was a graphic and moving story. The plot turned on the exact transmission of the telegraphed flower order.

Another unique public relations program consummated during 1959 was the National Flower Election. There had been before Congress for some time, requests for the selection of a national flower. Naturally, each state with an official flower was anxious to have its symbol selected. To poll the public for a national floral symbol, FTD conducted the National Flower Election, supplying member florist shops with ballot boxes and printed ballots listing 20 of the most popular American flowers, with space for write-in selections.

More than 5,250,000 ballots were distributed. This program gained the widest publicity ever obtained in an FTD promotion. It received the congratulations of senators, congressmen and governors and was commended by the President and Vice-President of the United States. First, second and third place winners were rose, carnation, and chrysanthemum, in that order. The prime value of this program to the membership was the direct tie-in which brought the voters into FTD shops to cast their votes.

By the end of June and the fiscal year, the Clearing House announced that the clearings for the 1958-59 year including FTD overseas orders was $60,129,653. This goal, which 10 years before would have seemed wildly optimistic, was comfortably attained. The chairman of the Sales and Advertising Services Committee, Joseph Hynes, was presented with a plaque, citing his 2-year leadership during which FTD had realized its first $8 million-month and its first $60 million-year. New estimates are now pointed toward $100 million and, in the light of past performances, that figure is not unreasonable.

By vote of the members at the Los Angeles convention in 1959, the name of the department was changed to "Marketing Division," and its responsibilities described as the total effort made up of all techniques used to advance the sale of a product. Business increases have been followed by intelligent rises in the Marketing Division budget which, in turn, have brought more business. The end of this self-powered spiral is nowhere in sight.

One of the most significant statistics of the Marketing Division is that, when the budget for advertising and sales promotion was tied to the 1 per cent and 1 per cent assessment on FTD business, the increase in orders averaged 165,000 per year. With the introduction of the 2 per cent and 2 per cent budget, this yearly average increase rose to 330,000 orders. There is undoubtedly a limit to this mathematical progression. But it is certain, from past experience, that the limit will not be reached until after the yearly clearings far exceed $100 million per year.

Since 1930, when FTD began a co-ordinated national advertising and promotion program, FTD sales have accelerated 60 per cent faster than sales in the rest of the florist industry. This clearly illustrates the impact of FTD's marketing programs over the years.

CHAPTER NINE

The FTD NEWS Story

THE FOUNDERS of FTD realized that the success of the Association must lie chiefly in keeping the members informed of the increasing membership, so that the transmission of flowers-by-wire would enjoy continuing growth, both in area and in service potential.

Only the secretary could be aware of the addition of new members. In fact, it was largely through his efforts in recruitment that the roster of members continued to increase. Through his letters, his articles in trade papers and his insistence that each FTD member owed it to the Association to enlist all the florists in his region, the story of FTD reached more and more retail florists. The readiness with which prominent members accepted and promoted the new Association was a favorable recommendation to those more hesitant and dubious.

From 1912 until 1919 there had been spasmodic attempts by the Headquarters staff to keep the membership advised of the locations and firm names of the scattered members, beginning with a list printed in the several trade papers catering to horticulturists. Later, Secretary Pochelon, from his Detroit office, began issuing lists of members at quarterly intervals and, when this was not equal to the rapid growth of the Association, he sent lists out monthly.

In an effort to achieve popular acceptance of these lists, several of them carried news items, merchandising suggestions and other interest-provoking material designed to inspire the retailer with an interest in the growth of his potential service area through telegraphed orders. The average florist was hard to sell. Although he realized that the leading men in the industry were enthusiastic over the possibilities of the FTD idea, he often lacked the initiative to accept and promote new merchandising ideas.

By 1919, FTD had approximately 1,700 members. It was realized that the membership, whose principal contact with one another came at the yearly business meetings, might become better integrated through the pages of a magazine of their own.

During the framing of the agenda for the 1919 convention in Detroit, Karl Baum and Max Schling, in discussing price differentials of flowers in different parts of the country, suggested that a trade paper, issued from the FTD offices, would be an excellent way to inform members of the price of flowers they were ordering by wire.

Acting upon these suggestions, Michael Bloy, assistant secretary, and Hilmer V. Swenson, a Chicago advertising man then doing some work for FTD, submitted a proposition to the Board, agreeing to edit and publish a magazine to be known as the FTD NEWS, on a commission basis. No commission was to be paid until the magazine showed a profit. This was accepted. The first issue was in August, 1920. Besides being mailed to the membership, copies were distributed to FTD members attending the SAF convention in Cleveland that year.

While the FTD NEWS was published at the national offices of the Association, it was not a "house organ." Rather, it was an authoritative magazine, devoted to the interests and affairs of the retail florists. Printed on enameled paper, the first issue contained 64 pages. A complete roll of the membership was carried. It is some indication of the size to which the Association had grown, that this list consumed 19 of the 64 pages. A list of the district representatives of the U.S. and Canada was carried. Foreign representatives in

Egypt, Cuba, France, Great Britain and South America were listed.

Flanking the center columns of the membership roll were 165 cards of different members, advertising their services. There were eight full-page displays and 31 advertisements of half, third and quarter-page size, an impressive amount of advertising for the first issue of any magazine.

Articles on the history of the Association, self-help and how-to-do-it instructions on publicity, management, credit and other phases of the florist business were contributed by Breitmeyer, Gude, Brown, Knoble, Baum, Harper, Schling, Ammann and others. Of the Headquarters staff, Helen Wick, Pochelon's first assistant, and L. F. Darnell, the Association missionary, wrote of their work. J. C. Williver, vice-president of Western Union, had words to say about the relation of his service to the Association. The first issue was a decided success. Congratulatory mail poured in from members everywhere.

Many of the letters contained suggestions for the improvement of the content. But almost without exception the format and photography of the new publication were praised.

The staff of the magazine consisted of Michael Bloy, business manager; Hilmer V. Swenson, advertising manager; and Norman Beasley, editor.

The first printing was 1,200 copies. It cost $3,171.52, an amount which was greater than the revenue it produced. But the quality and usefulness of the new magazine were such that the directors decided to back the effort. It was not long before it was on a paying basis, where it has since remained.

The FTD NEWS is considered one of the quality magazines in the trade field. Its path to that eminence has not been unfalteringly smooth, as will be seen, nor was its acceptance by the membership entirely wholehearted at first. But it has today reached a place of prominence in the publishing world and its value to the Association is inestimable.

Early in its life, the FTD NEWS had an opportunity to demonstrate its worth. The controversy over the proposed Clearing House program had evoked rumors, misconceptions and half-truths, not only confusing to the membership but often critical of the integrity and good faith of the proponents of the plan. Through this 2-year period, the FTD NEWS cut through mists of misinformation with the clear light of truth. After the favorable vote at Baltimore, which established the Clearing House on a voluntary basis, it was the FTD NEWS which kept the entire Association informed of the monthly growth of the clearings. It believed that success is its own best advertisement.

When it was realized that only through an enforced use of the Clearing House by all members was a strong financial structure to be erected, the FTD NEWS again proclaimed the truth and communicated the advantages of the operation and the approval of the leading members to all the florists. Authoritative articles by John Besemer were presented, explaining the financial basis of the Clearing House. Pochelon's contributions, urging the adoption of the mandatory procedure and showing the success of the plan between American and Canadian florists, were conveyed to the members. Breitmeyer, Knoble, Penn, Gude and others, to whom all retailers would look for advice, stated clearly their opinions on the efficacy of the system and its true value to the Association, through the columns of the FTD NEWS.

When the membership met in St. Louis in 1923, it was the largest convention ever held by the Association. The exposition of the Clearing House issue and the attitudes of members toward the plan brought to St. Louis a thoroughly informed group of florists to vote on the issue. From the first meeting, there was little doubt of the outcome. The vote for the mandatory Clearing House was intelligent and considered, thanks to the FTD NEWS.

The FTD NEWS also aided the young Clearing House

department by lending it $12,000 from the fund built up in
the magazine's short life. This amount was almost half of
the original operating fund of the Clearing House.

In the same year of 1923, the FTD NEWS published an
international edition, with articles in German, French and
Italian. The success of this issue and the awakening awareness of FTD in Europe were instrumental, beyond doubt, in
the adoption of a Mother's Day by German florists. President
Edward Sceery, speaking of the FTD NEWS, said, "The
advancement of our Association, especially when we consider
its growth in foreign countries, has, I believe, been largely
due to it."

The 1920's were a time of industrial expansion. New ideas,
procedures and techniques came into use, and increased
production and a rising business curve proved their usefulness. In keeping with this trend, the FTD NEWS constantly
improved its form and content. There was a gradual shift of
emphasis from floricultural subjects to information on
advertising, publicity, management, cost analysis and merchandising. The FTD NEWS tried to persuade the retail
florist of his status as a businessman with a product to
distribute. The rules of salesmanship and promotion applied
to all. This was a new concept for the florist. He had been
principally concerned with funerals, weddings and special
days. The FTD NEWS showed that his field of service was
not restricted, that he had a larger local consumer potential
and, through FTD, a vast international area through which
to distribute his product. He was urged to expand with the
expanding economy.

"The financial pages of our daily newspapers leave no
room for a Thomas doubting our prosperity," wrote the
editor. "Month after month somebody continues to break
records. Principal industries seem to operate at capacity
levels. Here and there you find someone who fears the pace
is too rapid, but such fears are evidently not based upon the
signs of the time." This was in early 1929, when it seemed

that the new industrial revolution had supplied the answer to all the ills that had beset the business world for ages.

In December of that year, the same editor advised the members to "be sane and join the optimists."

Hilmer V. Swenson resigned as advertising manager in that year, but Michael Bloy remained on a new 3-year contract as editor and business manager of the FTD NEWS.

As the country entered the depression period of the '30s, the FTD NEWS had gained sufficient maturity to enable it to "roll with the punch." Its editorial tone changed. It became the moral support of the member florists. Correctly gauging the extent of the slump, the FTD NEWS urged florists to use their time to improve their shops, their knowledge of flowers and their ability in design. They were advised that now was the time to re-assess their operations. With the public spending more conservatively, possibly flowers would be overlooked. It was the duty, even the obligation, of florists to use their increased spare time to devise ways of bringing the idea of flowers to the mind of the customers.

Bloy pursued this theme with articles and editorials. He wrote, "We have good reason to expect that in the future will come greater sales to the masses, rather than to a supporting class whose numbers are but 15 per cent of all customers." The FTD NEWS supported this idea with articles on styling and design, profusely illustrated. It conducted, through its pages, a design school for florists. These articles were contrived by the best men and women in the industry. Their names lent prestige to the content and to the FTD NEWS itself.

The florist industry has never felt business declines, depressions and wartime recessions to the degree that other businesses have suffered. Bloy emphasized this through his columns. He showed that the condition was because of predictable cycles and that, while recovery might seem slow, it had a tortoise-like persistence. It was automatic and inevitable.

The FTD NEWS backed up its preaching of improvement and optimism by practicing it. Attention was given to editorial page layout. The charm inherent in all graphic arts media was utilized to increase the attractiveness of the magazine's appearance. It rose to a place of prominence in its field. It was recognized, and it is today, as a leader among the nation's trade magazines.

The editor endorsed the thought that, out of the depression, would come not more florists, but better florists. To this end he began a series of contests for artistic window displays, made in the members' own shops. There was a subtle psychology back of this. Not only did it give the florist something to work toward, but it improved the appearance of his shop windows, making them more attractive to the passer-by, and increasing awareness of the availability and beauty of floral decorations.

The FTD NEWS joined in promoting flowers for shut-ins at this time, bringing to the membership notice of radio and newspaper exploitation of this feature and publishing the results of the campaign. Throughout this entire period, the stress was upon improved artistry and quality.

By the middle of the decade, Hollywood press agents had discovered the FTD NEWS. The editor was deluged with photographs of beautiful movie stars holding, looking at, smelling, wearing or surrounded by flowers. The quality of the enameled paper on which the magazine was printed, made reproduction of such photographs particularly appealing. There was prestige to be gained by a magazine from this association with Hollywood.

The FTD NEWS invaded the fashion marts of New York to demonstrate by photography the compatibility of flowers and the latest in women's styles. Through a feature called "New York Fashion Flashes," the FTD NEWS showed the florist how he might increase his business by suggesting to customers different uses of fresh flowers as fashion high-lights to their dress.

These artistic impulses fostered during the depression, plus the regular features of the magazine, brought to the FTD NEWS a sounder, more balanced formula for success.

In 1938, the FTD NEWS lost the man who had so success-fully guided its destiny. Michael Bloy died. There is no doubt that Bloy's contribution went far beyond the pages of the periodical he created. He was a skillful and intelligent editor. Through his 18 years of service, he watched FTD grow from a young and struggling Association to a virile and progressive organization of almost 8,000 members. He and the FTD NEWS had been a powerful force in uniting and educating the membership. While his absence would be deeply felt, he had wrought so well that the magazine could continue its progress without faltering.

Writing in the FTD NEWS, Max Schling, one of the first proponents of the magazine, ended his tribute to Bloy by saying, "All that I say here about Mike and the rest of my old associates is not merely honoring Mike or the others indi-vidually — it is a tribute to Mike for his splendid work, for what he gave to the FTD NEWS and the Association. We were all one body, one group that strove with might and main for better men in our profession. Now that Mike has left us it seems to me just the time to remind the old group, those that are still among us, that we should come together once in a while and drink a glass in memory of those that have gone on — and perhaps remind others outside of this group that the spirit of unselfish fellowship and devotion, the teamwork, co-operative getting and giving that now rules the flower world, was due to their pioneering."

The FTD NEWS continued under the direction of Viola K. Swindler, associate editor. In February of 1939, adver-tising rates were increased. This had been a matter of contention between the News Committee and Bloy. In the early days, when the magazine's income did not cover the cost of production, it had been suggested by the committee that good business practice dictated a raise in the rates to advertisers. Bloy protested strongly. He maintained that the salvation of the FTD NEWS lay in increasing its circulation; that, until the advertiser could be shown that with greater coverage he was reaching more customers, higher rates were not warranted. But Bloy's condition had been met. The circulation was now in excess of 8,000, with an estimated readership per copy of 3.6 persons. This rise was accepted by the advertisers without incident and, later in the year, the size of the card advertisements was reduced to permit a column of editorial material on each page.

There was also a progressive shift in editorial policy. More stress was placed on business articles, with a comparable reduction of the art and fashion content. The size of each issue was now close to 300 pages and, because this was bulky and heavy, the membership list and market reports, composing about 60 pages of each issue, were printed on colored stock for easier finding. Another popular feature was, "Add Another Candle," a salute to the birthdays of the original members. The first anniversary noted was Philip Breitmeyer's seventy-fourth birthday.

The search went on for a qualified editor for the FTD NEWS. In July, 1940, Robert B. Powers was appointed to the post. Powers brought to the editor's desk a wide experience in publishing, advertising, journalism and business management. Under his direction, more improvements were made in style and format, including more readable type faces and new headings for the town listings in the membership section. Page layout was made more attractive. The use of color throughout the magazine was much increased. There was a re-awakened interest in illustrative content, and the use of photographs and art work was increased by 30 per cent.

The FTD NEWS now had assumed a dual character. First in importance from the shop standpoint was the list of FTD members necessary for the transaction of FTD business. The other part of the book was the regular news section, filled with trade articles and self-help material. The magazine was published in two sections, one of which might be left in the shop for reference, and the other taken home to be read at leisure. As an experiment in publishing, this plan proved popular with the subscribers.

But a war was raging in Europe. The United States was busy with defense production, conscious of a troubled world but unprepared for the approaching holocaust of Pearl Harbor. Paper was one of the products being diverted from normal channels into the preparedness program. So the FTD NEWS, after several months, abandoned the issuance of two separate sections, in the interest of conserving paper.

The flames at Pearl Harbor had scarcely subsided when fire swept through the offices of the FTD NEWS. Beginning at 7 p.m. on February 12, 1942, a conflagration gained such headway that it required the efforts of 10 pieces of fire equipment to place it under control. The blaze originated in a short circuit in the FTD NEWS offices. The composition board of which the office walls were built offered encouragement to its rapid spread. An hour after the fire started, firemen were still trying to get lines into the second floor offices. Only a firewall, dividing the building, saved the FTD NEWS presses and the pages already printed for the March issue. But paper stocks were severely damaged. Many photographs and "carry-over" material for future issues were ruined. The damage to the building and the offices was estimated at between $150,000 and $200,000.

Moving into a hotel across the street, the FTD NEWS staff established itself as best it could and began work on the March issue. It was a night-and-day task. Office equipment was loaned by friends and dealers. Supplies were hurriedly brought into the emergency quarters. The staff pitched into their work with the same devotion and enthusiasm that still characterizes the FTD NEWS offices. The March issue was distributed on time.

During the entire war period, the FTD NEWS was indispensable to the membership. Besides the news features, which informed them of ways to meet the wartime rules on delivery, rationing and other deterrents to service and supplies, the magazine published lists of army camps and post exchanges, broadening the florists' service area and encouraging the interchange of flowers between military personnel and their families.

Field men kept the membership informed of national conditions in the flower industry, by reports which were condensed and printed in the FTD NEWS. Morale articles, such as Editor Powers', "Flowers are Moral Armament," helped to guide the industry through the emergency period and to maintain the optimism and enthusiasm of the florists themselves.

For the first time in its history, FTD held no convention in 1942. Acceding to a request from the government in view of travel difficulties, the meeting scheduled for New York was cancelled. It was the FTD NEWS that was able to bring to the membership a full report. It also carried the committee reports that would have been made on the convention floor.

The resolution canceling the 1942 convention left open the question of when annual meetings would be resumed. Consequently, when conditions had not improved in 1943, it was again decided to forego a convention. Stepping into the breach, the FTD NEWS decided to hold "a convention in print." This idea was enthusiastically accepted by the membership.

Under the heading, "We're Keeping Flowers in the Fight for Freedom," the magazine published a special section which carried cards of the members and as many photographs as possible to create the atmosphere and feeling of personal encounter. The mail columns of the FTD NEWS were filled with congratulatory letters.

On the more practical side, all the committee reports that would have been heard at an annual meeting were again published.

During the remainder of the war's duration, the FTD NEWS staff took on the extra work of producing two more publications. First was the WINGED MERCURY MESSENGER, a tabloid paper distributed to military service camps. This carried flower information and news of FTD service, besides articles promoting the telegraphing of flowers. The other was the NEWS-ETTE, a florists' "house organ" kind of paper, edited especially for flower shop personnel in the armed services. Both these papers were received with thanks during their short existence.

When the end of the war could be foreseen, the FTD NEWS began a "Plan Now" campaign, looking to the return of normal conditions, with the pent-up demand for much that would turn dollars into new directions. "The gift and luxury dollar, that so easily found its way into many a flower shop during the war," warned the editor, "will soon have other doorways to enter." As part of the planning program, the magazine ran a series of post-war shop designs, worked out to suit many architectural tastes and all sizes and shapes of real estate. Members were urged to consider their operations objectively, to view their shops and their premises as a stranger might do and to be prepared for the new time of peace with enthusiasm and a resolve to retain the quality and quantity of the wartime business, with attractiveness of surroundings and the highest type of floral service.

The postponed New York convention was held in 1946. The FTD NEWS was able to report in person what before it had called the "Convention in Print." Drastic changes in policy were in store. John M. Besemer had been desirous of moving the publication operation to Chicago for some time.

But he was deterred by the fear of losing the services of Editor Powers, who had maintained the quality and circulation of the magazine, through the troublous times of war. Powers had interests in Detroit which prevented his leaving the city. With the expiration of the Powers contract, however, it was decided to make the move.

Powers wrote in a farewell editorial, "To have been a part of the further growth and development of the NEWS as editor and manager in the past six mostly rugged wartime years has been a challenging publishing assignment. Even more, it has been a priceless adventure in friendship."

The translation of a major publishing effort from one city to another, with regard for publication dates, is not a simple matter. Difficulties developed in the moving. When it appeared that an issue of the magazine would have to be postponed, Powers and his staff, with the true instinct of writers for a deadline, stepped into the breach and the mailing was made on time.

The new editor of the FTD NEWS was Anthony C. Morgan, long an editor of FLORISTS' REVIEW. Under his guidance, the magazine continued in value to the membership and amply provided for its own improvement without cost to the Association.

By May of 1949, the size of the magazine had increased to 300 pages per issue, making a heavy book to handle. No reason longer existed for combining the two sections of general news and membership listings under a single cover. So, with the issue of June, 1949, it was decided to publish two sections each month. The reasons were the same as when the plan was used experimentally in 1941; viz., greater ease of handling and a means of leaving the membership section in the shop for ready reference, while taking the news section home for perusal after working hours. The practice of publishing two sections is still followed.

Morgan's tenure as editor reached a tragic end, when he was fatally stricken by a heart attack at the President's

Banquet, during the annual meeting in Montreal in 1949.

Ruth Marshall, associate editor, assumed the task of directing the publication during the ensuing search for Morgan's successor. With the help of the entire staff, she maintained the rigid schedule, quality of content and interest to members.

Kenneth S. Jacobs, of Chicago, was appointed editor in May, 1950. He had been managing editor of a public utilities trade magazine. His background included experience in all phases of publication work. Under his direction, there was a gradual policy shift toward increased editorial content, aimed at increasing the number of readers. This would be reflected in improved circulation figures which, in turn, would broaden the scope of product advertising and increase the income and earnings of the FTD NEWS.

There was also included, in each issue, a postpaid return card which readers might use to request further information about products advertised in the FTD NEWS, new developments, inventions, items mentioned or new literature offered by advertisers. This sort of card has become a standard feature of many industrial magazines. A market survey and analysis was instituted to bring circulation and sales information up to date.

The entire FTD NEWS staff collaborated in producing a Fortieth Anniversary Year Book, which amounted to a compendium of the history and growth of the Association, details of the Headquarters operation, a statement of the value and prestige of FTD membership, the principles and applications of design, and valuable instructions on store management and architecture. This 170-page, hard-cover book was distributed to members at the 1950 convention in San Francisco.

More color advertising was added to the FTD NEWS the following year. For the benefit of florists, an authoritative series of articles called "Sales and Management Clinic" was begun in the August issue, designed to help members apply the latest and most successful modern methods to their own operations.

Display and card advertisers increased. Although there was a slight drop in advertising billing during the first part of 1952, increased efficiency in the operation of the department resulted in a higher net income.

The growing business of the FTD NEWS required enlarging the staff. And the position which the magazine had gained in the publishing field necessitated that any new personnel should be experienced and well-grounded publication people. In his job as both editor and manager, Jacobs needed an assistant to share the load. He summoned Hal A. Shanafield, a former Chicago newspaperman, subsequently managing editor of Haywood Publications in Chicago and a member of the faculty of Northwestern University. Shanafield joined the FTD NEWS staff, November 1, 1952.

Also introduced that year was a new format which more clearly separated the two sections. Section One was adapted specifically to home reading, by including in its pages the feature editorial articles, national industry news, new product announcements, the trade calendar and other features which did not relate directly to shop operation. Section Two was arranged as a shop manual, containing the membership list, member display and card advertising, with region, unit and local news dispersed through the advertising pages, thus combining all the information necessary to transacting FTD business with short news items for spare-moment shop reading.

Rotation in the Membership List was changed. Where rotation had affected only those towns with 15 or more members, the plan undertook to rotate members in all towns, 11 times a year. Rotation consists of taking the name at the top of the list, in any one town, and placing it at the bottom of the list in the next monthly publication, thus moving the second shop to first place the following month. This rotation is not made in August, except in the towns which have 11 members. These names are rotated 12 times a year. The plan guarantees that the same shop will not head the list on the same holidays every year. It is a fair and equitable solution of the listing problem.

A further amendment to the membership list was authorized by the committee later. This was to remove all elements of the listing not essential to accurate transmission of FTD orders by telegraph, telephone or mail. All matter extraneous to this requirement was considered advertising and was deleted.

It became apparent that the printing firm that had been issuing the FTD NEWS since its removal to Chicago was having increasing difficulty meeting the deadline, because of the increased size of the publication and the growing use of color printing. The printing contract was awarded to a larger company, whose equipment insured prompt printing and mailing of each issue.

The enhanced reputation of the FTD NEWS among the members was emphasized by a survey conducted early in 1957. A detailed, four-page questionnaire was sent to every member and a satisfactory return was received, more than double what can ordinarily be expected. Analysis of the answers showed that the readership of the magazine had climbed to 4.9 per issue. This signified that more than 50,000 persons read each issue, a high figure for any publication, but remarkable for one in the industrial field.

On January 1, 1956, Kenneth Jacobs resigned as editor of the FTD NEWS and Hal Shanafield took over as editor and manager. Other changes were in the offing. In August, General Manager Bodette, with the approval of the Board of Directors, announced plans for the FTD NEWS staff operation to be moved back to Detroit and established in offices in the Lafayette Building where FTD Headquarters was located.

This move contemplated much preparation. It was to be assumed that most of the personnel would not care to leave their homes in Chicago to live in Detroit. This made it necessary to engage office help and staff members already in Detroit. The result was that only Shanafield, himself, made the move from Chicago. In July he interviewed and engaged a complete editorial and office staff. These new members went to Chicago on August 27 for a 2-week training period in the FTD NEWS offices there. They participated in the next issue, studied the files, advertising contracts, editorial carry-over and all other phases of the publication of the magazine. Then they returned to Detroit and went to work on the next issue. They proved their earnestness by making the transition without a hitch. The move was smooth and without incident. The FTD NEWS came back to the city of its birth.

A new phase of the magazine's life was introduced by Mr. Bodette, when he announced, "I believe that the quality of our magazine places us in an advantageous position to raise our national advertising rates, to encourage further color advertising, and to pursue actively the national advertiser with the thought of increasing the revenue of the FTD NEWS. Even if some of the income from the book should be subjected to taxation, the remaining portion would be sufficient, coupled with planned production economies, to enable FTD NEWS to become an income source of considerable circumstance, enabling us further to promote our Association activities."

To increase the usefulness of Section Two, Interflora Directory changes were again included in the membership listings, beginning in 1957. Later that year, the printing contract for the magazine was transferred to Nashville, Tennessee. These moves were dictated by the rapid development of the FTD NEWS. Further format changes, which slightly decreased the page size of the book, enabled the editors to take advantage of color printing facilities.

When the Clearing House adopted an earlier closing date, production and editing changes were instituted, which advanced the mailing date of the magazine appreciably.

Thus, the monthly changes in the membership listing became available to the members several days before the old date, promoting greater efficiency in the transmission of orders. Members in Canada benefited from another innovation: expedited delivery through the mailing department's use of clasp-type envelopes, permitting speedier customs inspection.

Matters do not remain static in the FTD NEWS. While editing is of prime importance, production and mailing procedures are reviewed periodically, for a smoother work flow. An active advertising sales campaign, backed by four-color, four-page promotion brochures, imply further improvements, which will inevitably increase the magazine's 11.3 per cent allocation of the general expense fund.

In 1958, General Manager Bodette conceived the idea of forming a Publications Committee, to supervise all the publishing projects of the FTD Detroit Headquarters. This arrangement was tested for a year. When its success and efficiency were established, it was accepted by the membership in convention at Miami Beach in 1958. The printing of the magazine was moved back to Chicago.

Besides the work of publishing the FTD NEWS, the Publications Division now includes an off-set print shop employing six persons, and fully equipped for press and bindery work in registered color or black and white in sizes from postcard to 14 x 20 inch stock. Most of the printing for the Association is done in this shop. The work turned out in the Publications Division includes printing the annual reports, committee reports, circulars and bulletins to members, unit notices, test order summaries, all single-sheet internal Headquarters forms, ledger sheets and internal accounting forms, form letters, financial statements and many other printing jobs which arise.

Some of these jobs are mechanized for speed and efficiency. An example is the printing of "Report of Orders Filled" forms. These are pre-printed, imprinted with the name and address of the member shop and member's code number, and numbered in sequence in one operation. The self-operation of this shop results in much saving to the Association. An instance of the difference in printing expense, between the FTD shop and one outside, is illustrated by a run of "Report of Orders Filled" forms. Estimates for the outside printing of these forms, consisting of 100 original forms and 100 duplicates, one pad to a member, ranged from $18,000 to $23,750. The FTD print shop was able to turn out the whole job for less than $11,000.

In addition to these advantages, the shop can provide immediate service. Three hours after receiving the final copy of a letter to members, the letters are folded for mailing. All this is a part of the efficiency which characterizes the operation of the Publications Division, assuring the members the ultimate in service. Manager of the print shop is Ashley Sayles, a 10-year FTD veteran.

Another important tool for the member florist in filling FTD orders is the Delivery Directory. This lists alphabetically more than 100,000 non-member towns in the United States and Canada and shows the nearest member town. If a member receives an order to wire flowers to a town without an FTD florist, he consults the Delivery Directory. The Directory is issued periodically in revised form. More than 3,000 changes a year, because of new members, change of ownership, change of address and other reasons, are processed for this book.

The Delivery Directory and all the information forms concerning its revisions and other connected services, are the special province of Isabel Elsbernd, an employee of FTD continuously since 1926. Her first work was done in the Clearing House, where she remained for 21 years. In 1947 she was given supervision of the Handy Book, and has continued in that position. She has an amazing memory of the cultural geography of the United States and Canada. She seldom has to consult the Directory for a quick answer to any question concerning the geographical distribution of FTD members.

The Answer Book is now also the responsibility of the Publications Division. This contains the rules and regulations concerning FTD procedures. It is a store of valuable information on all aspects of the Association and its operations, particularly valuable to new members and an important source of reference for the entire membership.

One more important publication comes under the supervision of the Publications Division under the new arrangement. This is the Numerical Membership List. As members know, each FTD florist is assigned a code number, which must be entered upon the "Report of Orders Filled" form when reporting to the Clearing House. This is the member's identification number for IBM machine purposes.

The Numerical Membership List is kept up to date by constant revision and is issued every four months. Revisions are necessitated by certain numbers being too close to other code numbers, in the case of florists doing large business with each other. Often a member will request his number to be changed to prevent confusion. When new members come into the organization, it is fair that their numbers be communicated to other members as soon as possible. The problem of multiple shops in one town and of changes of ownership also may require a change of code numbers. All of this is under the direction of the Publications Division.

The membership of FTD can be proud of the Publications Division. It is staffed with intelligent, experienced men and women who comprehend the problems of the retail florist and try to present to him, through the pages of the FTD NEWS, the latest information on merchandising, management, public relations, credit and collections, taxes, accounting, inventory control, and sales promotion, to help him increase his value to his customers. It also keeps him informed on the progress and business of the Association, that he may be perfectly informed on FTD affairs. It increases the camaraderie of the membership, by publishing letters and stories.

The division produces many of the working tools of the FTD retailer: the Membership List, Delivery Directory, Answer Book, and Numerical Membership List, without which the Association would suffer. It produces these adjuncts to FTD membership at less cost, and supervises their distribution more efficiently, than any outside firm could do; all this while contributing to the operational fund of the Association.

THE CHANGING FACE OF THE FTD NEWS

The changes in publishing tastes and trends are shown in the various types of cover design which the FTD NEWS has presented to its readers over the years. At lower left is a very early cover. A recent design is shown lower right.

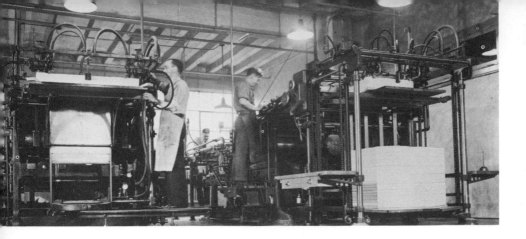

For years these presses met the FTD NEWS deadlines faithfully and competently. At times the magazine ran to more than 300 pages.

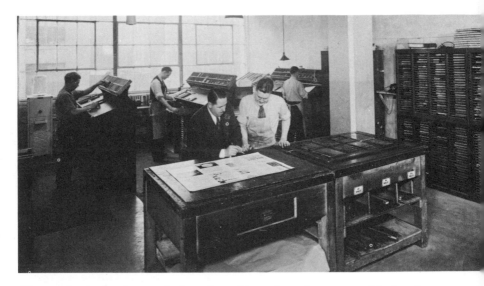

Changes in production methods and machinery have kept pace with the changes in FTD NEWS covers. A view of the composing "stone" and a corner of the first composing room is shown above.

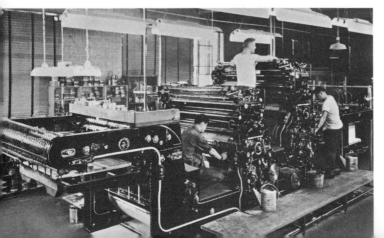

Now the most modern presses equipped for registered four-color printing are employed. The magazine ranks as one of the outstanding American industrial publications, both in quality of content and excellence of its graphic art reproduction.

Late in the evening of February 12, 1942, fire roared through the offices of the FTD NEWS, inflicting almost a quarter of a million dollars of damage to editorial material and paper stocks. Firewalls saved the presses, type fonts and other equipment.

◀ Not the result of a "hot story," but the editor's desk after the FTD NEWS fire was finally brought under control. Destruction of files and office equipment seriously threatened prompt issuance of the magazine then in preparation.

Quickly establishing makeshift offices in a nearby hotel, the staff plunged into the "round-the-clock" work of meeting the forthcoming deadline. Friends aided by lending supplies and equipment. The issue was mailed on time.

The FTD Answer Book is a compendium of information on practices and procedures of the Association. It attempts to answer any question a member might ask about FTD. In loose-leaf binding and updated regularly with new material, the Answer Book also contains a capsule history of FTD, Interflora data and a condensed catalog of FTD supplies.

The FTD Delivery Directory lists alphabetically more than 100,000 non-member towns by state and province with mileage to two nearest member towns, assuring FTD service to most of the United States and Canada. Hospitals, funeral homes, army camps and national military cemeteries are also included, along with many foreign listings.

The Numerical Membership List catalogs all members serially as to assigned FTD code numbers.

CHAPTER TEN

Evolution and Growth

F THE CONVENTION in St. Louis in 1923 had done nothing more than pass the mandatory Clearing House provision, it would go down in the history of FTD as a memorable meeting. But its importance is emphasized by another move which the Board of Directors took at that time, viz., the decision legally to incorporate the Association and make it Florists' Telegraph Delivery Association. There was much in that decision of prime importance to the individual members.

FTD had, since its inception, been a voluntary Association of individuals. The astute businessmen of the organization, like Knoble, Anderson, Penn, Gude and Breitmeyer, were concerned about the position in which they might find themselves, should legal action be brought. Said Knoble, in addressing the meeting on the subject of a revised Constitution and Bylaws, "I am wondering whether any of you in this room recognize the fact that when your Board of Directors went to a bank and borrowed $50,000 or $75,000, each and every one of you was responsible for the amount of money that was borrowed, if the organization could not take care of it. Think of that situation. It was a terrible condition, but it was merely one that grew out of circumstances of this organization being merely an institution that was gotten together for the interchange of some small amount of business, which grew up to what it is at the present time, something that will probably be, in a few years, a business running up to $10 million a year."

And then he made this significant statement: "The Constitution, as it will be drafted, will probably necessitate the incorporation of this organization."

In the discussions preceding the presentation of the Clearing House proposal to the membership, the committee had thought it expedient to consult a St. Louis attorney for advice. They had selected George B. Logan, a well-known lawyer of that city. He expressed himself as amazed that an association of such financial magnitude was unincorporated, advising that a charter be immediately sought, in the best interest of both the Association and the membership.

So drastic a change in the structure of the Association could not be submitted to the convention on short notice. But Knoble notified the meeting that, during the remainder of the year, they might expect to be called on for a mail vote on the proposition. This vote was subsequently held and the resolution authorizing the incorporation of FTD was carried overwhelmingly.

To neglect one more happening at St. Louis would be to ignore a development destined to culminate in a significant change in the leadership of the Association.

It would not be correct to say that antagonism existed between Secretary Pochelon and President Sceery. Each had high respect for the ability and loyalty of the other. But they differed as to how the organization should be directed. Each was exceedingly strong-willed. For more than 10 years, Pochelon had sat at the secretary's desk, with his finger on FTD's pulse. No one excelled him in knowledge of the Association's activities and standing. No one worked harder or more faithfully to advance the FTD cause.

Because of his special understanding of all the Association's activities, the earlier presidents had deferred to his judgment and endorsed his suggestions, leaving him virtually free in the management of FTD affairs. This is no reflection on those presidents. They were men with their own businesses at home. They received no salary. They may have been inclined to view the office chiefly as an honor.

Sceery came to the president's chair with a different view. He saw the president's function as that of a leader. He set out to exert that leadership by traveling widely, visiting members and speaking at meetings. He made himself a president in fact as in name, in the promotion of the Association's interests. In his 2-year tenure of office, he expended more than $14,000 of his own, plus tremendous physical energy, in his travels for the benefit of the Association.

He also believed it a function of the president to guarantee that the Board of Directors was staffed with men, successful in their own businesses, who could, without reference to geography, advantageously chart the progress of the Association. That is why he appealed to the members to elect Henry Penn to the Board to fill the place vacated by himself when made president. That is where he and Pochelon first collided. Pochelon thought the West should be represented on the Board. The argument was never satisfactorily resolved. Something less than perfect relations existed between the two stalwarts ever afterwards.

Sceery, in his formal address to the meeting in 1923, recommended that an executive secretary be appointed to assist Pochelon. Charles Grakelow was chairman of the Committee on the President's Address and he commented thus: "Now I would like to make a few remarks prior to the next motion to be acted upon. We have had in this organization for many years a secretary, an unusual man; and where we are today — and I do not want to strew him with flowers at all, but I believe in giving credit where credit is due — and where we are today is, in a great measure, due to the untiring and never-ending enthusiasm and pep of Albert Pochelon, of Detroit."

This brought applause. He went on, "Albert, if your ears burn, I will ask your indulgence until I have finished my remarks; and then, if the old saying is true, that a man's

ears will burn when something is said about him, your ears
will be on fire; in fact, they must have been on fire for the
first half hour that we were in that committee room on
account of the nice things that were said about you, some
of the nicest things I have ever heard.

"But the committee deems it advisable, due to the enormous business that this Association has taken on — and
agreeing with the president that the surface has only been
scratched — they feel that the time is about due when an
executive secretary should be engaged, not with any embar-
rassment to the present secretary, but with the idea of
co-ordinating with him and relieving him of some of his
work and making possible the retaining for a longer period
of a doggone good secretary; therefore, the committee makes
this motion: That the services of an executive secretary be
engaged, who can give his entire time to the duties of the
office, and that the Board of Directors be empowered to act
upon this recommendation at such time as they deem it
expedient."

The motion carried unanimously.

Albert Pochelon, on October 20, 1923, tendered his resignation as secretary to the Association he had served so long.
He announced this in a letter to all the members.

No one was prepared for the reverberations which followed. The tension between the two men had been kept well
concealed within the Board of Directors. But Pochelon's
resignation revealed it for all to see. There was almost
instantaneous reaction. Letters and telegrams flooded Headquarters, the FTD NEWS office and the members of the
Board.

Philip Breitmeyer, in a full page letter published in the
November issue of the FTD NEWS, said:

"To My Fellow FTD Members:

"I have had the pleasure and the honor to be
close to this man; his aims and his motives always
have been for the interest and welfare of his fellow

men, yes, and the women, too, who are so actively engaged in our profession and in whose interest he always dwelt. I say now that the Association, and I mean all of us, need Pochelon now more than ever. In every movement in which departments were formed, it was Pochelon whose earmarks were noticeable, every one of the departments were conceived by Pochelon and I feel that I am safe in saying this, and when we have such men, do not let them go but rather inspire him to go on and lead us in yet greater work, give him your loyal and loving support . . . Let us all agree that we will not accept his wishes as expressed in the letter, but promise him the loving and solid support which he has had so many years in order that we may function in the proper spirit of our motto, FAITH in him who has served us so well, loyal to TRUTH, and, DETERMINED to make our work scale the full 100 per cent.

Sincerely yours,
Philip Breitmeyer."

On the same page was published a resolution, telegraphed from the Philadelphia unit, which said: "We are not unmindful of the 11 years of untiring service rendered this Association by Mr. Pochelon. At a time when such as he gave could not be purchased at any cost, he gave it without any hope of gain; he neglected his own business that FTD might prosper and we, as a unit, protest most solemnly against allowing such a man to sever his connection at this time, a time when his good judgment, his unflinching honesty, his straightforward manliness, are needed more than ever. That he may regard these protestations and reconsider his resignation is our fondest hope, for in so doing he will be rendering the greatest service that the membership has ever asked of him. As the Association has suggested at St. Louis that we have a paid secretary, we, the Philadelphia unit, suggest that the man that has worked so hard for 11 years to make this a success and given his services for nothing should now, as the Association is able to pay, make Albert Pochelon the paid secretary at a salary of at least $10,000 per year, and all power invested in him to manage the office affairs as heretofore. Signed by all members present of the Philadelphia unit."

At the director's meeting in Detroit, a month after Pochlon's resignation, William J. Smyth moved: "We are all happy to know that Al and Ed are coming together; and I want to make a motion that Al Pochelon's resignation be not received; that he is our secretary, and is going to be our secretary." Said William Gude, "Would you not add to that a vote of confidence?" Continued Smyth, "And that we also want to vote him a vote of our confidence." Gude seconded.

"You have heard the motion duly made and seconded," announced Sceery.

A. F. Borden broke in with, "I do not know whether that covers enough of it, but it seems to me that, during the interim between our directors' meetings, Albert Pochelon should be supreme in all items of the work; that he should be in authority and have full control, between the directors' meetings and the convention; that anything he should say here would go with all the employees of FTD. I do not know whether he has that authority."

"He has that authority now," Smyth assured him.

"It should be pointed out that he has absolute authority on everything," insisted Borden.

The president put the motion and it carried unanimously. Pochelon was still the secretary, without an executive secretary to help him.

Sceery had been re-elected president at St. Louis, to serve for another year. Henry Penn, of Boston, and Herman Knoble, of Cleveland, were re-elected directors and Frank Gorly, of St. Louis, was named to succeed Max Schling.

Charles H. Brown became vice-president, and W. L. Rock continued as treasurer.

Between November, 1923, and January, 1924, the Board of Directors worked diligently on the changes in the Constitution and Bylaws necessary before a corporate charter could be granted by the State of Michigan. Working with them was George B. Logan, the legal counsel from St. Louis.

A special meeting of the membership was called for January 3, 1924, to consider these revisions. Thirty-eight members attended. The required number for a quorum was 11. This meeting was necessary, although by a mail vote the Board had been empowered to make the revisions. Logan explained that the mail vote was not in obedience to the Association's Constitution. A membership meeting, he told them, was the only means by which an amended Constitution could be legally adopted.

There was one other benefit in the revision. The amendments were written by Logan, from his experience as a corporation attorney. He pointed out to the directors many inconsistencies in earlier Constitutions. They were quick to see the need for new regulations, correctly and expertly drawn.

The meeting progressed methodically through the reading of the new provisions by Mr. Logan, comparisons with corresponding clauses in the old Constitution and any questions that the members put. All present had been supplied with copies of the new Constitution and Bylaws. They were ready with their requests for clarification. Logan led them through, skillfully and patiently, explaining the meanings of the Articles and the legal reasons for them.

The meeting extended into the night. When the last Article was read, approved and passed, the group delegated President Sceery, Secretary Pochelon and Director Breitmeyer to sign the application for the charter. This they did. And the Florists' Telegraph Delivery Association became a corporation.

Also at this meeting was much discussion of the Clearing House Plan which had become mandatory on the full membership, January 1. There was still an appreciable number of the members who objected to the plan. W. B. Brown, of Detroit, acted as a sort of "devil's advocate" in presenting their views. He was overwhelmed by the prevailing sentiment of the members present in favor of the Clearing House.

The work of the meeting was completed with the adoption of the new Constitution and Bylaws. When that was accomplished, late in the night of January 3, 1924, the meeting adjourned. A meeting of the Board of Directors was on the agenda for later in the month, January 24 and 25.

The first order of business at the directors' meeting was the administration of the directors' oath by the president to the members of the Board. This requirement was embodied in the new Constitution and is still in force. George Logan had come up from St. Louis to attend the meeting and give his legal advice. Certain aspects of the FTD governmental structure, following incorporation, required formal recognition by the Board. Among these were the various committees.

It had been the practice for the president to appoint members to certain committees of FTD, calling on those whom he believed best fitted. No official sanction by the Board had been necessary. Now, said Logan, the Constitution required formal appointment by the president, after which ratification by the Board was necessary, to make the committee a formal body within the structure of the Association. All committees were now provided for by the Bylaws.

The Committees of Finance, the FTD NEWS, Publicity, and Arbitration were all quickly approved. In order to formalize a Clearing House Committee, a new resolution was needed. This was passed by the Board without incident, empowering the president to make the appointments. A new Field Department was organized. A committee was empowered to oversee its activities. The Executive Committee was to be composed of the chairmen of the standing committees.

In order that the committee members should accurately comprehend their duties, Secretary Pochelon was delegated to write a short "description of duties" of each group for the instruction of its members.

Although FTD had been a corporation since January 3, 1924, legally it was without funds. All the property of the Association was still in the name of the former organization. It was necessary that a formal assignment of all its assets be made by the Association to the corporation, and accepted in writing by the Florists' Telegraph Delivery Association. This was done. The documents were signed by President Sceery, attested by Secretary Pochelon. All other formalities were accomplished under the legal supervision of Logan, and the FTDA was in business.

One of the important decisions at this meeting was the organization of the Field Department. As early as 1916, in the Constitution adopted at the first separate meeting of FTD, provisions were made for district representatives to be named on a geographical basis. Twenty-four were appointed, but no definite geographical limitations were placed upon them. They were leading florists in their areas, and their duties consisted in spreading the gospel of FTD to other retailers and soliciting their membership.

When Fred J. Ammann was appointed field manager, he worked under the direct supervision of Headquarters. His principal work was assisting the district representatives in their duties, carrying news of the Association to the members and, through contacts and talks to meetings, increasing the morale and fraternal bonds within the membership.

As early as 1922, Ammann's work had shown its value and there was interest in a stronger district organization. Early proposals had favored for each district a president, vice-president, Board of Directors, district representative and arbitration and investigation committees. This, however, was

considered to be premature. The recognition of the field
work by appointment of a committee and the establishment
of a department was further acknowledgment of this branch.
In 1924, $3,000 was appropriated for the first half-year's
maintenance of the field work and new rules were formulated
for the government of the district units.

These rules were drawn up by Karl P. Baum, who had
been named chairman of the Field Department. A chairman,
vice-chairman and secretary were provided for. The chairman was directed to appoint two unit members to serve with
the district representative as a Membership Committee to
pass on all applications for membership. Units were required
to hold at least one meeting a year and "as many more as can
be conveniently arranged for." They were given authority
to make assessments for intra-unit work, not to exceed five
dollars a year. This was a move to strengthen the Association
at the "grass roots" level, through better acquaintance among
the florists of any district.

The meeting realized that this fostering of fraternity
among the members added to the strength of the entire Association. So the move to adopt the new rules carried
unanimously.

Looking toward the convention in New York, the Board
adopted the Australian ballot. Nominations would be the
first order of business. Mike Bloy was made responsible to
see that the ballots were printed the first night, and ready
for the election the next day. Sceery appointed himself,
Vice-President Brown, and J. F. Ammann to arrange the
program for the convention.

Not too much had happened to the young corporation. An
extended directors' meeting was unnecessary at this time.
So, an early adjournment was called, with the next meeting
scheduled to coincide with the annual members' meeting in
New York in September, 1924.

That meeting proved to be the biggest in attendance yet
held by FTD. More than 800 attended and, as in St. Louis

the previous year, the members came to hear and to be heard. There were serious questions for consideration and, in the matter of their Association, florists are not the silent type.

There was still much dissatisfaction in certain quarters with the Clearing House. Certain important members seemed to believe that there was not enough control or supervision over the funds of the Clearing House. And, with the increasing amount of money channeled through that organization each month, a fear may have arisen that opportunities for peculation increased in proportion to the amount of the clearings.

One of the objectors to the Clearing House was President Sceery, who had strongly championed the plan the year before. Max Schling also questioned the financial statements of the Clearing House Committee, chaired by Herman Knoble.

Sceery had prepared a scathing address, pointing out what he considered derelictions of duty in the Headquarters offices, mismanagement of the Clearing House, failure to keep him informed of the affairs of the Association and gratuitous insults to himself as president by neglecting to invite him to the meetings of the committees.

The president did not read this address at the regular meeting of the Board. But, after the preliminary business was completed, he directed that the stenographer and all present, except himself and members of the Board, absent themselves, while the Board went into executive session for the presentation of the speech. When the president had finished his presentation, Grakelow, who sided with Sceery in most of his projects, moved that the report be withheld from the floor of the meeting, pending sober reflection.

"The chair declines emphatically to entertain the motion or to be guided by the sentiments therein contained," declared Sceery, hotly. "The recommendations made by the chair are specific and call in toto for a committee to be appointed from this Board for the investigation of certain matters. If, in the wisdom of you gentlemen, you do not see fit to grant the recommendations of the chair, I promise you that I will ask for it from the membership."

Throughout the discussion that followed — and rather heated it grew — Sceery insisted that he had not included personalities in his criticisms. This was not the impression gained by the Board members. They told him so. Breit-meyer, Gude, Bertermann and Knoble violently objected to the implications of the address.

Breitmeyer, especially, accused Sceery of petty jealousy toward Pochelon. "You know," countered the president, "that I have never in my life done anything to cause any friction between Mr. Pochelon and myself. There is no jealousy. You know there is no jealousy and your statement is wrong."

"There is petty jealousy," Breitmeyer stoutly maintained.

Sceery also criticized a trip made by John Besemer to Dallas and Oklahoma. Otto Lang, of Dallas, appointed to the Board the previous January by Sceery, explained, "Mr. President, the trip of Mr. Besemer, I think, was worth every dollar that was expended. His trip down there will help us in saving some $2,700 eventually. His trip through that territory which had never seen or heard anything of the Clearing House, was worth every cent of the money that was paid." Besemer's trip had involved the collection of delinquent accounts and the salvaging of a prominent member in Texas, who was about to withdraw.

Of the president's remarks concerning the Clearing House operation, the directors objected, almost to a man. They are quoted thus:

Gammage: "Mr. President, I think your report came as a thunderbolt to most of us tonight, and I am sincerely sorry that you should discredit the Clearing House force for the work they have done."

Breitmeyer: "It should not go to the meeting, as he intends to have it go. If he wants it to go to the meeting, let it go.

Men will take sides. I will be one of them. I will tell the people that things have been going satisfactorily."

Bertermann: "I take your letter (address) as an affront to this Board of Directors. I take it as an aspersion on a lot of good businessmen here, a lot of men who have been associated with this Association and who are of the highest character."

Knoble: "There are present in this room 14 men, and it would look, from the discussion, that the majority of them are opposed to your suggestion. In view of that fact, you ought to give that some consideration in presenting these things before the body. I will stand before that body with you, Mr. Chairman, all day long if necessary, and I will defend every single dollar the Clearing House Committee has ever spent, and I can point to the figures."

In the face of the opinions of these men, who had long demonstrated their loyalty and devotion to the welfare of the Association, it is hard to analyze Sceery's vigorous dissatisfaction with their management of FTD.

On the other side was the history of Sceery's dedication to FTD. He had spent himself, his money and his time. No president before him had entered upon his office with such single-purposed determination to promote the growth and acceptance of the Association among retail florists.

Before the Board meeting adjourned, Frank Gorly moved, in an effort to mollify both sides, that an efficiency expert be engaged to inspect the Headquarters office operations and advise short-cuts and improvements in procedure. The motion received only two votes.

Sceery was adamant. He delivered his speech before the convention the following morning. It did not stir the conflict on the floor which the directors had feared. But it is significant that the Committee on the President's Address, consisting of Edward McCarthy, J. S. Miller, George Asmus, Frank J. Clark, and Max Schling, in their report to the convention, either did not concur in his recommendations, or suggested that they be referred to committees for consideration. The Clearing House received a hearty vote of confidence, after Herman Knoble thoroughly explained its operation during the past year.

With the termination of the New York convention, Edward Sceery passed into the history of the Association. Although he continued to sit on the Board of Directors ex officio as a past president, he never again wielded great influence.

Charles H. Brown was elected president for the coming year. Karl Baum, of Knoxville, was named to the vice-presidency and Al Pochelon and W. L. Rock were re-appointed secretary and treasurer. Under the charter of incorporation it was necessary to elect two sets of directors for the year, one group to serve for four years and the other for three. As 4-year men, the members elected S. A. Anderson, of Buffalo; George Geraghty, of Toronto; and Edward J. McCarthy, of Brooklyn. The 3-year directors named were Frank McKenna, of Montreal; Dr. Walter A. Moore, of Seattle; and Olaf Olson, of St. Paul.

The New York convention of 1924 was a time of decision. There had been stormy times before, but probably no single occasion in the history of the Association had so vitally affected it. President Sceery's ideas and their rejection by the committee constituted a singular, unprecedented event.

Sceery persisted. At the January, 1925, meeting of the Board, he again brought up the matter, insisting that he had received no co-operation from the Headquarters staff, that Pochelon and Besemer were "at loggerheads," and that a situation existed in the Detroit office, detrimental to the Association. Pochelon, Besemer and Bloy all denied before the Board the existence of hard feelings. And there the matter rested.

President Brown took a firm hold at the first meeting of the new Board. He succeeded in ironing out any differences which might have affected the administration of Headquarters or the future of the Association. He demonstrated from the first his trust in Pochelon and the others. And, although a close friend of Sceery, he gave him no support.

By now the membership of FTD had grown to 2,440 in the United States, 117 in Canada, and 239 in foreign countries. This was a large foreign representation. Among his suggestions, President Brown proposed that a group of past presidents visit Europe, sometime during the next year, to bring Europeans into closer contact with their American and Canadian colleagues. It was time, he said, that FTD increased its range, through closer association with European florists.

This move assumed greater proportions during the year. The president's speech at the Atlanta convention of 1925 strongly urged the furtherance of the world organization. The foreign florists had the status of correspondents and not of members in the American sense. Otto R. Sielaff, recently appointed assistant executive secretary as an aide to Pochelon, presented a paper before the Atlanta Board meeting, outlining his view of the world organization. He pointed out that, under the new Constitution and Bylaws, foreign florists could become full members of FTD and that, through the use of the Clearing House, all florists in America and Europe could be linked in an organization which would spread the message of flowers-by-wire and redound to the benefit of all.

There was considerable discussion about holding the annual meeting in a European city in 1926 or 1927. The British group had requested that money be appropriated for propaganda in Europe. It was thought by the Board that a convention in London might be the impetus needed for the launching of a world organization. This convention was never held. FTD florists had visited England and the mainland of Europe in former years and had made reports to the annual meetings concerning their trips. But these visits were not official.

Now, the time was thought ripe for an official visit. President Brown was favorable to the trip, as was Pochelon. They began to plan the trip for some time following the close of the Atlanta convention.

When the ballots were counted at Atlanta for the election of officers for the coming year, it was found that Charles H. Brown had been re-elected president, with William J. Smyth, of Chicago, to assist him as vice-president. Named to the Board of Directors were Thomas H. Joy, of Nashville; Herman D. Schiller, of Chicago; and Gertrude Schultheis, of Scranton, Pennsylvania. The election of Miss Schultheis marked the first time a woman had been elected to a national FTD office. This must have caused some delighted smiles among those who could remember back to the Toronto meeting of 1921, when Philip Breitmeyer had been soundly trounced in a verbal encounter with Miss Hester Getz and Mrs. Helen M. Schlauraff on the question of the place of women in the affairs of FTD.

The year 1925 was a time of great business expansion in all lines in the United States. This prosperity was reflected in the growth of FTD and also by the organization of a sizeable rival association called American Telegraph Florists, or Amtelflo. About 800 florists were members of the new group, 270 of them also belonging to FTD.

The secretary of Amtelflo had secured his organizational experience by working as a bookkeeper for FTD for about five years. The Board of Directors of FTD ruled that the Association could not condone dual membership and, through the pages of the FTD NEWS, notified those members who had joined the rival group that they must resign from it or be removed from the rolls of FTD. The matter was allowed to rest at this point, pending the decision of those who belonged to both organizations.

With the coming of spring, President Brown and Secretary Pochelon put their plans for a European trip into action. They sailed from New York, May 8, 1926, on the S.S.

Carmania. Their itinerary was ambitious, including the British Isles, France, Italy, Austria, Czechoslovakia, Germany, Switzerland, Denmark, Sweden, Norway, Holland and Belgium, with plans to visit all the principal cities of those countries. The trip was fully reported in the FTD NEWS and an official report made to the Board at the Chicago convention. There was no doubt that the two men ably represented the Association in Europe, and that the work they did hastened the formation of the world organization.

At the 1926 Chicago convention, William J. Smyth was elected president. Herman Knoble was named to the vice-presidency and Alfred T. Bunyard, of New York; Laurent Clody, of Chicago; and Otto Lang, of Dallas, were elected to the Board. Al Pochelon continued as secretary and W. L. Rock as treasurer. These men inherited the dual membership problem. Realizing that the solution was not easy, the Board engaged an attorney, who wrote a letter to the members who had joined the other organization, directing them to resign immediately or face the penalty of expulsion from FTD. To the surprise of some of the directors, there was little opposition to the order. What had looked like a serious split in the ranks was healed with few objections from the members who had joined the rival group.

For the first time, the annual minutes noted the record of a meeting of the "Associate Division" in Chicago. This division was composed of representatives of allied trades serving florists, growers and wholesalers. They had long been regarded as influential in the promotion of membership in FTD. Their salesmen were in contact with both members and non-members and with every branch of the florist industry. They were able to appraise the opinions of florists, sometimes more accurately than the FTD field men.

It was pointed out at this meeting that many florists in smaller towns were excluded from FTD ranks by the size of the annual dues and the guarantee deposit. A strong suggestion was made to provide for smaller payments from retailers handling not more than $150 to $200 of telegraph orders in a year. Since, however, this aspect of the FTD financial structure was the concern of the Clearing House, it was decided that nothing could be done along those lines.

The membership of FTD had reached 3,300 and was growing satisfactorily. There was still dissatisfaction over the fact that often a member would not recommend his competitors for membership. This was causing hard feelings among retailers. In this field, the associate members could be of great help, and Herman Knoble, chairman of the meeting, suggested that the associates use their good offices to increase the goodwill among competitors. There was room, he urged, in FTD for all retailers who were ethical and upright businessmen.

The 1927 convention was held in Washington, D. C. It was a routine meeting with no serious problems for consideration. Business in the United States was the best it had ever been. The Association was growing in strength and it seemed that the future was rosy indeed. Even the matter of a convention city for the next year was disposed of easily by leaving it to the secretary to select either French Lick or West Baden. West Baden was eventually chosen. Elected president was W. J. Smyth for another term. The vice-presidency went to Henry Penn, of Boston. Henry Hornecker, of East Orange, N. J.; Tommy Luke, of Portland; and W. A. Saltford, of Poughkeepsie, N. Y., were named to the Board of Directors.

The rising tide of business brought up the subject of salaries of the office personnel. A resolution was passed by the Board in January, raising the salaries approximately 10 per cent. Another unusual matter came before the Board, which could be called a straw in the wind, indicating coming change in the administration of the Headquarters office. A motion was put before the Board by President Smyth that Albert Pochelon be formally elected executive secretary.

Elections by the Board had not been considered necessary, in the cases of Pochelon and Treasurer Rock, for several years. Why Smyth brought it up at this time cannot now be learned. It is possible that its roots lay in the sentiments between the secretary and Sceery, in the early Twenties. This move disturbed Breitmeyer, who had come to the meeting but could not remain. He was quick to point out that this was a procedure that had been dispensed with several years ago and he came to the support of Pochelon. The motion carried and both Pochelon and Rock were re-elected.

If one might read between the lines of the report, he might find an undercurrent of feeling there that Pochelon had outlived his usefulness. But there is a contrary suggestion in the statement of Sceery himself. He defended Pochelon and his record in strong terms. Pochelon was visibly affected by Sceery's speech. After the difference that had existed between the two, which itself is hard to explain at this late date, Sceery's defense of the secretary is even more confusing.

The annual meeting at West Baden, Indiana, proved to be one of the most interesting and far-reaching of all. It was also one of the most explosive. For some time there had been suggestions from various units to change the manner in which the directors were elected, to afford more equitable representation of the different regions of the United States and Canada. Directors had been elected on the basis of their popularity at the annual meetings. Some members did not consider this a proper way to apportion the representation. There had been resolutions from many parts of the country, suggesting that proper representation meant an equal geographical distribution of directors.

This contemplated regional zoning, with more local control over the affairs of each unit, and a local election of directors.

It was also thought by some prominent members, and especially by the associate members, that the Associate Division should be given a greater voice in the plans and programs of the Association.

One objection, which many members recognized as reasonable, was the lack of authority provided in the Constitution and Bylaws, by which this change could be accomplished. This introduced the topic of revision of the rules and regulations of FTD. A committee, consisting of Henry Penn, Herman Schiller, Philip Breitmeyer, Arthur Leidiger, William J. Smyth and Laurent Clody, had been appointed to draw up the revisions of the Constitution and Bylaws for presentation to the West Baden meeting.

The committee had done their work and had had the revisions printed in the form of ballots; one for the Constitution and one for the Bylaws, calling for a single vote on the total revisions. When these "ballots" were presented to the members, strenuous objections to their form were expressed on the floor. It had been the custom to offer each amendment to the Constitution and each revised Bylaw separately for the consideration of the convention. Offering only two ballots prevented a vote against some and in favor of others. Some members called this ballot form an attempt by the committee to "railroad" through the meeting certain changes not favored by the majority.

There is no doubt that the changes were substantial. Article II of the Constitution was to be amended to provide that the principal business office should be in Detroit but that the directors should have the power to establish such other offices as might be necessary.

Article IV was to be amended to provide for changes in the Constitution, by recommendation of not less than 50 active members voting by mail, or by a majority of the Board of Directors. Then such changes would have to be approved by two-thirds of the members voting by mail within 30 days on ballot forms supplied them by the executive secretary.

This last provision, the mail vote, was bitterly assailed by

Knoble, Sceery and Brown. It was as hotly defended by Clody and other members of the Committee for Revision.

The revision of the Bylaws included a plan for regional zoning, as requested by various units in past years. Through this new plan, the members in each geographical district, during the first 20 days of June on alternate years, would be supplied with nomination ballots by the executive secretary, by which they could vote for as many directors as their territory was entitled to have. These nominees would be notified by the secretary, within 10 days of the nomination. Then, in July, the secretary would submit ballots to the members containing the names of six times the number of directors to which the territory was entitled. The man receiving the highest number of votes was to be the new Board member.

The Board was also given power to elect the president, first vice-president, a second vice-president (who was always to be from Canada), the executive secretary, and the treasurer. The executive secretary was to be the operating executive officer of the Association and a member of all committees ex officio. He was to have general supervision and management of the Association, under the direction of the president, the Board and the Executive Committee.

Amendments and revisions of the Bylaws were to be made by a mail vote, as in the case of constitutional amendments.

The revised Articles of the Constitution were printed on a single sheet of paper, with the single proposition stated at the bottom: "Are you in favor of adopting the revised Constitution?" Two boxes, labeled "Yes" and "No," were appended for the voter's mark. The revisions to the Bylaws, which were extensive, were printed on four pages, with the same sort of voting provision.

The changes had been submitted to the members before the annual meeting, that they might study them and be prepared to render a verdict at the proper time. Many of them had not taken the time to do so. There seemed to be considerable backing for the formation of regional zones and this seemed to be the principal concern of the voters. They had overlooked what Herman Knoble called the most dangerous provision of the new Bylaws, the mail vote.

Knoble took the floor to criticize the revisions. He was halted several times by prolonged applause as he explained his opinion that no Bylaw could be properly explained in writing and that the proper way to cure the misunderstandings about revisions was always in open discussion. Knoble was popular with the membership and his views received great consideration.

He was followed briefly by Laurent Clody, who reminded the convention that only 10 per cent of the membership was present — an average attendance — and that such a situation meant that the laws of the Association were passed by only one-tenth of the members entitled to vote. The mail vote, he argued, would assure the participation of as much as 50 per cent.

Past President Brown took the floor to oppose the new Constitution and Bylaws. He pointed out that they called for the secretary to be a member of the Association, in other words, a florist. This would bar a man, trained in the administration of the office, from using his training in the executive position. He also pointed out that men whose names were signed to the letter to members which accompanied the revisions, did not in all cases sign, or even approve, the new rules.

Otto Sielaff, an attorney and Pochelon's assistant, was asked his opinion of the documents. He objected to them from a legal standpoint and on the basis of utility. He maintained that what was needed by the Association was a thorough investigation by a business counsel or "business engineer." Sielaff also denied that he had signed the letter, indicating he did not approve of the revisions.

David Roberts, an independent attorney retained by FTD, defended the legality of the Constitution and Bylaws. And so it went for most of the day. Clody finally managed to get a motion before the house that the discussion be ended and that the revisions be submitted to the membership the following morning. At the voting box the next day, the revisions carried.

Aside from the disagreement over the changes to the rules and regulations, the West Baden convention was a most fruitful occasion. The program had been replete with instructive talks by men high in the florist and horticultural fields. A model florist shop had been conducted in the lobby of the hotel as a training feature for the members. No attempt was made to make money from the shop, but it sold $800 worth of flowers the first day.

In the election of officers for the ensuing year, Charles H. Grakelow became president, S. A. Anderson, vice-president, and William L. Rock, Angelo Rossi, of San Francisco; and Mrs. Percy Waters, of Toronto, were named to the Board. Rock also continued as treasurer and Pochelon as secretary.

The dissatisfaction over the revisions to the Constitution and Bylaws was not immediately dissipated. There was still rankling over the subject when the Board met the following January, 1929, in Detroit. Charles Brown brought up the topic on the first morning. Grakelow knew he had his work cut out for him. Sceery was also present. Both he and Brown were strong-willed and argumentative. But Grakelow took firm hold of the meeting, denied Brown and Sceery votes as past-presidents under the new Bylaws, and thus removed their influence from the meeting.

Logan, the lawyer from St. Louis, and Roberts, of Detroit, expressed their opinions of the action at West Baden. Logan was convinced that the revisions were illegal and that the old Constitution and Bylaws still controlled. Roberts was of opposite mind.

Faced with this split opinion, Grakelow put the matter to a vote: Whether the Board would declare that the Association was operating under the revisions or under the old rules. The revisions won by a vote of seven to six. Thus the matter subsided for the moment.

The meeting in Detroit produced another close vote and one that caused surprise, shock and consternation to many members. On the second day of the Board meeting, when time came for the election of the treasurer and secretary for the coming year, Pochelon and Rock were requested to leave the room. This was accepted custom. The Bylaws provided that no member of the Board could vote upon a matter in which he was financially interested.

As the veteran secretary left the room, President Grakelow announced that nominations were in order for the position of executive secretary, to serve for the ensuing year.

Arthur Saltford said, "Mr. President, I wish to place in nomination for the office of executive secretary the name of Al Barber, of Cleveland."

The nomination was seconded by Henry Hornecker. There seemed no surprise around the table at this nomination.

Laurent Clody was recognized by the chair and he nominated Pochelon. Tommy Luke seconded. The nominations were then closed and the vote taken. Herman Schiller, the teller, separated the ballots into two stacks, counted them and announced the result. Pochelon had received six votes. Barber was the winner with eight votes.

A strange silence fell over the room. Breitmeyer, William Gude, Anderson, Penn, Sceery, Brown, Smith and Gammage, all members of the Association since its founding, sat staring at the table before them. They knew the work that Pochelon had done for the organization when it was a frail and faltering group. They could recall him standing before the annual meetings, his hands filled with sheaves of letters he had written and received, exhorting the members to be more aggressive in recruiting new florists for FTD. Maybe they remembered his "goat," his humor, his statistics and the collections for the publicity fund which were almost his trade-mark.

They must have recalled seeing him at the Board meet-ings, announcing the growth of FTD, insisting on public relations and advertising budgets, defending his conduct of the Headquarters office when needful, charging some with "petty politics injurious to the Association." Whatever the pictures the screen of memory showed them, they saw Albert Pochelon always as a dedicated and devoted member, a hard-working secretary and a firm believer in the future of FTD. He was a sentimentalist, stubborn perhaps when he thought himself right, but a man with only one purpose: to make the Florists' Telegraph Delivery Association a virile and efficient force for the transmission of the beauty and fragrance of flowers to the entire world.

Finally, William Gude rose. "Mr. Chairman," his great voice was strained and softened, "may I be excused at this time?"

"Are you coming back?" Grakelow asked.

"No," said the big man, simply.

"Mr. Gude," the president continued, "is there anything you would like to bring to the attention of the Board at this time?"

"No, not a thing." The former president turned without another word and slowly left the room.

"Mr. Chairman and members of the Board," said Gertrude Schultheis, as the door closed behind Gude, "it seems to me we have done today one of the hardest things that we have ever had to do in any of our meetings. I know it has been for me a very hard job to vote against Albert Pochelon, but it was an absolutely necessary thing to do. We have gotten to the point where it did not seem as if Mr. Pochelon knew how to operate, and it is just a pity; it is the greatest pity in the world to me." No one answered her.

"The old order changeth . . ." An era had ended. But even as it closed, another began. The meeting of the Board continued.

CHAPTER ELEVEN

The Great Depression

HEN THE BOARD OF DIRECTORS met in Detroit in January, 1929, with Charles Grakelow in the chair, it was faced with an enormous amount of work. Grakelow was well known to all the directors. He had an easy, pleasant way of conducting the meetings, but he could be firm when the occasion demanded, as it soon did.

Sceery, Brown and Smyth, all past presidents, who were entitled to vote in the affairs of the Board under the old "Bylaws," were denied that privilege by President Grakelow. He maintained that, since the members had adopted the revised Bylaws at West Baden after due discussion, he was under their mandate to uphold the law as established by their vote.

The new president was not arbitrary about this. He admitted that the question of legality disturbed him. To avoid the appearance of overriding opposition to the new rules, of which there was considerable in the Board, he appointed a Committee on Constitution and Bylaws, consisting of Past President Brown, chairman; and Directors Bunyard, Mrs. Waters, Schiller and Past President Bertermann. Their duty was to study the controversial provisions of the revised rules and prepare a report for the Boston convention in September.

With the retirement of Albert Pochelon as secretary, the subject of a permanent building for the FTD offices assumed major importance. The offices had been in the Pochelon

Building in downtown Detroit. Pochelon's L. Bemb Floral Company occupied the street floor of the building.

It was not entirely the former secretary's departure from the official family which prompted the desire for new offices. It was a time of feverish building with larger and larger edifices going up. Unprecedented stock market speculation was causing a corresponding building boom and companies that had never thought of erecting their own buildings were hurrying into construction. It was the style and spirit of the time.

There was one other consideration developing this thought among members of FTD. The Association had begun in the spirit of fraternity, besides that of business. The period of FTD's formation coincided with what might be called the "Temple Era" in American life. Just about every kind of co-operative group must have a "Temple." It had been mentioned at FTD meetings ever since the Association had taken form.

When the subject came up at the Board meeting, Grakelow asked for the report of the committee which had been appointed at West Baden to consider a building site. The report was not entirely harmonious. Much local interest was involved, each committeeman wanting the FTD Temple in his own home town. The expense of building was agreed upon at approximately $100,000. A committee, consisting of past presidents and members of the Finance Committee, under the chairmanship of Irwin Bertermann, was instructed to investigate the matter and report to the convention. No time limit was specified. It was thought that two years might be consumed in making the decision, but the committee was ready with its report much sooner.

Brown's Committee on Constitution and Bylaws was also ready much ahead of time. They worked so diligently that it was necessary for Grakelow to call a special meeting of the Board in Detroit, for May 21, 1929.

With the advice of legal counsel, the committee had completely revised the West Baden Bylaws and was ready to submit the results to the Board. The Articles were examined carefully, the Board having time to discuss each one at length, receive explanations from the committee and express a final opinion. This work occupied the entire morning and, when it was completed, Anderson moved that the Bylaws be adopted as a whole by the Board, for submission to the general membership at the next convention. This motion carried.

The revised documents were not complicated and they were free from many inconsistencies noted in the West Baden revisions. They drastically restricted the powers of the executive secretary, who had been given broad controls at the last convention. The president was made the chief executive officer, that duty being taken from the secretary. Brown had also restored the voting power of the three immediate past presidents.

There was some echo of West Baden still present in the regional zoning provision, which was retained with specific instructions for the election of regional directors to the Board. Districts were to be organized within the regions, with a district representative appointed by the president to serve each district for one year. A director-at-large was to be elected by the convention after free nominations. The executive secretary and the treasurer were barred from serving on the Board of Directors. The Associate Members' Division was empowered to name one of its members as "chairman of the associate members," and the one so named, on written certification of his legal election, was to become a member of the Board.

William Rock reminded the meeting that he had been promised an assistant and asked if one could then be appointed. Laurent Clody moved that Al Barber be named to that post, as he was not spending his entire time in the office. This was done.

It is noteworthy that when the Board voted Pochelon's

retirement, the executive secretary's salary was reduced from $15,000 to $3,000 per year. This may demonstrate the resolve of the Board to decentralize control. Barber had accepted this reduction, having a business of his own in Cleveland. Since his election, he had confined his activities to Board meetings. This left John Besemer as acting head of the Detroit offices, although his title was manager of the Clearing House.

This was not a happy arrangement. FTD had become so large that it needed the leadership of a man with authority to make decisions on the complete office operation, one who would be in a position to reach the president or members of the Board or committees for advice and consultation. Not enough time had passed to demonstrate the weakness of the situation, but, as the summer progressed, complaints arose about slowness of correspondence from the Detroit office and the looseness of the central control.

This was a chief point made by President Grakelow at the convention in Boston in September. Barber had also felt the sting of these criticisms. But since he was in charge of the coming Cleveland flower show, he felt he could not give full time to the office affairs.

Grakelow praised Barber's work and suggested that arrangements be made by the Board for the secretary's full time, at a commensurate increase in compensation. Arthur Saltford, who had nominated Barber for the position, moved that the executive secretary be asked to give full time to the Detroit office, at a salary of $1,000 per month, beginning immediately. Barber was absent from the Board room during this discussion. Anderson thought the proposed salary too great and suggested $9,000 per year, however, he was overruled. Saltford's motion was put and carried. Barber was called back and informed of the increase, but asked permission to complete his obligation to the Cleveland flower show. His request went unanswered and the suggestion was made that he turn over the flower show to Herman Knoble.

The Board next considered a troublesome question. After the Clearing House was established on the basis of a 2 per cent charge for collections processed through Detroit, it was hoped a refund would be made to the members when total clearings showed the operation could be accomplished at less cost. Clearing House advances were now comfortably ahead of its cost of operation, so certain members of the Board thought this promise should be fulfilled. A rebate of $25,000 had been made not long before to test the membership's reaction. One of the chief supporters of this rebate was Sceery, never quite reconciled to the Clearing House plan. Sitting now as an advisor with a vote, he brought up the matter. Besemer was consulted. He said that the cost of doing business during the year had been approximately 1.1 per cent and that the Clearing House could return to the members the amount of $25,000, without impairing its efficiency. Sceery insisted that this be done.

Grakelow was opposed to this move. So were Rock and Luke. The president had spent his time in office visiting members from coast to coast. FTD had gained 903 new members during his term, raising the total to 5,397. He felt that $25,000, apportioned among so many members, would be insignificant compared with the use that the Association could make of the money. Sceery argued that, if the Detroit office were run more efficiently, the collection charge could be reduced to 1 per cent. He favored bringing the question to the floor of the convention.

At this point, Grakelow relinquished the chair to Vice-President Anderson and addressed the Board on the danger of such a course. Grakelow could sway men with the power of his eloquence. Never had he used it more fervently. He had plans, formed during his travels, of enlarging the membership of FTD. He had decided that two field men, prospecting the West Coast, would greatly stimulate FTD activities in that area. He believed that with $25,000 this could be accomplished. But he could not convince the Board that his project was more important than the rebate to the members. The vote for returning the money was 11 to 4, in favor of the rebate. Grakelow was successful, however, in keeping Sceery's plan to reduce the 2% charge off the floor of the convention.

Two important advances took place at this Boston convention; viz., the adoption of the new Bylaws and the decision to buy a building in Detroit.

Irwin Bertermann reported to the meeting on the latter. He called on Philip Breitmeyer to describe the premises, for Breitmeyer, former Mayor of Detroit, had been named by Bertermann as chairman of a special group inside the New Home Committee. Breitmeyer knew property values in Detroit. He knew the needs of the Association. He knew the space requirements, the importance of a well-situated home, its accessibility to transportation lines and the general character of Detroit neighborhoods.

The house selected was the former mansion of Julius Haass, a Detroit banker, standing on Grand Boulevard East, near Vernor highway, Jefferson and Kercheval avenues, all principal thoroughfares. It was 80 by 50 feet, standing on a lot 150 feet wide and 200 feet deep. The price was $75,000 and Breitmeyer estimated that alterations necessary to convert the structure to an office building would cost between $8,000 and $14,000.

Belle Isle Park, one of the show places of Detroit, was within walking distance. Between 500,000 and a million persons passed the location in a week's time, a desirable feature from the publicity standpoint, since it was contemplated that the lawn would be landscaped in an eye-arresting way.

Breitmeyer believed that the property would increase in value over the years and the money invested would, in time, produce a gratifying profit, should another move be necessary.

When Breitmeyer finished his description, Grakelow took

the speaker's stand to explain that, by owning and operating its own building, the Association would save about $7,000 a year, the difference between maintenance of the new property and $16,800 yearly rent then being paid.

Herman Knoble, the financier, then arose to dispute the figures given the convention. He had made an independent investigation of the site, he said, and according to reliable information it was worth closer to $45,000 than $75,000. It was in a neighborhood not zoned for business and the cost of heating, janitor service, and general upkeep would much exceed the amount mentioned. He advised the members to consider the proposition with great care.

Knoble admitted, however, that the building was "an exceptionally beautiful place."

"I am told on good authority in Detroit," he said, "that the property was appraised by bankers at a present valuation of $300 a front foot. That would be $45,000. This banker also said that, if restrictions were removed, the price might go to $750 a foot, putting the valuation then up to the point of our investment."

Herman Knoble had a head for figures and an exceptional grasp of financial matters. But for once he had made a mathematical mistake. Bertermann was quick to note it. He sprang to his feet.

"Mr. President, Mr. Knoble said that the property would be worth $750 a foot. Is that right?"

"Yes," replied Knoble.

"Am I right," continued Bertermann, "in saying there is 150 feet of frontage?"

Knoble agreed.

"One hundred and fifty feet at $750 a foot is not $75,000," said Bertermann. "I know you said that inadvertently, and I am correcting you so that the audience will know."

Knoble admitted, "I intended to say $105,000."

There is no doubt that this was an honest mistake. But Knoble had destroyed his own argument. He had shown the

The Men Who Guide the Destiny of the F. T. D. Association

Meeting of the Board of Directors and Executives in session at F. T. D. Headquarters
815 Bates St., Detroit, Mich., April 11th and 12th, 1921

A meeting of the FTD Board of Directors held in the Board Room of FTD Headquarters in the Pochelon Building, Detroit, August, 1921. Seated, left to right, Wm. J. Smyth, Chicago; Max Schling, New York; Charles H. Grakelow, Philadelphia; Vice-President H. G. Dillemuth, Toronto; Edward Sceery, Paterson, New Jersey; Irwin Bertermann, Indianapolis; President Philip Breitmeyer, Detroit; Wm. F. Gude, Washington; W. W. Gammage, London, Ontario; A. F. Borden, Los Angeles; W. J. Palmer, Buffalo; Herman P. Knoble, Cleveland; Karl P. Baum, Knoxville, Tennessee. Standing, left to right, Michael Bloy, Business Manager, FTD NEWS; Albert Pochelon, FTD Secretary; George M. Geraghty, Toronto Retail Florists' Association; Hilmer V. Swenson, Advertising Manager, FTD NEWS; Miss Helen Wick, Assistant Secretary, FTD; Wm. L. Rock, FTD Treasurer, Kansas City; Arthur J. Munro, official stenographer, Buffalo.

In 1922, at Baltimore, Maryland, a persistent photographer managed to get most of the members to cease discussing the adoption of the Clearing House long enough to assemble them for this panorama. The size of the gathering indicates to some extent the rapid and

Festive hats and feminine finery featured this banquet of FTD members at the Hotel Commodore, New York City, in 1924. The photographer has added an international touch by labeling it Florists' Telegraph Delivery Association of U. S. and Canada.

A convention in Washington, D. C., is not complete without a visit to George Washington's home at Mount Vernon, as these FTD conventioneers demonstrated in 1927. The wide sloping lawn, with the stately columned mansion in the background, was a photographer's dream when it came to posing such a large group.

enthusiastic growth of FTD in the scant eight years that had passed since it decided to hold its conventions separately from those of the SAF. Many prominent oldtime members can be recognized in the photograph.

"On to San Francisco," was the cry as three trainloads of FTD members stopped in Denver and were entertained by the Mountain and Plain States Florist Association in 1930, during the 25-day "convention by rail."

When business is away, FTD members will play. Below is a scene taken at the President's Banquet and Ball in San Francisco in 1930.

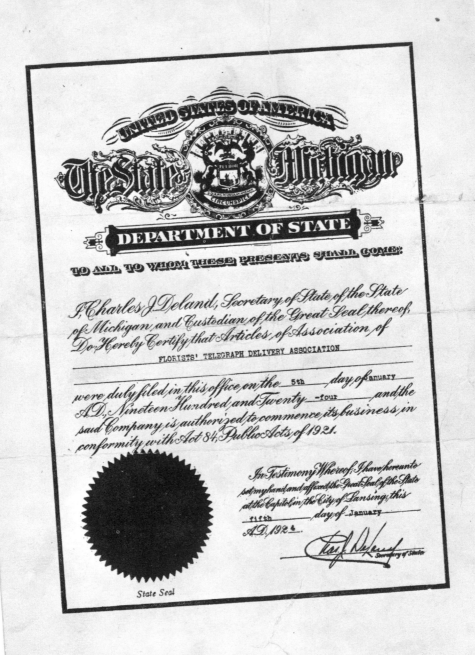

Five days after the establishment of the Clearing House as a mandatory procedure for FTD members, the Association became duly incorporated by filing Articles of Association with the Secretary of State of Michigan. Above is the original certificate.

members that the property they were offered for $75,000 was—or could be—worth $105,000.

The motion was quickly made and seconded that the property be bought. The vote was unanimously favorable. Treasurer Rock then framed the motion in the form of a resolution to liquidate the building fund and transfer it to the general fund for the purpose of purchasing the building. There was no dissent and nothing now prevented the acquisition of FTD's first self-owned home.

Grakelow had proved himself a hard-working and able president. He had accepted the office under the West Baden revisions which did not allow the president to succeed himself. This had not deterred him. He had traveled widely, presenting to the various groups an inspiring picture of the future of their Association. The charm of his eloquence and the warmth of his personality had endeared him to all new acquaintances, just as those traits had won him a place in the affections of those who attended the annual meetings.

The new Bylaws did not bar his renomination to the presidency. Breitmeyer was quick to take advantage of that. As Vice-President Anderson opened the nominations, Breitmeyer rose for recognition. He was greyer, somewhat slower and a little more stooped, but he showed the same commanding presence and dignity as when he had risen 17 years before in a similar situation and, through the force of his personality and logic, obtained the nomination of Albert Pochelon as secretary, against Valentine's advocacy of John Young.

"Mr. Chairman," he began, "when we have a president who has served us as well as this president has—and he is just in the beginning of his work—I feel we should be unanimous and even cast aside a Bylaw, which calls for nominating two men for president. I do not need to eulogize the president, because you know him as well as I do, and, therefore, I would like to place in nomination our president of today—I need not mention his name—and, in the same breath, I would like to move that the nominations be closed. Now, that may be against the Bylaw rule. But I hope the matter can be brought about, so that our president will have no opposition."

As the aging stalwart sat down, the thunder of applause which followed his words must have gratified him greatly.

Tommy Luke was on his feet before the applause died, to second the nomination. Brown and Gorly also praised Grakelow, in seconding his nomination and moving that nominations be closed.

Chairman Anderson would not entertain the motion since it was in violation of the Bylaws. He called for further nominations. But the members refused to name an opposing candidate. The chair was forced to close the nominations. The motion carried uproariously.

Grakelow resumed the speaker's stand and said, "Ladies and gentlemen, may I briefly, though nonetheless sincerely, to you my nominators and seconders, and to you, my gracious friends, express my appreciation for the wholehearted manner in which you have placed me in nomination for the presidency of the organization for the ensuing year, and just say, 'Thank you!' This is an occasion upon which actions speak louder than words. I will do my best, and it will not be tinged with regret. Thank you."

In the same way, no nominations were made to oppose Anderson, and he was re-elected vice-president unanimously. Under the new Bylaws, directors were to be elected from Regions 1, 4, and 7. They were: Sidney Hoffman, Sr., of Boston; Frank Schramm, of Toledo; and Arthur Leidiger, of Milwaukee, respectively. Henry Penn, of Boston, was elected director-at-large. San Francisco was selected as the next convention city.

Much had been accomplished at Boston. The dividing of the country into districts, done at West Baden and affirmed at Boston, was a notable improvement in FTD government. Seventy-seven district representatives had been named and more were in prospect. One disappointing feature was the omission to name field men to assist the district representatives in their educational work and to help create a virile continental organization. But this was an improvement soon to come.

The new Bylaws were modern, well-considered documents, powerful and fair. A hard-working crusader occupied the president's chair. And FTD, now mature and self-assured, faced the third decade of the Twentieth Century, a time of portent and promise. Business indices were higher than the country had ever known them. Wages and salaries were rising and the disposable income of the nations had reached new peaks.

But just ahead lay Black Friday, the unforgotten October 29, 1929.

By January, when the Board of Directors next met in Detroit, the magnitude of the stock market disaster was evident to most businessmen. Banks and other lending agencies were beginning to suffer. The steady falling of the business index proved that the condition was not merely an abnormal stock fluctuation. The word "depression" was beginning to be heard.

Said President Grakelow, in his opening address to the Board, "Every other business reports the most regrettable depression, while we show a 15 per cent increase over the previous year."

This increase was in the number of orders filled. Actually, the dollar volume of business was up only 5 per cent, because smaller orders were the rule. The depression, deepening fast, had decreased the size of the orders. But the heartening fact for FTD was that the field work in the regions and the organization work in the districts were increasing the area over which FTD could extend its service. This really resulted in more business, although spread over a larger area.

Emphasis on local organization was a watchword of Grakelow's two administrations. His wide travels and his speaking ability brought him into persuasive contact with many members. They, in turn, introduced him to florists who were not yet members, and it was a small task for the Grakelow personality to make applicants of them. This continual growth in membership was reflected in the manner in which the Association rode out the most difficult of times.

On the basis of enhanced efficiency in operating the Clearing House, the Board voted Manager Besemer an increase in annual salary from $8,700 to $10,000, despite considerable discussion on this point before the increase was ordered. There had been an over-all savings in the department of about $7,000 over the year. More efficient operation had enabled him to cut the staff slightly and, as soon as the new edition of the Handy Book was ready for distribution, there would be a further reduction in employees.

This was the first Board meeting at which a member of the Associate Division had sat as a voting member. The chairman of that division was C. C. Pollworth, Jr., of Milwaukee, and by virtue of his office he was a member of the Board of FTD. It had been recognized that the matter of the trade fair, generally held in conjunction with the annual meetings, was a troublesome factor. The practice was growing of placing exhibits in sample rooms throughout the convention hotels and keeping them open during the sessions. This caused some members to miss meetings. With the incorporation of the Associate Division into FTD, it was hoped that closer control could be exerted over this practice. Pollworth promised full co-operation of his division. He presented to the Board the rules adopted for the conduct of the Associate Division within FTD. They were heartily approved by the directors.

In the matter of the new building, the New Home Committee, through Breitmeyer, reported that progress was being made but that the city of Detroit had not yet re-zoned the premises. It was the former mayor's opinion that this would be done in a short time.

Before the meeting adjourned, early on the second afternoon, William L. Rock was appointed treasurer for the twentieth time.

President Grakelow now "hit the road" again, in the interest of increasing membership and forming more solid regional and district organizations. There had been agitation from certain districts for a change in their boundaries. In the West and South, where state feelings were stronger, suggestions were made that regional boundaries conform more closely to sectional divisions. The president wished to investigate this feeling.

He was also concerned with developing the membership in the western parts of the country and he wished to engage field men acquainted with that area. He had made this point at the convention of the year before, asking that the money to be rebated to the members be utilized for education and recruitment. He had failed in this but he was undaunted and his persistence was to pay great dividends.

On May 9, 1930, the president's travels were suddenly terminated. As his chauffeur drove him along a street in his beloved Philadelphia, a speeding car came out of a side street, struck the president's automobile and overturned it, pinning Grakelow and his driver under the demolished sedan. Luckily no fire resulted, but it was necessary to use axes and crowbars to open a door, so the wounded men might be removed. Grakelow, taken to the hospital, was found to have a crushed chest and serious head injuries. These confined him to his home for several weeks.

During this idleness, he put the finishing touches to a plan which he had first mentioned unofficially at the meeting the year before in Boston. Since the 1930 meeting was to be held in San Francisco, he saw the long trip from the East to the West as an opportunity for a grand FTD tour by rail.

With the help of agents of the Pennsylvania and the Santa

Fe Railroads, he perfected plans for a 25-day trip, via six special trains from Philadelphia to San Francisco, with entertainment, side trips and business meetings on the way. Few tours by rail have ever been conducted in such magnitude.

The trip was to begin in Philadelphia and move over the Pennsylvania and connecting roads through Chicago to Denver, the rendezvous point for other trains from north and south. From Denver, the route was south to Tuscon and on to San Francisco. As a sign of the times, the rates are interesting: for the 25-day trip, $388 for an upper berth, $420 for a lower and up to $485 each for two in a drawing room.

This was a prodigious project, even for normal times, and in late 1930 the depression was beginning to affect all lines of business. Nevertheless, the president went on with his plans.

On June 26, 1930, a check for $74,000 was drawn against the funds of FTD, in payment for the new home. The zoning restrictions had been removed, clearing the way for the purchase. The Association at last had a building of its own.

In earlier days, this might have been named the FTD Temple, but the "Temple Era" had passed. So the property was referred to simply as the "New Home." The value of the property was estimated at between $75,000 and $100,000. Chairman Bertermann, of the New Home Committee, praised his colleagues for their hard work and attention to detail in acquiring a permanent office building for the Association. Work began immediately on remodeling.

Meanwhile, plans for the president's rail tour were fulfilled. Grakelow's train left his home city at 3 p.m., August 20, 1930, carrying 163 florists and their families, bound for Chicago. Philadelphia, New York and Chicago were the rendezvous points for eastern and southern members. The entire eastern United States was represented aboard the three trains.

Converging in Chicago, the two eastern sections were welcomed by the Chicago Unit and royally entertained for the entire day. Three trains left Chicago for Kansas City, arriving shortly before noon, August 22. They were met there by officials of the Chamber of Commerce and 65 Kansas City florists, who brought enough flowers to festoon the trains. W. L. Rock and 15 more florists got aboard during the 20-minute stop. The trains headed west to Denver.

In Denver, the Mountain and Plains States Florists' Convention was in session. It welcomed the tourists enthusiastically and probably Denver has never seen a comparable florists' meeting. Over 1,000 florists were attending the convention when the trains arrived. The publicity given the traveling group, the camaraderie developed in the day-and-a-half stopover in the city, and the contacts made by the various members among the conventioneers, added immeasurably to the prestige of the Association.

While in Denver, President Grakelow, William Gude, Philip Breitmeyer, Irwin Bertermann, W. L. Rock, Alfred Bunyard, Al Barber, John Besemer and other members of the tour visited a cemetery where they laid a wreath upon the grave of J. A. Valentine, FTD's honored founder.

The trip continued through Colorado Springs, Santa Fe, Albuquerque, the Grand Canyon, San Bernardino and San Diego into Los Angeles, with stops for sight-seeing along the way. Visits were made to Tia Juana and Agua Caliente in Mexico and a tour of the movie studios and trips to Catalina Island were enjoyed by the never-tiring group.

North from Los Angeles, the tour went through Yosemite Valley and the big tree country, arriving in San Francisco early in the morning of Monday, September 1. The annual meeting of FTD was to begin Wednesday, September 3, 1930, which gave the travelers time for a breathing spell before plunging into the serious work of the convention.

Each train had carried dining cars, club cars and cars fitted for entertaining and dancing. Cars were also arranged to be used for meetings. So the trip had not been entirely frivolous. The entire Board of Directors was present, as were the official family from the Headquarters offices and the chairmen of several important committees, including Laurent Clody, of the Clearing House Committee; Otto Lang, of the News Committee; Arthur Saltford, of the Service Committee; and C. C. Pollworth, Jr., of the Associate Division.

As the trains left Santa Fe, early on the afternoon of August 25, 1930, President Grakelow had called a meeting of the Board of Directors. Heedless of the magnificent scenery flying past the windows, the directors listened until dinner time to condensed reports of the standing committees. One other directors' meeting was held on board. These two meetings had done much to streamline the conduct of the convention and only one other such meeting was held. Following dinner of the first day after arriving in San Francisco, the directors met to hear a talk by E. H. Toepke, the FTD field representative for the West Coast.

There was method in Grakelow's introduction of Toepke at this time. The president knew that he would have to convince the membership at the convention of the need of retaining the proposed Clearing House rebate if he was to have money for the educational program, including the expansion of the field service work. Toepke was an enthusiastic speaker and completely sold on the work he was doing. An extroverted, likeable chap, he had made many friends among the western florists. Grakelow had met him while visiting florists in that area in the exercise of his official duties. He had persuaded him to come to the convention, prepared to present his views on the value and necessity of field service expansion in the recruitment of new members.

Toepke impressed the Board with his enthusiasm and sincerity. Breitmeyer told him, "You have confidence in yourself, in connection with this work, as a result of your experience." Toepke agreed with the former president heartily.

By the time the convention opened on Wednesday morning, it was apparent that the long association of the Board members, the officers and the rank-and-file on the train trip had gone far to streamline the convention. The Board had had several days in which to discuss, informally, the agenda for the meeting. They had been able to canvass the members' views on several pertinent points sure to come before the convention. There were 300 working florists on the three trains and this represented the largest number of the membership ever brought together for so long a period. There was time on the trip to break down formalities and to express freely many different views on the problems and future of FTD.

After the opening formalities of the convention, President Grakelow introduced the candidates for the various offices and directorships. It was then permissible to nominate other candidates from the floor. Grakelow called for nominations and none was made. Nominations were officially closed and it was announced that the polls would open the next day at 8 a.m.

In his address, Grakelow stressed three points: first was the discontinuance of the refund to members from Clearing House collections and the retention of the money for an educational program to include more field men for recruitment of members, and more design schools for the education of members. It would also include the attraction to FTD of other florists and more state and regional organizational meetings for better acquaintance among regional members. Second was authority to appoint a committee to confer on the improvement of the district representative organization. Third was a recommendation that only one member of the Finance Committee leave office each year, obviating the necessity of an annual change of the committee's entire membership, with the consequent annual loss of all informed members.

Bertermann reported to the convention on the purchase of the FTD building. A bid of $27,000 had been accepted for remodeling the structure. The Board had also authorized a reserve of $10,000 to cover contingencies which might arise in the process of altering the building to fit the needs of FTD. This news was received with applause. Plans were made to move into the new building on November 1, 1930, and this was the date upon which the FTD NEWS began to designate the new home as the official mailing address.

Twenty-five associate members had exhibits at the convention, which for the first time they conducted themselves, under the supervision of C. C. Pollworth, the associate member of the Board.

When the report of the Committee on the President's Address was made by its chairman, Granville Gude, Grakelow left the chair in order to be on the floor for the discussion of any of his recommendations questioned by the membership. His suggestion to change the manner of election of the Finance Committee was adopted without comment, as were his other recommendations, until the discussion reached his suggestion that the rebate to the members be discontinued.

This provoked spirited argument but, in the end, Grakelow was able to obtain the adoption of his plan; i.e., to abolish the rebate and use the money for expansion of the educational program through field men and design schools.

The election of officers and directors for the ensuing year, 1931, resulted as follows: Thomas Luke, of Portland, Oregon, was named president. Alfred Bunyard, of New York City, was elected vice-president. H. Reeve Darling, of Los Angeles, was made director-at-large, and the regional directors named were Joseph F. Coombs, New Haven, Connecticut, Region 1; Edward Nelson, Tampa, Florida, Region 6; F. C. Weber, St. Louis, Region 8; and Herbert

Clausen, Denver, Colorado, Region 9. W. Ray Murphy, of Cincinnati, was later named chairman of the Associate Division and became a director ex officio.

From several standpoints the San Francisco gathering had been a great convention. Grakelow had been able to stop, for the time being, the rebates from the Clearing House fund to the membership, and to make possible the expenditure of this sum in furtherance of the general interest, through expanded field work and education through design schools.

The West Coast, from San Diego to Vancouver, had been made aware of the Florists' Telegraph Delivery Association through the vast publicity engendered by the passage of the special trains through cities and countryside. The western florists had gone to great lengths to furnish entertainment and co-operation in the traditional western fashion. Florists from the East and South had been able to meet and mingle with those from the Southwest and West, for the discussion of problems and plans of interest to all. It was an ambitious project and its execution had been faultless. Three hundred florists had made the trip to the Coast, many of them with their families. The total number of passengers on the three trains was more than 1,200.

When the 1930 convention closed in San Francisco, the trains left for Vancouver, via Portland, Tacoma and Seattle. East from British Columbia, the members saw Lake Louise and Banff, Winnipeg and St. Paul. Then they returned to Chicago, and from there to their respective cities. At each stop the local florists met the trains with photographers, reporters and entertainment committees, eager to show the tourists that their fame had preceded them and that flowers and fun awaited.

On the material side, the cost of the trip to the individuals, not to FTD, was about $750,000. The rail transportation was in the neighborhood of $200,000. It was estimated that the group spent $50,000 during the 5-day stay in San Francisco and a half-million dollars on the entire trip. That is a large sum of money but, divided among 1,200 persons, it is only $625 each, including railroad fare, a figure to awaken memories of the "good old days." The value of the publicity, nationally and in the visited cities, could be estimated in the millions.

The move to the new building, at 484 East Grand Boulevard, Detroit, was made in November, 1930, as planned. The transfer was done in one long day and was without incident. In 20 years, almost to the day, from the time of its founding in Rochester in 1910, FTD had developed from a nebulous organization with a frail hold on the future, into an Association of substance and strength. It had become a force in the world of commercial flowers, entitled by position and promise to purchase its own office building. And it is interesting to note that FTD was one of the first businesses to join the "move to the suburbs," which was greatly to affect business property for the next 30 years.

The first meeting of the Board of Directors in the new building was on January 20, 1931. Tommy Luke, incoming president, and the other officers and directors were installed by Irwin Bertermann, the oldest present in point of service. Frank Thatcher, of San Francisco, replaced Angelo Rossi, just elected mayor of San Francisco. Al Barber continued as executive secretary, and W. L. Rock as treasurer.

Those with personal recollections of the depression period, who might assume a gloomy treasurer's report, will be surprised. There had been some loss, as shown in Treasurer Rock's report. But this, he explained, was actually more of a bookkeeping adjustment than an actual depletion of funds. By reducing the budget by $6,000 over the preceding seven months, the ship of FTD had kept its water line level in the ebbing tide of business. There was, according to the Clearing House reports, some reduction in the size of individual orders, but the volume of business had remained satisfactory.

Communications from the units showed that there had been some retrenchment, but it was gratifying to the Board to learn that these reports did not show any desire by florists to withdraw from the active promotion of their business. Instead, there were widespread calls for more education in design, more field men to spread the gospel of FTD, better control of the membership and a closer attention to the ethics of the florist industry.

This was a wholesome attitude, especially recognized by the businessmen among the directors. The willingness to promote and grow during a time of crisis was, to them, a sign of optimism and courage, an unbeatable business combination.

The tone of the entire Board meeting was heartening. There had been no problems of moment since the meeting at San Francisco. The Atlantic City Convention Committee, reported Ed Sceery, was arranging a strictly business meeting. But he guaranteed that the opportunities for entertainment would not be curtailed and he expected the 1931 convention in New Jersey to be one of the best ever held. Mrs. Percy Waters, who had withdrawn the invitation to Toronto in favor of San Francisco, renewed the request to hold the 1932 meeting in the Canadian city, and the Board heartily acceded.

The Board ended its formal session early on the second day, January 21, 1931, and prepared for the formal dedication of the new building and the open house to follow. The directors were to serve as hosts.

The dedication, which lasted all afternoon and evening, was a memorable affair. Flowers, of course, were used in profusion, and the beauty and taste with which the Detroit florists decorated the new home was a triumph of their art. Philip Breitmeyer, former mayor of Detroit, introduced the dedication speaker, the incumbent mayor, Frank Murphy, who was later to be Governor of Michigan, Governor-General of the Phillipines, Attorney General and, finally, Associate Justice of the United States Supreme Court. Murphy praised not only the building but the spirit of co-operation and fraternity that made it possible. He honored FTD as an influence for beauty and dignity in the business affairs of Detroit.

The next two years were not a happy period in the United States. Unemployed workers staged demonstration marches in the large cities. Veterans sold apples on the corners. "Brother, can you spare a dime?" became much more than a song title. The republic was not unacquainted with depressions and business slumps, but none had disturbed the nation more than this one. And it was not only this country that was suffering, but the entire world.

That great showman, Tommy Luke, known affectionately as the "happy, round little president," did not quail. It was not his nature. He had built his business by working long hours and he did not forget that simple secret when he became the leader of FTD.

The 1931 Atlantic City convention opened in a tense atmosphere. All realized the necessity for a close examination of the affairs of FTD in the light of world conditions. President Luke opened the directors' meeting by saying, "I have kept the Board meeting today strictly to the members of the Board, feeling that we could have possibly a better expression from the Board members."

The reports from the various committees were guardedly optimistic. Grakelow, in his report of the Service Committee activities, still believed that money could profitably be spent in education and publicity through field men, but he was willing to reduce his estimate of the cost of such a program. He mentioned a matter that had plagued his administration, the reduction of the 2 per cent collection charge. He suggested that, if it could be reduced to $1\frac{1}{2}$ per cent, this was the time to do it. He was even willing that the question be presented on the floor of the convention.

To counteract this reduction, he recommended that an

additional tax of 1 per cent on all incoming and outgoing orders be collected to finance an advertising campaign. Breitmeyer expressed strong objection to any such increase in taxes to the membership, but the matter was brought to the floor and carried.

This was the most drastic change suggested at Atlantic City. The convention adjourned on the universal belief that the meeting had been an excellent morale booster. Not much business had been transacted. There was a general atmosphere of "wait and see." Circumstances had made the membership wary, but not discouraged. There was still talk of a convention on shipboard, enroute to Europe, for 1933.

Luke retained the presidency, but was given a new vice-president, Frank Baker, of Utica, New York. Ernest S. Simmons, of Toronto, host city for the 1932 convention, was elected director-at-large. The regional directors named were Robert Graham, Jr., Baltimore, Region 3; Don Johnston, Canton, Ohio, Region 4; John Weiland, Chicago, Region 5; H. Reeve Darling, Los Angeles, Region 10; and P. F. Rosaia, Seattle, Region 11. William F. Ekas, of Baltimore, joined the Board, by virtue of his election to the chairmanship of the Associate Division.

One week after the close of the Atlantic City convention, England went off the gold standard. This was a world sensation, almost comparable to the stock market crash. Business slipped more and more. By January 1, 1932, 15,000,000 people in the United States were unemployed. Florists marvelled at the stability of their business. But they were not without trouble. One of the first questions presented to the Board at their meeting in Detroit in January, 1932, was how to deal with members in receivership.

Legal counsel explained the precise meaning and effect of receivership. Secretary Barber announced that most members seeking receivership had been carried by FTD, a procedure against which Attorney David Roberts strongly advised. But President Luke suggested that every consideration be given embarrassed members and that they be dropped from membership only when there was no other recourse. This attitude of the officers and Headquarters staff persisted through the depression, promoting loyalty and redounding to increased faith and regard for FTD.

The year 1932 was a year of contrasts. While the subject of receivership was being dealt with in the Board meeting, Past President Grakelow was urging a shipboard convention for the next year and receiving much encouragement from the membership. The success of the train tour to San Francisco was still strong in the memories of many. They saw in the European trip a possible duplication, not only of the camaraderie of such a trip, but of increased publicity in Europe, which might expand their operations greatly.

Grakelow, Darling and Weber supported the move to authorize the European tour. Vice-President Baker, Graham and others were opposed to it. Mrs. Waters, Leidiger and Nelson were willing to vote for the convention, if it appeared that the membership had shown strong interest in it at the Atlantic City meeting. Nelson contended that the trip had been recommended by vote. When Grakelow finally put the motion, a vote by Australian ballot showed that the Board favored making the trip by a vote of 12 to 4. This decision demonstrated the inherent enthusiasm of the typical florist. In the midst of a great world crisis, florists were giving more thought to advancing the future of the Association than to their own business affairs. With banks and businesses failing every day, they saw only the benefit of FTD in the years to come.

Such was the tone of the directors' meeting. With great things promised for the 1932 Toronto convention, the Board adjourned. But much affecting FTD was to happen before that meeting. With the coming of warm weather, veterans' groups in all parts of the country began a "bonus march" on Washington. The Insull utility empire collapsed and the crash echoed in business throughout the nation. Great

Britain abandoned its historic free-trade policy and developed a system of imperial preference tariffs, further restricting international trade and deepening the gulf between America and its overseas markets.

Even in the midst of such economic gloom, FTD was optimistic. In July, 1932, an international FTD school was held in Detroit, with the astounding attendance of 1,056 florists, representing 40 states and two Canadian provinces.

That fact expresses the spirit of an Association which, in the midst of vast economic disaster, could send almost a fourth of its membership, many over long distances, not to discuss overhead or cut prices, but to study ways of improving the attractiveness of their product and to promote the distribution of fragrance and beauty throughout the world!

As President Luke expressed it, "The Association never stands around on one leg, waiting."

There was, however, some retreat from the enthusiasm manifested at Atlantic City. One of the first matters to come before the 1932 Toronto convention was a motion from Past President Grakelow to rescind the recommendation that the Board of Directors decree a shipboard convention enroute to Europe in 1933.

There was considerable opposition to this motion. Many had looked forward to the trip, and did not wish to see the plan changed. But wiser heads prevailed and the trip was canceled. In the end, the convention was awarded to New Orleans, but the dream of a session on the sea remained fresh in the minds of many members for years.

The most evident result of the depression was a decrease in the dollar volume of orders. The $1.00 and $1.50 orders were becoming the rule, rather than the exception. Was it fair for a member to accept a $1 order and expect the filling florist to deliver the flowers? This was a problem that came before the meeting. It was moved that commissions on orders of less than $1.50 be eliminated. But the true sentimental character of florists was quickly illustrated. There was strenuous objection to the move.

Said President Luke, "The one dollar order of today is the ten dollar order of tomorrow." Mrs. Waters told of a boy who came to her store every Saturday night and bought a single rose for 10 cents. She knew, she said, that each Mother's Day she would get an order for 50 cents and the pleasure of filling those two orders repaid her a thousand times for the lack of profit. The consensus was that the florist, as a duty, should fill small orders, even at a loss. The motion was overwhelmingly defeated.

It is a fact that business conditions had caused some curtailment and some laxity. Harry Ramm, of New York, a district representative of Region 2, offered a motion that the Board of Directors give to any accredited representative of FTD the power to examine any member's order file and slips, "in connection with the transmission of orders from the shops of members of this Association."

The previous motion had awakened the sentimentality of the florists. This one aroused their ire and their independence. The motion never came to a vote. It was howled down.

The most spirited discussion at the Toronto convention arose over the 1 per cent tax on incoming and outgoing orders, the money to be allocated for advertising. Morton Goldfarb, of New York City, objected strongly to this tax, claiming that to maintain it in the face of declining business was not only to overcharge the members but was to be wasteful and extravagant at a time when every prudent measure should be employed. Grakelow, chairman of the Service Committee, with jurisdiction over the advertising expenditures, took exception to Goldfarb's words and their implication. He praised the honesty and diligence of those who had contributed to the work of the committee. He was joined by Adolph LeMoult, Jr., of New York, who, although not a member of the committee, had given much time in the furtherance of the radio advertising program then being sponsored.

Max Schling, whose appearances at the conventions were growing fewer, but whose influence remained strong, summed up the FTD position on advertising in these words: "If you want to cut down advertising then, first of all, close down your shop. Stop buying flowers and stop talking people into buying flowers. But, if you want to carry on your business, go ahead and spend your little share to let people know that you are right. Forget about the period of 1930, 1931, and the beginning of 1932. It is past. There is a new era coming, and the man who lies down is going to be laid down. The man who carries on is going to be the winner." The tax was retained.

The Toronto meeting was brief, lasting only a day and a half. But members left it feeling that, even if small progress had been made, none had been lost. In view of the world situation, florists were better off than most businesses. This realization, strengthened by a knowledge of conditions in other regions and areas, sent the members home with a conviction of well-being.

Elected for the year 1933 were: Frank Baker, of Utica, New York, president; and Arthur Leidiger, of Milwaukee, vice-president. Adolph LeMoult, Jr., of New York City, Region 2; Charles W. Siebrecht, of Winona, Minnesota, Region 7; Jack Allen, of Glendale, California, Region 10; and Ernest S. Simmons, of Toronto, Region 12, were named to the Board of Directors. Miss Rachel Butterworth, of Framingham, Massachusetts, was elected director-at-large. William F. Ekas continued on the Board, representing the Associate Division.

CHAPTER TWELVE

Recovery and Progress

T THE JANUARY meeting of the Board of Directors in Detroit, President Baker presented what he called "the Baker plan" for the operation of FTD. It was a comprehensive document, covering all the activities of the Association, looking particularly to the subject of publicity. The plan was received with applause by the Board. It showed the president had not been idle. "The platform of this administration," said Baker, "boils down to two substantial planks — education and publicity."

But President Baker had to construct his platform without a knowledge of coming events. On January 30, 1933, five days after the Detroit meeting, a man named Hitler became chancellor of the German Reich. On March 4, 1933, Franklin D. Roosevelt was inaugurated president of the United States. These two men, as far apart as the poles, were to play a great part in the administration of President Baker.

One of Roosevelt's early acts was to appoint General Hugh Johnson administrator of the National Industrial Recovery Act, a Congressional effort to lift the country from the depth of the business slump. Many of the points advocated in the Baker plan had to be curtailed because of the government's limitation on promotion of funds for advertising.

Under the National Industrial Recovery Act — popularly known as the NRA, or Blue Eagle — it was necessary for florists, as for all, to conform to a standard code of practice, which involved minimum salaries and established prices. On

June 14, 1933, President Baker called a meeting in Detroit of representatives of the florist industry, for the purpose of drawing up a tentative code for the business.

This code required the approval of General Johnson's office in Washington. With the help of David W. Roberts, the FTD counsel, the code was drawn and presented to General Johnson's office and, although it was approved, it did not meet the wholehearted endorsement of the florists who were forced to abide by it.

Roberts appeared before the convention in New Orleans to explain and justify the code from the legal standpoint. He faced much questioning and some criticism, as architect of the rules and regulations under which the industry would be required to operate. But he was not to blame for those conditions. Never before in history had such drastic measures been necessary. There was a vital question of the constitutionality of the NRA. Even lawyers differed as to its application, its power and its scope. Roberts had done a masterful job of writing the code. President Baker and the Board praised him for his efforts.

On March 6 of that year, President Roosevelt decreed the famous "bank holiday." FTD was not particularly hurt. It had become the practice of the Clearing House to maintain two accounts. One was carried in the Bank of New York and the other in the Northern Trust Company in Chicago. Neither of these banks was in trouble, and the closing caused only a slight delay in the clearings.

FTD did not suffer any loss of money due to bank failures during this time, but, to facilitate clearings, two loans were negotiated: one for $50,000 from Traders Gate City Bank, of Kansas City; and another for $45,000 from the Fifth Avenue Bank of New York. Credit deposit fund bonds were pledged as collateral for these loans. Getting the money was not easy because of the current state of the Bylaws which gave to the Executive Committee "full authority over all departments" between meetings of the Board of Directors.

Treasurer Rock offered a resolution, clarifying the power of the Executive Committee, to which Director Charles Siebrecht objected strenuously. In the end, the resolution carried.

The closing of the First National Bank of Detroit had disturbed Treasurer Rock, who was also chairman of the Finance Committee. To protect the funds, Rock distributed them in five banks: the Fifth Avenue Bank, New York; the Northern Trust Company, Chicago; the Traders Gate City Bank, Kansas City; the National Bank of Detroit; and the Imperial Bank of Canada, in Windsor, Ontario. Clearings were made from the Chicago and New York banks. The Detroit bank was used as a collection agency for members' checks and the payment of current purchase accounts. The Executive Committee approved the arrangement.

There remained in the closed First National Bank, $122,000. The bank was being investigated by a grand jury, but John M. Besemer believed the money to be safe. He told the Board of Directors, "There has not been a witness who has testified that the bank ever was insolvent, either then or now."

Altogether, FTD came through the bank holiday satisfactorily. The National Florists' Council was formed in Detroit on June 26, 1933, to adjust the many problems which had troubled florists since the beginning of the depression. Only 51 FTD members withdrew during the hard times. At the annual meeting in New Orleans, the membership was announced as 6,363, a consistent growth of the organization since its founding almost 25 years before.

President Frank J. Baker was re-elected at the New Orleans convention. Otto Lang, of Dallas, became vice-president. Mrs. Bert Schiller McDonald, of Chicago, was named director-at-large. John J. O'Brien, of Boston, was named to the Board of Directors for Region 1; Peter A. Chopin, of New Orleans, became regional director for Region 6; O. K. Sanders, of St. Louis, represented Region 8; and C. E.

Wademan, of Houston, became director from Region 9. Representing the Associate Division on the Board was N. A. Benson, of Denver. Denver was awarded the convention for 1934.

By the time the Board of Directors met in Detroit in January, 1934, business had "turned the corner" and there was optimism over the outlook. Treasurer Rock, in his report to the Board, pointed out that expenses for the past five months had exceeded income by $12,823.05. There had been in the past month, however, some upturn in business.

The credit deposit fund now stood at $165,123, and the general fund amounted to $226,973.34. Cuts had been made in salaries. The secretary had been receiving $15,000 a year, the chairman of the Clearing House was paid $10,000 and the editor of the FTD NEWS received a commission of $22,000, out of which he paid contributing editors and convention expenses. Under the new arrangement for salaries, the combined income of the three men had been reduced to $18,000, a substantial savings.

The value of the real estate had been written down by 35 per cent and was now at $34,229.17. This indicates the severity of the readjustments in the Association's finances during the depression.

There was no thought of canceling the Denver convention, although Laurent Clody, of the Finance Committee, foresaw a deficit of $10,000 for the year. Most of the money was being spent by the Service Committee, conducting schools for the members. There was also the membership in the National Florists' Council, which would cost between $5,000 and $7,000 for the year. Rock's report showed $3,500 in delinquent accounts over the past month, $859 of which had been through bankruptcy. An additional $100 was believed uncollectable. But even with these reports, there was a general air of faith in the future. Before the Board adjourned, approximately $78,000 was appropriated for an advertising campaign, and the question of an exhibit at the

Century of Progress Exposition in Chicago, to cost $5,000, was left for a later decision by the president.

In view of the depressed business conditions which the Association had suffered during the preceding few years, these decisions were remarkable. They demonstrated again the courage of the Board and the willingness to expend every effort to improve the business of the membership.

The fears of those who saw the expenditures for advertising and publicity as unwise were never realized. Increased business during the summer, plus the general business upturn, absorbed the expenses voted in January. Rock's report to the Denver convention showed that income had exceeded expenses by $13,284.51, a heartening development. There was also good news about the bank account in the First National Bank of Detroit. The federal government had arranged financing of the bank's receivers, enabling FTD to salvage about $36,000. An increase in clearings of 12 per cent had been registered for the year.

Otto Lang, of Dallas, was elected president at Denver in 1934, and was re-elected for another term at Pittsburgh in 1935. Herbert Clausen, of Denver, was named vice-president and relinquished that office the following year at Pittsburgh, to Ernest S. Simmons, of Toronto. Mrs. Amelia Gude Thomas, of Washington, D. C., was elected director-at-large. She was succeeded at Pittsburgh by Emily Dunn, of Cleveland. Regional directors named at Denver were Ed Ludwig, of Pittsburgh, representing Region 3; Willard Crain, of Cincinnati, from Region 4; Homer Lange, Chicago, from Region 5; and Carl T. Kipp, of Spokane, from Region 11. The Associate Division chairman was Howard Hook, of Pittsburgh, Pa., who remained in this capacity for three years.

In the second year of President Lang's administration, the following were elected regional directors: Lou N. Anderson, Montclair, New Jersey, Region 2; James H. Dale, Houghton, Michigan, Region 7; Fred Seulberger, Jr., Oakland, California, Region 10; and Charles Cooper, Toronto, Region 12.

President Lang's administration was characterized best by the one word, "Work." Although times were slowly improving, there was still much to be done for florists and for the Association in general.

At the January, 1935, meeting of the Board, in Detroit, it was recognized that the country was on the road to recovery and that FTD should keep alert to the possibilities of more and more business. A new advertising program was agreed upon, to be conducted in a carefully chosen group of magazines. It was the consensus that smaller advertisements would give the Association more exposure than the large displays in use. In this way, the advertisements could be run in eight national magazines instead of four.

It was also decided to postpone the revision of the Handy Book and devote the money saved to advertising. There was a general tone of enthusiasm over the rise of the business curve. Albert Barber issued an optimistic announcement on business conditions: "Business is gaining! We are returning to normalcy!"

The 1935 convention in Pittsburgh reported a gain of 205 members for the year, bringing the membership to 6,698. A Service Committee, under Chairman Grakelow, had sponsored six major design schools around the country. There was a gain of 12 per cent in clearings over the year. Said President Lang, "Our organization has made a gain every month this year. This advance is substantially more than any other business in the United States can show."

Amendments to the Bylaws were passed, changing the boundaries of the 12 regions. Other amendments provided for the appointment of district representatives by the president just before August 1 of each year, and also clarified retail memberships. The sum of $91,000 was appropriated for national advertising, not without argument on the floor. There were some who considered the national advertising campaign a waste of money. But it was the wholehearted decision of the convention that the gains made in the sale of flowers proved the efficacy of the campaign.

In an effort to get business, many members had been accepting orders from non-members and this had caused some loss. Al Barber reported to the Board meeting in January, 1936, that $16,534 was currently owed to members by non-members. He requested that the directors urge at their district meetings that accounts be more promptly reported to the home office.

This was a matter for the field men, of which there was a dearth. At the 1936 FTD convention in Dallas, Director Fred Seulberger made a plea for a field man for Regions 10 and 11, covering nine states on the West Coast. It was not only the quality of the shops and the way they were run that disturbed Seulberger. There was also the fact of competition from a rival organization, which had caused the service charge to be voted down at the San Francisco convention in 1930. E. H. Toepke had visited the West for several months and had been excellently received. But his time was limited in each region. Seulberger moved the hiring of an additional field man. Grakelow, always aware of the worth of Toepke, amended the motion to suggest the hiring of four, no one of whom was to have a territorial designation. Thus they could range over a wide area and, at the same time, show no sectional favoritism. It was realized by the Board that there should be more education and morale-building as was offered by field men. But there were always those who objected to hiring more men.

Carl T. Kipp, of Spokane, director of Region 11, suggested: "Speaking for Regions 10 and 11, we feel that it is impossible for the regional director to cover the field as it should be covered. There are a lot of (rival) members on the Pacific Coast. Some of them, of course, would not be eligible for FTD membership; but there are some who are eligible, and they have gotten away from us just because there was no one available to give it proper attention. Mr. Toepke has done a wonderful work . . . but any trained man there would serve the purpose just the same."

Offered Grakelow, who had traveled the area extensively, "Some of the shops are a disgrace, and we would not be proud to have our emblem displayed in them. There are also some beautiful shops. We have other sections where there is a dried-up rubber plant in the window, with a ribbon saying, 'Asleep in Jesus.' While I do not feel that we should go in for dictatorial powers, I do think that we should do what we can."

Grakelow next suggested that the matter be held over until the January, 1937, Board meeting, at which time the Service Committee would offer a definite outline, with an estimate of the cost.

President Lang realized that an expanded future for FTD lay in greater activity of the units. He had, therefore, refused to ratify certain elections in the units, when groups, listing membership of 75 to 125 florists, had cast only 10 votes at annual meetings. He accented the fellowship and co-operation that was possible on the unit level and severely censured local organizations which had shown less than full attention to their meetings. But he was happy to announce in an eloquent address: "The big investment in futures we have made has been in the direction of national advertising. The result was monthly increases in FTD business . . ."

The 1936 Dallas convention saw Charles Grakelow's retirement from active participation in the government of FTD. The devotion to the Association of this gifted and eloquent speaker is hard to overpraise. Elected president in 1928, he had served in an official capacity ever since, with two years as president, and the remainder of the time as chairman of the Service Committee. He had great influence in the councils of FTD, but he never stooped to use it to his advantage. He brought to every question the benefit of his experience and his wise judgment. The encomiums which followed the announcement of his retirement brought tears to his eyes.

Irwin Bertermann took the convention floor to offer a resolution which outlined to the group some of the things for which Grakelow had been responsible. He ended by saying, "This is a grand privilege to show your love, consideration, and respect for an outstanding gentleman who has done so much for all of us."

Instantly, the floor was filled with men wanting to move the resolution. President Lang recognized Past President Dauernheim, of SAF, also a member of FTD, who moved the resolution. It was seconded by Peter Chopin, Adolph LeMoult and President Lang. When the motion was put, it carried by a rising vote of acclamation.

One of the far-reaching developments of the year had been the association with certain members of Fleurop. This was an organization of continental European florists, about 4,500 in number, with headquarters in Zurich, Switzerland. It had been founded in 1927, along the same lines as FTD. Max Hubner, well-known florist of Berlin, was its first president. Other quasi-official organizations for the transmission of flowers-by-wire had previously existed in Europe, similar to the early arrangement among American retailers for the same purpose.

By 1936, Fleurop had grown to an impressive size and had been the subject of discussion in the councils of FTD. Petitions from some Fleurop members for membership in FTD had been received, but nothing had been done toward admitting them on the same basis as the British members, because of the monetary exchange situation.

The Board of Directors decided to make an arrangement with certain well-qualified Fleurop members, using the Swiss franc as the medium of exchange and 221 Fleurop members were transferred to a separate listing of that organization's members. These were accorded something like a Clearing

House privilege, operating not through FTD, but through the Fleurop offices in Switzerland. The Board felt some apprehension about this arrangement, but such a vast field for expansion existed on the continent of Europe that they considered it worth the experiment. The fears, of course, were caused by the international situation in Europe. Hitler was gaining enormous power in Germany. The neighboring countries were becoming nervous and wary of his aims. The concern of the Board was well-founded.

Elected president at Dallas was Ernest S. Simmons, of Toronto; vice-president was Peter A. Chopin, of New Orleans. Irene Hayes, of New York, was named director-at-large. Directors elected were: Dan Gallivan, Holyoke, Massachusetts, Region 1; William E. Joy, Columbus, Georgia, Region 6; H. Rollo Mueller, Columbia, Missouri, Region 8; and Gordon Boswell, Ft. Worth, Texas, Region 9. Howard Hook continued on the Board, representing the Associate Division. Philadelphia was chosen as the next convention city.

Simmons was singularly successful in his objectives. During the year, 421 new members were added to the rolls, spreading representation to 117 more cities and towns in the United States and Canada. "Increasing demand for flowers-by-wire service has been met by increased membership. The widespread use of flowers-by-wire service dictates a future policy of development in non-member towns," he told the convention.

The recruitment program in non-member towns had been forwarded by 16 design schools, held throughout the nation and Canada during the year. These had a two-fold purpose: to interest non-member florists in joining FTD, and to improve the quality in floral design and shop operation for those attending the schools. The days of indiscriminate enlistment of shop owners were over. It was now realized by FTD that, before a florist could become a member, it would be necessary for him to demonstrate his artistry, his credit reputation and his ability to operate an attractive and modern shop.

The Fleurop experiment, after a year, had encountered some difficulty. Germany, with the largest floral business on the continent, had decreed that no money leave the country, except under rigid restrictions. This greatly interfered with the payment by German florists of their foreign bills. Such a condition had been reached that the Fleurop Clearing House in Zurich refused to handle any German business. Only those countries which had trade agreements with Germany could get money out of that country. The United States was not one of them.

Ernest King, representative of the British FTD Unit, attended the 1937 Philadelphia convention and made a request for a loan of $5,000 to help the British group to carry the accounts of the Germans until payment could be made through the English trade agreements. He stated specifically that an actual loan of $5,000 cash was not required. The endorsement or guaranty of the amount to a British bank would, he said, be sufficient.

This loan was allowed on the condition that the British Unit establish its own guarantee fund by assessing members, that they improve their accounting system and that they modify the structure of their organization along the lines of the American organization. But with war so near, the question of how to conduct business with the German florists became academic.

Again the question of hiring more field men was presented to the Board, and as before, it was voted down. The governors of FTD, so progressive in other matters, seemed reluctant to put more representatives in the field to further general improvement and morale of the membership. There is no question that Toepke, wherever he went, had done a great good. The Board did not disparage his efforts, but apparently they considered him unique.

Charles Grakelow had not relinquished his idea of a

European convention. As usual, he had no lack of ability in voicing his sentiments. On his own responsibility, he had investigated the subject with steamship companies and he was ready to present to the convention an economical plan. His idea was to engage a well-known orchestra, which would broadcast each night from the ship, informing the world that FTD was in convention on the high seas.

A Paris style show would be held each evening. Selfridge's, in London, he was sure, would present a fashion show especially for the FTD members. "The amount of publicity, with this steamer so bedecked with flowers," he explained, "would make it of international news value that would bring us great results without a question of doubt. I have an unusual yen for spectacular theatrical stuff, which comes natural." This was not an overstatement.

President Simmons agreed with Grakelow that the trip would be of advantage to the Association. So forceful were the arguments of the two men that Grakelow was requested to outline his plan in writing for the consideration of the Board so that they could canvass their members and be ready to vote on the trip at the next Board meeting in January.

Three thousand persons, members and families, attended the Philadelphia convention. There was the old relaxed spirit and conviviality, reminiscent of the conventions of the pre-depression period. Business was booming. The old enthusiasm had returned. Ernest S. Simmons was re-elected to serve another term as president, with Willard Crain, of Cincinnati, as vice-president. Alice Flick, of Ft. Wayne, Indiana, was named director-at-large. Elected to the Board of Directors were: Granville Gude, Washington, D. C., Region 3; Bruno Smoke, Detroit, Michigan, Region 4; Edward W. Gould, Chicago, Region 5; and Hans Niklas, Portland, Oregon, Region 11. The new Associate Division chairman was Herbert M. Sauber, of Washington, D. C.

Portland, Oregon, was selected as the convention city for 1938.

Under the leadership of President Simmons, FTD entered 1938 in probably the soundest condition of its life, both financially and from a membership standpoint. Business continued good, with an increase of 11 per cent in the final months of the past year, with every prospect that the percentage would go higher.

The new membership rules, adopted by the Board during the year, came up for consideration. The consensus was that they were operating successfully. These rules removed the consideration of applicants for membership from the individual units and gave the function to the executive secretary, based on facts and reports from the district representative and a confidential committee. This step was thought necessary to eliminate any antagonism on the part of competitors in the consideration of new members. There had been rumors from some New England units that such an attitude was influencing the consideration of well-qualified applicants.

At the Board meeting in January, 1938, Charles Grakelow was able to get his proposed plan for a shipboard convention accepted, by the vote of 9 to 8. There was a little hedging by the Board. They selected an alternate convention city as a safety measure. The situation in Europe was alarmingly unsettled. The directors voted St. Paul as the alternate city.

Convention Committee Chairman Tommy Luke and his colleagues went "all-out," to make the Portland meeting memorable. For months preceding it, full page advertisements were run in the FTD NEWS extolling the virtues and entertainment possibilities of the "Rose City." Two special trains, reminiscent of those which bore the conventioneers to San Francisco a few years before, were run from Philadelphia and New York, gathering florists along the way. For the more adventurous, the airlines ran Florists' Special flights to the West Coast.

Several stops were made by the trains along the way where

FOUNDED 1910

Florists' Telegraph Delivery Association

MEMBER'S CREED

My Obligation as a member of the Florists' Telegraph Delivery Association, to my Association and to the public which I serve is identical to my obligations as a citizen.

I recognize that my business and that of my Association must be conducted fairly and ethically at all times.

I recognize the trust placed in me as a member of the Florists' Telegraph Delivery Association by my customers and my fellow members, and shall at all times conduct my business in a manner commensurate to that trust.

I pledge my unwavering support to the high ethical and business standards upon which my Association was founded.

I further pledge my skill, faith and cooperation in the advancement of the service my Association guarantees.

Every FTD florist receives a copy of the MEMBER'S CREED when he is granted membership. The sentiments of this statement of member obligations were developed from the FTD Pledge, written by Michael Bloy, first manager of the FTD NEWS, and distributed to members at the Toronto convention of 1921.

The FTD member using this 1904 model van had to be sure that his flowers were fresh so that they would not shatter as those solid tires rumbled over the cobbled streets of the day. Drivers had to be accustomed to chain drive, cranking the 2-cylinder engine on the side, lighting the oil lamps and hearing cries of, "Get a horse!"

Not so this driver, who already had a horse . . . and a sleek and well-groomed horse, at that. Delivery service, local or by wire, has always been a watchword with FTD members.

(*Above, left*) Delivering a modern arrangement from a modern (for that time) van. Note that mud-guards protect driver and pedestrians during wet weather.

(*Above, right*) Pneumatic tires and acetylene headlamps (note tank on running board) stamp this vehicle as the last word in floral delivery.

Modern Mercury-marked florists' delivery trucks are familiar sights in the concrete canyons of great cities or the quiet streets of local neighborhoods. Prompt and efficient delivery service is as important now as it was 50 years ago.

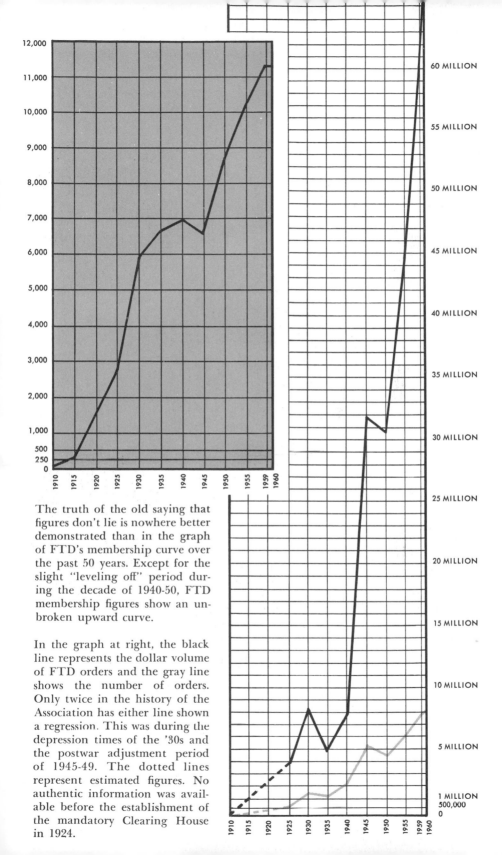

The truth of the old saying that figures don't lie is nowhere better demonstrated than in the graph of FTD's membership curve over the past 50 years. Except for the slight "leveling off" period during the decade of 1940-50, FTD membership figures show an unbroken upward curve.

In the graph at right, the black line represents the dollar volume of FTD orders and the gray line shows the number of orders. Only twice in the history of the Association has either line shown a regression. This was during the depression times of the '30s and the postwar adjustment period of 1945-49. The dotted lines represent estimated figures. No authentic information was available before the establishment of the mandatory Clearing House in 1924.

EVOLUTION OF MERCURY EMBLEMS

1914

1928

FLORISTS' TELEGRAPH DELIVERY
FTD
INTERFLORA · WORLDWIDE

1959

FLOWERS-BY-WIRE
ANYWHERE   ANY TIME
"Say it with flowers"
FLORISTS TELEGRAPH DELIVERY ASSOCIATION
INTERNATIONAL

1936

FLORISTS' TELEGRAPH DELIVERY
Send Flowers Worldwide
INTERFLORA

1957

FLOWERS - BY - WIRE
AUTHORIZED FLORISTS' TELEGRAPH DELIVERY SHOP

1939

Changing his stride only once (between 1914 and 1928), Mercury has continued
at breakneck speed to deliver flowers-by-wire for FTD members for more than
46 years. This familiar emblem is known around the world as the hallmark of
floral quality and artistry.

entertainment by local florist groups provided welcome interludes in the monotony of travel. The trains passed through Portland and went on to Seattle for the week end, and then back to Portland for the beginning of the meeting on Sunday, September 4, 1938.

Quoting the report in the FTD NEWS, "No decided changes were made in the present policies of the Association, and appreciation was expressed for endeavors and accomplishments of committees acting during the past year." This would indicate that the affairs of the Association were running smoothly and well. The Portland convention was notable for its entertainment more than for the business transacted.

But Charles Grakelow saw his boat trip to Europe again rejected, in favor of St. Paul in 1939. The situation in Europe was deteriorating. Hitler had moved into Austria. The Sudeten crisis was at its height. There was a real possibility of an entire convention membership being stranded in Europe by the outbreak of war. So, although the trip had received the approval of the Board of Directors at the January meeting, it was now decided that the St. Paul convention would be the wiser course.

Willard Crain, of Cincinnati, was elected to the presidency, with Ed Ludwig, of Pittsburgh, vice-president. Yvonne Benafel, of Los Angeles, won the post of director-at-large. Elected to the Board of Directors were: S. A. Anderson, Jr., Buffalo, Region 2; Leo J. McKenna, Montreal, Region 12; Hans Rosacker, Minneapolis, Region 7; and Alfred Serveau, San Francisco, Region 10. Herbert M. Sauber was re-elected chairman of the Associate Division.

If proof were needed of the growing strength of FTD in the industry, it was given during the latter part of 1938 and the beginning of 1939. There had been a sentiment of some vigor inside the Associate Division for a separation of the associates and the growers. Certain members of the division

who were also growers had proposed that, if they were
formed into an entity of their own, they could have representation on the Board of Directors, just as the Associate
Division did under the prevailing plan.

This desire of the growers for a separate division came
before the Board of Directors in Detroit in January, 1939.
As a measure of its importance and the consideration already
given it, it was presented to the Board by Past President
Simmons, following the recommendation of the National
Advertising Committee, and had been endorsed by the
Executive Committee. President Crain believed that the
growers, as a group, were not happy with the predominance
of suppliers in the Associate Division. He thought that their
interests would be better served with their own director on
the Board.

There was then in the SAF a plan for reorganization of
that society. A serious question arose as to how they would
view the formation of a growers' division in FTD. After a
lengthy discussion of the problems, S. A. Anderson, Jr.,
moved the adoption of the resolution creating the new
division. It was carried, with only Granville Gude in opposition. But such a drastic move is not constitutional by the
directors' decision alone. On advice of counsel, it was decided
to let the planned revision await the St. Paul convention,
when it would be presented to the membership as an
amendment to the Bylaws.

At the same time, a motion was offered, raising the dues
of the Associate Division to $10 a year, an increase of 100
per cent. This also required further consideration by the
total membership and was left to the convention.

The Association had allocated $15,000 to the St. Paul
Convention Committee. The meeting was to begin September 3, 1939, in the Twin Cities. However, the convention
had been budgeted by the committee at $14,950, dangerously
close to the allocated amount. It was explained to the Board
that this figure had been necessary because of the increased

prices of all services in the Twin Cities over the amount spent in Portland the year before. Director Hans Niklas then moved that all registrations, beyond one for each member, be charged for at the rate of $5, and the extra amount thus realized be turned over to the St. Paul Committee. Director Gordon Boswell moved an amendment to the original motion that the $15,000 allocated by the Association be made to cover 1,500 registrants, and that $5 each for all registrants over that number be paid into the general fund to be drawn upon by the local committee if necessary. In this form, the motion passed.

The spring and summer of 1939 was a period of strange contrasts. The upheavals in Europe increased in intensity, creating a universal nervousness reflected in some businesses and leaving others unaffected. FTD went ahead with plans to make its meeting in St. Paul a "bigger and better convention." Al Barber wrote in the FTD NEWS, "The Florists' Telegraph Delivery Association, and the entire floral industry, have made progress and moved steadily forward."

Robert H. Roland, executive secretary of SAF, was telling subscribers that "the florist business in the United States is in a sick condition. Volume has been inadequate, prices have been declining, costs have been increasing, and the industry, which formerly enjoyed a reasonable profit, has been facing constantly declining profits, which, in many cases, have run into actual losses."

SAF decided to engage a firm of business consultants to recommend remedial measures. This situation was not apparent to the retail branch of the industry. It was only the growers and wholesalers who were so adversely affected by world conditions.

Three months before the St. Paul convention, all available floor space for the trade fair was sold out. There was a growing list of prospective exhibitors willing to take any quarters available.

Early on the morning of September 1, 1939, German

troops, on order of Adolph Hitler, crossed the Polish border. Before the day was over, Europe was again aflame with war. England and France declared war on Germany, September 3, 1939.

On this same day, the Board of Directors of FTD held their meeting in St. Paul, preceding the opening of the convention the following day. War in Europe seemed far away. There was no great anxiety over the involvement of the United States. This thought was expressed to the convention by Merlin H. Aylesworth, publisher of the NEW YORK WORLD-TELEGRAM, and by Governor Harold Stassen, of Minnesota, both of whom addressed the meeting on the morning of the second day.

These distinguished visitors had hardly finished speaking when the following cable was received from James Rendall, of the FTD British Unit:

"Please note that from the commencement of hostilities and for the duration of the war, all international business, both inwards and outwards, has ceased. Letter follows."

Whether it so desired or not, FTD was involved in the war. John M. Besemer, who read the cablegram to the convention, immediately advised the members not to accept any orders for Canada or England until he could obtain clarification of the message. Ernest S. Simmons had already discovered that it was impossible to send a cable to England. The situation as to Canada was still in doubt. Besemer strongly suggested that the members wait until he had received the letter mentioned in the cable before accepting any orders for either Canada or England.

Before the day's meeting was over, President Crain had received a telegram from Western Union, advising him that cables would be accepted to warring nations but that they were subject to censorship. So the matter rested for the duration of the convention.

Although the St. Paul convention lasted only a day and a

half, several significant changes were introduced into the Bylaws on the recommendation of President Crain and the Board. A Growers' Division was provided for, with the chairman of the group to have a seat on the Board. Finalization of the plan for the group was left to the present Board, to be reported at the meeting of the directors the following January. The Finance Committee, the Sales and Advertising Committee and the FTD NEWS Committee were made standing committees, their members to be appointed by the president, with the approval of the Board, as soon as possible after taking office.

At least one member of the Board was to be appointed to each standing committee, except the Finance Committee, and that member was to be chairman. Some changes were made in the duties of the Nomination Committee, permitting the presentation of nominations to the members in the various regions well in advance of the fall elections.

A new Mercury emblem was adopted and its display made mandatory. This new emblem was a dignified black and gold circular plaque, containing the figure of Mercury surrounded by the title of the Association and the simple legend, "Flowers-By-Wire."

In the election of officers for the ensuing year, Willard Crain was renamed to the presidency. W. E. Joy, of Columbus, Georgia, became vice-president. Margaret Blackistone, of Washington, D. C., was elected director-at-large. Regional directors elected were: W. F. Holbrow, Dorchester, Massachusetts, Region 1; James Donn, Miami, Florida, Region 6; William Hasselmann, Independence, Kansas, Region 7; and Lon Foster, Oklahoma City, Region 9. B. J. Clarke, Columbus, Ohio, was named chairman of the Associate Division. The appointment of a chairman of the newly formed Growers' Division was left to President Crain, with the concurrence of the Board.

In the meeting at St. Paul, much was accomplished. It was a business meeting in the strict sense of the term. The affairs of the Association were handled efficiently. But, as FTD entered the fourth decade of the Twentieth Century, the rapid changes in world events presaged sweeping changes in the structure and service of the Association. It could not afford to be left behind by world developments. It had never failed to rise to the occasion, with both men and plans. There was no doubt that it would meet the future with fortitude and resolution.

Before the Board of Directors could meet in Detroit, in January, 1940, death struck the membership two serious blows. William Hasselmann, who had been elected director at the last convention, died suddenly at his home in Independence, Kansas. He had been one of the principal florists of his region, a life-long member of the profession and a man of charm and influence in the Association. And, just as the Board was assembling for the meeting in Detroit, word came of the death of William F. Gude in Washington, D. C.

The worth of this great florist to FTD was inestimable. As president, director and counselor, Gude had given strength and wisdom to the Association in its early days. He had been a pillar of faith in its future. His death was especially calamitous at this time, with the country on the brink of another World War. It was he, perhaps more than any other, who had, through his acquaintances in high places in the nation's capital, been able to steer FTD through the maze of rationing, cutbacks and restrictions which, in the first World War, had threatened the organization's existence.

He had been a tireless worker for the Association since its founding. He had served as a director in the preliminary organization, before the formation of the Florists' Telegraph Delivery in Rochester in 1910. Although illness had handicapped him in his last years, he never lost his interest or his faith in FTD. The growth and success of the Association remained one of his great prides.

To fill the place of Hasselmann on the Board, President

Crain appointed Herman Swoboda, of Omaha, Nebraska, to serve until the election in September. Another appointee to the Board was the representative of the Growers' Division, John Lemon, of Richmond, Indiana.

John Lemon was a director without an organization. The Growers' Division had been slow in forming. Lemon, in his report to the Board, said that he had nothing to report because, to date, he had nobody to represent.

He further informed the Board, "There is no question regarding the fact that, in our industry, there is a great deal of distrust and lack of trust between all of the members of the trade and between different branches of the same division; in other words, the retailers do not trust the growers, the growers do not trust the wholesalers and the wholesalers do not trust anybody; that the retailers do not even trust each other, and neither do the growers."

This was a curious analysis of the attitude of the industry, since the growers themselves had requested permission to form their own division. Lemon asked for suggestions from the directors as to what he could do for his organization. The consensus was that the matter would have to develop of its own force in hope that by the time of the convention in September, a brighter picture might be presented.

The federal income tax question, which had been dragging along in the courts, came before the Board for consideration. It was decided, on advice of counsel, to retain the top tax attorneys in Detroit to expedite the settlement and determine the status of FTD. This was ordered by unanimous decision.

Over the past two or three years, it had become apparent that some dissidence existed among the Board members over the operation of the Headquarters offices. There was no suggestion of bad faith, but part of the Board considered that the interior structure of the Association, particularly as it concerned the Headquarters operation, needed overhauling. The spokesman of this group was S. A. Anderson,

Jr., and he brought the matter up as a motion to appoint a committee of Board members to study the advisability of a change in the organizational structure and to report to the Board at the coming convention.

Anderson considered the arrangement under which FTD office procedures were carried on at that time as antiquated and inefficient. They had been set up 15 or 20 years before, when the Association was not doing comparable business. FTD was at this time spending between $200,000 and $300,000 a year. He proposed an Auditing Committee, to oversee the financial structure of the Association and report to the Board. He pointed out that the Board now met only twice a year and that, in the January meetings, decisions had to be taken for the following nine months. He favored three or four meetings of the directors every year.

Anderson stated further that, in his opinion, "there should be an executive officer of our Association with absolute, full control of the Association, such as in the case of savings banks and other organizations; and that such officer should sit on the Board and have a voice with the rest of the Board members." He added that he felt there was a great deal of room for improvement and that the slight additional cost would be saved a thousand times over.

This was a strong view and Anderson argued it ably. It did not meet wholehearted approval of the entire Board, however, and some fear was expressed of the political effect of such changes. Members of the Finance Committee and the Executive Committee objected to the implications of Anderson's views, but he stoutly maintained that there was a division of authority between those two committees, which was inefficient and might be wasteful.

Anderson presented his ideas so earnestly that they had some effect on the directors. When they suggested that his motion be tabled until the next convention, Anderson chose to withdraw it rather than have it tabled. Nevertheless, the motion to table carried.

Anderson's father had been a member of the Board. The young man had grown up in the florist industry, under the influence of FTD. His ideas seem to have been a quickening breeze among the younger members, blowing in the direction of stronger central organization and closer control over the Association's activities.

All through the spring and summer of 1940, Hitler's forces continued their successes on the European continent. Denmark and Norway were invaded and conquered in April. A month later the Germans moved into Belgium, Holland and Luxembourg. On that same day, Winston Churchill succeeded Neville Chamberlain as prime minister. Soon thereafter, Churchill made his famous "blood, sweat, and tears" speech. Dunkirk was evacuated on May 26, 1940.

Meanwhile, in the United States, President Roosevelt was setting up the Office for Emergency Management, the framework within which the defense and war agencies were organized and operated.

Italy "stabbed France in the back" in June. Germany occupied Paris in the same month, causing the capitulation of the country and the formation of the Vichy government. In July, German planes began bombing English cities. Russia hurried to annex Latvia, Estonia and Lithuania.

Despite world conditions, the business of FTD florists showed an increase. There was also an increase in membership and in the number of cities and towns in which the Association was represented.

The members convened in Cincinnati on Monday, September 9, 1940, with the Board and the Executive Committee meeting on Saturday and Sunday, preceding the convention. One of the first matters to come before the Executive Committee was Anderson's suggestion at the January Board meeting that a committee be appointed to study a structural change in the Association. Things were not too favorable at the home offices in Detroit. Al Barber had been ill for some time. Members complained that FTD personnel seemed to remain on their jobs only until they could find more profitable places elsewhere. There was a constant turnover. The efficiency of the operation, some felt, had badly deteriorated. A report of the salaries paid the employees on the first floor of the FTD Building, where the stenographers and telephone personnel worked, showed 12 persons with an average weekly wage of less than $20.

There was discussion about replacing Barber. It was finally decided to leave the matter to the Executive Committee.

John Lemon, chairman of the Growers' Division, again reported that nothing had been done about his group. There was a hint that opposition within the industry was hampering organization of the growers into a definite group within FTD, but nothing substantial could be found to sustain this apprehension. There were 52 growers listed in the Associate Division, but it appeared that proper organizational methods had never been employed to get their co-operation in the new division. Lemon's report was accepted without comment.

There was cheer for the members in the president's annual address, which revealed that the year's increase in business had amounted to 6 per cent, in spite of greatly decreased Canadian business and a bare trickle of "bon voyage" orders. There was, in his report, the first intimation that the war in Europe was vitally affecting florists in America, whose industry before had enjoyed a singular immunity.

One amendment to the Bylaws was offered at the 1940 Cincinnati convention and adopted by the membership. It called for the expulsion of any member violating any part of the Constitution or Bylaws, except the reporting rules of the Clearing House. In the event of violation, an affidavit containing the facts of the violation was to be filed in duplicate with the secretary of the Association. The member was to receive a copy and, unless adjustment was made within 30 days, a date would be set for a hearing before the Board or the Executive Committee. These groups might also delegate the responsibility for the hearing to a district representative or a regional director. If an adverse finding was made, the member charged was to be immediately expelled.

President Crain had been so assiduous in the conduct of his office for two, years that the Cincinnati convention presented few difficult problems to the members. The meeting was smoothly run and happily concluded, with a banquet at which the new officers and directors were introduced.

William E. Joy, of Columbus, Georgia, was the new president. Assisting him in the office of vice-president was Bruno D. Smoke, of Detroit. Mrs. Lauretta Rausch, of Chicago, became the new director-at-large. Regional directors elected were: John H. Claus, Germantown, Pennsylvania, Region 3; Charles I. Kent, Cleveland, Region 4; Phillip E. Scanlan, Chicago, Region 5; Herman Swoboda, Omaha, Region 8; and William F. Peters, Spokane, Washington, Region 11. Ben J. Clarke, of Columbus, Ohio, remained in the post of chairman of the Associate Division. John Lemon, of Richmond, Indiana, was reappointed chairman of the incipient Growers' Division.

Although the registration for the Cincinnati convention was 12 short of the all-time high reached in Philadelphia in 1937, it showed the greatest number of votes ever cast for the officers and more member shops represented than any earlier convention.

The health of Al Barber did not improve during the remaining months of the year, and one of the pressing matters before the Board in January, 1941, in Detroit, was that situation. He had been on leave of absence for some seven months at full salary. Some of the directors felt that this money could be better utilized. There was nothing but sympathy for the secretary but, as a matter of business and in deference to the welfare of the Association, it was necessary that someone assume his duties. Barber, himself, realized that he was physically unable to continue as executive secretary. He appeared before the Board, asking that some post without so much responsibility be found for him in FTD. This was not considered wise by the majority of the directors.

It was decided after much discussion to terminate his salary as executive secretary as of February 1, 1941, and to pay him $200 a month for the following year, after which responsibility toward him would cease. But Barber did not survive this arrangement. He died on April 2. John Besemer was promoted to this post, at a salary increase retroactive to October, 1940.

Good news was given the Board by the Finance Committee, which announced that all the funds of the Association, frozen in the depression closing of the First National Bank of Detroit, had been paid in full.

The Growers' Division had once again failed "to get off the ground," reported Chairman John Lemon. He earnestly asked the Board members for suggestions of how to proceed with the organization of that group. He still expressed the hope that, by September, such a group would be established in operating form.

President Joy ended the meeting by saying, "Gentlemen, I wish to say that I appreciate your patience with me. I have been a little nervous as this has been my first Board meeting as President. I thank you so much for staying with me until I finished. Now, let's all go back to our regions and put FTD where it belongs!"

No apologies were needed for Joy's conduct of the meeting. It had been smooth and expeditious. Discussion of all the problems, including that of the executive secretary, had been abundantly held. Every director had received full freedom of expression. It had been a profitable meeting and the directors adjourned, feeling that much was accomplished for FTD.

World events moved swiftly during the spring and

summer. Roosevelt was inaugurated as the first third term president in history. At his urging, Congress passed the Lend Lease Bill. This principally aided Britain but later was extended to Russia when Hitler, disregarding his non-aggression pact signed with the Soviets two years before, invaded Russia. United States Marines occupied Iceland at the invitation of that country. Roosevelt and Churchill met on a battleship in the Atlantic Ocean and announced to the world the signing of the Atlantic Charter.

Of much more intimate effect on the members of FTD was the drafting of men for America's peace-time army. This move by the government was beginning to curtail the working forces of many florists. Deferments granted to men employed in certain designated war plants did not apply to the employees of florists. Many skilled designers, growers and sales representatives had been called to the colors.

Government spokesmen still insisted that the United States would remain the "arsenal of democracy," not actively engaged in the combat, but florists who had been in the business during the first World War were apprehensive.

The natural urge of florists to fraternize was again demonstrated in planning for the 1941 convention in Los Angeles. Railroads were crowded with troop and war material transportation. Passenger coaches were in short supply. Despite this, Edward W. Gould, of Chicago, chairman of the Transportation Committee, arranged for two florists' specials, the "Rose" and the "Orchid," to leave Chicago on August 25 for the West Coast. In advertisements, published in the FTD NEWS, members were warned to make their reservations early, because it would be impossible to obtain additional cars.

Adolph LeMoult, who had intended to run his famous "Green Special" on another West Coast trip, was forced to cancel his arrangements. His train conflicted with those planned by Gould, in charge of transportation. Also the length of the trip from New York and the arranging of so many cars for one special purpose, made difficulties. He published a letter in the FTD NEWS, explaining his cancellation and urging all to support the Chicago trains. His letter ended, "There shall be but one shepherd and one fold."

The trains which left Chicago were equipped with cars for entertainment, for dancing, for meetings and for all the regular railway services. Special stops were made at Colorado Springs, Salt Lake City, Reno and San Francisco. Mayor Angelo Rossi, an FTD member, met the trains in San Francisco with a bagpipe band and, although this trip did not approach in length of time or entertainment Grakelow's famous specials, the five days to the Coast were a memorable occasion for more than 400 FTD members. A daily newspaper was printed on the train.

The Los Angeles convention broke all West Coast records. Once more President Joy demonstrated his skill at presiding. There was no wasted time or effort. The affairs of the Association were conducted and settled with utmost dispatch.

John Lemon, chairman of the Growers' Division, made a report to the opening meeting of the Board that was a classic for its incisive examination of the circumstances which had kept the group from becoming an entity inside the Association. At the end of his report, he suggested that any attempt to unite the growers into a separate division be abandoned. So well received was his address that, upon motion, it was published verbatim in the minutes, as valuable enough to be referred to in later years. Lemon was reappointed chairman of the Growers' Division, with a seat on the Board. His suggestion that efforts toward uniting the growers be abandoned was tabled for further consideration.

A new note in FTD service was struck; i.e., helping the serviceman send flowers to his home from wherever he might be training, with the greatest aid promised those who wished to remember their loved ones with floral gifts on special occasions. Further educational assistance to members was promised with the engaging of Horace Head, of Rochester, N. Y., as FTD official flower stylist.

William E. Joy, of Columbus, Georgia, was re-elected president. A. H. Serveau, of San Francisco, was elected vice-president. Named director-at-large was Annabelle Smith, of Pasadena, California. Regional directors elected were: Richard T. Broderick, Yonkers, New York, Region 2; Victor L. Scott, Winnipeg, Manitoba, Region 7; J. Fred Seulberger, Jr., Oakland, California, Region 10; and Ernest S. Simmons, Toronto, Ontario, Region 12. Samuel S. Pennock, Jr., of Baltimore, Maryland, was named new chairman of the Associate Division.

President Joy's address was a proud recital of growth and progress over the year. It was not boastful but an optimistic report of the increased advancement in the many fields touched by the Association. The operation in the Detroit Headquarters was becoming more efficient and routine. The affairs of all other branches of FTD were in good condition. Joy felt no need to make recommendations in his speech, beyond the continuation of the program of the Association as it was being conducted.

The gravity of the war situation in Britain was forcibly brought before the convention in an address by Mrs. Basil Rathbone, wife of the actor, speaking in behalf of her husband, who could not appear because of studio commitments. Rathbone had been helpful in arranging entertainment for FTD members during their stay in Los Angeles. Now, through his wife, he appealed for florists' aid in British War Relief. Steps were immediately taken to enlist the full support of the Association in this work, details to be determined later. Mrs. Rathbone received an enthusiastic reception by the convention.

The Los Angeles convention was a meeting to gladden the hearts of all florists who attended. And this was good, for it was to be the last convention for some time. Unknown to the members who celebrated so lightheartedly at the functions furnished by the Association and the city, Fate had written an end to the easy, joyful days in America for a long time to come. A wind was gathering across the Pacific that was to chill the heart of every American and the ferocious force of its striking was not far beyond the horizon.

CHAPTER THIRTEEN

The Second World War

HE SERENITY OF A Hawaiian Sunday morning, December 7, 1941, was shattered by waves of Japanese bombing planes screaming out of the skies to the north of the islands to drop their deadly cargoes upon the placid place below. When the raid was over, the Pearl Harbor Naval Base and important segments of the Pacific Fleet lay in shambles. Hickman Field, the Air Force headquarters for the Pacific, was severely damaged. More than 3,000 Army and Navy personnel were dead from Japanese bombs and bullets. The quiet that over-spread Hawaii was the stillness of a stunned and incredulous people.

Later in the day, Japanese bombers repeated the strike at Clark Field, near Manila, crippling the striking force of the United States in that area. Raids followed at Guam, Wake and Midway Islands. America was thrust into its second world war in a generation.

The next day, before a tense and haggard Congress, President Roosevelt described "a day that will live in infamy," and asked that a state of war be declared between the United States and the Imperial Japanese Government. There was only one dissenting vote.

Italy and Germany declared war on the United States on December 11, 1941, and a conflict began which was to rage over four-fifths of the world.

The suddenness of the Japanese attack was not immediately comprehended by the average American. To those of FTD

271

who remembered the days of 1917-18, there came a feeling
of familiarity. These were wartime conditions, with regulations to come. But it is doubtful that anyone was truly
prepared for all that impended.

There was no immediate increase in war preparations. The
United States was already on a defense footing. The sight was
familiar of uniformed men on the streets and long lines of
troop trains conveying soldiers to training camps. Nothing
was greatly changed by the time the FTD Board of Directors
met in Detroit, January 24, 1942. One important governmental move had been made. The War Production Board
was established on January 16, 1942.

In his opening remarks to the directors, President Joy
forecast some of the problems bound to confront the industry.
He emphasized that this was the time to sustain the morale
of the membership. He called upon the Board to endeavor,
in visits to the membership, to keep florists in a comfortable
state of mind and not "let them get the idea that the florist
business is going to the dogs."

He urged that flowers are a necessity, not a luxury. All
through the meeting of the Board, he proclaimed the thought
that the public must be taught the need for flowers for the
general morale. So it was decided to return the public relations program to the Detroit office, where a closer contact
with the membership could be maintained and more
attention given to the details of publicity for flowers-by-wire.

The wisdom of holding the convention, already scheduled
for New York City, was carefully considered and it was
decided to continue plans for the meeting. There were good
reasons for not canceling. There was no way, at this time,
to predict the war situation. There was a general feeling in
the country that the entry of the United States would
shorten the struggle. The FTD members believed that
normal conduct of the Association would soon be re-established. It was also felt that cancellation of the annual meeting
would be detrimental to morale and that holding the

convention as planned would imply solidity of the industry and the confidence of the directors in the future.

There was also a more practical consideration. The substantial increase in the business of florists over several months indicated that there were problems to be discussed on a national basis. The decision to hold the convention as planned was definite. John Besemer was named convention manager, with control of all the arrangements.

Anticipating many special wartime problems for FTD members, it was necessary to review the schedule of Board meetings. Some of the directors thought the practice of holding Board meetings only in January and at convention time, as provided for in the Bylaws, did not give Board members enough contact with the affairs of the Association. This matter had been discussed at the Los Angeles convention and reserved for further examination at the January, 1942, Board meeting. President Joy, using his constitutional prerogative, called the next meeting for July and, in order to set definite dates for future meetings, the first Tuesdays after the twentieth day of July and January were named as meeting dates.

John Lemon, chairman of the Growers' Division, did not attend this session of the Board. It was clear that not enough interest had been shown by the growers to entitle them to group representation. So, on motion of Richard Broderick, it was voted to discontinue any effort to organize them. They remain part of the Associate Division and are represented by the Associate Division chairman.

Florists everywhere entered ardently into the government's war program. Corsages composed of war stamps were devised. Facilities of individual shops were offered as sales depots for war bonds and stamps. Units in several regions held meetings to explore the ways by which the florists in the nation could best contribute to the war effort.

At the January Board meeting, Charles I. Kent offered the following resolution:

"That this Association go on record that we, the Board of Directors of the FTDA, support all local and national movements in the government's conduct of the war, to promote the sale of defense stamps and bonds, and engage willingly in the conservation efforts, and so advise the President of these United States, and that the secretary take the necessary steps to do this."

This resolution was adopted and FTD, less than seven weeks after Pearl Harbor, became one of the first national organizations to express its unqualified help to the nation's war effort.

Events moved swiftly. On January 30, 1942, Congress passed the Price Control Act. The Office of Price Administration was established to control rents and commodity prices. On April 28, 1942, the OPA froze the prices of all major items affecting the cost of living in an effort to check wartime inflation. Sugar rationing began in May. Gasoline rationing was instituted in 17 eastern states during this same month and extended to the entire nation after December 1, 1942.

All these drastic steps had been taken before the Board of Directors met in Detroit on July 21 and 22, 1942. So rapidly had conditions altered that a complete re-appraisal of the position of FTD became necessary. Many earlier decisions were subject to reconsideration. One of the most important was the decision to hold the forthcoming annual convention, scheduled for New York City.

Before the Board at this time came A. M. Dauernheim, of New York, general convention chairman. He was reluctant to suggest cancellation of the meeting, but he asked that the membership be told that all entertainment would be drastically curtailed.

He then presented, as the first mention of such a plan, the suggestion that, if the convention were canceled, a "process of freezing the present officers" in their positions be adopted. He read to the Board a letter from C. R. Beckert, president of Thomas Young Nurseries, of New York. In a serious and considered communication, Beckert "unalterably opposed" the convention. He said, "While not questioning the obvious benefits resulting from the serious side of the convention, no part of that side is apparent to the public. But the social aspect of this or any convention is apparent, at times noticeably so, and the impact of such concentrated gaiety upon those whose sons, relatives or friends are in the service, or whose names may have already appeared on the casualty lists, is too deep an affront to feelings already stalked by tragedy."

Also appearing on this occasion was Mr. Hoenig, a representative of the Waldorf-Astoria Hotel, in New York. Hoenig renewed the hotel's invitation to FTD to hold its meeting but said that, due to present conditions, the hotel would abide by the decision of the Board, despite contracts already signed and reservations confirmed.

Discussion developed and it appeared that the Board was divided on the question of holding the convention. Serious restrictions on rail travel had been imposed and gasoline rationing was in effect in the eastern states. There was also the labor problem for florists, many of whom were endeavoring to fill vacant places on their staffs by doubling their own hours. The announced intention of the government to call up married men in the next draft was a further drain on the working forces of many shops.

President Joy permitted full discussion of the problem, without expressing his own opinion. He did state, however, that he had met increased difficulties in his own travels for the benefit of the Association and was thoroughly acquainted with the national situation.

Director Victor L. Scott finally offered the motion that all conventions be postponed for the duration of the war. Joy called for a show of hands on the motion and it was carried.

The postponement of the convention settled one problem but presented another. According to the Bylaws, it was necessary for elections to be held for officers and directors each year.

This question was submitted to Guy Jensen, the FTD legal counsel, who advised that, according to the laws of FTD, as well as the laws of the State of Michigan, annual meetings could not be eliminated for the duration, but only postponed, subject to the call of the president of the Association, a majority of the Board, or by a petition signed by at least five per cent of the membership of FTD. He informed the directors that the courts were reluctant to interfere with the internal affairs of such associations. He expressed the belief that, if a vote could be taken from the membership that annual meetings be indefinitely postponed, subject to proper call, the good faith of the Board would be established. Nobody, he said, could legitimately interfere with that action.

On June 19, 1942, the Office of Defense Transportation had issued a request to the American people to "defer all meetings, conventions and tours of groups not closely related to the furtherance of the war effort," stating that if this request were observed, "there is good reason to hope that no drastic control over travel will be necessary." It was also realized that the New York City civil defense regulations governing blackouts, dimouts and mass meetings, on top of the fear felt by many coastal cities of the danger of sneak air raids, would much diminish the probability of a successful convention.

Jensen suggested that a resolution be framed and printed in the FTD NEWS, advising the members of the action taken by the Board to postpone the New York convention and that a return postcard be sent to each member, asking his concurrence. This, in the opinion of the attorney, would be the equivalent of offering the resolution to the annual meeting. This step was taken and the reaction of the members was almost unanimous in favor of the postponement.

Fred Austin, president of SAF, appeared before this

meeting of the Board to request that FTD "come into SAF as an affiliated member." He said that "he desired real co-operation between the two organizations."

Austin told the Board that SAF now represented 31 florists' organizations and desired to have FTD as the thirty-second member. The advantage of associating with SAF would be that the society would then be able to tell Washington that it represented the entire industry and was the proper channel for all directives and war orders concerning florists. He wanted FTD to agree to permit SAF to represent it in all its dealings with government rationing and allocating agencies. As a membership fee for this work, Austin suggested 25 cents for each FTD member, or a flat fee of $1,500 per year. A rival wire organization was to pay $1,000 a year if it decided to affiliate.

The money was necessary, explained Austin, because SAF had been forced to suspend its flower shows, its principal source of revenue for operating expenses.

After Austin ended his talk and left the meeting, the directors discussed the proposition at length. There was the utmost friendliness for the parent organization, but FTD had had 31 years of handling its own affairs, wherever they might arise, so there was a reluctance, on principle, to delegate this duty to another. The war was not going well for the Allies. Matters were likely to get worse before they got better. Undoubtedly representation in Washington would be required to adjust the restrictions on business which might be fatal to the continued existence of FTD.

Ernest S. Simmons, of Toronto, made the most telling argument against Austin's plan. He informed the meeting that the same plan had been advanced in Canada by the Canadian Florists' and Gardeners' Association, an organization comparable to SAF. But the Canadian retailers had insisted on being represented on any committee or group which had the duty of dealing with the wartime restrictions. This insistence had resulted in the formation of the Cana-

dian Florists' Advisory Council, made up of representatives
of all the florists' organizations in that country. As a result,
matters had been conducted satisfactorily.

Simmons was a man of great influence in Canadian florists'
councils, as he was in FTD. He had had three years of
rigorous cutbacks to deal with in Canada before the United
States entered the war. He suggested to the Board that the
same kind of organization could be set up in this country
and he believed it should be done. He knew Ottawa and
Washington were co-operating closely on all war matters. He
felt, since the Canadian government had publicly expressed
its pleasure at the co-operation of the Florists' Advisory
Council, a similar move by United States florists would be
received warmly in Washington.

Much had been done in this respect by Robert Roland,
executive secretary of SAF, who spent a great part of his
time in Washington in contact with government officials,
explaining the plight of florists, the necessity for flowers in
wartime and the importance of the florist industry to a
nation at war.

Roland was greatly assisted in this work by Granville
Gude, whose wide acquaintance with Washington and
established prestige in that city were placed at the disposal
of the florists' cause. In accepting this responsibility,
Granville Gude raised many echoes of the past, for it was his
father, William F. Gude, during another war, who had given
his time and substance to gain official recognition of the role
of florists in the country's war effort. And the footsteps of
that immense man were not too far apart for the lengthening
strides of the son.

President Joy had a close knowledge of the situation in
Washington and was quick to inform the Board that SAF
did not object to FTD being represented in any action which
concerned florists, but it was Roland's fear that, unless
the two organizations co-operated fully, two separate committees might be formed. It was foreseeable that two such

groups might find themselves at cross-purposes and destroy the very point they were trying to maintain.

This was not a simple question. In the interest of harmony within the industry, Otto Lang moved that FTD co-operate with SAF, that $1,500 be paid to SAF and that a request from FTD be entered for equal representation on any committee conferring with the government on matters pertaining to the industry. The motion, however, was to be subject to approval by FTD's legal counsel on the question of liability. In this form, the motion was seconded and passed. This was by no means the end of the matter.

Before the Board adjourned, meeting dates were changed to the last Wednesday in July, the second Wednesday in November and the first Wednesday in March. It was felt that, without the annual convention, more Board meetings were necessary. After routine reports by the standing committees, the meeting adjourned until November 11, 1942.

Throughout the rest of the summer and early fall, florists did not sit idly waiting for a move in Washington. No group in the country entered more sincerely into the war effort. The entire Headquarters staff in Detroit joined in this work. The FTD NEWS, edited by Robert S. Powers, ran a complete page of the names of shops over the country whose employees were investing 10 per cent of their salaries in payroll bond buying.

The loyalty and patriotism of FTD members were apparent to the government officials in Washington. On August 6, 1942, the following letter was received in the Headquarters offices:

"Dear Mr. Powers:

Please give my thanks and appreciation to the members of the Florists' Telegraph Delivery Association for their aid to the War Bond Program.

I am glad to know that a large percentage of your Association's members has adopted the Payroll Savings Plan. This is intelligent and practical

patriotism. Our country's need is great, and it can
only be met by all of us cutting down our personal
spending to the things we absolutely need and
investing every penny we can spare in War Bonds
to buy the weapons of victory.

Very sincerely yours,

H. MORGENTHAU, JR.

Secretary of the Treasury."

The members also entered wholeheartedly into the
conservation of gasoline and rubber. When the Office of
Defense Transportation released procedures for conservation,
FTD members began using bicycles, Shetland ponies, horses
and almost every conceivable means of transportation that
did not require gasoline or rubber. Many shops ran full-page
advertisements in newspapers, asking co-operation of the
public in cutting down delivery schedules.

Joseph B. Eastman, national director of the Office of
Defense Transportation, upon learning of the cancellation
of the annual meeting, wrote to Headquarters: "It is
apparent that the members of your Association are making
many valuable contributions to our war effort and I was not
surprised, therefore, to see that they readily subscribed to
this additional contribution of foregoing this year's meeting."

But the communication from Washington which did most
to raise the morale and hopes of the membership came from
the White House under date of August 7, 1942. It said
simply:

"Dear Mr. Powers:

Flowers add to our joys and comfort us in our
sorrows, and I am sure that in war time we will
need them more than ever.

Very sincerly yours,

ELEANOR ROOSEVELT"

A reproduction of this plain missive, set at a dramatic
angle against a royal blue background, adorned the cover
of the FTD NEWS for September, 1942. It was repeated,

surrounded by a scroll design, on an inside page. The reaction to this letter by the membership was immediate and overwhelming.

By unanimous demand, a facsimile was made available to members for window and wall posters, small statement stickers, larger package stickers and envelope stuffer blotters. No finer message about flowers had come out of the wartime period. It was a virtual endorsement, by a great lady, of the florists' efforts toward victory. Similar statements were received from Frances Parkinson Keyes, Katharine Cornell, Mary Roberts Rinehart and Ruth Bryan Owen. To the public it was an encouragement and an incentive to use flowers more generously than ever in the coming anxious months.

Before the next Board meeting, November 11, 1942, the Office of Defense Transportation issued an order requiring the registration of all commercial vehicles. This strongly suggested to FTD members that more stringent restrictions on the use of delivery vehicles was contemplated. Shop owners did not wait for the blow to fall. They immediately began "delivery pools." Four, five or six retailers joined in each locality and pooled their delivery cars. Only one car was used each day. Delivery schedules were arranged, to afford each shop equal facilities. Both gasoline and rubber were thus conserved. The customer was encouraged to place his order early, in anticipation of the rigid schedules. There was excellent co-operation from the buying public.

Other business restrictions were faced by FTD members before the summer was over. Many hospitals, because of curtailed staffs, had discouraged the delivery of flowers to patients. In some cases, florists were able to alter this attitude by agreeing to deliver arrangements only. The governor of Indiana issued a proclamation barring flowers from hospitals in that state. But prompt action prevented the order from being enforced.

Congratulatory telegrams were banned and there was fear that this directive might extend to telegrams for flowers-by-wire which contained congratulations. But this never came to pass.

With all this narrowing of opportunities to serve the public, the Board, which met in Detroit on November 11, 1942, was pleased to hear some good news.

The number of overseas floral orders, from soldiers to families and loved ones, for the coming Christmas season, had been estimated by the Army Exchange Service, which handled these orders through the various PX installations in Europe, as 23,000. This estimate, since orders were received until mid-December, was revised upward to a minimum of 25,000 Christmas orders.

But even good news must have some contrast. The drawback was that the Army Exchange Service in New York declared that it lacked the personnel to handle such volume and that new methods must be devised for forwarding this business. This meant that no time was to be lost in arranging for the business that could be expected to double for the prime holidays of Easter and Mother's Day.

The Christmas business was handled through the office in Detroit. The estimate proved amazingly accurate. So it was decided to place FTD personnel in the Army Exchange Services building in New York, for more efficient forwarding of overseas orders for Easter and Mother's Day. Posters were placed in all PX's overseas to remind soldiers of the opportunity to send flowers-by-wire on those days. As a result of these reminders, plus the natural desire of overseas soldiers to remember their loved ones, Easter business reached approximately 50,000 orders. Mother's Day orders exceeded 70,000. These were received in the Army Exchange offices in New York, where they were taken over by FTD personnel and re-routed all over the country.

In view of the rush to set up the New York facilities and the amazing flood of orders, few errors were made. There was, to be sure, room for improvement. Re-evaluation of the system was begun, to prepare for the holidays to follow.

With transmission and delivery problems eased for the moment by the establishment of the receiving office in New York, a more serious development threatened not only the reputation of FTD but its basic structure. For more than 10 years, despite the tremendous increase in business in flowers-by-wire, the reserve for working capital of FTD had not been increased. This, in addition to the $120,000 tied up in Britain by the inability of the British members to send money out of the country in payment for flowers, suddenly caught the Association with inadequate funds for prompt payment of American and Canadian members' Clearing House credits.

In February, 1943, the Finance Committee had recommended that the British Unit members be put on a cash basis with payment expected monthly. Looking to the expected increase for the coming holidays, John Besemer was advised to visit England and arrange for the most expeditious release of the frozen funds, if practicable. But estimates of the coming business were revised upward so rapidly in the ensuing weeks that the wisdom of this trip disappeared almost before he could pack his bag.

By the time the Board met in March, 1943, the situation was critical. Besemer estimated that between $500,000 and $600,000 would be needed to handle the clearings for the impending holidays. According to Besemer, the total available security against which FTD could borrow funds to support the Clearing House amounted to $300,000, not only far too little collateral for the amount needed, but security which should be kept free of lien for emergencies.

The secretary had been in consultation with David E. Roberts, re-engaged as general counsel by FTD. They had drawn up a resolution, which Besemer now offered to the Board as the quickest and most equitable way in which to raise the necessary funds. The resolution, approved by the

Executive Committee, called for the Clearing House to withhold 10 per cent of each incoming order, for a period not to exceed six months, or until $600,000 had been raised.

This was a drastic move and one that caused some consternation among the members of the Board. Many arguments were advanced against it. President Joy permitted the widest possible consideration of all phases of the project, but in the end there was nothing else to do. The urgent need for such a large sum of money could be met in no other manner. The resolution was adopted. The Board ruled that the funds thus obtained as working capital were to be credited to each member's credit deposit and that, as soon as the emergency was over, it was to be returned to each member, in proportion as it was collected, as a personal emergency savings fund. The plan was placed in immediate effect.

To inform the membership of the revolutionary action, "pink sheet" stuffers were inserted into all reports sent out by the Clearing House. The "pink sheet" was a news bulletin sent on special occasions when it was desirable to tell members of some unusual fact or action at Headquarters. The full story of the Board's decision was carried as the feature story in the next issue of the FTD NEWS.

In the discussion which preceded the adoption of the resolution, there had been concern over how the members might accept such an extreme decision, without having any voice in it beyond that of their elected representatives. But fears were groundless. The membership, aware of the tightening wartime demands, almost unanimously accepted the move. With personal problems in their own shops to worry about, they were well content to leave to their trusted representatives the larger tasks of international finance, service and customer satisfaction.

As a mark of the enthusiasm with which the members sprang to the aid of the emergency credit deposit fund, the amount accumulated during the short period allotted to the 10 per cent collection was $687,000. The Board, in gratitude for such a generous gesture, voted that the fund would pay 4 per cent interest to the contributors. Thus, not only did the members help FTD when help was needed, but they established for themselves a healthy savings account, accumulating to their credit about $27,480 per year.

The situation in Washington was touchy. John Clements, FTD's New York public relations counsel, was spending most of his time in the capital, observing developments in the rationing picture which might affect FTD members. At his suggestion, President Joy, accompanied by Directors Sam S. Pennock, Jr., Charles I. Kent and Victor L. Scott, visited Washington, where they appeared before Joseph B. Eastman, national director of the Office of Defense Transportation, and Paul V. McNutt, chairman of the War Manpower Commission. To these busy men, they offered all the facilities of FTD in the prosecution of the war effort. They were graciously received and the fact that they came to offer help instead of requesting favors made a favorable impression.

Of much more concrete effect in showing FTD's willingness to aid in the conservation of war materials, Clements advised that the Sales and Advertising Committee immediately call into New York all field men and set them to organizing delivery pools. This was done and, beginning with the larger cities and extending into the smaller towns, these field men organized more than 200 delivery pools, with an average saving of 40 per cent on florists' deliveries.

The Office of Defense Transportation was informed of this voluntary action by FTD, and the Association received warm recognition of such intelligent, all-out co-operation. FTD was told that it was the first industry to throw itself so completely into the war effort on a voluntary plan of co-operation.

Some time later, when the full effect of the pooling arrangements became apparent to the Office of Defense Transportation, Director Eastman inquired of the John Clements organization if it would be possible to have the

FTD field men come to Washington to work with the ODT on a proposed national pooling plan. Clements replied that, while he had no authority to order this, he was sure that the Board of Directors would be delighted. The Office of Defense Transportation further asked FTD to compile a record of the plans and procedures used in forming so quickly such a significant number of motor delivery pools and submit this record to the Washington office.

As a result, Harold Hewey, then manager of the FTD Sales and Advertising Department, and Erwin Hamme, veteran FTD field representative, joined Robert Roland, secretary of SAF, and presented a workable pooling plan which was later adopted by ODT. Erwin Hamme then took a leave of absence at the request of ODT to counsel other industries in the establishment of delivery pools.

All this recognition was gratifying to the officers and Board of Directors of FTD, but they were sobered by the information, relayed by Clements, that the transportation situation was exceedingly grave. A survey was in progress to determine what facilities existed for the shipment of vegetables north from Florida and other southern truck areas. Despite his appreciation of the efforts of FTD so far, McNutt had declared in plain terms that the florist industry was not essential.

Any differences attending the formation of the National Florists Advisory Council were ironed out and the committee, composed of President Joy, Charles I. Kent, Samuel S. Pennock, Jr., Granville Gude and Robert Roland, was formed. Pennock was named secretary of the council.

It had been thought that the work of the advisory council would consist of monthly meetings, limited to the considerations of affairs on the Washington scene, which might be affecting the florist industry or which might tend to do so. But this proved a rosy dream. The group became almost immediately an integral part of the Washington maelstrom.

WARTIME BOARD OF DIRECTORS

The Board of Directors which served throughout World War II. To them fell the problems of rationed supplies, delivery cutbacks, transportation restrictions and the countless other wartime problems. (From left to right) Directors: Victor L. Scott, Winnepeg, Manitoba; Herman Swoboda, Omaha, Nebraska; J. Fred Seulberger, Jr., Oakland, California; John H. Claus, Germantown, Pennsylvania; William F. Peters, Spokane, Washington; Phillip E. Scanlan, Chicago, Illinois; Vernon R. Frank, Decatur, Georgia; Lon Foster, Oklahoma City, Oklahoma and Ernest S. Simmons, Toronto, Ontario; Director-at-Large Mrs. Annabelle Smith, Pasadena, California; President W. E. Joy, Columbus, Georgia; Executive Secretary John M. Besemer, Detroit, Michigan; Treasurer W. L. Rock, Kansas City, Missouri; Court Reporter Bernard Sharkey; Director Charles I. Kent, Cleveland, Ohio; Associate Division Chairman Samuel S. Pennock, Jr., Baltimore, Maryland; Past President Otto Lang, Dallas, Texas; Directors Richard T. Broderick, Yonkers, New York and W. F. Holbrow, Dorchester, Massachusetts.

Probably the first general meeting of District Representatives with FTD officials in the early 1920's. DR's were first instituted in 1916, but not until 1921, at Toronto, was a thorough plan for district unit organization considered by the Board of Directors. At the same time, the slogan, "Faith, Truth and Determination," was adopted. The loving cups were probably awards for excellence in membership recruitment, principal function of DR's at that time.

Above, President Marion Fisher's informative report is enthusiastically received by a group of DR's assembled at Seattle in 1956. District Representatives perform an invaluable liaison service between the official echelon of FTD and the general membership.

Below, scene at a general indoctrination meeting of District Representatives held at Detroit in November, 1958. Acquaintances formed and common problems discussed at such meetings are instrumental in strengthening the entire organizational framework of FTD.

President Irving Allen poses with a group of DR's assembled in New York City for advanced training and education in new FTD policies and procedures. Concentrated instruction at such gatherings enables DR's to carry out their duties with greater efficiency and effectiveness.

Above, a reorientation meeting of DR's in Kansas City hears President Allen explain the latest decisions of the FTD Board of Directors. DR's in turn, carry these explanations to their own unit meetings, thus keeping the membership fully informed on FTD policies.

Below. Word by word analysis of any changes in FTD practices and procedures is given to District Representatives by FTD officials. Copious note-taking by DR's assures proper transmission of the information to members in their respective units.

FAMOUS WOMEN
ATTEST TO FLOWER POWER

The finest expression of the worth of flowers to a warring nation came from Mrs. Franklin D. Roosevelt. Members welcomed and displayed the sentiment in window and counter cards, statement stickers and stuffers.

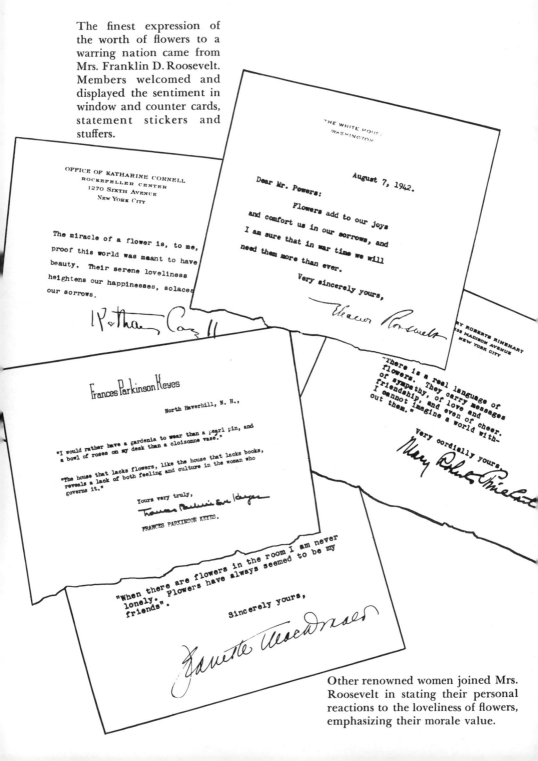

OFFICE OF KATHARINE CORNELL
ROCKEFELLER CENTER
1270 SIXTH AVENUE
NEW YORK CITY

The miracle of a flower is, to me, proof this world was meant to have beauty. Their serene loveliness heightens our happinesses, solaces our sorrows.

THE WHITE HOUSE
WASHINGTON

August 7, 1942.

Dear Mr. Powers:

Flowers add to our joys and comfort us in our sorrows, and I am sure that in war time we will need them more than ever.

Very sincerely yours,

Eleanor Roosevelt

MARY ROBERTS RINEHART
MADISON AVENUE
NEW YORK CITY

"There is a real language of flowers. They carry messages of sympathy, of love and friendship, and even of cheer. I cannot imagine a world without them."

Very cordially yours,
Mary Roberts Rinehart

Frances Parkinson Keyes

North Haverhill, N. H.,

"I would rather have a gardenia to wear than a pearl pin, and a bowl of roses on my desk than a cloisonne vase."

"The house that lacks flowers, like the house that lacks books, reveals a lack of both feeling and culture in the woman who governs it."

Yours very truly,

Frances Parkinson Eve Keyes

FRANCES PARKINSON KEYES.

"When there are flowers in the room I am never lonely. Flowers have always seemed to be my friends".

Sincerely yours,

Jeanette MacDonald

Other renowned women joined Mrs. Roosevelt in stating their personal reactions to the loveliness of flowers, emphasizing their morale value.

All through the summer, the members spent more time in Washington than in their own shops.

There was discussion, at first, of engaging a public relations man, available in Washington at all times for consultation. The FTD members favored retaining John Clements, for the work he had already done for the Association. The members of the council who were representing SAF preferred the services of Marshall Stewart, with whom they had had some dealings. In the end it was decided, that since the entire committee was spending most of its time in Washington, they could conduct their own public relations.

The strain of the frequent meetings and the countless details to which the members of the council had to give their attention, proved too much for Chairman Pennock's health. His absenteeism increased until finally he was hospitalized from overwork. To relieve him as much as possible from pressure, Robert Roland was named secretary of the council, and instructed to move from Chicago to Washington. When this change was accomplished, the National Florists Advisory Council assumed the form which it retained throughout the war.

Because of the press of business and war work at home, James Donn was forced to resign from the Board of Directors during the early part of 1943. He was a high official in the Red Cross of Florida, was busy with the developing and camouflaging of air fields near Miami and was also occupied with several fraternal organizations. He regretted having to tender his resignation. He said, "to be fair to the Association as well as myself, I feel that this is the only solution." In his place, President Joy appointed Vernon Frank, of Decatur, Georgia, who had been Donn's opponent at the last election.

Past President Willard Crain was also obliged to withdraw from the Board during this period, because of the closing of his business in Cincinnati, brought on by war conditions and attention to other interests.

On February 12, 1943, occurred the passing of Max Schling, perhaps "to sit beside a quiet street and tend a little shop with a small greenhouse," a picture of Paradise he had himself drawn in his letter at the death of Mike Bloy. Schling had been an intense little man and a master florist. His ardent support of the young FTD was an important factor in its early life. He left many friends among the membership.

Death also took another man who had played a long and vital role in the meetings and conventions of the Association. This was Arthur J. Munro, of Buffalo, the court stenographer who for 24 years had taken and transcribed verbatim minutes of the conventions and Board and committee meetings of FTD. A master of his profession, he was the inventor of the Munro system of shorthand, widely known in court reporting.

By the time the Board met in November, 1943, the attention of the Florists Advisory Council was directed principally toward three targets: the delivery situation, now under the control of the Office of Defense Transportation; the shortage of corrugated boxes; and the shortage of wire. It had been hoped that, as the war routine tended to stabilize, the delivery problem would be eased and that a better over-all view by the government would permit the lightening of rigorous restrictions on the use of tires and gasoline. This had not proved true. The hardships suffered by businesses all over the country with the sudden rationing of gasoline and tires had caused the ODT to be flooded with requests for permits and for clarifications of rules.

The council was spending most of its time trying to incorporate, into one permit, all the needs of the florists. These included additional holiday deliveries, the use of hired passenger cars to aid such deliveries, and increased hospital deliveries. There was optimism about the petitions now being processed through the ODT, but the earlier fate of similar petitions made the council cautious about prophesying. The corrugated box picture was even less heartening.

Food packers were having trouble securing enough corrugated containers for shipping their products and, if this situation continued, the chance of florists getting an adequate supply of boxes was remote indeed. For the wire shortage, it was possible to use string and other substitutes, but they were far less satisfactory. Wire was made of steel and, with so much of that metal going into war production, it appeared that florists would have to be content with makeshifts.

To assist in the increased work of the Florists Advisory Council, President Joy had appointed John Lemon as a representative of the growers, increasing the membership to six.

For all the excellent work under emergency conditions that FTD had done for flowers-by-wire service to overseas camps, little along that line had been done at home. There was perhaps a sound reason for this. There were many FTD members in towns near the army camps in this country, and Headquarters had waited for them to make contact with these camps, offering the service, instead of proceeding as an Association service. But in many cases the florists had not done this. They would naturally work to serve their regular trade first and, with almost everything in short supply, sometimes it was not possible for the retailer to seek increased business. However, wherever the local member could afford to make contact with the Army Exchange Service at a particular post and arrange to take flower orders, the results had been excellent.

After some discussion, it was decided that a committee should be appointed to work with the Army Exchange Service to make FTD service available in every camp not at present served by a local member. This expanded the potential business greatly and promoted early preparation for the coming Christmas season when, with increased domestic trade and the estimated growth of orders from overseas, consideration would have to be given to a more efficient handling of holiday business.

The war fortunes of the Allies had taken a decided upturn. The North African campaign had ended with victory over Rommel's German troops. Sicily had been taken in July and Italy invaded in early September. This was followed by the unconditional surrender of Italy. But the Germans continued the fighting in that country.

In the Pacific, too, American power was fighting back successfully from the first damaging blows by the Japanese. Tarawa was taken in November as a step on the road to Tokyo. Roosevelt and Churchill met Chiang Kai Chek in Cairo in the same month and went directly from that meeting to the Teheran conference with Stalin. These meetings did much to persuade North Americans that a victorious end to the war could be foreseen.

Further to fortify these hopes, it was known that war material was being poured into Europe in ever increasing amounts. While this kept the retailer scrambling for supplies, he could do so with a good heart, knowing that the darkness presaged a brighter dawn.

FTD was looking to the future. This was evidenced in a motion by William L. Rock that President Joy be empowered to appoint an international board for FTD, to deal with all matters of international nature with regard to world-wide flowers-by-wire service. This board contemplated five members from the United States, two from Canada and one from the British Isles. President Joy was also empowered to appoint representatives from other countries, as necessary. Ernest Simmons ventured the thought that representatives of New Zealand, Australia and South Africa would closely follow FTD ideas and give the American group ample strength to take care of the European situation.

From July 1, 1943, to January 1, 1944, more than 130,000 overseas orders for flowers were processed through the Army Exchange Service offices in New York. Careful planning and an intelligent estimate of the sudden rush of Christmas business enabled the FTD personnel to redistribute these orders efficiently and promptly. As a further check on this business and how it was handled, postcards were sent to 500 people who had received flowers through this service at Christmas, asking if the flowers were delivered and whether they had any comments. Out of 360 replies, only seven persons reported that the flowers were never received and five reported that the flowers were wilted.

On the strength of this record, the Board, meeting in Detroit in March, 1944, considered setting up a similar arrangement on the West Coast to serve the entire Pacific war area. Before this office could be established, a censorship was imposed on all communication with Hawaii. This forbade any and all private communication.

Director Victor L. Scott, chairman of the FTD Post-War Planning Committee, gave this meeting of the Board a most enlightening report on what florists might expect with the end of the war. He stressed the new efficiency, learned by florists from the war experience, stating, "We have learned to economize, because we have been forced into pooling, and many of us have learned a great deal more about merchandising, because the Government has insisted that we keep records. These things have all had a tendency to bring up the standard of the flower business."

He continued, "It is quite possible that when this war ends, it will come to a close just as quickly as it started, and the position our committee is taking is that we must not be caught unprepared. The only yardstick we have to measure by is what happened after the last war."

Scott went on to enumerate the problems which the committee was anticipating: a depression, although he considered this unlikely; the rehabilitation of returning men and women; the growth of airplane transportation, as it might affect the florists; the continued shortage of florists' supplies until the need for other consumer goods was satisfied; an intensified educational program for FTD members; the continued rationing of gasoline and rubber; and the recapture of markets and customers lost due to the war-caused lack of opportunity and supplies.

The report concluded, "Let it not be said that we won this war but lost our business, which had grown to large proportions during the war, only because we were not prepared for the postwar period." The report demonstrated the wisdom of the appointment of the committee and also showed the broad lines along which they were thinking concerning the end of the war.

The matter of continuing himself and the other officers and directors in office concerned President Joy. Not only was he kept from his business more than he liked, but he feared that the membership might get the impression that no effort was being made to hold another convention. This was not true. The subject arose at every Board meeting. This time, however, Joy undertook to get an expression from the membership on the subject of a convention, or at least a streamlined business meeting, in 1944.

To determine the temper of the membership about a convention in 1944, cards were sent out requesting opinions. The return was not heartening. Most of the members neglected to reply. Those who did return the cards were almost evenly divided. There was a small, but definite, majority against a convention. Members were almost entirely opposed to any sort of "streamlined convention."

On investigating the hotel and transportation situation in New York, it was found that no hotel would contract for a convention of more than 25 persons. And the plight of travelers, both by rail and by motor car, was worse than when the convention was originally canceled. So it was again decided to postpone.

In Washington, reported Pennock of the Florists Advisory Council, the outlook was for more, not less, restrictions on supplies, on rationing and on deliveries. Although pooling arrangements made by members in the various cities showed a mileage saving of 55.8 per cent over a similar period in 1941, the ODT was not pleased with the picture of the delivery situation in all industries. Discrepancies had been detected in the reports of other businesses and the ODT was considering a crackdown on all offenders.

Pennock urged that FTD members carefully observe the existing regulations. He underscored the good work done by FTD field men in their pooling operations and he strongly advised the continuance of this work. He was guardedly optimistic about retaining the present status of the delivery permits, or even softening them somewhat. But he could offer no encouragement in the case of corrugated boxes or florists' wire.

A new Handy Book was issued in 1944, despite the wartime worries. Double the size of the preceding edition, it contained 400 pages and listed more than 106,000 towns and cities. The issue of 8,200 copies, containing many maps of service areas, was the most ambitious edition of this invaluable florists' tool yet attempted. It was especially helpful in the handling of thousands of overseas orders received by the Armed Forces Order Division.

At the March, 1944, meeting, President Joy announced the death of two veteran members of FTD. They were Past President Frank Baker, former Mayor of Utica, New York, and Herman Knoble, of Cleveland, the former director who did much in the early days of the Association to apprise members of the financial details of the industry and who served long and well as the first chairman of the Clearing House Committee.

Since the enormous increase in the overseas business over the Christmas holidays, the Armed Services Committee, under Victor L. Scott, had been busy preparing for the coming Easter and Mother's Day orders. On the basis of past experience, the estimate was 80,000 orders for Easter and 120,000 for Mother's Day. To be ready for this, it was decided that more space was needed. Arrangements were made to move the New York FTD offices to 480 Lexington Avenue, New York. John Besemer superintended the move. It was not a day too soon and, even with the expanded work area, the staff was hard put to keep pace with the flood of orders. In the period from the March Board meeting until after the second Sunday in May, which was Mother's Day, the New York FTD office staff accepted and redistributed more than 720,000 overseas orders for flowers. These were received from the Army Exchange Service on long lists. Order forms had to be typed from these lists. Each order had to be checked for errors and then allocated to the proper FTD member.

At times, more than 20,000 orders were delivered, processed and routed in one day. Total amount of this business was almost $4 million.

When things quieted down, plans were begun for the Christmas business. It was realized that a limit must be put on the amount of orders that could be accepted. Rationing, definite quotas and other war-familiar plans were suggested, but each of these had a connotation that was not compatible with the thought of flowers. It was finally decided to set an early time limit for the taking of orders in the posts overseas. This date was set tentatively at November 1, 1944, and the Army Exchange Service advised all posts that, to assure proper delivery for Christmas, overseas flower orders must be in the hands of the FTD New York office on or before December 15, 1944.

The success of the overseas flowers-by-wire project went much farther than the most optimistic imaginations could have pictured it. It furnished the soldier with a dream-visit to his family and loved ones. It supplied a release from tension to a man who lived with tension. When the soldier placed his order, he became for that moment a creator of beauty in a stark world, and the fragrance of his gift drove from his mind the sordid scent of war. To the recipient, the loveliness of the gift and the thought behind it brought something of the presence of the sender and, across the reaches of an ocean, two separated loved ones were suddenly close together through the simple sincerity of a gift of flowers.

So psychologically beneficial was the flowers-by-wire program for the men overseas, that the Army Engineer Corps made a short film, showing a soldier placing an order for flowers. The film followed the order through until it was received, then showed the pleasure the gift caused at home. This picture was made available to Special Service officers wherever soldiers were stationed.

The commanding officer of one European post wrote, "I feel that the flower service is proving most helpful to the men who wish to send a remembrance to relatives or friends and who would be unable to do so without the arrangement which has been established through your organization." Surveys, made 15 years later, found ex-soldiers who remembered, and still used, this FTD service.

The summer of 1944 was a season of paradoxes. On June 6, allied forces landed in Normandy, establishing the beachhead which the Germans could not dislodge. All the news from Europe, both in France and Italy, was of success.

But at home, consumer goods grew shorter in supply, the pinch of government restrictions grew tighter and the production of war goods accelerated to a feverish pace.

On August 25, 1944, American and French troops marched into Paris and, by September 11, the Americans were on German soil. The end of the war was thought by many to be in sight. On October 20, General MacArthur returned to the Philippines. On both sides of the world, the enemy was in retreat.

The agenda for the Board meeting in November, 1944, was not too heavy. It was definite that no convention could have been held and enough members had expressed themselves to forestall any idea of a streamlined meeting. Units of Region 2 especially requested that no sort of meeting be held which would interfere with New York City as the site of the first postwar convention.

As an indication of approaching Christmas business, the overseas load had already reached 125,000 orders and the quarters at 480 Lexington Avenue, where between 50 and 60 persons were employed, appeared inadequate. Properly to handle the Pacific business, a Navy office had been opened in Seattle, similar to the New York operation.

With the end of the war imminent, serious discussion was given over to postwar planning. FTD was in a unique position. Through the simplicity of the flowers-by-wire plan, by which a soldier could send a gift to America without the inconvenience of packing, mailing and worrying about its safe arrival, the Association had built a foreign business that was phenomenal.

During the time of the actual hostilities it had been, of necessity, handled through co-operation with the armed forces. But with the cessation of fighting, it was probable that the business would revert to the practices of all free enterprise countries and depend on the effort expended. To let this volume of orders be lost through neglect or through lack of facilities would be a catastrophe.

That FTD was aware of its duty and the task before it is shown in the address delivered by Victor L. Scott, chairman of the FTD Post-War Committee, to the SAF convention in Chicago in the summer of 1944. In his talk, Scott detailed his committee's suggestions for a complete postwar industry plan.

This envisioned the establishment of an industry-wide central office, under the direction of an executive manager, which would, through a governing board of directors, formulate and direct advertising, public relations, marketing control, business management and other elements for the stabilization of the industry for a successful future.

To implement this central office, it was suggested that FTD

subscribe $100,000 and SAF a like amount, with other organizations contributing as their abilities permitted.

"It would be most unfortunate," said Scott, "if our industry were to lose many of the advantages gained during the present era when many definite improvements have been made in the air of government controls. If we are to maintain and improve our present position in the industry, it is vital that we do not return to the previous haphazard and individualistic basis of operation which was more or less the same at the beginning of the war as it was 25 years previous, in spite of the fact that most other industries had found it necessary to organize themselves in order to maintain a successful effort."

He drew a plan of advertising, public relations and marketing which would enable the industry to sell more flowers to more customers. He projected a system of marketing areas, each supervised by a member of the board of the greater industry plan, where, through contact and co-operation, the factors of production, distribution and grading could be standardized. Shortages in one area could be met by transportation from other localities. Supply and demand could be predicted and the result would be more and better flowers, at prices which would attract more customers, thus broadening the service potential of the industry and making fresh flowers available to a greater part of the population.

With this plan would go a program of scientifically conducted clinics and research projects for all members of the industry, to improve accounting, growing, distributing, advertising and marketing, for the betterment of the entire industry.

Particular care would be taken in organizing this plan, so that no one branch of the industry could dominate, by money or membership, the affairs of the organization; but that democratic principles of government should everywhere prevail.

Scott reported that SAF was then conducting a campaign

to raise money for its own promotion work, but that they had declared any funds they could raise above those for their own program would be placed in a fund which they hoped to build for "Flower Industries, Inc." This was the name chosen by the Post-War Committee for the projected organization.

Scott told the SAF convention, "It is the sincere desire and hope of the directors of the Florists' Telegraph Delivery Association that the Society of American Florists will agree to work with us and together we may be the common means of bringing about a better and greater industry in the post-war period. Our committee stands ready to meet with the committee from the SAF and make plans, so that together in harmony and comradeship, we can lay the cornerstone of a greater structure."

This was an ambitious and far-reaching program. It was a plan to apply the principles of industrial engineering to horticulture, just as government agencies were later to direct the production and distribution of agricultural commodities. That the program never came to fruition is due to no inherent lack of merit or of enthusiasm on the part of its promulgators.

A development that gained FTD wide publicity during 1944, and established it forever in the hearts and memories of servicemen, was the work of the Armed Services Seed Committee. In co-operation with Burpee Seed Company, this committee had packets of flower seed prepared to send to soldiers in rear camps overseas, on the theory that planting and cultivating flowers would alleviate the tedium of inaction.

When this was proposed to Army officials, they suggested that it first be tried on inmates of hospitals in this country, where men wounded in battle were recuperating. Its success was almost immediate. Later on, packets were prepared containing 12 varieties of annuals, including calendulas, poppies, cosmos, cornflowers, two varieties of marigolds, nasturtiums, petunias, zinnias, mixed annuals and sweet alyssum. These were packaged in red, white and blue envelopes imprinted, "With the compliments and best wishes from the Florists' Telegraph Delivery Association, Inc., 484 East Grand Boulevard, Detroit, Michigan." They were delivered to each contingent of soldiers or sailors which left for overseas duty. The reaction from men and officers was most gratifying. More than $15,000 was spent on this program.

The Board of Directors met in January, 1945, forsaking the wartime plan of three meetings a year and returning to the schedule of a meeting in January in Detroit and again before and after the convention. The war was not over, but there was every indication that it would not last much longer. The heavyhearted days of the "Battle of the Bulge" were over. Germany had spent herself in that one last struggle. The end was imminent. The Board could proceed cautiously with its postwar planning.

The principal work accomplished by the directors at this meeting was a review of the Bylaws and the adoption of suggestions for their modernization and broadening. This would enable FTD to enter the postwar period with unhampered plans for expansion at home and, especially, into the fertile foreign fields so recently pioneered by American soldiers. With this task completed, the meeting adjourned.

As wars end, history moves swiftly. On April 28, 1945, Mussolini was captured and executed by Italian partisans. On the next day, the German army in Italy surrendered. Berlin, caught in the pincers between converging Allied and Russian armies, capitulated after being almost bombed out of existence during May 1 and 2, 1945. Weary German commanders announced that Hitler had shot himself and his wife, Eva Braun, in their impregnable concrete bunker near the Chancellory. May 7 saw the final unconditional surrender of all German forces in the field. "VE Day" was proclaimed, May 8, 1945. One phase of the combat was over.

Halfway around the world, desperate Japanese forces were preparing to defend their home islands against the invasion they knew they could not prevent. But already in their future was a terror so ghastly in its power that few minds in the world could conceive of it.

A super fortress streaked through the skies, high above Hiroshima, on August 6, 1945. The bomb bay opened and, out of the dark cavern of the speeding plane, a new age fell upon the helpless city below. In a flash of fire and unimagined force, the Atomic Age was born as a city disappeared in a surge of white heat that rivaled the surface of the sun. Only the stunned disbelief of the Japanese postponed their surrender to August 14, 1945.

Motorists riding down the streets in rationed America, listening to their car radios on August 15, heard the government announcement that gasoline rationing was ended. Whether they needed gasoline or not, long lines of motorists pulled into filling stations and ordered, "Fill 'er up!" until the station tanks were empty. Laughing attendants stood in their driveways waving grinning drivers on to other stations. The long war was over. All rationing would soon end and normal times were just around the corner.

But no war ends suddenly. Ahead lay long months and years of occupation and readjustment, and a generation of Americans was to be stationed abroad.

The influence of these military men and women on the peoples they lived among would be long and lasting. It remained for the Florists' Telegraph Delivery Association to exploit this opportunity to spread the message of flowers-by-wire to all the lands of Europe, through the legions of Americans and Canadians who already understood the pleasure of expressing emotions through the gift of flowers bestowed a half-world away.

International organization was the key to the future. Toward this goal the energies and influence of FTD were turned.

CHAPTER FOURTEEN

Extending The Service

S A WAVE STRIKES the shore and recedes into the waters from which it arose, so the wave of soldiers that America and Canada had sent to Europe began to recede toward its homelands, almost as soon as the armistice was signed. Many of these did not return alone. They came, bringing brides from England, France, Italy, Scandinavia and wherever Allied troops had been stationed. Thus, the ties between America and Europe were multiplied and strengthened. Many thoughts would continue to flow across the ocean.

The burgeoning families of the foreign brides in America would present ample opportunities for floral gifts to new mothers, and birthdays and anniversaries in the old countries would stir the sentiments that only flowers can express. Later, the same would be true of brides from Hawaii, Japan and Australia. It was imperative that the progress in international business, accomplished during the war, be prevented from returning to former haphazard procedures. A strong and well-integrated international organization was needed, built upon a high plane of ethics and co-operation, with an equal division of responsibilities and rights and a firm purpose to turn war-created opportunities into lasting benefits.

On June 22, 1945, President Joy called a meeting of the International Committee in New York to outline a plan of international co-operation to be presented to the president of the British Unit, John Hunt, and his officers, and to Elfried Stump, president of Fleurop, and his officials. Three tentative plans of action were drawn to serve as a basis of negotiations with the European groups. The principal purpose of each plan was "to extend and enlarge world flowers-by-wire service. The committee agrees that the possibilities of increasing our services are now unlimited."

This blueprint of the proposed organization contained plans for apportioning the interest of each of the three groups, for the manner in which meetings would be held, for the financial structure and for a general statement governing the formation and employment of an advertising fund to be applied in all the member countries.

Almost immediately upon the completion of the plan, Victor L. Scott, chairman of the Post-War Committee, left for Europe with John Besemer. They first visited Hunt in Dundee, where they were enthusiastically received by a group which included Geoffrey Lewis, of London, vice-president of the FTD British Unit. To the surprise of the Americans, it was found that the British group was more advanced in its thinking along international lines than the visitors were.

In a conference with the British, a memorandum was drawn up outlining the plan agreed upon between the two groups. This was to be presented to the representatives of Fleurop for their consideration. But it was agreed between the American and British members that, if Fleurop did not desire to come into the organization, the various national associations which made up Fleurop would be invited to join. If this was not successful, the leading private florists in the continental European countries were to receive invitations, either to join the British Unit or to join the plan on their own. This arrangement seemed to imply some doubt that Fleurop would be wholeheartedly favorable to the projected association.

Armed with this agreement and the good wishes of the British Unit, Scott and Besemer went to Zurich, where they were welcomed by Elfried Stump, the president of Fleurop, Secretary Max Schneider and other officials and members of the continental group. Any fears the Americans might have felt about the attitude of Fleurop were quickly calmed by Stump and Schneider who, like Hunt and Lewis, had thoroughly considered the formation of such an association and were elated that the strength of FTD could be depended upon for the furtherance of the plan. They privately promised the full co-operation of their association. But, officially, it was necessary for them to solicit the concurrence of each national group before a firm commitment could be given. They foresaw no difficulty there. This was a distinct achievement for Scott and Besemer.

Returning to Britain, the Americans met again with the British officials and a detailed plan of incorporation of the new association was perfected. This plan accepted as a fact the future co-operation of the American and British branches of FTD, with the assimilation of national groups or individual European florists, if Stump was unable to deliver the organized affiliation of Fleurop.

A world emblem and slogan were deemed essential. A provisional title, "Flowers International," was considered for the purposes of organization. Spheres of influence of the participants were to be charted. The rules of the international association were to control the conduct of all business inside the organization. Standard policies, procedures and currencies were to be established, all looking to the general purpose expressed, "To organize, promote and direct a world-wide flower relay service."

The financial structure of the new association was to be that of a stock corporation, incorporated under the laws of the state of Michigan and capitalized at $100,000. Of this amount, FTD was to subscribe $50,000; the British Unit, $10,000; and Fleurop, $10,000; with $30,000 left unsubscribed. This last provision left open the possible subsequent acceptance of other national or continental groups wishing to affiliate with the international organization.

Control of the new association was to be vested in a Board

of Directors, composed of three members each from FTDA, FTDA British Unit, and Fleurop. There would also be an advisory body called the World Federal Council of the International Association, to be composed of one member from each national unit.

The plan was submitted to the Executive Committee of the British Unit, before Scott and Besemer left England, and their full approval was obtained. The British members were impatient to see the new association established. As evidence of the full participation of British and American groups, the following memorandum was signed before the FTD representatives left for New York:

"Agreement between the British Unit and the FTD Association (America), for the promotion of world-wide flowers-by-wire service. It is agreed that funds shall be made available immediately as follows:

BRITISH UNIT..............................$ 4,000
FTDA 20,000

To be put aside for organization and promotion expenses of world-wide flowers-by-wire service.

Signed on behalf of: FTDA

Victor L. Scott
John M. Besemer
BRITISH UNIT
John Hunt
G. P. Lewis"

On their return to America, Scott and Besemer communicated the results of the British meeting to President Stump in Zurich, outlining the plan and concluding: "Because in our opinion there are many orders which will be sent as soon as normal trade relations with Europe and other world groups can be resumed, may we respectfully urge you to call a meeting of your International Committee and the presidents of your national groups, as quickly as possible, in order that there may be no delay in establishing this world-wide flower service?"

When the FTD Board of Directors met in Detroit, September 24 and 25, 1945, consideration of the international plan was the principal order of business. Surprisingly, opposition to the plan was manifested by various members of the Board. Victor L. Scott was detained in Winnipeg by illness. The burden of convincing the directors of the efficacy of the plan, with its fairness and its future, fell on John Besemer.

There seemed to be two main objections to the plan: one, the disproportionate amount of money to be invested by FTD and the contributions of the other two groups; and two, the equal representation of the three groups on the Board of Directors. Some directors felt, since FTD was contributing the lion's share of the capital of the association, it ought to be represented in proportion to its investment.

Besemer pointed out the danger of insisting on an uneven division of the Board. "We did not go over there with the idea, 'We are the big shots around here and we want everything our way.' We tried to give and take, in order to arrive at some international understanding. The easiest way would be to give the management to the three respective groups, irrespective of the amount of capital they have invested. If anything ever happened, we still would have $50,000 worth of stock, and we could take the thing over ourselves — the whole business."

Besemer further argued for disproportionate investment by showing the Board that the membership of the participants was also disproportionate. FTD had approximately 6,500 members. The FTD British Unit had only about 1,000 and Fleurop, in all continental Europe, could count only about 2,500 florists as members.

Certain directors remained unconvinced. They advanced the idea that if a Canadian member of FTD were to be elected to the Board, the chances were strong that he would vote with the British members, thus giving that Unit four votes to only two votes for the Americans.

Ernest Simmons, of Toronto, pointedly allayed fears on that score. "As far as Canada is concerned," he stoutly maintained, "we are an independent nation — a part of a commonwealth, it is true — but I think you can well feel sure that any representative you might have from Canada in this group would be much closer to the interests of the United States than to any of the foreign parts of Europe, or to England. I do not think you need have any misapprehensions in that regard."

And so the discussion ran for the better part of two days. In the end, John Hunt, who had come over from Dundee to attend this meeting, stated flatly, "When Vic Scott and John Besemer agreed to the '3-3-3' principle, we were very happy indeed, and I am quite certain that, had you asked for more, my members would not have accepted." This made success or failure of the plan specifically depend on the equal division of the Board of Directors in the new association.

Vernon R. Frank, of Decatur, Georgia, entered the impasse with: "Mr. President, may I speak one word? I think this will be an investment, and it will be a money-making proposition; and if it is a money-making proposition, we will share five times in the profits to England's once, regardless of the number of votes."

Vernon Frank, after further debate, moved that the Board adopt the plan as suggested by the committee. Ernest Simmons seconded this motion. Suddenly, Charles I. Kent broke in with, "Right here may we interrupt and get some idea on how the British Unit adopted it? Was it at a general meeting, or piecemeal? Or, just how did the British Unit go about the adoption of that? We have a membership of 6,600 odd that we have to satisfy, and we would like to know if we can use the same yardstick in getting the approval of their membership."

John Hunt explained, "We had the thing considered and

called a council or Board meeting. We notified every member of the plan, and told him that the Board meeting was being held on a given day; if they objected to the plan, if there was any question to ask about the plan, that they write us before the Board meeting, and the Board would consider their views." Hunt's thickly-burred Scots voice rose a little. "We had only two letters and both of them said words to the effect, 'It's damn high time it was here.' Only two letters! The Board considered the matter. They thrashed it out as you are doing now, and after that I was authorized to sign on their behalf."

Once more John Besemer read the plan from beginning to end to refresh the memories of the directors. "Gentlemen," announced President Joy, "I think it is time we voted, unless you want some more information." Apparently the Board was satisfied. Voting was by a show of hands and the plan carried. There was one dissenting vote.

After a full day and a half of earnest consideration and discussion, FTD had taken a momentous step. The union of the three strongest flowers-by-wire services into a single, integrated association, combining the outlets and service facilities of the world's leading florists, was unique in the history of industries based upon the distribution of a perishable commodity. Out of it was to come a system of distribution that functioned without regard to the problems of international currency exchange, or the boundaries between nations. For beauty has no bounds and fragrance cannot be fettered. The blessing of flowers is for the entire world. With full knowledge of the facts and a solid basis for previewing its course, the international plan had been adopted because it was a sound, progressive and natural step.

Despite the time devoted to the organization of the international association at the September, 1945, Board meeting, there were other important decisions made. The National Florists' Advisory Council, which had functioned so zealously in guarding the rights and interests of florists throughout the war period, was disbanded. This group, consisting of Samuel S. Pennock, Jr., William E. Joy, Charles I. Kent, Granville Gude and Robert Roland, had done great service in keeping before the rationing and control officials in Washington the minimum requirements of the entire florist industry.

Moreover, they had kept those officials acquainted with the contributions to the war effort, in terms of morale, money and man power, which had been made by the floral industry. As a result, even though rationing and shortages had cut deeply into the supplies and delivery facilities of the shop owners, the industry had been able not only to stay alive but to expand enormously into markets not considered practicable before. With the end of rationing, the reason for the existence of the council disappeared and, with the thanks of the entire membership, it was disbanded.

It was also decided at this meeting to return to the individual florists their share of the emergency deposit fund which had been collected by a levy of 10 per cent on wire orders. The need for this fund had also disappeared. In the dark days, when FTD money was tied up in Europe, and the amazing flood of soldier orders from war camps made a greater sum necessary for the operation of the Clearing House, this money had assured the payments to members. Now that the emergency was over, the money was made available to those who had so willingly consented to its use by FTD.

Also disbanded was the Post-War Committee. All its educational programs were turned over to the Sales and Advertising Committee. One of the worthwhile projects, initiated by this committee, had been the establishment of a fully equipped florist shop at Percy Jones Hospital in Battle Creek, Michigan, the pioneer rehabilitation clinic for wounded service personnel. Regular floral design classes were held and interested veterans had opportunity for practice.

Doctors and officers at the hospital were high in their praise of the therapeutic value of these classes to handicapped men and women. Several dramatic stories of complete recoveries by maimed or shocked soldiers came out of this school.

The Board meeting of September, 1945, was adjourned with the observance of a period of silence in respect for Irwin Bertermann, second secretary and second president of FTD, who had died on June 8, 1945.

It would be hard to estimate the value of this man's contribution to the Association. He was one of the 15 men who met on August 18, 1910, in the Seneca Hotel in Rochester, New York, to call the Association into being. He made the motion to adopt the original Constitution and Bylaws, promulgated by John Valentine. It was he who resigned as secretary, only to find himself elected president, when other officers and directors were resigning from pure apathy toward the new Association.

Through all the years of his membership, he had been a rock of strength and wisdom, never questioning the future of the Association and never slackening in his devotion to the industry. To the last, he was planning for the years ahead, in which he foresaw the progress of the aviation industry adapted to the swift distribution of flowers. It is a measure of his foresight that the air lines now carry, in daily flights, orchids from Hawaii to California, flowers from California to Puerto Rico, carnations from Denver and flowers from mid-America to all the markets of the continent.

The field service operation, which was a part of the Sales and Advertising Department, had entered the year of 1944 with four field men: Willis B. Corwin, James P. O'Malley, Erwin Hamme and James E. Kelly. These were more properly called "field representatives." They were the men who, during the war, were principally concerned with the organization of delivery pools and other war conservation measures, as applied to the florist industry. Theirs had not been too happy a lot during the hectic days of the war.

Shortages of tires and gasoline had forced them to give up their automobiles and resort to buses and trains to cover their territories. The inefficiency and lost time occasioned in scheduled transportation had greatly handicapped their work. But their enthusiasm did not waver and they continued, as best they could, in their rounds of individual shop owners. The fact that they were called to Washington to advise the Office of Defense Transportation on the establishment of delivery and transportation pools is a measure of their zeal and attention to details.

The tradition of the field men in FTD is one of the oldest in the Association, beginning with the employment of L. F. Darnell, on February 1, 1919. While his work was principally to secure new members for FTD, he also, through his experience in the florist business, was able to advise shop owners on the conduct of their business, on advertising, customer relations, marketing and many other phases of flower retailing. It was quickly recognized that Darnell's work, and that of others who might come after, carried the potential of uniformity in an industry which tended to be stubbornly individualistic.

Following Darnell's tenure, J. Fred Ammann, who had been president of SAF, assumed the post of field man for FTD. Ammann was also an experienced florist. He had a considerable growing business at Edwardsville, Illinois. His title later was changed to "field manager," but his duties closely resembled those of a modern field service representative, combined with the recruiting work initiated by Darnell. Edward Sceery, FTD's first "traveling president," spent much time in the field with Ammann and praised his work highly. He was the first president to bring sharply to the attention of the Board of Directors the importance of constant liaison among the Detroit Headquarters, the Board of Directors and the full membership.

Ammann was forced to resign as field manager by the press of his own business. For a time FTD was without any representation in the field. By 1930, the growth of a rival organization on the West Coast began to concern FTD members in that area. So it was decided to revive the field service work. E. H. Toepke was the only representative in the field from 1930 to 1936, and his efforts were confined to California and the other West Coast states.

With the resignation of Toepke, FTD was left without a field force for the second time. This condition continued until early in 1941 when Paul C. Kimball, the new sales director, reconstituted the field service force by engaging five field service representatives. Willis B. Corwin was re-engaged and four new men, Barnum Coolidge, John J. Jones, Herbert E. Palaith and Ralph Robinson, were hired. In September of that year, E. H. Toepke returned to the fold. This made a total of six field men, the nucleus of the present field organization.

During the days of war rationing, with all the demands of draft boards and other war-created emergencies, this force shrank to three. By the time the war was over, the force had again risen to five. One of these men was Erwin Hamme, still a member of the field representative staff today, who was on leave of absence to counsel ODT on delivery pools. The field force has constantly grown in numbers, in the qualifications of its personnel, and in service to the membership.

Before the Board of Directors adjourned in September, 1945, they voted to continue the seed distribution program, which had so importantly added to the recreational activities of veterans' hospitals over the country. General Bethea, of McCloskey Hospital in Temple, Texas, wrote: "On behalf of the staff and patients of McCloskey, please express our thanks to each member of your Association for this tangible evidence that you remember and appreciate what these wounded heroes have done for us all."

Another letter said: "Even the toughest soldier, although he may not show it, has an inner appreciation for the beauty of flowers."

Such expressions were enough to prove the morale value of the simple gifts of flower seeds and to spur the directors to extend the service. The Graves Registration Corps of the United States Army was engaged in locating the burial places of Americans slain in battle and removing the bodies to military cemeteries abroad, to be returned to the United States at the desire of relatives. The commanding officer of the Corps expressed a wish for flower seeds for the beautification of the new cemeteries. FTD responded with a gift of 33,807 packets for the use of graves registration groups all over the world. As a result, the relatives of those who lie in foreign fields may be solaced to think that over their dead bloom flowers from the lands for which they gave their final gift, with the colors of the flags for which they fought forever reproduced in the living beauty of flowers.

With the meeting of January 22 and 23, 1946, the Board of Directors returned to its old plan of meeting in January and again before and after the annual convention. It had been decided that the convention would be held, although the current hotel situation made impossible the guarantee of sufficient space for the convention and the trade fair. Besemer suggested as a practical plan that the Associate Division hold an open booth fair, utilizing the hotel ballroom instead of private quarters, as in the past. These details, however, were left for later resolution. The important thing was that the annual meetings were to be resumed after five years.

General Manager Besemer's report to the Board was short, but it was long enough to contain some humor. Of the $657,000 remaining in the emergency deposit fund, which had been collected from members to finance the war orders from Europe, $602,000 still remained unclaimed. Only $55,000 had been returned. It seemed that the members knew a good investment when they made one. This amount was lying in FTD's coffers and paying 4 per cent interest to the members who had contributed it. At this rate, FTD was paying over $26,000 a year interest on money it no longer needed. The Board quickly voted to return the money to the members before the end of June.

The overseas business, which had been so profitable during the active days of the war, continued, though reduced in volume. Almost $1 million had been cleared through FTD on this business in the six months preceding the meeting of the Board. Almost a third of this represented the Christmas trade alone. Most of this came direct to the FTD offices through Mackay Radio. With the establishment of permanent occupation posts in Germany, much of the European business was channeled through "Deutsche Bundespost," allied with the American PX's. These orders were transmitted through RCA Radio.

The question of the international organization was again discussed in detail. David Roberts, legal counsel, had drafted the Constitution and Bylaws of the proposed corporation, which he presented to the Board at this meeting. Many of the same old objections were raised again and were thoroughly threshed out. The conclusion was that the international organization be incorporated. The name adopted at this meeting was "World Wide Flowers, Incorporated." Roberts said the name would remain subject to change by the directors but that some name was required for the incorporation. Actually, Articles of Association were filed under the name of "International Telegraph Florists, Inc." The directors were to serve for terms of four, three and two years, and three were to be elected. President Joy called for nominations. Willmore F. Holbrow, of Dorchester, Mass., was elected for the four-year term; Charles I. Kent, of Cleveland, for three years; and Alfred H. Serveau, of San

Francisco, for a two-year term. William E. Joy served as an ex officio member during the remainder of his term as president of FTD.

This was an important forward move. Much planning and revamping of the new association would have to be done before it approached the smooth operation of FTD. But the launching of the new project placed the horizon of FTD in Eastern Europe and added an entire continent to the service area of American and Canadian retail florists.

The organization of the international association did another thing of perhaps even more importance. It demonstrated that the thoughts of florists go far beyond the walls of their shops or their immediate delivery area. Through planning and co-operation, they have developed a method of retailing a fragile and delicate commodity over the entire world. No other purveyors of perishable products have ever been able to match the system.

The work of the field men had increased steadily since the removal of rationing. During 1945, they made 2,283 member calls and visited 104 non-members, also making more than 90 special investigations for the Membership Department. According to Ernest Simmons, chairman of the Sales and Advertising Committee under which the field men worked at that time, the work would be accelerated during the coming year. In a meeting at Detroit in December, Harold Hewey and the members of the field staff had analyzed the needs of the membership. This information was desired by Hewey as a basis of laying out the specific work of the men in the field for the next year. Reports showed that instruction was needed in accounting and costs, salesmanship, store management and local sales promotion.

With the help of the field men, business clinics were scheduled for Little Rock, Atlanta and Houston in February, and for Albany in March. These clinics proved to be so helpful to those who attended that it was decided to continue until convention time. Twelve clinics were held, with more than 1,000 shop owners or managers taking advantage of the lectures and information offered. Instruction was given by outstanding bankers, accountants, personnel directors and sales promotion consultants, engaged by FTD because of experience and ability at analyzing florists' problems and supplying simple, logical solutions.

Besides these clinics, the field men, both on their personal visits and in their printed reports in the FTD NEWS, encouraged retailers to discuss their problems. The experience and training of the men in the field, and the ideas which they picked up in their contacts with other florists, often came to the aid of a troubled merchant. This was the function of the field representatives. They were able to elevate the level of merchandising, sales promotion and customer relations for the entire region they served. An incidental advantage was the development of a more co-operative attitude among florists, a readier interchange of sales and merchandising ideas and a strong loyalty of the members to the Association.

Events moved swiftly toward the New York convention dates of August 19 through 22, 1946. As the time approached, it could be seen that all was not as smooth as expected. Curbed wartime travel across the Atlantic had kept New York City crowded almost beyond its capacity. There seemed little chance that this pressure would subside before August. By the middle of May, more than 1,000 hotel reservations had been filed with the New York Convention and Visitors' Bureau. So the problem of finding more room for florists was acute. The FTD NEWS, in its June issue, carried a feature story on the coming convention and detailed the trouble which members might encounter if they did not make hotel reservations immediately.

With innumerable last minute changes because of the crowded conditions of the city, the FTD NEWS was not able to print a program of the convention. However, the Convention Committee gave constant attention to the hotel situation, assuring undecided members that rooms would be found if they made last minute plans to attend. By careful co-ordination, all convention visitors were accommodated.

The FTD convention opened on August 19, 1946, in the ballroom of the Hotel Commodore in New York. This was the "victory convention," the first annual meeting of the membership since 1941. Almost 4,000 persons attended, despite the unpleasantness of crowded transportation systems and the distances many had to travel.

The FTD members were welcomed to New York by Mayor William O'Dwyer, and his address was answered by FTD's own Angelo J. Rossi, who had served 13 years as mayor of San Francisco. After the opening formalities, the convention got down to serious business. There was much work to be done after a hiatus of five years.

In his address to the members, President Joy reviewed the past five years and called attention to the progress which FTD had made, even through the darkest days of the war. In the years since the last convention, the gross clearings of sales had risen from $8,788,959 to $30,822,257, an increase of 400 per cent over the 1941 figure. He noted the valuable work that the field men had done, both in building the membership in times of adversity and in aiding present members in their rationing and merchandising problems.

The membership in 1946 amounted to 7,210, including active, associate and foreign members, compared with 6,975 in 1941. This was not a remarkable growth unless viewed against the history of the period. Then it assumed importance. Many retail associations had suffered severe losses in membership during this time.

The formation of the international organization, advances in advertising and public relations, the rehabilitation program for handicapped servicemen and the seed donations to the Graves Registration Corps were all mentioned as accomplishments of his administration. Joy concluded by saying:

"We have every right to be thankful for the progress of the last six years. It has not been the achievement of any individual or a small group; it is the product of the co-operation of all."

President Joy, at the conclusion of his talk, introduced the foreign visitors present. These included: John Hunt, president of the FTD British Unit, recently elected president of International Telegraph Florists, Inc.; Geoffrey P. Lewis, vice-president of the British Unit; and Robert Fowler, Jr., another vice-president of the same group. Also there from across the Atlantic were Carl Jorgenson, of Copenhagen, and Cornelius Thim, of Amsterdam. Elfried Stump, of Zurich, president of Fleurop, had been expected, but following a meeting of the international organization in Copenhagen, he had gone on to Stockholm to visit members in that Swedish city and had succumbed to a heart attack while there. Representing Fleurop at the New York convention was Max Schneider, of Zurich, the secretary of the European organization.

The convention accomplished a great amount of work in the 2-day meeting. There was a soberness and a tenseness about the group that was not characteristic.

Little of the good fellowship of pre-war days affected the deliberations on the floor. The 5-year period since the last meeting had exposed some serious weaknesses in the Bylaws of FTD. The Board, meeting in January, 1945, had reviewed the weaknesses and suggested changes to be brought up at the convention.

It was the adoption or rejection of these suggested changes that occupied most of the time of the meeting. One amendment to the Articles of Association was adopted. Forty-two amendments to the Bylaws were offered; 31 were adopted, nine were defeated, and two were eliminated. These decisions took much time. Charles H. Grakelow was often on his feet, questioning incisively and demanding explanations of the need and the reasons for the changes offered. His was another demonstration of the loyal gadfly technique, often employed by serious FTD members when issues were hazy or background lacking on certain questions. At the end of the meeting, Will Holbrow thanked Grakelow for his "wonderful array of questions." There is no doubt that the votes of the members were founded upon full knowledge of the issues.

The principal changes introduced into the Articles and Bylaws were:

Clearing House fee reduced from 2 per cent to one per cent, effective with current clearings.

Maximum dues shall not exceed $50 per year regardless of the volume of net incoming orders handled.

Each member must issue a receipt to every customer for each cash FTD order at the time the purchase is made.

Membership shall not be granted to owners of shops operating temporarily in locations where there are one or more active members of the Association in good standing.

No active, associate, or grower member shall permit the use of the Florists' Telegraph Delivery Association membership list by any non-members for any purpose.

No ex-presidents shall be eligible to hold any elective office in the Association for a period of three years subsequent to the end of their terms on the Board of Directors as past-presidents; and regional directors shall not be eligible to succeed themselves as regional directors for a period of three years subsequent to their elected terms on the Board of Directors.

In the event of the failure of the Association for any reason to hold an annual members' meeting, the election of regional directors shall be held as

In 1926, Secretary Albert Pochelon (standing left) and President Charles H. Brown (standing 3rd from left) visited Europe to sound out European florists on the subject of an international flowers-by-wire organization. Here they are with Scottish friends on the lawn of the Tarbet Hotel, Loch Lomond, Scotland.

The tour of Brown and Pochelon covered most of the cities in 12 European countries. Here they are given a reception in the grand manner by a group of Italian florists in Rome.

The original Board of Directors of Interflora as they met at New York City in 1946. Seated (l. to r.): J. M. Besemer, FTD general manager, Detroit; John Hunt, Dundee, head of overseas service; Edward J. McCarthy, Brooklyn, new president of FTD; standing: Geoffrey Lewis, London; Robert Fowler, Southampton; Carl Jorgensen, Copenhagen; Cornelius Thim, Amsterdam; Max Schneider, Zurich; Charles I. Kent of Cleveland and Willmore Holbrow of Boston, U. S. members of international governing board.

The Interflora Board, in session in London, 1959. Left to right: Jack Shearn, vice president, London; Jack Dobson, Glasgow, Scotland, past president; Eugene Daudelin, Chicago, FTD Interflora director; President-elect Victor Stein, San Francisco; Maurice Debrie, Paris, outgoing president; E. M. Deichman, Copenhagen; and Franz Kommer, Bremen, Fleurop representatives. Not shown in the picture is Harold Kayton of San Antonio, Tex., FTD Interflora director.

ORIGINAL INTERFLORA AGREEMENT

Hermed dokumenterer vi, at der i København d. 22. Juli 1946 af Repræsentanter for Fleurop, Florists' telegraph delivery Ass'n. British Unit og Florists' telegraph delivery Ass'n. America er grundlagt en Verdensforening for Forsendelse af Blomster.

Det er vort store Ønske gennem denne Forening at kunne styrke Venskabet mellem alle Nationer.

This commemorates the founding of The international telegraph florists association, organized to further the overseas business of all members of Florists' telegraph delivery Ass'n. British Unit, Florists' telegraph delivery Ass'n. America and Fleurop.

For our respective associations we pledge to further its interests so that the world may be better served, and the friendship of nations cemented through the medium of flowers.

Hiermit dokumentieren wir, dass am 22. Juli 1946 in Kopenhagen, durch die Vertreter der Fleurop, Florists' telegraph delivery Ass'n British Unit, Florists' telegraph delivery Ass'n America in feierlichen Weise eine weltumfassende Vereinigung zur Vermitlung von Blumenspenden gegründet worden ist.

Damit soll ein grosser Wunsch durch Blumenspenden die Freundschaft zwischen den Angehörigen aller Nationen zu verstärken, in Erfüllung gehen.

Copenhagen, 22th July 1946.

Fleurop.

Florists' telegraph delivery Ass'n.British Unit.

Florists' telegraph delivery Ass'n. America.

What appears to be the last page of an official document in Dutch, English and German is in reality the entire text of the original Interflora agreement signed in Copenhagen by representatives of Fleurop, FTD British Unit, and FTD. This was the official beginning of a trade agreement destined to make the international transmission of fresh flowers available to the entire western hemisphere, with eventual extension to the whole world.

provided in the Bylaws; and upon affidavit of the certified public accountant as to the result of such election, the secretary shall be empowered to certify such election, and such directors will take office at once.

It was plain that no more "frozen boards" were desired and the members, finding little fault with the actions of the Board during the preceding five years, felt that the constant rotation of directors made for a healthier situation and maintained members' interest in the conduct of affairs of the Association.

The "frozen board" during its 5-year tenure had worked hard. It had held meetings under trying circumstances. Its members had devoted many days, taken from their busy and shorthanded shops, to the affairs of FTD. They had faced many situations for which there were no precedents, either in the past of FTD or their own business experience. Decisions had been required almost upon the instant. That these were not always the best was due more to lack of time for full study than to any meagerness of ability or any imperiousness of attitude. The pace of war is rapid even for those who only stand and wait. Faced with the pressing problems and harsh conditions of a nation fighting for its existence, and representing an Association which the government had labelled "nonessential," the Board had succeeded in keeping its FTD members in business. That incomes and bulk of business grew greatly during this period, in spite of vital shortages, cannot all be credited to the enormous flow of money during the war. Part of it must be attributed to the management of the Association, which caused its members to benefit from the unusual temper of the times.

The election of officers and directors at this meeting was short. Votes had been cast for directors in 1941 and had been impounded, awaiting the time when the results could be announced to the assembly. When the ballots were opened at New York, it was found that Paul M. Carroll, Houston, Texas; Vernon Harris, Birmingham, Alabama; Allen W. Hixon, Worcester, Massachusetts; and James S. Wilson, Des Moines, Iowa, were to be the new members of the Board. The Associate Division elected James Sykora, of Chicago, their chairman.

Edward J. McCarthy, of Brooklyn, was named president; Mrs. Bert Schiller McDonald, Chicago, vice-president; and Eugene C. Butler, Niagara Falls, director-at-large. John Besemer continued as secretary and W. L. Rock as treasurer.

Ed McCarthy, the new president, was an outstanding florist and had been a member of FTD since 1920. His Irish wit made him a favorite with members everywhere. Once, in opening a convention, after the invocation had been given by the Right Reverend McCarthy, of Chicago, the president began, "Madam Chairman, Father McCarthy . . ." Then he hesitated. Turning to the priest, he said, "I hope I pronounced the name right!"

He was active in the affairs of the Benevolent and Protective Order of Elks in his native Brooklyn and had served as Exalted Ruler of his lodge. The regard in which he was held forecast a successful administration.

Although much was accomplished during the two days of the meeting, entertainment was not slighted. The New York committee had outdone itself in making the members' visit interesting. But the meeting was not the notable event that many had expected. Although a great number of amendments to the Bylaws had been adopted, it is probable that, if conventions had been held regularly during the war years, the exigencies of the times would have dictated these same changes. But they would have been made on a yearly basis, instead of all at once.

This ready adaptation to changed conditions has always been a characteristic of FTD. The Articles and Bylaws have never been considered traditional or permanent. Their susceptibility to change and the willingness of the members to adopt new provisions, or to substitute more modern procedures, has kept FTD a flexible and forward-looking organization, unfettered by outmoded rules. That this course is desirable is proved by the constant growth and progress of the Association.

Immediately following the convention, the first regular meeting of the Board of Directors of International Telegraph Florists was held. In attendance were: John Hunt, Dundee, Scotland, president of the new group; Willmore Holbrow, vice-president; John M. Besemer, secretary-treasurer; David Roberts, general counsel, and the following directors: Charles I. Kent and Alfred Serveau, representing FTD; Robert Fowler and Geoffrey Lewis, of the British Unit of FTD; and, representing Fleurop, Cornelius Thim, Amsterdam; Max Schneider, Zurich; and Carl Jorgensen, Copenhagen.

During an all-day meeting, the framework for an international service was composed. The service was to be in effect by November 1, 1946. One of the important accomplishments was the creation of an international monetary medium for use in the exchange of flower orders. This exchange unit was the "fleurin," equal to 25 cents in American money, with a rate to be established later in all countries served by the new organization. This "fleurin," with the ultimate stabilization of its exchange value in the markets of the world, became and still is the only currency freely accepted in world trade which is not backed by a sovereign government.

CHAPTER FIFTEEN

The Mid-Century

*A*MOVEMENT HAD BEEN on foot in FTD for several years to move the Headquarters offices into downtown Detroit. The building at 484 East Grand Boulevard had outlived its usefulness. Quarters were cramped. Extensive repairs to the building were imperative, and the expanding personnel required an easier access to restaurants, transportation and other facilities found only in a downtown location. The problem of prompt mail delivery, better obtained downtown, was also a factor.

A satisfactory buyer for the Grand Boulevard property was found and, on November 1, 1946, the Headquarters of the Association was moved to the second floor of the Lafayette Building, not far from Woodward Avenue, Detroit's principal thoroughfare. This new site was across the street from the Federal Building, containing the main Detroit Post Office, and a short stroll to the billion-dollar waterfront beautification project of the city.

The transfer of physical equipment, which included files, machines and countless items of office necessities, was no small task. It was accomplished without any interruption in the conduct of the Association's affairs. Office work ceased Thursday evening, October 31, and all office furniture was moved to the new location the next day. Members of the office staff came in on Saturday to put their desks in order. Business was resumed as usual on Monday, November 4, 1946.

Although the International Telegraph Florists had gone

into full operation, it had shown a loss by the time the Board met in January in Detroit. This was to be expected. Willmore F. Holbrow, vice-president of the new organization, presented a full report of the affairs of the group to the Board. There had been a great decrease in soldier orders from overseas. The Army Exchange Service had ceased to handle flower orders. But the Army, aware of the morale benefit of whatever orders the occupation troops wished to send, instructed Western Union, Mackay Radio and Commercial Cables to continue to accept flower orders, and to have them processed through International Telegraph Florists.

This was a victory for the new organization over any possible competitors in the international market, since it had official recognition by the Army.

A bank account had been opened in England to expedite the handling of business from Britain. Another was contemplated for Zurich for the use of Fleurop members. A separate office for ITF had been set up at 111 Broadway, New York, and the staffing and operation of this facility accounted for the greatest part of the loss shown on the balance sheet.

The balance sheet showed total assets of $91,640.67; liabilities of $38,220.07; for a total net worth of $53,420.60. The net loss in operations had been $16,579.40.

Holbrow emphasized the potential for business on Memorial Day and other holidays in wiring floral pieces for the decoration of the graves of American dead, more than 160,000 of whom slept in foreign fields.

Membership lists of European and British members of ITF had been supplied to FTD members in the United States and Canada, with complete instructions and order report forms. The future of ITF seemed promising. The Board thanked Holbrow heartily for his concise and interesting report. It was accepted unanimously.

One of the most far-reaching decisions made by the Board in 1947 was the complete mechanization of the Clearing

House operation through the leasing of a full complement of IBM electronic accounting machinery. According to John Besemer, the use of this equipment would cut the cost of operating the Clearing House from $750 to $1,000 a month. But it would also place more burden on the members, because reports would have to be rendered punctually on a weekly basis. Without this promptness, the advantage of the machines would disappear. Also in the installation of electronic machines, it was necessary to give each member a code number, so that the equipment could properly process all reports. This was the origin of the members' code number system, in use ever since.

The directors took another important step at this meeting, not without objection by some members. With the slackening of overseas soldier business and the reduction of the Clearing House discount to 1 per cent, it became impossible to continue the member service program in its present dimensions without impairing the capital of the Association. President McCarthy announced that there was enough money available to keep the program going for the remainder of 1947. But, after that, if no way of financing was found, it would have to be abandoned. No one wished to see that happen.

The member service program had been a double benefit to FTD. It had increased the members' interest in the organization and their consciousness of the advantages of belonging to FTD and adhering to its principles. And through design schools, merchandising aids, sales promotion instruction and other aspects of the service, the general quality of the entire retail florist operation had been improved. The member service program was producing better florists and better FTD members. It was imperative that it be continued.

To supply the needed funds, it was moved that an assessment of 4 cents on each outgoing FTD order be imposed on the members. Three directors expressed doubt that such an action would have the support of the membership. One Board member was in favor of increasing the assessment to

6 cents. The outcome of the discussion was that the Board adopted the 4-cent charge, three members dissenting; the continuance of that discount to depend upon the will of the membership, as expressed at the coming convention in Chicago. The assessment was effective immediately.

One other decision of the Board concerned the district representatives. Prior to the war, it had been the practice of the district representatives to meet at the annual convention. But rationing and travel difficulties had caused FTD to abandon this policy. Now that the war was over, several of the regions had forwarded resolutions to the Board, asking that these national meetings be resumed. Again, the directors were not in complete harmony.

It was argued that there was a lack of time properly to instruct the district representatives if their meeting was to be held concurrently with the convention. And to prolong the meeting an additional day would increase the expense of the members and of the convention. On the other hand, it was recognized that the district representatives received much helpful and wholesome information at the convention which they could take back to their districts. This increased their value to their constituents. And the members who could not attend the convention benefited from the knowledge brought them by the district representatives.

As a compromise, it was decided to have regional conventions in the zones where the national conventions were not scheduled. (Previously, the North American continent had been divided into five zones, among which the national conventions were to be rotated.) The district representative in each zone would be expected to attend his own regional convention during the first year of his 2-year tenure. And on the second year, he would be brought to the national convention. In this way, half of the district representatives would attend each national meeting.

The importance of the work of the district representatives had so impressed President McCarthy that he believed their activities should be co-ordinated with those of the field men and with the general membership supervision. Until this time, acceptance or rejection of new members and the disciplining of defaulting members had been wholly within the jurisdiction of the secretary of the Association.

One of McCarthy's first moves, after the crowded agenda of the 1946 convention had been covered, was to lay before the Board his plan for a new standing committee, the "Membership Committee." It would be the function of this group to pass upon the applications of prospective members and also to hear the appeals of rejected applicants. This accomplished three things. It eliminated the harshness of a one-man, unappealable rejection of an application by the secretary, based solely upon the report of the district representative. It established the Membership Committee as an intermediate appellate body on membership questions, with a further right of appeal to the Board of Directors. And it provided closer scrutiny by the Board of the immediate membership affairs of the Association.

The duties of the committee, as laid down in 1946, have not changed materially since. They have been altered only as dictated by conditions incident to changing times and growth. The formation of this committee was the origin of what is now known as the Membership Fulfillment Division of the national FTD Headquarters. This division is now a major branch of the Association.

Evidence that FTD had settled into a smooth and efficient postwar routine was seen in the rapid disposal of items on the business agenda for the national convention held in the Stevens Hotel in Chicago, on September 2 and 3, 1947. This was more like conventions of other days. The upsurge of business that followed the settlement of most of the world's diplomatic problems — for the time being — had cheered the members, enabling them to express their naturally optimistic and enthusiastic natures. The Chicago Convention Committee, headed by Laurent Clody, had made available all the facilities of that convention-wise city to the FTD visitors. To some degree, entertainment overshadowed the business deliberations of the Association.

Business affairs were by no means slighted. But FTD operations were running so smoothly that little change or improvement could be suggested. However, ample time was given to convention matters to enable everyone to speak his piece.

The establishment of the Membership Committee had proved a popular and valuable move. In the president's address to the members, McCarthy praised the work of this group. He also announced that of the $800,000 accumulated in the Clearing House reserve fund, a result of the 10 per cent assessment on members during the late war, $230,000 had been returned to members, which was approximately 30 per cent of the total. "This method of distribution of these reserves will continue," he stated, "without reducing the balance beyond a proper level.

"During the past year, the volume of business done was far in excess of the amount anticipated, and I am extremely happy to state that we reached the sum of $28 million," continued the president. "This really is proof that we are keeping up in front with our business, and I feel sure we shall keep up and very probably exceed this splendid record."

International Telegraph Florists was now firmly established under the name, "Interflora, Incorporated." The new title had been suggested by the European members on the theory that a name derived from the Latin would be more comprehensible to all the continental countries and would better convey the international idea. The wisdom behind this overseas organization had been proved on Memorial Day in 1947, when more than 2,500 floral pieces were wired to foreign countries to decorate the graves of war dead in United States and Canadian war cemeteries.

The meeting also heard that the Graves Registration

Corps, since the inauguration of the FTD flower seed program, had planted American flower seeds on 167,000 graves of American and Canadian dead, in 67 military cemeteries around the world. Letters from military officials indicated sincere appreciation of that effort. More than 350,000 packets of seeds were contributed.

The first hint of the present quality control program came to the members at this convention. The Bylaws provided that the filling florist acknowledge to the sending florist the receipt of the order and of delivery. This, contended Edward Chopin, Sr., of New Orleans, was an outmoded regulation. He moved that the acknowledgment be dispensed with and that, in its stead, a system of "spot checking" be introduced through the service department to ascertain how members were filling orders received by wire.

Under existing provisions of the Bylaws, this was not possible at the present convention. Chopin then suggested that a resolution be drawn for presentation at the next convention, to amend the Bylaws so that the acknowledgment could be eliminated and "spot checking" begun.

From this plan of periodical spot checks on members, the present "test order" program grew. The test order procedure is now one of the most valuable tools for testing the adherence of FTD members to the ethical and business standards of the Association. It strongly implements the over-all quality control program.

The 1947 meeting was the last appearance before the assembled members of Albert Pochelon, the celebrated man whom someone had called the "insistent" secretary of FTD for 17 years. He died on June 14, 1948, before the next annual meeting. Almost single-handedly, he had held the Association together through its foundling days and guided it into its maturity. At the Chicago meeting, the allied florists presented to Pochelon and to William Rock, both ardent fisherman, elaborate sets of trout fishing equipment, as recognition of their long service to FTD.

In the election of officers came more evidence of a return to old times. Victor Scott, of Winnipeg, and Angelo J. Rossi, of San Francisco, nominated for president and vice-president, withdrew their names from the ballot and recommended the re-election, on their records, of Edward McCarthy as president and Mrs. McDonald as vice-president. The members unanimously confirmed the recommendation. Ben F. Siebrecht, of Aberdeen, South Dakota, was named director-at-large, and new members of the Board were: G. Wright Defenthaler, of Detroit, and later of Royal Oak, Mich.; Otto Heck, of Reading, Pennsylvania; Clarence LeMar, of Chicago; and Nick Schroeder, of Portland, Oregon. William E. Joy, of Columbus, Georgia, was elected to the Board of Interflora. James Skyora was re-elected chairman of the Associate Division.

Soon after the close of the 1947 convention, an honored name again became associated with FTD. Julius Pochelon, son of Albert Pochelon, joined the organization as assistant secretary and aide to John Besemer. He was an experienced banker and it was thought that his presence would be of benefit to William Rock, long the FTD treasurer, and also relieve some of the pressure of official duties on John Besemer, whose health was failing. Besemer had been forced to miss the 1947 convention.

Following his annual report to the Board of Directors, preceding the 1948 convention in Miami Beach, October 23-27, Besemer tendered his resignation as general manager of FTD. There were many expressions of regret at this action and some suggestions that the resignation be rejected, but the Board, at the meeting following the convention, accepted the resignation, effective January 1, 1949. Thus ended Besemer's 28-year association with FTD, one of the longest official tenures in the history of the organization, second only to that of William Rock, the perennial treasurer.

The Membership Committee, the "pride and joy" of President McCarthy, made its first full-year report to the

Miami Beach convention. This group, composed of James Lawrie, as chairman, with Laurent Clody and Charles W. Pappas, had spent a busy year, holding 17 meetings. Lawrie announced that the membership consisted of 7,790 active members, 700 associate members and 154 foreign members, a total of 8,644. This was the largest enrollment of florists in FTD to that date.

The swift growth of the Association following the war had inspired the suggestion that the membership be closed. There was a feeling in some quarters that the members who had pioneered the Association, and proved their loyalty and support over the years, should not have their influence diluted by constant addition of new members.

The objections to this plan were that there were still areas where FTD service was not available and that to close the membership would freeze the geographical pattern of FTD, deny its benefits to rapidly developing areas and open the field to competing services.

The closed membership faction answered that it was not their purpose to restrict FTD service. They advocated a plan of contracting with outside florists to supply FTD's world-wide facilities on a franchise basis, but not to admit those florists to voting rights or membership. This was never seriously considered by the Membership Committee. The ranks of FTD have always remained open to reputable quali-fied florists.

The Membership Committee had acted upon Chopin's suggestion to "spot check" florists, and had instituted a test order program during 1948. Three hundred and sixty-eight shops had been tested on the following points:

1. REPORT ON SENDING FLORIST:
    a. Description of sales person and kind of flowers ordered.
    b. Statements itemizing costs and advising whether receipt was given.
    c. A general statement regarding salesman-

ship, courtesy, telegraph charges,
receipts, etc.
2. REPORT ON RECEIVING FLORIST:
a. Description of and number of flowers
delivered.
b. Length of stems.
c. The container in which the flowers were
delivered.
d. A general statement regarding quality,
freshness, attractiveness, etc.

The test showed that the most prevalent infraction of FTD rules was failure to give the customer a receipt for his order. Only 25 deliveries were reported unsatisfactory. The test was conducted by the Willmark Service System of New York.

Lawrie concluded his report on the test order program in these words: "We believe that this program can be extremely beneficial to the improvement of our flowers-by-wire service, and request your approval to continue such a program for at least an additional year. A large part of the value to be gained from this test program lies in the fact that the membership has now become aware that test orders are being conducted on a regular basis and will feel an increasing responsibility for better delivery of all their telegraph orders."

More than five times the original allocation is now spent yearly on the test order program and the words of Lawrie are as true today as when they were first spoken. Members have never objected to this procedure, realizing that self-regulation is a strength in itself. In the last survey, 580 shops were tested, with only seven unsatisfactory performance reports.

The matter of contracting for outside firms to use FTD facilities arose again, but in a slightly different manner from that mentioned above. By the time the members convened in Miami Beach, in 1948, the movement had reached such proportions that it was fully considered by the Board during the convention. Present at Miami Beach was H. A. Wiecking, an FTD member from Marion, Indiana. Wiecking had organized Flowers-By-Wire, Inc., an Indiana stock corporation, which proposed to establish flowers-by-wire service desks in the country's leading department stores. The stores were not to sell flowers directly, but only to accept telegraph orders from customers for transmission.

As Wiecking explained his plan, these orders would be channeled through FTD florists for delivery. The store would retain 20 per cent of the gross amount of the order for its services. Wiecking would operate a clearing house for all disbursements to delivering florists, deducting five per cent of the gross order for his commission. In other words, on a $10 order the store accepting the order would retain $2. The telegraph order would be sent immediately to an FTD florist for delivery. The bill would be sent through Wiecking's clearing house, which would deduct 50 cents, and pay the delivering florist $7.50 for delivering the $10 gross order.

This was not the first time that the question of department store florist shops had come before the Board. The general feeling of the directors had long been that such shops were not properly constituted for FTD membership. Wiecking was aware of this. He reminded the Board that his plan did not include the sale of flowers, but merely the acceptance and forwarding of orders. It could be handled, he suggested, with only the installation of an order desk and attendant in some suitable spot in the store.

Wiecking explained further that, if the Board ruled favorably on his plan, he could begin immediate contacts with FTD members. He stated that he had already presented his proposal to about 600 department stores in the country and had received enough encouragement to prompt him to put this question to the Board. "I am not asking the approval of this Board," he concluded. "I am asking if I am doing something that is jeopardizing their memberships, or your membership, or anybody else's who happens to be in this organization."

After Wiecking left the room, it was moved by Victor Stein and seconded by Allen Hixon that a committee be appointed to investigate Flowers-By-Wire, Inc., and report to the Board at its January, 1949, meeting.

The Flowers-By-Wire question was one of the more serious matters to come before FTD since the war. H. Rollo Mueller, of Columbia, Missouri, inherited the problem when elected to the presidency at the 1948 convention. To assist him, John Claus, of Germantown, was named vice-president; and Geraldine Hale, of Dallas, became director-at-large. The four regional directors who took office were: Louis Hoebel, of Fort Lee, New Jersey; James Lawrie, of Toronto; George Rentschler, of Madison, Wisconsin; and Victor Stein, of San Francisco. Laurent Clody, of Chicago, was nominated to the Interflora Board with his term to start in July, 1949. The new Associate Division chairman was John Henry Dudley, of Lansing, Michigan.

In the short time between the Miami Beach convention and the January, 1949, Board meeting, H. A. Wiecking had intensified his organizational activities. Many of the most prominent members of FTD had embraced the scheme. Some of them had invested money in the stock of his corporation. The Flowers-By-Wire question was thoroughly discussed at the January, 1949, Board meeting. When the matter came up, President Mueller threw the question open for full discussion.

Victor Stein, Paul Carroll and John Claus spoke at length on the information they had acquired about the project since the Miami Beach convention. It was generally decided that association with Flowers-By-Wire, Inc., was inimical to the best interests of the members of FTD.

This decision by the Board seemed conclusively to dispose of the matter. In actuality this was not so. The problem arose later to cause the Association considerable expense in an antitrust action by Wiecking, and to dictate a drastic revision in FTD policy concerning membership.

Whether the plan would have been a successful addition to FTD facilities is problematical. Upon motion of Louis Hoebel, seconded by George Rentschler, a decision was made to set up a series of department store installations to test the value of the plan. One of these test stations was established in the J. L. Hudson store in Detroit. This is the second largest department store in the United States in gross sales volume and square footage of sales area. Only Macy's in New York exceeds it.

The test station was opened April 11, 1949, and a complete audit of its affairs was made by June for a report to the Board. Some interesting statistics were revealed. In the 43 sales days of the station's operation, 425 orders were written for delivery in the United States and Canada and four orders were recorded for foreign countries. These orders ranged in value from $3 to $10, with the $5 order being the most popular. The average of these orders was $6.10. One hundred seventy-five were cash orders, amounting to 40 per cent. Of the remaining 60 per cent charged, 37 per cent were bought by employes of the J. L. Hudson Company. At this time, Hudson's employed approximately 12,000 people. They were allowed a 10 per cent discount on all purchases.

An FTD evaluation of this project showed the following negative and positive apparent results:

On the Negative Side

1. Failed to be self-supporting.
2. Aroused to some degree the ill will of local members.
3. Proved very costly to organize further in other cities.
4. Proved that the novelty of method is responsible for some of the sales.
5. Proved an embarrassing operation to deal in the

same store with a live flower department adjacent.

On the Positive Side

1. Thousands of potential customers are contacted.
2. 12,000 regular employees became potential steady customers due to the attractive employee discount.
3. FTDA receives favorable publicity.
4. The major portion of sales are new business.
5. Charge accounts are used.
6. Type of merchandise sold is easily delivered by florist at delivery end.
7. Accounting (J. L. Hudson's and Headquarters') presents no problems.
8. Department store employees work long hours but have added advantage of getting shopping passes to shop on company time within the store.

On the basis of the opinions from both Hudson's and FTD, no further serious consideration was ever given this sort of operation.

The retirement of John Besemer had left FTD without a general manager. Julius Pochelon had taken the reins, pending the engagement of Besemer's replacement. Shortly after the announcement of Besemer's retirement, President Mueller appointed a committee to investigate the qualifications of applicants for the position. This group consisted of Granville Gude, chairman, Edward Goeppner, Henry Forster, Sr., and Frank Schramm. These men had met in Detroit the previous November, better to acquaint themselves with the problems of FTD's Headquarters and to form a basis of judgment on those who were seeking appointment to the vacant position.

They had been in session at the Statler Hotel in Detroit for two days preceding the January, 1949, Board meeting, at which they appeared to report their conclusions to the directors.

In those two days, 12 men had been interviewed for the post. Ten of them had come to Detroit and two were questioned by telephone. No time or effort was spared to give the applicants full opportunity to be heard and to present themselves and their qualifications to the committee. Sessions for the two days lasted from 9 a.m. to 10 p.m. The final decision was not easy.

The committee at last reported to the Board that its consensus was that Philip W. Jones best met the requirements of FTD.

Jones was a native of Chicago. He had majored in industrial management and administration at the University of Illinois. He had gained wide experience in these fields throughout North America and, by the end of the war, he was eastern manager for a firm of business and public relations counsels. With the expansion of the Hilton hotel chain, he had joined that organization as director of industrial relations and was still connected with that firm when he applied for the FTD position.

After a short discussion, the Board acted upon the recommendation of the committee and elected Jones general manager and secretary of the Association. He was the third man in the 40-year history of FTD to hold the top administrative position. Harold Hewey, head of Sales and Advertising, was made assistant to the manager. Julius Pochelon was promoted to chief accounting officer.

Jones assumed his new position on February 1, 1949. He moved slowly in suggesting changes to Association procedures which had been developed through 20 years of Besemer's administration. But by the time the FTD membership met in Montreal for the 1949 convention, Jones was able to report: "The past eight months at Headquarters have been exceedingly busy ones. Co-operation and healthy employee relations had to be re-established. We could not give you the service you most certainly should receive until all employees felt that they were working for FTD and not just the Clearing House, the Membership Department, etc. Frequent staff meetings are held, and key employees frankly argue the merits or disadvantages of problems.

"Despite world unrest, the frontiers of the future lie invitingly before us. They stretch to fabulous horizons — all holding promise of increased floral activity. But these frontiers of tomorrow call for bold enterprise, for optimism, and for the united efforts of all members."

Jones made a good appearance before the 1949 Montreal convention, and the members accepted him wholeheartedly.

There were not many pressing problems to be laid before the convention. For some time there had been in the Sales and Advertising Committee the thought that an increase of the advertising contribution of the members from 1 and 1, to 2 and 2, would more than double sales. This was one of the first motions to come before the membership. It was thoroughly discussed. There was spirited opposition to such a move, as well as solid support for it. In the end, the motion put by George Rentschler, chairman of the Sales and Advertising Committee, carried. However, President Mueller was forced to announce later that the amendment had not been properly advertised to the membership and was therefore illegal. Upon advice of Ward Arbury, new FTD counsel, Mueller reluctantly declared the amendment out of order. No other way to pass the increase could be found. It was finally decided that the increase would have to lay over to another meeting.

After almost 40 years as treasurer of FTD, William Rock offered his resignation to the convention. It was regretfully accepted. To honor the man who had devoted so many years of his time to FTD, Rock was made treasurer emeritus, with his full salary to continue for the rest of his life. Julius Pochelon was elevated to the position of treasurer of FTD.

San Francisco was selected as the 1950 convention city. The Montreal meeting and the deliberations of the Board of Directors adjourned on a note of sorrow and respect for the memory of Anthony C. Morgan, editor of the FTD NEWS, who had died of a heart attack during the president's banquet, on the evening of October 5, 1949.

H. Rollo Mueller had been re-elected president of FTD and Allen W. Hixon was named vice-president. Elizabeth Bertermann, of Indianapolis, was made director-at-large. The four new directors elected to the Board were: G. Stewart Barnaby, of Brookline, Massachusetts; Ed J. Barnes, of Kansas City, Missouri; J. M. Caruthers, of Orlando, Florida; and Harold Kayton, of San Antonio, Texas. John Henry Dudley continued on the Board as Associate Division chairman. H. Rollo Mueller, who had also filled a vacancy on the Interflora Board created by the resignation of Willmore Holbrow in June, 1949, was nominated to the Interflora Board.

At the January, 1950, Board meeting, legal counsel suggested and secured extensive changes in the Articles of Association and Bylaws to bring them into line with recently developed practices and procedures within the Association, and also to make them conform to the requirements of the Michigan General Corporations Act which had been passed by the Legislature since FTD was founded.

Serious consideration arose in 1950 concerning a private telegraph network for the transmission of FTD orders. A company specializing in the establishment and maintenance of such networks was called into consultation and, after analyzing FTD's situation, presented its report to the July, 1950, meeting of the Board in Detroit.

On the basis of 20 major cities studied for 30 days, the monthly traffic flow amounted to approximately 73,000 messages. According to the consultant, FTD could install this private network and operate it seven days a week, 14 hours a day, for a monthly expense of $27,000. This included the wire charge and 70 operators' salaries.

By establishing a flat rate of 20 cents per message, to be charged florists transmitting orders, FTD could realize $1 million annually, based on a total of 5 million messages a year. It was plain that this was an ambitious project. Several of the largest companies in the country were at that time using such networks. The arrangement had passed the experimental stage. There was no doubt of its efficiency.

The consultant who presented the plan was not a high-pressure salesman. He did not ask for a quick decision. Instead, he suggested further exploration of long-range possibilities. Clarence LeMar had been appointed by President Mueller to investigate fully the feasibility of the private network and it was he who brought the consultant to the meeting. After listening to the presentation, the Board recommended that LeMar and Jones study the plan further and be ready to report their findings to the membership at the 1950 convention in San Francisco. This ended the matter for the time being.

Throughout 1950, a series of test orders was run in Detroit, New York City, Los Angeles, St. Louis and other cities. A full report containing pictures of the arrangements delivered was carried in each issue of the FTD NEWS. Analysis of these deliveries showed that there was a serious degree of carelessness in flowers-by-wire orders. This had a poor effect on the morale of the Association. The Membership Committee reported to the Board that it wished to continue the test orders and asked for an appropriation of $10,000 to underwrite the program. This amount was granted to the committee and it was complimented on the conduct of the test order program.

The suggested changes to the Articles and Bylaws of the Association, which were to be presented to the membership at the San Francisco convention, occupied considerable space in the FTD NEWS.

This extensive revision of the Association's rules and regulations provoked a heightened interest in the coming convention. The test order program also caused much discussion and kept the members on their toes. The FTD NEWS carried a full report of the suggested changes, so that an informed membership would be ready at the convention to act on the proposed new Articles.

The San Francisco meeting convened September 1 to 5, 1950. In its pre-convention meeting, the Board of Directors voted unanimously to proceed with the establishment of a private communications system and it appropriated $50,000 for that purpose. It was estimated that such a network would save the flower-buying public as much as a million dollars a year. The preliminary hookup was to link the cities of Chicago, Detroit, Cleveland, Washington, Philadelphia and New York, an area which included approximately 60 per cent of the country's buying public. The saving to the public would be occasioned by the low flat rate for message transmission. No commitments were to be made for 60 days, pending further study and research. But plans were made to extend the system within three years to insure that every FTD member should be within 100 miles of the network system.

Another far-reaching action of the general convention was the unanimous adoption of the 2 per cent (gross) on all outgoing orders, and 2 per cent (gross) on all incoming orders. This would provide a 44 per cent increase in funds available for Association promotion. The 4-cent outgoing order charge was eliminated. The revised Articles and Bylaws, as suggested by Frederick J. Kennedy, legal counsel, were adopted after explanation by Louis Hoebel, chairman of the Legislative Committee, of the necessity of bringing FTD into line with new Michigan corporation laws. The total registration for the meeting was 1,571.

In the election of officers and directors, Granville Gude, of Washington, D. C., became president; and Victor Stein, of San Francisco, was named vice-president. Maude Howard, of Salt Lake City, was elected director-at-large. The new directors were: Carl E. Bohnert, of Charleston, West Virginia; Clarence Muelleman, of Chicago; Jerry O'Neill, of Seattle, Washington; and Victor Stoll, of Hamilton, Ohio.

Frank W. Fredenhagen, of Burbank, California, was later appointed to the Board to fill the vacancy caused by the elevation of Victor Stein to vice-president. Julius Pochelon, of Detroit, continued as treasurer and Philip Jones as secretary. A. J. Grigsby, of Cleveland, was the newly elected Associate Division chairman.

Leo J. McKenna, of Montreal, Quebec, Canada, was nominated to the Interflora Board to fill the vacancy created by the resignation of Laurent Clody and Granville Gude of Washington, D. C., was nominated for a full term.

The importance of the idea of a private communications system for FTD caused President Gude to appoint a Communications Committee, consisting of Clarence LeMar, chairman, Rollo Mueller and Edward McCarthy. Further study of the project was necessary, because the network would have to be licensed by the Federal Communications Commission. There was also the matter of competition between Western Union and American Telephone and Telegraph Company for the leasing of lines to FTD.

The engineering firm with which FTD was discussing the project was the Communications Engineering Company, of Chicago. This was an independent engineering company, represented by its vice-president, John McEnerney, who was in a position to bargain with the two major wire-leasing services for the more favorable rate.

Mike Mitchell, vice-president of Western Union, asked the privilege of meeting with the committee to discuss his company's interests and to consider a volume rate for the transmission of messages over his lines. The meeting was held in Washington on September 28, 1950. But Mitchell had nothing concrete to offer, beyond repeating a proposal that his company was tendering to the United States Government for a similar network.

He did, however, offer his company's help in clearing the project through the FCC. Mitchell, it appeared, was willing to help only if his company was assured that its lines would be utilized. According to LeMar's report to the Board of Directors in Detroit in January, 1951, "Mr. Mitchell made a threat that should the FTDA pursue the network program, his company would be ethically proper in entering the flowers-by-wire business."

It was agreed that Philip Jones should supply all available statistics concerning FTD's wire business, to enable Western Union to survey the possibilities. A month later, Western Union informed FTD that it would not be good economy to install the network on a six-city basis, as proposed; and that, for further quotations, Western Union would require more time for study.

The committee also approached the Bell Telephone System for a proposal on the network from them. The telephone company did not care to make a commitment until the plan had been cleared by the Government.

Here the matter rested. In view of the Korean war and the shortage of supplies, it was the opinion of the committee that "it would be unsound even to start a project so great at this time."

The first report of the new Member Service Committee was made to the Board in January, 1951. This committee, consisting of Chairman Harold Kayton, Maude Howard, Ted Boesen, Ed Ludwig and John Liesveld, had been organized after the San Francisco convention. Its function was to assume all activities pertaining to member services, such as the field force operation, distribution of sales promotion materials, the design schools and other educational projects for local members. The program of member-support through national advertising remained with the Sales and Advertising Committee.

A tentative committee of FTD, called "Say It With Flowers — Today" was considering ways and means of combatting the "Please Omit" problem. Because of its wide and harmful effect on the entire industry, this problem had been the concern of all branches of the business. Victor

Stein, the FTD representative to SAF, reported to the Board that SAF was interested in allying the entire industry in a move against "P.O." He reported that the Executive Committee of FTD considered the matter of prime importance and agreed to join the FTD committee with the efforts of the general movement, also further to implement the work with a contribution of $25,000, provided the other branches of the industry contribute $50,000. George Rentschler placed Stein's suggestion in the form of a motion and, seconded by Maude Howard, it carried.

This was the first FTD recognition of what later grew to be the "Florists' Information Council." As with all movements of first importance in the history of FTD, the matter of the appropriation and the projected plans for the industry-wide campaign came before the membership for thorough discussion during the annual convention held in Washington, September 1 to 7, 1951. It was there announced that contributions from the industry for the furtherance of the fight amounted to $76,000. It was agreed that this was not an amount to accomplish great headway on the problem. But it did indicate an awareness of what was facing the industry.

An industry-wide committee, consisting of three FTD representatives, three representatives from SAF, and four from other branches of the business, under the chairmanship of Sam Pennock, former president of SAF, and former director of FTD, had been established to administer the affairs of the campaign. The FTD representatives were Walter Mosmiller, Jr., Harald Thompson and Victor Stein. Public relations counsel was engaged and the name of the committee was officially made Florists' Information Council.

As usual with important matters, the discussion of this campaign by the membership was not without some disagreement. But after thorough explanation by those who supported the FIC, the members heartily endorsed it. Their first objection had been that money would be taken from the

Sales and Advertising Committee that could be better used
for the general promotion of the sale of flowers. It was shown,
however, that the appropriation did not come from the
Sales and Advertising Committee fund, but from the Member Service Committee's allotment. Since this was definitely
member service, the contribution was proper.

Another reason advanced against joining this movement
was that it was a discriminatory expenditure of money, as
all areas were not affected by the "P.O." problem. So appropriation of $25,000 for the benefit of some members
discriminated against others who did not need the campaign
in their locality.

Proponents of the FIC showed that the problem was at
its beginning; that its potential for growth was great; and
that the time to take action against it was now. The vision
of those who espoused this attitude was prophetic. This
"business deterrent" became, and continues to be, one of the
major concerns of the entire floral industry. The FIC
remains active against it.

FTD has also conducted its own surveys on the problem,
whenever and wherever it has arisen — over radio, television,
in newspapers and among funeral directors. This does not
seek to supplant or interfere with the work of the FIC. It
is directed to immediate counteraction against "P.O." where
it affects members at the local level.

It should be emphasized that FTD does not object in any
measure to the suggestion of memorial contributions to
charities or institutions. Rather, it seeks to eliminate the
negative implications inherent in the "Please Omit" and "In
Lieu Of" announcements which often appear in obituaries.
The expression of condolence, sympathy or respect by anyone as he chooses is a basic and cherished right, according
to FTD.

The Washington convention was a smooth and friendly
occasion. President Gude's address expressed his confidence,
gained through wide travel in the interest of the Association,

in the welfare of FTD. The agenda he had prepared was efficiently presented. No drastic changes in operation had been proposed. The matters that came before the members were disposed of quickly and easily.

Granville Gude was renominated president, opposed by S. A. Anderson, Jr. But Anderson withdrew and moved that Gude be re-elected unanimously. This was done amid hearty applause. James Lawrie, of Toronto, was elected vice-president and Marion Fisher, of Syracuse, New York, became director-at-large. Frank Fredenhagen, of Burbank, California; Douglas I. Macklin, of Sarnia, Ontario; Alfred K. Petit, of Mineola, New York; and Harald Thompson, of Rochester, Minnesota, were named the new regional directors. Philip Jones continued as secretary, Julius Pochelon as treasurer and A. J. Grigsby became Associate Division chairman. Henry Forster, Sr., of Detroit, was nominated to the Interflora Board.

At the directors' meeting following the adjournment of the convention, Harold Kayton announced that the member service program now encompassed plans to add two new members to the field staff. This would necessitate a reduction in the areas of the existing field territories and provide for better service to members. The department also proposed to publish a book of FTD policies for distribution to members and prospective members.

A recommendation by Philip Jones, that FTD take steps to extend the availability of FTD service to men and women in the armed services outside the continental United States, received the full support of the new Board. An appropriation of $15,000 was authorized for its promotion.

Remembering the success of overseas efforts during the war, and recognizing that rival organizations were attempting to capture the military flower business in its entirety, the Board authorized a strong promotion in this field for the benefit of FTD members.

Much progress in establishing alliances with post exchanges

overseas was reported when the Board met in Detroit in January, 1952. The objective of the program was to acquaint the thousands of men and women of the overseas military forces with FTD's service and its availability. It was thought this would have a more lasting and beneficial effect than the immediate garnering of flower orders from army and navy personnel. It was not too long to remember back to the favorable impression of FTD brought home by men and women returning from Europe. To gain and hold their confidence was the principal aim for the present.

The proposed private communications system was still problematical. The shortage of electronic equipment made progress in this field difficult. Two other factors indicated that careful study of the project was needed. First, the Federal Communications Commission had issued a ruling described as somewhat vague. The Commission had tentatively agreed to grant the permit for the system, but the difficulty was in figuring the basic charge to FTD members under the FCC ruling. It seemed that FTD would only be able to assess the members using the new system enough to recompense the commercial lines for the use of their services, without collecting enough to repay FTD for its time and expense of installation and operation.

The second deterrent to installation of the system was FCC's ruling that no congratulatory or sentimental messages could be contained in wires transmitted over the network. To do so would be to compete with the common carriers — the telephone and telegraph companies — who were already franchised for such operations. Only the bare flower order could be transmitted. This did not seem adequate to the Board, and the plan was left in abeyance for the time being.

Through FTD's quality control program a series of tests had been conducted during the past fiscal year which proved so satisfactory that the Board voted to continue the program. Of more than 300 florists tested in seven target areas, more than 98 per cent scored acceptable or better. The publicity given these tests through the pages of the FTD NEWS was a stimulus to florist readers to produce first class work. The shop reports, published with pictures of the test arrangements, were fair and factual capsule comments. No effort to intimidate members was made and no warnings of impending tests in other cities were issued or implied. The tests and the articles spoke for themselves and informed members that high standards and strict observance of the FTD Code of Ethics was expected at all times. The program was recognized as one of the most valuable ever conducted by the Membership Committee.

The Board met again in Detroit, June 25 and 26, 1952. No single momentous decision was reached. But many troublesome problems were solved. The general effect of the meeting was to assure a smoother operating organization during the next fiscal year.

Of particular interest to members was the Board's decision to reduce the appropriations from $50,000 to $5,000 for the study and development of the private communications system. This was to be presented to the membership at their 1952 convention. The unsettled conditions in the world and the many governmental and legal problems connected with the plan indicated that there was little to be gained by further exploration.

An important personnel change had taken place since the January Board meeting. Julius Pochelon, treasurer of FTD, had tendered his resignation, to take effect July 1, 1952. John P. Beitler had been engaged to replace him. The position of comptroller was created for Beitler and he prepared to assume complete administration of all the accounting and financial affairs of the Association.

Beitler, a certified public accountant, had a broad background in finance and accounting, beginning with the Mellon Enterprises in Pittsburgh in 1939. Later, he spent four years in the accounting department of the Westinghouse Company and then joined the staff of Price, Waterhouse and Company, national auditing firm. In 1946 he became a member of the comptroller's department of the Pittsburgh Plate Glass Company, and came to Detroit in 1951 for the Ford Division of the Ford Motor Company. He was a competent and aggressive administrator. Not only was he thoroughly trained in his profession, but he understood fully the intricacies of the post he was assuming.

The general tone of the meeting was one of success, achievement and profound assurance for the future. President Gude reviewed the past fiscal year and predicated his optimistic view of the coming year upon the accomplishments of the 12 months just completed.

The Board adjourned, to meet again preceding the annual members' meeting during the week of August 25, 1952, when, after 29 years, FTD was returning to St. Louis for its convention.

CHAPTER SIXTEEN

Trials and Prosperity

N CONTRAST WITH the uproarious St. Louis convention of 1923, which saw the establishment of the mandatory Clearing House after a bitter debate, the 1952 meeting of FTD in that city was smooth and quiet. President Granville Gude had prepared an agenda that kept the meeting active and yet was flexible enough to permit ample discussion of various issues presented.

One of these issues was the revived question of a private communications system for the transmission of FTD orders. Only about $2,500 was spent in the preliminary survey and Clarence LeMar, the original proponent of the plan, brought the matter before the members again. Further study was made of the cost of operating the network and LeMar asked that a committee be appointed to review the proposals of the engineering company seeking to put the system into operation. An extended examination of the plan was made, with the benefit of comprehensive data from engineers concerning traffic expectancy, availability of personnel and cost per message. Enough merit in the proposal was demonstrated to prompt the members to adopt LeMar's resolution. This move kept the matter alive, although it was not expected that actual work on the system would start immediately.

There was hot debate on the plan to return to the general fund the money carried as a "reserve for losses." In the end it was rejected. This reserve fund was established in the earliest days of FTD, when it was feared that members, who left the Association for one reason or another, might also leave unpaid accounts on the books of the Clearing House. The reserve, which was collected from, and belonged to, the members, was a hedge against unpaid accounts. Over the years, the money had been invested and interest had increased it to its present amount.

Experience proved that such a sum was not needed and the auditors suggested it be returned to the general fund. There was considerable reluctance to authorize such a return. The thought persisted that, in the event of a business decline, the money might be needed as originally planned. Despite the explanation by the accountants that the transfer to the general fund was nothing more than a bookkeeping transaction, the membership voted against the change.

The St. Louis meeting saw the formation of the National Junior Florists' Association. Children of members had been attending the conventions as a part of their summer vacations and the junior association was seen as a chance to bring these young people into the industry, with a design school of their own and a general strengthening of their interest in the business through personal participation in certain affairs of the annual meetings.

Six of the juniors demonstrated their designing skill to the membership. Although the young people's experience covered only six months to two years and they ranged in age from 13 to 18 years, adults were surprised and delighted with the designs they turned out.

Bill Schray, of St. Louis, chairman of the junior session, introduced the young commentator, Amelia Gude Thomas, of Washington, D. C. She was the daughter of Amelia Gude Thomas, who had often attended the conventions with her father, President William Gude, and entertained the members with amusing recitations.

As a demonstration of junior skill, Kem Branin, 16, of Syracuse, vice-president of the junior group, made a pick spray of red roses and fern with a red satin bow. His brother,

BOARD OF DIRECTORS
DETROIT, 1950

(Left to right) Directors Clarence LeMar, Chicago, Illinois; Otto H. Heck, Wyomissing, Reading, Pennsylvania; G. Wright Defenthaler, Detroit, Michigan; G. Stewart Barnaby, Brookline, Massachusetts; Victor Stein, San Francisco, California; James Lawrie, Toronto, Ontario, Canada; Treasurer Julius Pochelon, Detroit, Michigan; Secretary & General Manager Philip W. Jones, Detroit, Michigan; Director-at-Large Elizabeth G. Bertermann, Indianapolis, Indiana; President H. Rollo Mueller, Columbia, Missouri; Vice President Allen W. Hixon, Worcester, Massachusetts; Attorney Ward Arbury, Buffalo, New York; Court Reporter Alex Checkaway, Detroit, Michigan; Director Louis Hoebel, Fort Lee, New Jersey; Associate Division Chairman John Henry Dudley, Lansing, Michigan; Directors Nick Schroeder, Portland, Oregon; Harold Kayton, San Antonio, Texas; J. M. Caruthers, Orlando, Florida; George Rentschler, Madison, Wisconsin; Ed. J. Barnes, Jr., Kansas City, Missouri; Past President Edward J. McCarthy, Brooklyn, New York.

Design schools are an integral and important part of FTD conventions. Here a group of members gains pointers on technique and artistry from a master designer.

Besides private demonstrations, large class exhibitions are held, featuring artists and designers from America and Europe, with running commentaries and instructions by America's foremost teachers of floral design.

Special classes, symposiums and seminars are held on such specialized design subjects as weddings, Mother's Day, Valentine's Day, church decorations, Christmas flowers and other specific applications of the florist's art.

Design schools are well attended and form one of the most valuable and rewarding phases of FTD conventions for FTD members. Through such large-scale demonstrations, members are kept abreast of new trends in flower arranging.

BOARD OF DIRECTORS
1959-1960

(Left to right) Directors Charles R. Hum, Los Angeles, California; Ralph W. Bachman, Minneapolis, Minnesota; James Ludwig, Pittsburgh, Pennsylvania; Marshall B. Gifford, Portland, Oregon; Associate Division Chairman O. Ben Haley, Denver, Colorado; Directors Arthur C. Clemensen, Chicago, Illinois; Earl Tobler, Kansas City, Missouri; Mrs. Alma Pratt, Hamilton, Ontario; Treasurer Andrew H. Strang, Philadelphia, Pennsylvania; Director-at-Large Mrs. Bessie Pawson, Santa Ana, California; Vice President Joseph Hynes, Chicago, Illinois; President Irving Allen, Bremerton, Washington; Executive Secretary & General Manager John L. Bodette, Detroit, Michigan; Assistant Secretary Miss Virginia Roberts, Detroit, Michigan; Director Joseph Casey, Melrose, Massachusetts; General Counsel Richard C. Van Dusen, Detroit, Michigan; Directors Marty Swartz, Dallas, Texas; Peter D. Tryforos, New York, New York; Ralph C. Hunter, Charlotte, North Carolina; Robert C. Cherry, Paducah, Kentucky; Mrs. Doris Remis, Schenectady, New York; John M. Carey, Detroit, Michigan; Past President Stanley C. Minshall, St. Petersburg, Florida.

Without the "Trade Fair," sponsored each year by the Associate Division, a great deal of the convention "flavor" would be missing from FTD's annual meetings.

Florist supply salesmen performed valuable service for FTD in the Association's early membership drives. Today, as the Associate Division, they continue to aid FTD members by exhibiting the latest in services and supplies at the annual meetings.

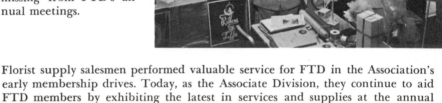

A view of the "midway" of a typical FTD Trade Fair. Besides showing the latest florists' products, the Associate Division contributes substantially to the entertainment of FTD convention visitors.

A model florist shop established as a central feature of a recent Trade Fair by the Associate Division. Lecturers, business consultants and suppliers demonstrate the most recent developments in florists' supplies.

Well-attended annual business meetings have been characteristic of FTD throughout its 50-year existence. Free and frank discussion of important policy matters by members from all parts of North America have kept the Association strong and flexible. Shown above is the 1946 meeting at the Hotel Commodore in New York City.

Regional seating and designation by placards for purposes of voting was originated at the Houston convention in 1953. This is a scene showing the floor during the presentation of nominees. Some members have left their seats to caucus or campaign.

Social events highlight all national conventions of FTD. Here, relaxing after a busy day planning the future of the Association, members dance and dine in elegant atmosphere during the 1955 Seattle convention.

Mercury bestrides the opening of the 1959 convention in the Statler-Hilton Hotel in Los Angeles. While the grace of flowers lends a festive air to the meeting, efficiency and acumen keynote the meeting.

Flowers-by-wire bring florists-by-plane. These members from South Africa are shown registering for the convention at Los Angeles, 1959, after a trip by air from the other side of the world.

President Jack Branin, 17, assisted by Treasurer Jane Hunt, of Humboldt, Tennessee, devised a muff and headpiece for a wedding attendant. Cymbidium orchids were used on brown velvet and the muff had a brown net skirt on one side.

The promise shown by the young designers proved the value of directing their energies toward the florist profession through the new National Junior Florists' Association.

At this convention, it was decided to increase the membership fee from $10 to $25 and the inspection fee from $25 to $35. This required an amendment to the Bylaws, which was quickly voted by the members. Another amendment adopted at this meeting provided that only one past-president would serve on the Board of Directors.

In the election of officers, James Lawrie, of Toronto, became president and Ed J. Barnes, of Kansas City, Mo., vice-president. Miss Emma Louise Pochelon, of Detroit, was named director-at-large, and H. Rollo Mueller, past-president of FTD and president of Interflora, was nominated for re-election to the Interflora Board. New directors who took their places on the Board were: Robert L. Cason, of Corsicana, Texas; Phil M. Harrison, of Nashville, Tennessee; Vern A. Oppenlander, of Denver, Colorado; and James Scott, of Providence, Rhode Island. The new Board named G. Stewart Barnaby, of Brookline, Mass., as treasurer. Oscar G. Carlstedt, of Jacksonville, Fla., was the new Associate Division chairman.

In retiring from the presidency, Granville Gude stressed the policy that FTD must be run on the principle of "What's right," not "Who's right." He promised continued efforts toward the growth and prosperity of the Association.

Before the end of 1952, FTD membership hit an all-time high. On December 31, 1952, the rolls listed 9,475 florists as members of the Association. For the first time in the history of the organization, the field staff had been able to call upon every member shop during the year.

The first meeting of the Board of Directors under President James Lawrie met in Detroit, January 28 and 29, 1953. Because of the many problems on the Board agenda, it was found necessary to extend both days' meetings into the evening hours.

Reporting on the first half of the 1952-53 fiscal year, Treasurer G. Stewart Barnaby noted increases of 3.6 per cent in the number of wire orders and 6.9 per cent in the dollar volume over the previous fiscal year. Christmas clearings had risen nearly $750,000 above those of a year ago. Advanced accounting procedures and other internal control practices had been installed to provide still more efficiency in the Finance Department.

Both the Membership Committee and the Member Service Committee gave optimistic reports to the Board. Membership had increased by 132 shops, extending FTD service into 53 additional areas. A new publication known as the "Answer Book" had been distributed to members. This book undertook to answer virtually any question concerning FTD that could occur to a member. It was considered a notable contribution to the promotion of efficiency within the organization.

It was at this meeting that Philip W. Jones, general manager and secretary, met disagreement from some Board members over his method of administering the Headquarters operation. He tendered his resignation. After a lengthy deliberation in executive session, the Board voted to accept it, although the vote was not unanimous. Jones wished to be relieved of his duties immediately. The Board granted a waiver of the contract provision for notice.

Harold R. Hewey, who had been head of the Sales and Advertising Department of FTD since 1941, was named acting general manager and secretary to direct the Headquarters operation until a replacement for Jones could be found. Hewey was well acquainted with FTD affairs and with the industry. His capabilities gave the Board ample time to make an unhurried selection of a permanent man for the Headquarters operation.

After the close of the January meeting of the Board, one of the trade journals carried an article stating that another "F.T.D.A., Inc.," had been organized as a New York corporation. Its original board of directors and incorporators were announced as John Besemer, former FTD general manager; David E. Roberts, former FTD legal counsel; and Gladys Besemer, nee Martin, who had been a member of the FTD Headquarters Staff in charge of overseas orders. (Following his resignation from FTD, John Besemer had gone to New York and organized International Flower Service, Incorporated, a firm engaged in handling overseas flowers-by-wire orders.)

The same article said that Interflora, Inc. had also been chartered in New York, with the same directors, officers and incorporators.

Several members of FTD wrote to the Board informing them of these new corporations. The directors deemed the affair of such importance that it should be referred to the FTD legal counsel for investigation.

After determining the facts of the case, Donald Flintermann, FTD attorney, engaged counsel in New York to bring suit there. FTDA and Interflora, Inc., both Michigan Corporations, were plaintiffs. FTDA, Inc., and Interflora, Inc., both New York corporations, were respondents. On the face of it, the case was confusing.

The Besemer organizations appeared by counsel, filed an answer to FTD's complaint and asserted an affirmative defense. The important charge was that the assistant secretary of Interflora had registered the respondents' name in Europe under the Geneva Convention; i.e., had registered International Flower Service, which was John Besemer's organization.

The case came up at the end of May and, on June 15, 1953, the court gave its opinion. The court found that the action of respondents was wrongful, that it was in violation of the New York Penal Code, that Mr. and Mrs. Besemer and Mr. Roberts held positions of trust in both the plaintiff organizations, which precluded their engaging in this activity, and that their affirmative defense was without merit.

On June 23, 1953, a decree was entered, ordering the Besemer organization to cease immediately using the name, "Florists' Telegraph Delivery Association," and the name, "Interflora," or any similar terms, labels, trade-marks or designations, and that the cable addresses of these two organizations be removed from the Central Bureau of Registered Addresses, New York.

The effect of this was to cure the confusion caused by the similarity of titles and leave to FTD the sole proprietorship of its names, Florists' Telegraph Delivery Association, and Interflora, Inc.

This welcome news came just before the Board of Directors met in Detroit, June 29 to July 2, 1953. At this meeting, the engagement of a new general manager was announced. After interviewing numerous applicants for the post, the Board had chosen John Paul Ostrander, 41 years old, a native of Detroit, who had been sales manager of the Marine and Industrial Engine Division of the Packard Motor Company. His background in sales and sales promotion also included service in the sales departments of the Chrysler Corporation and of Bendix Aviation. He began his duties July 1, 1953.

Earlier in the year, President Lawrie had appointed, for the first time, a Headquarters Committee, consisting of Vice-President Ed J. Barnes, Jr., chairman, G. Stewart Barnaby and Victor Stoll. This committee was to visit the Detroit Headquarters for one day every three months, observe the operations there and report to the Board the information obtained from conferences with the general manager and the department heads and from observation of the efficiency and general tone of the operation. Any complaints about associates, work load, wasteful routine or other deterrents were to be investigated by the committee and recommendations made to the head of the department or to the general manager.

The committee found that four visits a year were not necessary and changed their schedule to three, one to be held during the regular January Board meeting. The appointment of this committee may have reflected some apprehension about the conduct of the Detroit office. But the committee had nothing but praise for the staff and the management of Headquarters.

The 1953 convention was held in Houston, Texas, August 30 to September 2. That great Southwestern seaport brought out its most capacious ten-gallon hats and its highest-heeled boots to welcome the florists with openhearted hospitality. Although President Jim Lawrie was arrested by the Sheriff's Posse and imprisoned for some time in a mock jail in front of the hotel, not all the Houston happenings were high jinks. Much serious business was transacted.

This convention saw the first meeting of the Board of Interflora since 1948. The cost of transportation of the members had been the principal deterrent to yearly meetings. Present for the Houston gathering to represent FTD America were Interflora President H. Rollo Mueller, Granville Gude, Henry Forster, Sr., of Detroit, and Gilbert Van Dongen, manager of the FTD Clearing House and assistant secretary and treasurer of Interflora. FTD British Unit members of the Board were Robert Fowler and Geoffrey Lewis, of England; J. Dobson, of Scotland; and James Rendall, British Unit secretary and Interflora assistant secretary. Fleurop was represented by Cornelius Thim, of Amsterdam, Holland; George Ehrhardt, of Berne, Switzerland; Carl Jorgensen, of Copenhagen, Denmark; and Max Schneider, of Zurich, Switzerland, secretary of both Fleurop and Interflora. Franz Kommer, of Bremen, Germany, newly elected director of Interflora, representing Fleurop, attended as an observer.

Emphasis was placed on the rapid growth of the membership of the international group. The FTD British Unit reported 2,100 members in its ranks, including South Africa, Tasmania, Australia, New Zealand, the Malay States and other members of the Commonwealth. Fleurop was described as being composed of 12 separate units, with more than 7,000 members sending 2 million Interflora orders annually. Optimism was the keynote of the meeting. Carl Jorgensen, of Copenhagen, stated: "We must first make our members proud to be Interflora members, conscious of the prestige that goes with the ability to send flowers world-wide. The importance of it is not entirely one of making money; the service is one of the most effective instruments for developing understanding among the peoples of various nations."

New Interflora officers elected at Houston were: Robert Fowler, president; George Ehrhardt, vice-president; Max Schneider, secretary; Jim Rendall, assistant secretary; and J. Paul Ostrander, assistant secretary and treasurer, contingent upon the approval of the Board of FTD. The Executive Committee consisted of Robert Fowler, George Ehrhardt and H. Rollo Mueller, the retiring president.

As the new general manager of FTD, Paul Ostrander made his first report to the annual meeting at Houston. Although he had been in office since July 1, 1953, the report held a note of apology: "I am not as yet an authority on the structure and operation of your Headquarters; but with the assistance of the Headquarters team, I fully expect to perpetuate the efficient, friendly and sincere management, which has progressed so outstandingly for the past several months under the guidance of your good friend, Harold Hewey.

"Being a newcomer, it is difficult for me to speak on the specific progress of each department of your Headquarters. However, separate reports have been submitted by the executive heads of your Headquarters, which will provide this information."

A drastic change in the members' voting procedure was

instituted at Houston. A Voting Procedure Committee, consisting of Peter D. Tryforos, of New York City, chairman; Sylvia MacGuffog Valencia, of Westboro, Massachusetts; and Charles N. Pappas, Jr., of New York City, recommended to the convention that the floor of the hall be divided into 12 sections, each identified by a sign indicating a region, and each section equipped with a microphone over which the vote of the region could be announced. The regional director would sit with his members, poll the delegation's vote, and announce the result to the chair. The chair, or any qualified member, would then have the right to challenge the vote of any region and call for an individual poll of its members. This system, with some minor variations, is still in use.

The continuance of the Florist Information Council was seriously threatened at the Houston meeting. Allen Hixon, of Worcester, Mass., FIC chairman, presented a financial report covering contributions and expenditures of the Council during the past year, noting that FIC funds were exhausted. He pointed out, however, that a recent letter of solicitation had resulted in better-than-expected commitments for additional funds for the "Please Omit" program. Still, he said, FIC would be definitely limited in its program until January, when part of the SAF marketing funds would be made available for continuing the crusade against "P.O."

Following testimony by several members to the efficacy of the FIC program in their areas, H. Rollo Mueller placed a motion before the convention that FTD subscribe $10,000 for FIC. The motion carried. FTD had, in previous years, contributed a total of $75,000 to FIC, while the rest of the industry had contributed less than $52,000.

In the election of officers, Clarence Muelleman, the Nominating Committee's choice to run against the incumbent president, announced his withdrawal in favor of President James Lawrie and moved his re-election by unanimous vote. The members approved the action without a dissent. Ed J. Barnes, Jr., was named vice-president for a second term and

Mrs. Jane Hunt, of Humbolt, Tenn., was elected director-at-large. Eugene Daudelin, of Chicago; Rudy Luepke, of Vancouver, Washington; Edward Lutey, of Detroit; and William C. McMullen, of State College, Pennsylvania, became the new regional directors. Oscar Carlstedt, of Jacksonville, Florida, was re-elected chairman of the Associate Division. Clarence Muelleman, of Chicago, was appointed treasurer and J. Paul Ostrander continued as executive secretary. President Lawrie was also nominated to the Interflora Board.

The outlook for business in 1954 was not so bright as in the previous year. Many economists saw a slight decline in all lines, and leading members of the florist profession translated this trend in terms of its effect upon their business. No depression was expected; but all signs pointed to some recession.

To meet this condition, FTD went about making plans for a better handling of European orders. Arrangements were made with the Statistical Tabulating Service in New York City to handle orders from the Deutsche Bundespost. These orders had been coming directly into Detroit, through FTD's registered cable address, Flortelde. It was found, however, that personnel was not available to take care of this business during holiday rush periods.

Statistical Tabulating Service asked for 30 days to study the arrangement, before setting a price for their service. This was granted and, after the trial period, a contract was signed with the service for relaying overseas orders to the proper FTD members.

General Manager Ostrander was able to report to the Board of Directors at their 1954 January meeting that more than 600 orders had been received through Flortelde at Christmas, 1953. Immediately after the holiday, arrangements were made with Bundespost to transmit mail orders, as well as cable orders, through the New York affiliate. This service was in operation by January 15, 1954.

In this report to the Board, Ostrander also suggested that one of the field men be sent to Europe to promote overseas business through the many Army Post Exchanges operating for military and civilian personnel in Europe in connection with the occupation. It was Ostrander's opinion that a field man could advantageously spend three to six months in Europe, after which he could be sent to South America to observe the business in those countries. Japan also had about 25 excellent florists who had asked to be admitted to FTD as soon as satisfactory currency transmission procedures could be worked out.

The Board did not concur in this plan, fearing that members of the FTD British Unit and Fleurop would be opposed to it.

In a supplement to his report, Ostrander asked that the Board resolve certain variances in their decisions of August 30-31 and September 1-2, 1953, and those of June 29-July 2, 1953, relating to the signing of a contract with Radio Corporation of America for the transmission of flowers-by-wire orders from Europe and the Pacific area.

The general manager reported that he had arranged a meeting with Mr. Pitts of RCA for February 1, 1954, in the FTD Headquarters and that he needed an expression from the Board before he could proceed with the negotiations leading to the contract. "I should like advice from the Board on how this matter should be handled," he requested. "I should also like advice from the Board on who they feel should represent this Association in our discussion with Mr. Pitts on February 1 and whether the agreement can be finalized without again bringing it before the Board."

The Board was apparently cool to the suggestions of the general manager and, upon motion, it was ordered that his report, with its supplements, be received.

On March 18 and 19, 1954, the Headquarters Committee visited the Detroit offices unannounced. The committee reported to the Board that Mr. Ostrander expressed resentment of this visit and threatened that, unless the committee gave him its endorsement before it adjourned, he would resign. The committee had already decided that Mr. Ostrander lacked qualifications they desired in a general manager and so informed the Board. On April 3, 1954, J. Paul Ostrander's services with FTD were terminated.

With the departure of Ostrander, Harold Hewey again stepped into the position of interim general manager. Shortly thereafter, properly to evaluate the Headquarters operation, the Headquarters Committee engaged the firm of Hall and Liles to make a survey of the Detroit offices to measure the morale, efficiency and over-all staff capabilities. On June 30, 1954, a preliminary report was submitted to the Board indicating that "The departments, in general, are well-organized . . . department heads are well acquainted with the work of their departments. Supervisor-subordinate relations are good . . . Technically, there are several office procedures in Headquarters that are outstanding in the field of labor saving and cost reduction. Each staff member is performing capably in his assignment. There is a strong feeling of teamwork . . ." This was a heartening report, both for the Board of Directors and for the Headquarters staff.

John P. Beitler, FTD comptroller, was appointed acting secretary and treasurer of Interflora with instructions to attend the scheduled meeting of the Interflora Board at Frankfort, Germany, both in an official capacity and as an observer representing FTD. As a spur to overseas business, the Board, at the request of Fleurop, agreed to engage a representative to visit military installations and other sources of flower orders in Europe to solicit orders for FTD. The cost of this venture was limited to $3,000.

Carl E. Bohnert, advisor to the National Junior Florists' Association, reported to the Board on the continued growth of the junior movement, with a membership of 577 and a bank account of $737.53, without any debts. Great strides had been made in the educational phase of the program, with a model curriculum for high school students in pre-floriculture, including "on-the-job" training. This work had been spearheaded by Director Ed Lutey, working closely with the Detroit Board of Education. An annual budget of $7,500 was requested and approved, with a view to expanding this service into other school systems.

By the time of the annual meeting, in Buffalo, August 22-26, 1954, the Headquarters Committee had decided that it was unnecessary to engage a new general manager at this time. A full report from the firm of Hall and Liles had stated, "The need for a general manager under the present conditions is not apparent."

It was the sense of the report that there was a "very active and close relationship between the individual committees and the key personnel at Headquarters who are assigned the job of carrying out the approved policies and procedures. In our opinion, the present plan of organization of Headquarters is very effective because of two factors: first, each committee is very active and very zealous in discharging its responsibilities; second, each staff member is capable and experienced. In the future, we can foresee the need for a general manager when one of the following conditions occurs: lack of harmony and co-operation between the key personnel at Headquarters; retirement of your secretary; less active participation of your committees."

In spite of the optimism of the report, a somewhat ominous note was sounded in the concluding paragraph, which stated: "There appears to be a certain amount of member unrest which has been directed at Headquarters, but could logically be dissatisfaction with the present over-all program of services. We suggest that a careful analysis be made of the needs and desires of the membership for services expected from FTDA."

This report prompted the Headquarters Committee to suggest that, instead of hiring a general manager, Morris Liles, the author of the report, be engaged on a continuing

basis to act in an advisory capacity to the officers, directors
and department heads when deemed necessary. This suggestion was adopted by the Board of Directors.

The members appeared to believe that, with more responsibility placed upon their shoulders by the decision to abide
by the Liles Report, it was their duty to name their best men
to office. Ed Ludwig, veteran member from Pittsburgh, was
elected president for the coming year. To assist him, Mrs.
Marion Fisher, of Syracuse, New York, was made vice-president. Named director-at-large was Miss Nellie Whitley of
Hamilton, Ontario. President Ludwig was also nominated
to the Board of Interflora. Jack B. Kaufman, of Chicago,
represented the Associate Division on the Board. Steven P.
Dalsimer, of Cedarhurst, Long Island, New York; Arthur
M. Forth, of Rhinelander, Wisconsin; Lew James, of Galt,
Ontario; and Al Simon, of Culver City, California, were
announced as the new regional directors. Harald Thompson
of Rochester, Minnesota, was appointed treasurer by the
new Board.

It might be asked if this convention produced the first
ominous rumblings of the "member unrest," referred to in
the Liles report. When President Lawrie, near the close of
the meeting, opened the subject of new business, a member
arose whose question had been earlier declared out of order.
He again called for a specific breakdown of the expenditures
of the various branches of the Association. Clarence Muelleman, the treasurer, endeavored to answer. But the proffered
information did not satisfy the questioner. Next, John
Padgett, of the accounting firm of Lybrand, Ross Brothers &
Montgomery, explained both the budgetary and control
procedure, used in certifying the annual reports of FTD
Headquarters. Several other members joined in the discussion, until the president had to rap for order.

The veteran Charles Grakelow asked the privilege of the
floor and moved that further discussion of the financial
affairs of the Association be tabled. His motion was seconded

by Joseph Hynes, of Chicago, and, upon a call for the question, the motion carried.

This was an incident of which the new Headquarters Committee could well take note, and apparently they did. President Ludwig had appointed to this committee Vice-President Marion Fisher, chairman, Clarence Muelleman and Frank Schramm. They met in Detroit on September 19 and 20, 1954, for their first inspection of the Headquarters operation. After discussing the office affairs with Morris Liles, they submitted the following memorandum to all department heads: "The Headquarters Committee would like to put the responsibility of efficient operation of the office upon the shoulders of Harold Hewey, secretary. At times Mr. Hewey's decisions may not seem acceptable to you — however, we ask you to accept his decisions on a fair trial basis. If it doesn't work out after a fair trial, go back to Mr. Hewey and reason it out once more. If an impasse is reached, let it be decided by Mr. Liles."

They also decided that a Procedure and Policy Manual should be immediately compiled for the use of each department. Such a book would answer many questions about the interrelation of departments and, it was hoped, make for more harmonious co-operation among them.

President Ed Ludwig visited 34 out of 92 FTD units, appearing before FTD groups at the rate of more than one a week in all parts of the United States. He totaled a mileage that would have carried him around the world at the equator.

One of the visits he made was to the Tournament of Roses in Pasadena, California, for the famous New Year's Day Parade, in which FTD had entered a float. At the start of the parade, he was introduced to the television audience as head of FTD, by James Wallington, NBC announcer. Throughout the whole spectacle, he was repeatedly called upon by the announcer, as an expert to describe the floats. Ludwig's knowledge of the subject and his facile descriptions added greatly to the viewers' enjoyment of the telecast. As a result of his appearance and his assured, competent vocal style, the president gained much newspaper and magazine publicity for FTD, in addition to telling the FTD story to an estimated 35 million watchers. It was a public relations triumph. In addition, FTD's float, in its maiden entry, won the President's Trophy, the award for the most effective use of roses.

President Ludwig also appeared on the nationally televised Art Linkletter Show, on the occasion of the presentation to Linkletter of a plaque from all FTD members, naming him their favorite TV personality. Once again, the president's gracious personality and relaxed presence were the subject of much favorable comment.

But Ed Ludwig did much more than travel and make public relations appearances. Grave problems arose during his administration, the settlement of which required the concentrated energy and effectiveness of the entire FTD official family and the Headquarters executive personnel.

Back in 1949, at the January Board meeting in Detroit, the directors, upon the motion of Victor Stein and Louis Hoebel, had emphatically rejected the plan offered to them by H. A. Wiecking at the Miami convention of 1948 to co-operate with him in his Flowers-By-Wire corporation. This firm had asked that FTD members be permitted to fill orders sent to them by Flowers-By-Wire installations in department stores and other business establishments.

Flowers-By-Wire was not a filling florist organization. It was merely an owner of stations for the reception of wire orders. The Board concluded, however, that the filling of orders for Wiecking's establishments would not be in the best interests of FTD.

Shortly after this rejection of his plan, Wiecking filed suit in Federal District Court in Indianapolis, alleging violations by FTD of the Sherman Anti-Trust Act. He sought, in the same action, to restrain FTD's enforcement of its dual membership rule, alleging that such enforcement was causing him and his business irreparable damage.

The petition for a temporary injunction came on for a hearing in Indianapolis on October 13, 1954. The hearing assumed the proportions of a major trial. The transcript fills more than 2,500 typewritten pages. Particularly telling testimony for FTD was given by Comptroller John P. Beitler and by Harald Thompson, FTD treasurer at this time. Beitler was able to give the court a clear picture of the financial structure of the Association, the operation of the Clearing House and the other Headquarters divisions. He demonstrated, by accurate membership figures, that FTD had less than 30 per cent of American and Canadian retail florists as members and that Wiecking had ample outlets for his business among non-FTD retailers. Harald Thompson, a devoted FTD veteran, sketched the history of the founding and growth of the Association and showed the court that the dual membership rule had been an absolute necessity for the development of FTD at the time it was adopted.

In the end, the court ruled in favor of FTD and the injunction was denied. Attorneys for Wiecking gave notice of appeal and both sides filed voluminous briefs. On June 21, 1955, the appeal was withdrawn and thereafter a settlement was reached and the case dismissed on September 19, 1955.

While all the action of this case did not take place in Ed Ludwig's tenure as president — it had covered some six years — the hearing at Indianapolis was during his term and, although he did not appear, he lent every possible assistance, both official and personal.

At the January, 1955, meeting, the directors heard another Liles report on the Headquarters operation which stated in part: ". . . during these last few months, one pronounced change is apparent in the organization: a growth in confidence among its key personnel. The lowered morale resulting from last year's crop of rumors has been replaced by a feeling of optimism and hope for a better understanding of the respective role and functions of elected representatives, staff and general membership."

The report included the following suggestions:

"Stay within the scope and limits of respective authority, i.e., Headquarters do Headquarters' job and Committees do Committee jobs.

"Recognize the differences in personality and background of key members in organization; or, stated in a different way, try and understand the other person's viewpoint.

"Develop a better system of communications within the FTD family to minimize the unfounded rumors which destroy confidence and tear down morale."

Over against this hopeful analysis was a resolution, placed on record by one of the larger units, recommending that a general manager for FTD be hired as soon as possible and that he be a person with an outstanding record as a successful florist in the United States.

There was evidence that the Board saw a need for new offices in Detroit. History was repeating itself. Many members favored owning their own building. President Ludwig presented to the Board a resolution that $100,000 be set aside for the purchase of a suitable site in Detroit or the metropolitan area for a new home for FTD Headquarters. This was reminiscent of the "Temple Era" of the early days of the Association. There was a lengthy discussion of the possibilities of this idea and, in the end, the resolution was adopted. FTD was now looking forward to its own modern building in Detroit, designed and engineered for its particular use. But, as with many another desirable event, time was to elapse before fruition.

Morris Liles' engagement as advisory general manager was extended for six months, from March 1, 1955, and the Board adjourned, looking toward the August convention to be held in Seattle.

On June 20-21, 1955, the Headquarters Committee met in Detroit for their scheduled visit to FTD Headquarters. They echoed the sentiment, expressed in the Liles report, that the tensions and lack of interdepartmental co-ordination, which had been observed on their first visit, had completely disappeared. Each person interviewed had shown a better spirit of co-operation and a keener interest in Headquarters operations. Some apprehension was shown, however, in the last paragraph of the report, which said, "We have been very concerned about Mr. Hewey's health and his being able to continue his leadership at Headquarters. Mr. Hewey advises us that his doctor has given him a clean bill of health and has advised him to continue working. We, therefore, feel that the present setup should function well and should continue in such a manner until a general manager has been selected."

In the entire period since the departure of J. Paul Ostrander, the close observer might have noted a sort of double standard of analysis: the realization of an essential weakness in the departmentalized administrative structure of FTD on the one hand; and a fervent, almost prayerful hope on the other, that by some miracle of business magic the Association would outlast the tremors that afflicted it. The inherent sentimentality of florists was in part the basis of this hope. But much more important was the fact that the Association was growing taller than its structure, if such an odd metaphor may be used.

The projected income of FTD, suggested somewhat timidly in 1950, had been "50 million in the 50's." At mid-decade there was reason to believe that this figure would be easily passed. That such an organization, of such rapid growth in importance and income, could be successfully directed by a combination of committees and personnel co-operation on a voluntary basis, denied all the history of business experience.

A strong hand was imperative at Headquarters. There must

be a centralization of direction and leadership, a concentration of control, a single source through which the officers, directors and members could transmit their wishes to the Headquarters division. Key personnel at Headquarters were able and competent. But those precise qualities may sometimes prevent harmonious co-operation. Ability and competence are dissipated if not properly directed. The more capable persons there are to work to a common end, the more strictly their capabilities must be channeled.

The Seattle convention, August 24-27, 1955, was a typically hospitable Western convention. There was plenty of entertainment and pleasure, but not to the detriment of business. The election of officers produced one of the major surprises of FTD history.

Nominated by the committee for president were incumbent Ed Ludwig and Mrs. Marion Fisher. When nominations were opened, there was one more name offered from the floor. Victor Stein, of San Francisco, was made the third nominee for president.

Predictions of a close election led to excitement. A brief delay, after the conclusion of the business sessions and before the arrival of the chairman of the Election Committee, increased the tension. Breathless silence greeted Joe Leshyn, Election Committee chairman, as he entered the ballroom. Silence continued as he announced the elections of Harald Thompson to the Interflora Board, who was later also reappointed FTD treasurer, Cel Scherrer as the new director-at-large, and Vern Oppenlander to the office of vice-president.

Then came the news that Victor Stein had been elected president. Pandemonium broke loose — an intermingling of ecstatic shouts from those with successful candidates and the cries of the disappointed. But, in true FTD fashion, the election was accepted as the will of the majority, without rancor or recriminations.

The four new directors who took oath of office were:

Ed Bradley, Jr., of Omaha, Nebraska; Luther Eubank, of Waxahachie, Texas; Stanley C. Minshall, of St. Petersburg, Florida; and Mrs. Sylvia M. Valencia, of Westboro, Massachusetts. Jack Kaufman continued as Associate Division chairman.

The election of Stein had broken a 44-year tradition of second terms for incumbent presidents. The question was in many minds whether this signaled the discard of other traditional concepts, and whether, if so, it was good or bad.

CHAPTER SEVENTEEN

The Recent Years

ICTOR STEIN brought to the office of president of
FTD a dynamic, driving quality that was the
opposite of the quiet efficiency of Ed Ludwig,
but no less effective. The new president assumed
his responsibilities with positively conceived
ideas and a definite purpose. He believed that firm business-
like direction of FTD was imperative for its security and
advancement. His program included a powerful general
manager, in whom the Headquarters operation would be
centered, and through whom all orders, instructions and
suggestions from officers, directors and committees would
be channeled to the appropriate departments.

Although Morris Liles had been named general manager,
this was recognized as an interim appointment, because of
his committed interest as a partner in the firm of Hall and
Liles. Harold Hewey served as secretary of the Association
and was nominally in charge of Headquarters affairs, but
most of his time was devoted to the direction of the Sales
and Advertising Department.

What Stein visualized was someone who should be competent and ready to accept full responsibility for the smooth
operation of Headquarters. He would need to be a man of
executive experience and one willing to answer finally to the
officers and directors of FTD for the results of his administrative decisions. In establishing these criteria, the president
knew that he was demanding more than had been asked of
any prior administrator. He realized, too, that such a man-

ager would require a higher salary. But he believed that this would be more than repaid by increased member satisfaction and by eliminating the questionable committee-department co-operative sort of administration currently in use.

President Stein desired one more quality in his ideal general manager. He wished to see the office filled by an "idea man" — a man with the business background and economic knowledge to enable him to project a course for the Association, plus the ability, after concurrence of the officers and directors, to carry that project through to a successful conclusion.

With this and other important questions in mind, President Stein called a special meeting of the Board of Directors in Detroit for October 10 and 11, 1955.

One of the first motions offered at this meeting was by Director Bill McMullen, seconded by Director Al Simon, that a committee consisting of the president, vice-president and three Board members be appointed to consider the engagement of a general manager. President Stein appointed to this committee Directors Eugene Daudelin, Steven Dalsimer and Stanley C. Minshall, in addition to himself and Vice-President Vern Oppenlander.

The urgency of action by this committee was emphasized by two occurrences. Comptroller John P. Beitler submitted his resignation as chief financial officer of the Headquarters operation. Secretary Harold Hewey asked for a leave of absence because of ill health.

The loss of these two stalwarts, upon whom so much of the office administration had depended, was of serious concern to the Board. Beitler was leaving to enter private business. Under his guidance, the Clearing House had continually increased its service to the membership and all the financial programs had been astutely handled. Hewey's long service and broad knowledge of FTD structure had made him uniquely valuable to the present administrative organization. The rigors of the Flowers-By-Wire hearing in

Indianapolis and the strain of the Seattle convention had done much to undermine an already weakened constitution, and doctors had advised Hewey that continued work might have serious consequences.

Morris Liles, acting general manager, submitted to the Board at this meeting a comprehensive analysis of the FTD organization. In it he outlined the duties of each officer for the best conduct of Association affairs. Of the future general manager, he said, "The scope and importance of the general manager's job will be in direct proportion to his abilities and stature. A small man will create a small job, and a timid person will make a stab at performing the job." Liles agreed with Stein that obtaining a general manager was a first order of business.

Also of importance at this meeting was consideration of the motion to charge a 50-cent service fee on each wire order, the money to be retained by the florist. This was an old, persistent question. Several versions of such a plan had been presented to the members at the Seattle convention. The resolution which finally came to a vote provided that the 50-cent service charge supplant the present 2 per cent and 2 per cent charge, and that 20 per cent of the total amount of the service charge collected yearly would be allocated for service to members, mainly to support the sales and advertising program. Many members saw in this resolution a danger to the orderly budgeting of the sales and advertising program.

Victor Stein, from the floor at the Seattle convention, had succeeded in amending the motion and tabling the resolution, pending further study by the Sales and Advertising Committee. A quirk of fate or a strong coincidence may be seen in this successful move by Stein, for it was he who, by a strong speech from the floor of another convention, had helped forestall the adoption of a similar resolution.

At this special meeting the Sales and Advertising Committee presented a proposal for study of the service charge plan. It involved the legal aspect, considering its effect on the tax structure of FTD, and the business aspect, including its influence on the advertising budget and the danger of creating customer resistance. The suggestions of Sales and Advertising were adopted by the Board.

With the close of the October meeting, the committee for the selection of a general manager bent all its efforts toward that end.

Morris Liles was instructed to interview likely candidates, screening out those he considered unqualified and arranging for those with possibilities to be seen by the committee. The members of the committee came to Detroit on December 2-3, 1955, by which time Liles had talked with approximately 170 applicants and had recommended eight to be interviewed. None of the eight was found satisfactory by President Stein's group.

January and February passed without the presentation of any acceptable applicants. The members of the committee kept in constant communication with one another by letter and telephone. The dwindling prospects of finding the right man was beginning to cause concern.

President Stein, with the help of Granville Gude, approached a management procurement firm in Washington, D.C., and presented his problem to it. Assurance was given that men would soon be available for interviews.

On Saturday, March 17, 1956, the committee met in Washington, responding to an urgent call by the president. Five management prospects were present. The committee was particularly impressed with the caliber and the potential of the men selected by the agency.

One of those interviewed was John L. Bodette, who at that time was serving as president of Vulcan Press, Inc., a division of Elton B. Stephens & Associates of Birmingham, Alabama, and as executive vice-president of ARMY-NAVY REGISTER, the oldest military weekly publication in America. The decision of the committee was spontaneous

and unanimous that Bodette exhibited the desired qualities
to a greater degree than any of the others. At four o'clock
that afternoon an agreement was reached between the committee and Bodette.

Stein went to New York from Washington and, two weeks
later, telephoned Bodette, who was vacationing in Wisconsin,
to join him in New York. There, President Stein introduced
Bodette to some of the leading florists of New York. They
agreed that Bodette appeared to be the man for the job.

On April 19, 1956, the General Manager Committee
reported their conclusions to the Board of Directors assembled in Detroit and recommended the confirmation of John
L. Bodette as general manager of the Florists' Telegraph
Delivery Association. The motion was put by Eugene
Daudelin, of Chicago, seconded by Luther Eubank, of
Waxahachie, Texas, and carried unanimously. The Board
voted to terminate the services of Morris Liles on April
27, 1956.

The new man brought to the top position in the FTD
Headquarters operation a sound background in managerial
experience, backed by extensive work in sales promotion
and direction. A 1943 graduate with honors from Wisconsin's
famed Ripon College, he had added two years at the
Columbia University College of Law to his academic education, after performing active military service. He had served
at staff level in the National Guard and the Army Reserve.
He volunteered as a private, rose through the non-commis-
sioned grades and received a commission, after completing
the course at the Fort Benning Infantry School.

He saw combat service with the 159th Infantry Regiment
in France, Holland, Belgium and Germany and served for a
year and a half in the Office of Military Government at
Heidelberg and Stuttgart, Germany. Subsequently, he had
spent his time exclusively in the administrative phases of the
magazine and book publishing field.

The new general manager began his tenure with a searching analysis of the entire FTD structure and operation, as affecting their relation to the administration of Head-quarters. Starting with the definitive evaluation embodied in the Liles Report of October 10, 1955, Bodette applied the recommendations of the report, modified by his own organizational experience and the results of his interviews and observations, to the drafting of a comprehensive appraisal of FTD's position. This complete picture of the Association he considered necessary as a basis of the administrative procedures he thought imperative.

The thoroughness of Bodette's investigation was not the work of a week. Long hours went into studying, planning, weighing and determining the measures necessary to bring FTD to the peak of operational efficiency, thus assuring the members maximum service. All this had to be done in the two months before the Board of Directors met in Detroit, on July 2-6, 1956.

When President Stein called the Board to order on the morning of July 2, 1956, the general manager had his report ready. In it he proposed a nine-point program, the principal provisions of which were consolidation of certain departmental functions to eliminate duplication of effort, a re-assessment of the national advertising program, a return of the editorial offices of the FTD NEWS to Detroit and certain promotional projects which he believed desirable. He asked, further, that the Board take note of, and adopt, that section of the Liles Report which detailed the functions and duties of the general manager and his sole and primary responsibility to the Board of Directors.

Bodette's presentation of his report and his obvious grasp of the situation demonstrated to the Board that here was a man neither afraid of authority nor awed by the magnitude of his office.

The Board considered each of the nine points separately. There was little discussion. They were adopted unanimously.

The next move of the directors was to name John Bodette

executive secretary of FTD, thus combining in one man
the two highest administrative jobs in the Association. And,
since the interest of FTD in Interflora would also come
within his purview, he was elected by mail as assistant secretary and treasurer of the international group.

Bodette's report was not the only important business to
confront the Board at this time. There were other matters
requiring serious consideration. At the 1955 Seattle convention, Victor Stein had successfully moved that the question
of a service charge be deferred for further study. In the
intervening time, a survey had been conducted from the
FTD offices to determine the attitude of the membership
toward the increased advertising revenue embodied in the
measure. The entire membership, consisting of more than
10,000 florists, was circularized, asking for their views, with
addressed, stamped postcards supplied. The unprecedented
result was 4,373 replies. Of these, 1,157 were in favor of
adding the service charge or otherwise increasing the advertising fund. There were 182 answers advocating a reduction
in advertising; 881 answers were inconclusive; and 2,153
were in favor of leaving the charge as it was. There is no
doubt that this reflected the majority opinion. Stan Minshall
moved, seconded by Eugene Daudelin, that the members be
so informed at the next convention in Boston.

Ed Ludwig, James Lawrie and Harald Thompson were
appointed FTD's "true and lawful attorneys" to vote the
Association's stock in Interflora at the next meeting of that
group.

Throughout the summer, an intensified program of sales
and management rallies sparked the enthusiasm of the members and pointed toward an increased promotional drive to
bring the public to a greater awareness of flowers-by-wire.
As a means of meeting and becoming better acquainted with
FTD members, General Manager Bodette attended as many
of these rallies as his schedule would permit. His talks on
"Every Dollar Counts" emphasized the efficient use of

dollar-power in advertising, sales promotion and shop administration.

The 1956 convention met in Boston, August 17-23. There were 1,416 registrations and the local committee had arranged picnics, sight-seeing trips and other entertainment. But there were also serious Association problems and plans to be discussed. Victor Stein's administration had been active and forward-looking. He had kept in almost constant touch with the Board and with as many members as possible. He came to Boston with an agenda that left little free time.

President Eisenhower and Governor Christian Herter, of Massachusetts, sent their greetings to the meeting. An international note was struck by a wire from President and Mrs. Ramon Magsaysay, of the Phillipines, congratulating FTD for providing a means of "expression between friendly people in friendly countries."

One of President Stein's first acts, following the opening formalities, was to explain the signing of a consent decree with the United States Justice Department terminating a suit brought against the Association by the United States of America in the Federal District Court in Detroit, alleging violations of the antitrust laws and seeking an injunction against certain trade practices. This act was the end of the FTD restrictions against dual membership. As a legal means of assuring that FTD would not return to the practice of exclusive membership — a situation not contemplated — the United States Justice Department had required the Association to sign a consent decree, agreeing to permit its members to join, or transact business with, other organizations for the transmission of flower orders by wire.

President Stein explained this to the membership and asked that the rule providing for exclusive membership be rescinded. This was done. Other amendments were offered to the Articles and Bylaws, most of them the result of suggestions by Bodette and discussed by him with the Board at the meeting the previous July. Bodette considered the practice of earmarking funds for specific purposes to be inflexible and detrimental to the proper exercise of the funds. There was also a needed revision in the structure of the standing committees. In all, 11 amendments to existing Articles and Bylaws were placed before the membership and all carried.

The members were eager to accept the recommendations of the president, the Board and the general manager when they were shown that the suggested changes were for the purpose of streamlining and strengthening the administration of the member service phases of the Association. As Stein explained, "I urge you to vote affirmatively on each measure. Your Board has given long and careful study to each of these proposals, and feels that adoption of each of them will be for the benefit of the entire membership."

The Boston convention was John Bodette's introduction to the assembled members. He demonstrated in his report that, during the four months since he had assumed the administrative leadership of the Headquarters affairs, he had acquired a wide knowledge of FTD's structure and formed definite opinions about the Association's position in the business world. He recognized that the social and fraternal bonds among the members, great elements of strength in the early days, must now become subordinate to the business and financial importance of FTD.

"I submit to you," he told them, "that FTD is big business, whether it wants to be or not, and by the very nature of its size, it will always be a target easily identifiable by those who would seek to destroy it. Because of its size, FTD must of necessity conduct its affairs in keeping with the scope of its activities. This means close attention to financial requirements, both in terms of guaranteed credit between members, as well as in the disbursement of millions of dollars in support of increased sales. Very frankly, the financial structure of FTD is not in keeping with the requirements of a $50 million business, particularly, when viewed in the light of the fact that it must not only be a service organization but a sales promotional organization with all the characteristics of a commercial banking institution."

In short, Bodette recognized that the tremendous growth of FTD during the mid-century decade was not fully realized by the average member. He sought to picture to them the edifice they had built in its true dimensions. FTD had emerged from the period of haphazard management. It had attained power and dignity in financial circles. It required "big business" treatment and "big business" thinking.

Bodette's talk did much to explain to the membership the reason why, in the program he had first presented to the Board of Directors, he had asked for a strong hand in the conduct of the Headquarters operation. Some changes were necessary for the efficiency of the Association's operation. There was no doubt that FTD had grown taller than some of the personnel who administered its affairs.

The impression made by the new general manager upon the membership assembled at Boston was solid and reassuring. There was a secure feeling of co-operation. The entire spirit of the meeting was prophetic. It was as if a pause were made in the steady forward progress, for a new look at the road ahead; as if strength and purpose, born of a fresh realization of size and power, were now urging the members on.

The membership of FTD was announced, as of this convention, as 11,213 in the United States and Canada, with members of Interflora raising the number to some 20,000 with direct communication between 92 countries.

New regional directors elected to begin their terms following the convention were: Irving Allen, of Bremerton, Washington; Lou DiVito, of East Cleveland, Ohio; Joseph Hynes, of Chicago; and Andrew Strang, of Philadelphia.

A shadow fell over the election of president. Nominated for the office were Clarence Muelleman, of Chicago; Allen

Hixon, of Worcester, who withdrew before the election; James E. Scott, of Providence; and Mrs. Marion Fisher, of Syracuse.

Before the convention opened, Mrs. Fisher was called back to Syracuse to the bedside of her eldest son, Louis, ill with pneumonia. The young man did not survive.

In her absence, Mrs. Fisher was elected to the presidency. She had seriously considered withdrawing her name from nomination, but the counsel of her remaining sons and many friends prevailed. Her son, Jack Branin, came to Boston in time to represent his mother in the presentation of the victors to the convention. Mrs. Fisher was the first woman ever elected to the highest FTD office, and she remains unique in its history.

Carl E. Bohnert, of Charleston, West Virginia, was elected vice-president and Cel Scherrer, of San Antonio, was re-elected director-at-large. Mrs. Scherrer was the first two-term director-at-large. Past-President Victor Stein was nominated to the Board of Interflora. James E. Kelly, of Rochester, N. Y., represented the Associate Division.

At the meeting of the new Board of Directors, the engagement of General Manager John Bodette was affirmed, as was his appointment as executive secretary. Ed Lutey, the retiring chairman of the Finance Committee, was named to the post of treasurer, succeeding the veteran Harald Thompson, of Rochester, Minnesota.

More had happened at the Boston convention than appears on the surface. There had been a marshalling of strength and a greater concentration of management and direction. No legal obstructions lay ahead. The Association had taken a new look in its own mirror and, like a boy who suddenly realizes that he needs to shave, had acquired new pride, a fresh sense of importance. Members left Boston telling themselves again that theirs was a great organization, capable, through combined efforts, of reaching business heights not thought possible a few years before.

The week following the Boston convention, President Fisher visited Headquarters in Detroit for a conference with Bodette. She completely reviewed the operation of the Detroit office and together they made a careful canvass of the entire situation. The result was a plan of operation covering all national aspects of the Association's affairs.

Leaving Detroit, Mrs. Fisher visited units and organization meetings in Tacoma, New Orleans, Los Angeles, New York, Philadelphia and other cities. Bodette joined her for the New Orleans meeting and a press reception in Los Angeles. Before she reported to the Board meeting in Detroit in January, she had travelled 30,000 miles.

Vice-President Carl E. Bohnert also "hit the road" for the Association, visiting many of the organization meetings impossible to include on the president's time schedule.

Mrs. Fisher reported to the Board in November that she was satisfied with the operation of the Headquarters staff. She praised the spirit that Bodette had infused into the office staff and called the directors' attention to the amount of work that the Detroit operation entailed.

The Board met in Detroit November 12-15, 1956. Bodette had not prepared a formal report of Headquarters activities, preferring to talk extemporaneously. From notes, he presented a comprehensive talk, outlining the innovations and changes that he was in the process of introducing.

He had taken the opportunity, while in Europe for the Interflora meeting, to confer with Air Force Exchange System officials and representatives of the American Express Company regarding the transmission of overseas flowers-by-wire. He was also successful in arranging a contract with the European Exchange System, whereby FTD would soon begin to benefit greatly. Preliminary moves had been made, looking to contacts in Turkey and the Near East, Spain and Japan.

Returning to Detroit, he had tackled the personnel problems. Turnover in the clerical staff had been a serious matter with the Detroit offices. The periodic demands made by heavy industry in the Motor City, particularly for trained key-punch and verifier operators in the Clearing House staff, prevented the stabilizing of a dependable, satisfied group of operators. The expense of training new personnel, investigation showed, was often more than the salary paid the employee.

The general manager instituted an incentive pay system in the Clearing House, based on average hourly production, dependability, co-operation and seniority, worked out after consultation with an employees' committee. The system appreciably increased the efficiency of the Clearing House staff, and also permitted certain dependable workers to increase their monthly earnings in sums from $5 to $36.50.

For the executive personnel, Bodette introduced psychological tests by a reputable firm of industrial psychologists. This, too, met with the full co-operation of the administrative staff and gave the general manager an authoritative evaluation of the quality of his assistants.

Field staff members were brought into Detroit for a two-weeks' conference. The field men were divided into four working committees, each assigned a definite mission, to develop information and procedures. These assignments were reported to the general conference for discussion, criticism and correction. From this conference, a definite field program was compiled.

The "P.O." problem, that perennial headache, had again grown acute with the publication in READER'S DIGEST magazine of an article advocating the establishment of "Living Memorials," institutions, scholarships, endowments and the like, instead of flowers for funerals. FTD was an advertiser in the magazine. Objections to the article, from members all over the country, poured into the Headquarters offices. A conference was arranged with the editorial staff of READER'S DIGEST and the magazine agreed to publish an article by Dr. Frederick Brown Harris, Chaplain of the

The main entrance to FTD offices. The soft voice and pleasant manner of receptionist Marian King have been familiar to FTD callers for 14 years. In the background, Lorraine Fearn, of the Interflora Department, has 15 years of service. The girls pictured on this page represent more than — shhh! — 150 years of FTD employment.

Dean of women employees at FTD was Jennie Prendergast, who, until her recent death, had been with the Association longer than any other employee.

These three senior members of the FTD office force are still efficiently fulfilling exacting positions in Association affairs. Left to right, they are Lauretta Dennis, 34 years; Isabel Elsbernd, 34 years; and a virtual newcomer, Dorothy Smith, 22 years.

Albert Pochelon's original shop occupied this corner at 153 Bates Street, Detroit. A back room became the first permanent FTD office in 1912. Later the building was enlarged and remodeled into the Pochelon Building, shown here, and renumbered 815 Bates Street. FTD offices remained here until the move into the "New Home," in November, 1931.

The "New Home," below, was a remodeled mansion on East Grand Boulevard, one of Detroit's most sumptuous residential streets. More than a million persons drove past these beautifully landscaped grounds each week on their way to and from Belle Isle, the city's largest park, an easy walk from Headquarters.

The address, 200 Lafayette Building, is familiar to florists in 188 countries of the world. The present FTD offices occupy the entire second floor of this 14-story building in downtown Detroit. The FTD Mercury emblem is visible in the corner window. Inset shows the building entrance on Michigan Avenue and the prominently displayed bronze nameplate of the Association.

NEW INTERNATIONAL HEADQUARTERS

At its June, 1960, meeting, the Board of Directors approved the plans for FTD's new office building in Detroit. As shown in the architect's drawing above, the design is modern and functional, furnishing 20,000 square feet of office space on two floors. A basement houses mechanical and electrical equipment. Exterior materials are brick, precast quartz-surfaced concrete, aluminum and glass. A movable partition system permits ready adaptation of the interior to all conditions called for by department growth and efficient work flow. The interior is acoustically engineered and completely air-conditioned for winter and summer. Decorative appointments feature living plants and flowers from all over the world. The site of the building occupies approximately 100,000 square feet in the new urban redevelopment area of Detroit's billion dollar waterfront beautification project. Grounds will be landscaped to harmonize with the area plans. Parking space is available for 72 cars. Ground-breaking ceremonies are expected to be held in July.

United States Senate, praising the use of funeral flowers. With this assurance, FTD continued its advertising contract with the magazine.

Up to this time, FTD had borne the financial burden of the campaign against "P.O." Bodette suggested that the other branches of the industry be invited to contribute as their share an amount at least equal to that contributed by FTD, which was approximately $71,000. Acting on this suggestion, the Board voted that the matter be transferred from the Sales and Advertising Services Committee to the Finance Committee, for a thorough presentation of the subject to other branches of the floral industry and an intensified effort to enlist support for the campaign from others who would benefit.

Much was accomplished at the November, 1956, meeting of the Board and more was planned for the January meeting. Several matters could not be explored in November and these were held over for consideration after the New Year. In the accelerated pace of FTD operations, this time passed quickly.

By the time the Board met in Detroit, January 21-25, 1957, an answer had been received from the Associate Division in reply to the suggestion that other branches of the floral industry match FTD's contribution to the "P.O." campaign. The Associate Division was in sympathy with the movement, but regretted its lack of sufficient current funds to permit an increase of its participation in the campaign. It did promise, however, to take the plan under advisement and attempt to find means of co-operating more extensively.

The Board heard at this meeting that during the fiscal 1956-57, membership in FTD had not increased appreciably, dispelling any notion that removal of the dual-membership restriction would cause a rush of new members. However, the top 10 states in growth of membership showed that in those areas membership had increased 11.8 per cent. In all, FTD had added 1,120 new member shops.

At Headquarters, the Bookkeeping Department and the Clearing House had been combined into one Financial Department, for more efficient administration and operation, with Gilbert Van Dongen named manager of the combined departments. This allowed Comptroller Al Moore, who had followed John P. Beitler into the post, to devote his time and attention to the supervisory duties of the financial operation.

General Manager Bodette summed up the accomplishments of the past three months by saying, "I believe we are on schedule. This is a year of gradual change and consolidation behind the program started in 1956. Much remains to be done on unit attendance, field service, membership fulfillment and in the area of local advertising. These areas will command more of our attention as we move into the new year."

There was prophecy in this statement. But prophecies often come true through the hard work of the prophet. By the end of the 1956-57 fiscal year, the Board, meeting in Detroit June 26 to July 3, 1957, learned that the field service representatives had completed 1,226 sending tests, with 348 members as subjects of receiving tests. In addition, the field men had made 5,309 service calls and, in the quality control program, each field man was conducting an average of 105 tests per month. This indicated that the activities in the field had markedly increased.

A Public Relations Department had been established to develop a program along three basic themes: first, to create, develop and build member understanding of, interest in, and lasting loyalty to their Association and its management; second, to build member prestige at the local level; third, to develop a co-ordinated program with other sections of the industry, effectively to combat the "Please Omit" problem.

In establishing this department, FTD acknowledged that public relations composed an essential phase of management responsibility, thus bringing itself into line with the major industries of the country. The great growth of public relations activities, and the influence of such growth on the consuming public, had been proved repeatedly by the most rigid surveys and studies. It was accepted, as it still is, as a natural and necessary part of sales promotion and as a major tool in making the consumer aware of the product, creating an incentive to buy and informing him of the product's availability. Without criticism, it might be said that this phase of sales promotion had been too long absent from FTD.

Other changes in employee relations had been introduced at Headquarters. The Board approved these innovations. Lines of communication had been drawn between the departments, between departments and the general manager and between employees and management.

The personnel was divided into three groups to insure efficient operation. The first consisted of the management staff, composed of the general manager and the department heads. This group met once each week, often joined by legal counsel and a representative of FTD's auditing firm. The junior executives and section supervisors composed a second group, which met with management once a month for an information seminar on such subjects as leadership, office procedure, handling of personnel and group discussions. Finally, employees had indirect access to the top management team through an Employee-Management Committee. This was composed of three representatives elected by the employees, and three members appointed by the general manager from the management team. As a result, a marked reduction was noted in personnel turnover.

In the selection of a convention city for 1959, conventions being scheduled two years in advance, there was some humor over the dilemma of the Board. Seeking to plan for a special Fiftieth Anniversary convention, it was not known with certainty when this anniversary would fall. Some members believed that FTD was organized in 1909. Others were convinced that 1910 was the first year. Treasurer Ed Lutey, appointed chairman of the planning committee for the Fiftieth Anniversary Committee, held the opinion that the birthday would fall in 1960. Investigation proved him right. Detroit was selected as the site of the mid-century meeting.

To assist the Florists' Information Council in its campaign against "P.O.," the Board appropriated $5,000. Another $2,500 was voted to SAF as FTD's payment as dues for its members. The FTD Associate Division also donated $2,500 to FTD to further research through survey work in coordinating the "P.O." program with FIC.

Frank Schramm, of Toledo, was appointed to the Interflora Committee to replace the recently deceased Harald Thompson, whose long and faithful services to the Association were recognized by the Board.

It was the sense of the Board meeting, in January, 1957, that notable new impetus had been given the FTD cause by the new management. Improved relations and efficiency in the Headquarters operation with the induction of competent and able department heads and the elimination of much of the employee turnover, plus an enhanced sense of loyalty and security, were seen as certain to permeate the entire Association, to heighten pride in membership. Closer contact among members, created by the new public relations program, would inevitably increase the strength of FTD and ultimately benefit the entire conception of flowers-by-wire.

The Board meeting adjourned, with all eyes turned to Chicago for the next annual meeting on August 16 to 23, 1957.

During the period before the Chicago convention, General Manager Bodette continued his established pace of membership visits and intense work in his office. Matching him in concentration on the business of FTD were President Marion Fisher and Vice-President Carl Bohnert. Members of the Board also found that more and more of their time was demanded by Association affairs as the tempo in the membership ranks increased. There was a growing awareness of the importance of membership. Members were almost every day reminded that the lines of communication from each shop led into a constantly growing number of communities and countries.

Further to strengthen the administrative team at Headquarters, John P. Beitler returned to the position of comptroller on July 27, 1957.

That the "big business" thinking, first advocated by General Manager Bodette, was beginning to inspire the general membership of FTD, was demonstrated by President Fisher in her opening address to the Chicago convention. She said, "Today we live in a complex and dynamic business world, a world which is constantly undergoing great changes — politically, socially and economically. Today we must either keep step with these changes or drop by the wayside. No business, no group or individual can escape it. It has been apparent for some time that our Association has been changing — that it *is* keeping in step with the rest of the business world — that it is no longer largely a social organization of members who had banded together to insure delivery of flowers over long distances. It has grown into a powerful business organization of men and women with definite economic goals." She recognized and commended the changes that had been made, depicting them as an integral part of "the new era of the new FTD!"

There were more changes to come. Ready for presentation to the membership at Chicago were 16 revisions of the Bylaws, which would further strengthen FTD's position in the business world. Not all these revisions were received wholeheartedly. Many veteran members regretted the subtle but inexorable changes occurring within the organization to which they had given so many years and so much devotion. Others, naturally of a cautious nature, thought that further consideration was required, before the membership could properly evaluate the changes. In the main, the important revisions were accepted.

The attendance at Chicago was the largest registration of FTD members since the Chicago convention of 10 years before. It represented almost 10 per cent of the membership. There were 1,909 registrations, a proper forum before which to present such important measures.

The question of a service charge was familiar to the membership. It arose again with a force that could not be stemmed. For the past several months, Manager Bodette had caused a test program to be undertaken in 92 florist shops across the country to measure the response of the public to such a charge. He told the meeting that, of the 6,634 orders on which the service charge was added in the 92 shops, there had been no comment whatever from 6,226 customers. Of the 408 who commented, 206 were satisfied after explanation, 124 were dissatisfied and refused to pay the charge, and 74 appeared dissatisfied, but paid.

A motion to table the service charge question failed. Charles H. Grakelow, Director Stanley Minshall and a strong southern group sharply opposed the charge. Joe Hynes, Herbert Berg, Mrs. Sylvia Valencia, Mrs. Christina Tinger and others were as strongly in its favor. After some parliamentary maneuvering, a vote was called for and the service charge carried, 339-118. Thus the membership resolved, without acrimony, a question that had arisen regularly throughout the life of FTD.

In his report to the convention, the Secretary informed the members that 11,424 florists and associates now composed the membership. There were 242 new member shops, 146 of which were the only florists in their respective cities. This growth reflected a much wider service area, for the expansion was principally in the Far West, the Midwest and the South, with Florida and Texas showing the most gain.

Bodette then posed the serious question, "Do we want to

achieve more member shops in sparsely populated areas with the thought to provide direct service and in so doing perhaps compromise some of the high standards for which the Association stands?" The question was by no means rhetorical. Its subject had become increasingly important with the growth of FTD. No answer was expected, but the query contained the basis for much sober reflection.

The general manager, as before, had been dividing his time between his office and meetings with members all over the country. He now asked that he be allowed to spend the next six months in his office, without having to accept speaking dates. This was granted.

A spirited election campaign developed when Eugene Daudelin, of Chicago, and O. K. Sanders, of St. Louis, were proposed for the presidency by the Nominating Committee. When Sanders withdrew his name, Mrs. Marion Fisher was nominated from the floor for re-election. Daudelin was elected to the office. Ed Lutey, of Detroit, was elected vice-president and Mrs. Kay Carron, of Biloxi, Mississippi, director-at-large. Harold Kayton, of San Antonio, was nominated to the Board of Interflora. New directors were: Ralph Bachman, of Minneapolis; Charles Hum, of Los Angeles; Mrs. Alma Pratt, of Hamilton, Ontario; and Peter Tryforos, of New York. James Kelly held over as chairman of the Associate Division. The new Board appointed Steven P. Dalsimer as treasurer and retained John Bodette as executive secretary and general manager.

In delivering the report on the president's address at the convention, former President Edward McCarthy said, "We highly recommend our president for her sincere devotion to her duties during the tenure of her office and the very efficient manner in which she guided the destiny of our FTD organization for the past year. We concur in her commendation of Mr. John Bodette in his program of efficient management at Headquarters and the formulation of a forward looking program for the further and progressive development of our Association."

There was no doubt that the plan for launching FTD fully into the stream of business commerce was recognized and appreciated. Those at first dubious about the wisdom of emphasizing the commercial over the fraternal were now applauding the change as promoting better times ahead for the entire membership.

The new Board met in Detroit, November 18-19, 1957, for a busy session. There had also been much activity by the officers and directors since the convention. Vice-President Lutey reported that he had attended seven unit meetings and two standing committee meetings. President Eugene Daudelin had been present at 15 similar functions. The directors had been busy in their respective regions.

Of paramount interest to the membership was the decision to return $300,000 to members who had advanced money for the operation of the Clearing House, this to be done before the coming Christmas. A recommendation, advanced by the Finance Committee and adopted, was that wherever possible any disagreement between members should be resolved by the members themselves. Director Stanley Minshall, chairman of the Membership Committee, took a practical view of the matter and observed that there would probably always be disagreement and that Headquarters would have to continue to act as referee. But he supported the recommendation.

New emphasis was laid on the National Junior Florists' Association. Mrs. Alma Pratt, chairman of that committee, reported that an extensive program, with prizes and gift certificates, was being prepared to induce more juniors to join. She suggested that students over the age of 21 years and studying floriculture in college be permitted to join the NJF Association. The Board was of the opinion that this program would be better developed at the local level, since the budget had already been completed for the year.

On the eve of 1958, the belief was expressed by the Board that the coming year held promise of a rise in gross national spending. It was time for FTD to prepare its service and advertising for its share of the consumer dollar.

The adoption of the 50-cent service charge at the Chicago convention had apparently caused no trouble for the members. But, by the time the Board met in Detroit on February 24-26, 1958, there was evident great variation in the procedure among the various shops for collecting it. The charge was not mandatory but optional. Furthermore, there were different tax laws in different states. Western Union was concerned, when the transmission fee and the service fee were combined, since this violated a ruling of the Federal Communications Commission. All this Manager Bodette reported to the Board.

He explained to the directors that he had instructed John Beitler, on his resumption of the comptroller's position, to make a thorough study of the FTD accounting system, anticipating a reorganization of the practices and procedures within the accounting department. Beitler appeared before the Board and reported his results. He advocated continued acquisition of electronic accounting equipment as it became available. Detailing the advantages of developments in this field, he showed the Board how savings of hundreds of thousands of dollars could be made, with increased efficiency in the handling of members' reports. He asked the Board to study his recommendations. "We will have faster dissemination of information for Board members and management," he said, "so that decisions can be made in the light of current operating facts." FTD now has a full complement of the most modern accounting equipment.

Bodette took the Board through the full range of FTD activities. He reviewed the advertising and sales promotional activities, and paid special attention to the campaign with newspaper editors to eliminate the "P.O." announcements from obituaries. The Speakers' Bureau, especially the services of Ian Stuart, was explained and its wholesome effect noted. Stuart was present to tell the Board about some of his appearances.

The Board decided that, in general, things were going well. President Daudelin summed it up in these words: "In talking to many prominent members in various parts of the country, they are very content with the Association as it is being conducted by its Board of Directors and management, and are most happy with the continual rise in sales which no doubt is generated by this good work."

By the time the Board met again, June 25-26, 1958, a change had also been made in the duties of the field men. Relieved of initial inspection of applicants' shops, they had more time to pursue the objective of visiting each member in his own territory once a year. The Board had ruled that the upgrading of members' shops was a first responsibility. This would result in improved quality control and service control to supplement the orientation supplied by district representatives. More attention to the unit meetings was also considered of importance for the field men.

The creation of two new regions was recommended. One of these would result from dividing the New York region into two. The other would be made by rearranging the geographical distribution of certain units.

General Manager Bodette recommended to the Membership Committee that a new plan of district representative indoctrination be adopted. He suggested that, in addition to being brought to Headquarters for a 2-day conference following appointment, the district representatives also be assembled for a one-day meeting at 6-month intervals at a central location in each region. There they would hear talks by the regional director, a Headquarters representative, district representatives and the field man for the region. This would keep them all in closer touch with administration thinking and procedures.

The Board met once more before the Miami Beach convention. This was on August 20-21, 1958, in Detroit, and was one of the most fruitful of recent meetings.

The services of Keyes, Madden and Jones Advertising Agency, of Chicago, had been engaged to handle the FTD advertising program, replacing the Grant Agency. It had not been an easy selection. The Sales and Advertising Services Committee, under Chairman Joe Hynes, had carefully considered several agencies before deciding on the Chicago firm.

The Florist Information Council which had been made an interim committee of the Society of American Florists, in 1957, was now made a permanent committee of the society. Its name was changed to Florist Information Committee.

The increased importance of the "P.O." fight caused the Board to appropriate $25,000 to the FIC. It was felt that FTD had registered progress in its own battle to overcome the threat, but it was the concensus of the directors that more could be achieved by operating through an industry-wide organization, such as the Florists' Information Committee.

General Manager Bodette presented three recommendations. They were the establishment of a "pilot city" for a national youth program; the creation of a national institute of retail flower selling; and the development of a Plans Committee.

Discussing at length his recommendation of a Plans Committee, the general manager expressed the opinion that, in time, such a committee could easily become of enough importance to warrant its permanence. He proposed that, in the meantime, a special committee be formed to begin the work.

A plan to introduce the sale of candy into florist members' shops was presented by the Sales and Advertising Services Committee. After considerable deliberation by the Board, the plan failed to pass.

The Board adjourned, satisfied that progress in harmony

with the general tone of business had been accomplished and that the convention would be a proper sounding board for the Board's proposals.

The Miami Beach convention was a combined vacation and business trip which attracted 1,500 registrations. That these convention visitors did not let vacation interfere with the affairs of their Association was soon shown by the resounding defeat of a proposal to permit the appointment of more than two directors to standing committees. This made plain that the general membership valued their authority to have members on the standing committees, who did not fill the dual role of committee member and regional director.

The proposal to redefine the territories of certain regions and to establish two additional regions encountered unexpected opposition. In the end, the project carried by an overwhelming vote, an example of the democratic discussion of issues, always a characteristic of FTD conventions. FTD has always recognized that the airing of different views serves to inform the general membership of the issues at stake, and the result is an informed vote.

An attempt to eliminate the 2 per cent and 2 per cent plus 1 per cent Clearing House charge in favor of the 50-cent service charge was also defeated. The members had operated for several years under that system and knew its value. They hesitated to adopt another financing plan, when the one in use had proved so successful.

General Manager Bodette presented one of his most optimistic reports to this convention. His suggestions had previously been, in the main, presented to the Board. He now explained his thoughts for the future of the Association, stating that more of them would be heard during the coming year. He concluded, "I think I could sum up the report of the secretary very simply. We have strong policies, a capable Board of Directors, a farseeing group of committeemen. I think that the requirements of the future are being properly assessed. I think we have a management team that is capable of translating policy into a working plan that will bring new profits to your shop. In other words, I say that the goal of $100 million in the '60s is still very realistic."

The optimism of future gains is often the springboard to their realization. It was certain that FTD was going forward into the coming year with every expectation of great advances.

In the election of officers, Stanley C. Minshall, of St. Petersburg, Florida, became president. Steven P. Dalsimer, of Cedarhurst, L. I., New York, was elected vice-president. Mrs. Kay Carron, nominated from the floor, retained her director-at-large office, and Past-President Eugene Daudelin was nominated to the Interflora Board. New members of the Board of Directors were Joseph Casey, of Melrose, Massachusetts; Ralph Hunter, of Charlotte, North Carolina; Marty Swartz, of Dallas, Texas; and Earl Tobler, of Kansas City, Missouri.

The steady advance of FTD in the business world continued through the next year. President Minshall proved to be another of the long line of traveling and working presidents. He established an office in the Detroit Headquarters and could often be seen back of the wide glass window, working on reports or meeting with Headquarters personnel. Minshall was no stranger to administrative labor. He had served as mayor of St. Petersburg and as a member of the Florida Legislature.

At the Board meeting, held February 17-19, 1959, General Manager Bodette framed his report around a series of questions, such as, "What is the evidence that FTD renders an essential service well and has dealt fairly with its members?" The talk was entitled, "Management — a Self-Evaluation." Speaking informally, he used the method of topic questions to lay before the Board the complete operation of the Headquarters affairs. He detailed the advances that had been made in management personnel capabilities with the introduction of new and better equipped employees. He reminded

the directors that it had been said of him and his plans that
they would overlook FTD's character as a members' organization. "When I cease to be conscious of that fact," he said,
"I will be unconscious. Eleven thousand people never cease
to remind me of the fact. It is an awareness that leads toward
pride on my part that my direction and leadership in
management affairs is seemingly recognized by the rank and
file membership for what it is."

There is no doubt that Bodette's ideas, with the constant
support of officers, directors and committeemen, had wrought
well for FTD. The proof was in the increased revenue, the
larger clearings and the closer control of quality and service,
all elements of sound business management.

The formation of two new regions, voted at the Miami
convention, added two directors to the Board. The oath of
office was administered to Mrs. Doris Remis, of Schenectady,
New York, and to Robert C. Cherry, of Paducah, Kentucky.
O. Ben Haley joined the Board as chairman of the Associate
Division. Mrs. Sylvia Valencia had been appointed to the
office of treasurer.

The history of the 50-cent service charge had been rather
rough. An opinion had been asked of FTD's legal counsel
as to the position of the Association in the collection of the
charge. According to the attorneys, extensive amendment
of the Association Bylaws would be necessary. There was
also the possibility of the Internal Revenue Bureau's finding
in the provision a reason to exact an income tax from FTD
on the money collected. This was particularly probable if
the charge was made mandatory. And there were other legal
implications in the service charge which counsel considered
important. On the strength of the legal report, it was moved
by Director Hynes and seconded by Director DiVito that a
special committee be appointed to study the service charge
matter and report to the Board. To this committee President

Minshall appointed Joseph Hynes, chairman, Steven P. Dalsimer and Robert C. Cherry.

There was another committee report given at this meeting of the Board, which held the promise of definite future advantage to the Association. The National Junior Florists' Association, founded along the lines of FTD, had not attracted the expected membership. Victor Stein conceived the idea of a trust fund to further the education of students interested in the industry. At the suggestion of General Manager Bodette, President Minshall had appointed a special committee to study the advisability of organizing a trust arrangement, to be called Foundation For Future Florists. This plan would offer tuition grants to students for the purpose of helping them pursue a course in floriculture in the college of their choice, provided the college had approval of the committee.

This committee, composed of Mrs. Alma Pratt, chairman; Camilla Pickering, of Fall River, Massachusetts; Cel Scherrer; Bud Bailey, of Chicago; Joseph Casey, and Burt D. Moore, of Dayton, Ohio, had met in Detroit two weeks before to consider plans for the Foundation. Also in attendance were President Minshall and General Manager Bodette. By unanimous vote, the committee decided to recommend to the Board that $25,000 be appropriated as the initial Foundation fund. From this amount, scholarships amounting to $250 each would be made available to qualified applicants.

This recommendation was later rescinded and the amount of the appropriation from FTD fixed at $5,000, with other organizations and individuals invited to participate in the fund by contributions. A trust agreement, appointing the National Bank of Detroit trustee, was drawn up and the Foundation formally established. At the Los Angeles convention, President Minshall announced the 13 recipients of the first tuition grants.

The Board of Directors, meeting in Detroit, June 10-12, 1959, agreed that all district representatives should attend the

1959 convention, scheduled in Los Angeles during August, for a general meeting and all four sessions of the annual meeting. Plans were perfected for intensive training of the district representatives in the latest concepts of their work.

An innovation was introduced regarding the change of ownership of member shops. It was decided that, when a change was made in the ownership of a member shop, the 90-day guarantee of account would be exercised and that the former owner could hold his member's voting privilege until the expiration of the 3-month period.

In London, July 19-20, 1959, nine delegates, representing 188 countries of FTD's international arm, Interflora, met to attend the thirteenth annual meeting of the international group to discuss policies and to elect new officers. Victor Stein, past-president of FTD, was named Interflora president and John L. Bodette was appointed secretary-treasurer.

At the conclusion of the meeting, newly elected President Stein sent a cable to Nikita Khrushchev, requesting that Russian florists be allowed to join the Interflora organization to permit the free transmission of flower orders to and from Russia. There are known to be about 94 florists in Moscow and other potential Interflora members in the principal cities outside the capital. Considerable promise for enlarging the scope of Interflora lies in completing arrangements with the Russian government. Efforts to that end are continuing.

CHAPTER EIGHTEEN

Now and The Future

LOS ANGELES banished its smog and presented to the FTD conventioneers a week of lovely weather for the annual meeting, August 16-20, 1959. It was soon apparent that the members had not come to enjoy the sunshine, but to plunge into the work of the convention.

Early in the Board meeting preceding the annual members' meeting, the directors voted to increase the appropriation for public relations and to adopt the recommendation of the Sales and Advertising Services Committee that $25,000 be allocated to the FIC program to further combat the "P.O." menace. A suggestion by the Finance Committee that $178,098 of the Clearing House reserves be returned to the members also carried.

The recommendation of the Relocation Committee that the purchase of a site for an FTD office building in Detroit go forward was upheld with the tabling of a motion to continue in the present offices for five years.

At the general members' meeting, the attending florists heard heartening reports from President Minshall on the growth and acceptance of FTD, which he had found in his many miles of travel since assuming office. Victor Stein reported briefly on the progress made by Interflora and the goals it hopes to achieve in the future. John Walker, executive secretary of SAF, spoke for the absent President Charles Pennock and thanked FTD for its co-operation and support during the year. He informed the gathering that because of FTD's financial aid, 241 cities had been visited by FIC field men and 199 newspapers had agreed to refrain from using "Please Omit" phrases.

General Manager Bodette told the audience the results of the change-of-name survey conducted during the year. Contrary to what many believed, the rigidly controlled sampling of the survey had shown that the best known phrases for carrying the idea of flowers-by-wire were now being used by FTD.

This revelation was ample proof of the influence of the Association's advertising and public relations campaigns. Bodette encouraged all members to make lavish use of these terms, suggesting that "Florists' Telegraph Delivery Association" be used as a formal name, "FTD" as a working name, and "Flowers-By-Wire" as a publicity slogan.

Recognizing the growing value of FTD membership, the meeting voted to increase fees for active members from $25 to $50 and inspection fees for applicants from $35 to $50. Some members thought that $100 was not excessive for the privilege of membership and a motion was introduced further raising the fees. It was declared out of order, but a second motion recommended that the Board consider such an increase for presentation at the next convention.

A motion to eliminate the office of director-at-large caused little discussion and was soon carried. The director-at-large to be elected at the Los Angeles convention was declared to be the final person to hold that office.

A third Bylaw amendment changed the name of the Sales and Advertising Services Committee to Marketing Committee, thus recognizing the broader area in which this division now operates.

But entertainment was not lacking in Los Angeles, either. Trips to Disneyland, a beautiful 1,400-year old ritual performed by Japanese children at the opening of the design school, an early morning "fizz" breakfast at the Los Angeles flower market, all contributed to the enjoyment of the meeting.

A one-hour musical spectacular, "Cash On Your Line," was presented by the Bell Telephone System. It featured Stubby Kaye and was replete with songs, fun and valuable suggestions on proper telephone selling for FTD members. This "business clinic" attracted over 2,000 registrants — a record of its kind.

The smooth handling of the registration of members attending the Los Angeles meeting is credited to the 14 men of the Field Service Section, under William G. Lee. Familiar to most of the members were two veteran field men — Erwin Hamme, with 18 years of service, and Simon (Si) Weaver, 16 years with FTD in field service.

The results of the election of officers showed that Irving Allen, of Bremerton, Washington, was the new president, with Joseph Hynes, of Chicago, vice-president. Named to serve as the last director-at-large, since that office was to be discontinued, was Mrs. Bessie Pawson, of Santa Ana, California. Lou DiVito, of East Cleveland, Ohio, was nominated to the Board of Interflora. John L. Bodette was reappointed general manager and executive secretary, and Andrew Strang, of Philadelphia, became treasurer.

New directors who took their seats on the Board were: John M. Carey, of Detroit; Arthur C. Clemensen, of Chicago; Marshall Gifford, of Portland, Oregon; and James Ludwig, of Pittsburgh. O. Ben Haley continued on the Board as Associate Division chairman.

The Los Angeles convention ended on a note of optimism and accomplishment. The year 1959 was closing with Clearing House transactions reaching the highest totals in history, exceeding by $10 million the early estimates of "50 million in the '50s." Membership was stable, and quality control had assumed an important place in FTD affairs. Business volume was rising and members could look ahead to increased results from advertising and public relations.

A short meeting of the Board of Directors was held in Detroit on October 19-20, 1959. A resolution was adopted at this time that FTD go ahead with the acquisition of land for a new building, the cost of both not to exceed $500,000. The President and General Manager were authorized to engage architects to draw preliminary plans and estimates for the construction. It was decided that in any question concerning immediate action on the procurement of the building site, the requirement of 10 days' notice for a meeting of the Board would be waived.

It was apparent that the directors wanted nothing to interfere with the procurement of the site. Their presence in Detroit on short notice could be counted upon.

So FTD moved into 1960, the Golden Anniversary Year.

The Board held its regular meeting January 19-20, 1960, in Detroit. One of its first moves was to honor its commitment of $25,000 to the Foundation For Future Florists for the fiscal year 1960-61. The budget for that period also included the expenses of the Committee of the Foundation For Future Florists. This scholarship arrangement was gaining in popularity and its value in putting trained and capable personnel into the industry was everywhere recognized.

The budget for the Fiftieth Anniversary convention, presented by Convention Chairman Harold Hutchings and Convention Manager Hubert Beudert, was presented to the Board. The directors were deeply interested in the forthcoming meeting and, in the interest of making the FTD mid-century gathering a high point in the history of the Association, voted an additional allocation. The tentative program for the convention was approved.

A site had been chosen for the new Headquarters building, and General Manager Bodette outlined the steps that had been taken toward its acquisition. President Allen and Bodette were given authorization to proceed with the architectural arrangements.

With the granting of statehood to Alaska and Hawaii, the Board recognized that Alaska now became eligible as an annual meeting place. Hawaii was made a part of Region 10, but a Bylaw limiting annual meetings to continental North America made a convention in Hawaii impossible for the present. The question of adding Alaska to Region 11 was left to be answered in a proposed Bylaw change at the 1960 convention.

Acceding to the request of Interflora that it be allowed to increase the size of its Board to 12 directors in order to provide for better representation of its constituent member countries, the FTD Board drew up a proposed Bylaw change. This would call for two nominees to be selected from the membership of FTD each year for the Board of Interflora, increasing to four FTD's representation on the international Board. The request indicated the growing awareness of countries in the FTD orbit of the ease with which flowers could be transmitted around the world.

It demonstrated, too, the increasing size of Interflora. It will be remembered that John Bodette, in his first report to the FTD Board after attending the Interflora meeting in London, announced that 92 nations were linked in the network of flowers-by-wire. Since that time, the size of the group had more than doubled. At present, Interflora florists in 188 countries now relay an average of one flowers-by-wire order every two seconds around the clock. Recent developments point to further growth.

President Irving Allen reported on his travels. He had devoted an enormous amount of time to visiting members and unit meetings, with trips to Detroit for interviews with Headquarters personnel. He was impressed with the smooth progress of Association affairs on a national level, and the general relaxed state of the membership. He had particularly noted that FTD members everywhere had expressed complete approval of FTD progress. The president, one of their own, brought them reassurance.

The general manager presented a comprehensive report of FTD's present condition and a look at the future. Within a 10-point frame of reference, he emphasized the powerful potential of FTD in the years ahead and submitted his recommendations for a program, to begin immediately, which would help to realize that potential.

He was concerned with whether FTD Headquarters had sufficiently close contacts and open channels of communication with the individual members to enable it to render to them the most efficient help and service in their business. Although the field service representatives made their regular calls and offered their help and advice when requested, they were, after all, representatives of Headquarters, and there might be a reticence on the part of individual members to talk freely with them regarding ideas and opinions they might have of the Headquarters operation.

Bodette suggested that the Board study the wisdom of engaging an outside opinion-sampling firm to make a study of the present member service situation, and, on the basis of its finding, recommend ways and means by which FTD's service to members could be improved.

In the same way, the quality and service control test program was reviewed. There had recently been government and industry investigations into the bad faith of certain practices in radio, TV and industry. Regarding advertising and public relations, Bodette was particularly anxious that no finger should ever be pointed at FTD's test program with the insinuation or accusation that it was not strictly conducted and in utmost good faith. To this end, he recommended that it be divorced entirely from any aspect of membership participation and be made an independent function of management, to be controlled directly from Headquarters. This would eliminate any suspicion that pre-information to the florist being tested colored the authenticity of the shop evaluation.

For better communication with the membership, and to

supply them with current economic and business news as well as information and notes on FTD affairs, the general manager proposed that a weekly newsletter be prepared by the Publications Division. This newsletter would be mailed to each member so as to reach his desk on Monday morning. In suggesting such a letter, Bodette meant to bring FTD into line with other large associations and business organizations. While commercial newsletters are available to florists, as to others, a letter channeled specifically to their interests was thought to have sufficient value to them to be worthwhile. This new publication would not interfere in any way with the publication of the FTD NEWS, but would keep the florist-member apprised of current conditions which might affect his business.

Recent authoritative appraisals of the international scene had indicated that business in Europe was at the dawn of a great revival. War damages and attitudes had been largely overcome. Factories were in production again. European consumer income was rising, and there was every reason to predict a boom in the continental countries. Bodette saw this as a rich opportunity for the promotion and exploitation of every facet of the Interflora organization to the benefit of FTD members. However, this would be a full-time operation. Since he was secretary of both FTD and Interflora, this meant that any time devoted to the expansion of Interflora would, of necessity, have to be taken from the attention he was pledged to give to FTD. This was a division of duties which he did not consider to be in the best interests of either organization.

As an alternative, he proposed the establishment of a separate Interflora Division within FTD Headquarters. This Division would be under the close supervision of Bodette, but would be conducted by a manager familiar with the European business scene and able to write and converse in the principle continental languages. His secretary and clerk would supplement his knowledge of languages and attend to the ministerial duties of the Interflora effort. Thus, all translations would be made at Headquarters, and a specialized drive for Interflora business would be possible. To begin with, this operation would be budgeted through the Clearing House until, through growth of intercontinental business, it became self-sustaining.

Three of the general manager's points related closely to retail selling. First of these was a "Flora-Cheque," a certificate in the nature of other merchandise gift certificates, but calling specifically for an arrangement of flowers of the recipient's choice. This Flora-Cheque would have the advantage of being easily mailable anywhere. It could be purchased from an FTD florist before a certain holiday, mailed to the person to receive the flowers in a do-not-open-'til-Christmas manner and opened on the proper day. The recipient would then take the certificate to his favorite FTD florist and receive the arrangement of his choice to the amount specified in the Flora-Cheque. The Flora-Cheque would then be cleared through the FTD Clearing House in the regular manner.

An added advantage of this plan is that it would defer the filling of the gift order until after the particular holiday, thus lightening the load of the filling florist.

Next offered was a plan to supply from Headquarters a mail promotional service for local florists. Realizing that many small shops have neither the personnel nor the time to conduct an aggressive direct mail promotional program in the interest of their business, the general manager suggested that a **Direct Mail Department** be established within the Marketing Division to offer a regular follow-up direct mail promotion program to the individual florist. The florist subscribing to this service would submit to the Marketing Division a list of his customers and prospects to receive advertising and sales promotion material on a regular schedule. These lists would be closely guarded, and would be available for no other purpose than that for which they were submitted. This mailed matter could be had upon a weekly, bi-weekly, monthly, or bi-monthly basis to keep the customer and prospect constantly informed and aware of the availability of flowers for all occasions at the shop of the subscribing member.

Closely tied in with the last two points was the National Institute for Retail Flower Selling which encompassed a comprehensive merchandising education program. This would be part of a plan to establish certain standards which a florist or designer must attain in order to qualify as a certified retail florist. This compares to other industries and their educational programs, such as the National Institute of Banking or the National Institute of Certified Life Underwriters.

Another point offered by General Manager Bodette was the establishment of a statistical department within the Marketing Division to maintain current break downs on all phases of the florist industry. In form for ready reference, the information would apply to all situations where such statistics are indicated, either for the international network or on a local level.

It was also suggested that a special committee be appointed to study a plan for furnishing free architectural and marketing advice to members. This information would be compiled and delivered by qualified architects and marketing specialists. It would relate directly to the members' local situation regarding remodeling, relocation, advertising and sales promotion, meeting competition and other aspects of his local market which vitally affected his business.

There was no doubt that the 10-point plan was ambitious and farseeing. It contained nothing that was not well within the possibility of accomplishment if prosecuted with vision and vigor. It was founded upon the premise that only by increasing its efficiency, the quality of its member shops and the competence of those who direct it, can the Association continue to overshadow all competition. Said Bodette, in summary, "I have never felt more secure in the ability of my associates and employees to give the Association superior man and woman power capable of fulfilling each assignment rapidly, capably and efficiently."

The management team assembled under Bodette's tenure is indeed apt and able. Each member is highly skilled in his respective field. The Headquarters operation is now separated into five major divisions: Administration, Finance, Marketing, Membership Fulfillment and Publications. The heads of these divisions make up the Management Executive Committee which reports direct to General Manager Bodette. The convention manager also reports direct to him.

The Administration Division is headed by Hubert Beudert, office manager, who is also convention manager. This division has charge of the Members' Group Insurance Plan, the Mail Department, and the Personnel Department. Personnel does not present a problem. The average tenure of clerks and secretaries is 3.28 years — a remarkable record in a city where personnel turnover is probably the highest in the nation. Two employees have been with FTD for 34 years each.

More than 3,500,000 pieces of mail are handled by the Mail Department each year. This is equivalent to the volume of a U. S. Post Office in a city of 100,000 population. Closely allied with the Mail Department are the Purchasing and Receiving Departments, both directed by F. M. Hollingshead.

The Finance Division is the compiler and guardian of the FTD budget. At its head is John P. Beitler. Allocation of finances to the various divisions are made in this office. All international business is also handled through this division, which includes as one of its departments the Clearing House. The Clearing House is really the "heart" of FTD. The marvel of electronics is nowhere better shown than in this big room filled with humming, clicking machines which, with superhuman speed and accuracy, process the accounts of the more than 11,000 FTD members and 13,000 members of Interflora.

Perhaps the Membership Fulfillment Division comes closer to the individual members than any other division. This direct contact is supplied first through the district representatives in their attendance at unit meetings and, next, through the visits of the field service representatives. Both of these groups report to this division. Vernon Michalke is in charge of the division, ably assisted by William G. Lee. Lee is an ex-field service representative and thoroughly understands the work of his men. The staff of 14 field men is available nationally for service, advice and information on all aspects of Association activities.

All members are familiar with the FTD NEWS, one of the top industrial magazines in the country. The editor is Hal Shanafield. This magazine is the concern of the Publications Division. Besides the FTD NEWS, the Publications Division issues the Delivery Directory, with which all members are familiar; the Answer Book, a valuable information tool; and compiles and maintains the numerical listings of the members. This division also includes an offset print shop employing six people, and fully equipped for press and bindery work in registered color or black and white in sizes from postcard to 14" x 20" stock. The print shop turns out printed annual reports, circulars and bulletins to members, unit notices, test order summaries, all single-sheet internal Headquarters forms, ledger sheets and internal accounting forms, form letters, financial statements, and many other printing jobs arising in the course of FTD procedure.

Advertising and public relations under the modern concept of sales promotion cannot be overemphasized. In this type of service to members, FTD is one of the national leaders. Gordon Conn is director of this, the Marketing Division. This division has the responsibility of wisely allocating more than $2,100,000 a year in advertising and public relations. Manager of Public Relations, a part of this division, is Ann Standish. The wisdom of decisions made in the

Marketing Division is shown in the steadily increasing volume of both orders and clearings over the years. Even through the depression days of the '30s, FTD rode through the bad times with hardly a break in the upward swing of its business curve.

The newest project of this division is Monitor, a sales training service and telephone technique evaluation presented by field service representatives in local meetings with members across the country.

Newspapers, radio, television, and magazines are all part of the advertising outlay of this division. So that the Marketing Division will have the benefit of specialists in the advertising industry, Keyes, Madden and Jones, an expert Chicago advertising agency, is retained on a yearly basis to advise and assist in the placing of advertising, evaluating its effectiveness and planning future programming.

The publicity program at FTD Headquarters is concerned principally with promotion of intra-FTD affairs, serving members at the local level. A national public relations program, closely coordinated with the local office, is administered by FTD's public relations agency, Edward Gottlieb & Associates, of New York. Continuous campaigns result in publicity in national magazines, network radio and TV programs, and in the nation's press through news and wire services.

Assistant executive secretary of FTD is Virginia D. Roberts, who first came to work in the Association in 1949 as secretary to Harold Hewey. She has a vast knowledge of the membership and the internal affairs of the Association.

President Irving Allen, FTD's "travelingest" president, will have visited every unit of the Association in the United States and Canada before his tenure ends. This is something that no other president has done, and it is even more remarkable since President Allen is a victim of poliomyelitis and must walk with the aid of crutches.

His prime interest and concern is to maintain and increase

a spirit of teamwork among the Board of Directors, management and the various committees, to the end that an atmosphere of effective accomplishment in all phases of the FTD operation is assured. He has been particularly successful in achieving this goal.

He carries this spirit of harmony to unit meetings, and there imparts to members the sense of well-being that exists between their elected and appointed representatives. Thus, a closer feeling of unity and co-operation is engendered throughout FTD. When the close understanding at the top, filtering down through the FTD pyramid, meets the loyalty rising from the local level, the sturdy strength thus formed makes FTD unique among the nonprofit organizations of the world.

Speaking of his travels, President Allen states: "Built on the foundation of the work of our pioneers, FTD has emerged as big business. As we enter this 50th year, we seem to have hit our stride in operating in a smooth, efficient, ever-expanding manner.

"As I have visited the membership, I have sensed a feeling of pride and confidence throughout the United States and Canada.

"Much credit for this efficient business operation must be given to General Manager John Bodette, with his outstanding executive abilities, fund of progressive ideas, and dynamic leadership.

"In this first four years of his exceptional service, his organization of a most productive staff, his thinking far ahead into the future, his quick grasp of the problems and needs of the industry have all resulted in the attainment of goals which, at first, seemed impossible. They have already been surpassed, and sights are set far ahead.

"An overwhelming number of our members have come to know and respect our general manager and to depend upon him for help with their many problems."

In referring to the above statement, President Allen

mentioned specifically the general manager's now well-known "Clear the Decks" letter. This communication went out to the entire membership over Bodette's signature on November 21, 1958. It told the membership that he, personally, wished to know if there was any service, adjustment or information that had been requested of Headquarters that had not been fully supplied. If so, he told them, he wanted to "clear the decks" and at the same time extend the services of the entire Headquarters facilities to each member. A self-addressed envelope, to be opened only by Bodette, was enclosed for a reply.

Members took advantage of the invitation. They returned 1,034 replies. Of these, 582 were complimentary, while only 48 contained complaints. These complaints were acted upon immediately. Four hundred and four of the letters required direct answers and these were dictated and signed by Bodette within 48 hours — something of a physical feat in itself. Mention is still heard of the "Clear the Decks" letter.

Concluding his statement, President Allen said: "The staff at Headquarters works as a most efficient team. In fact, team work is the key word in the deliberations of the Board of Directors, the work of the District Representatives and the field staff as well. There seems to be no question in anyone's mind but that the progress of FTD will be ever more rapid in the years ahead."

Time and maturity often tend to regroup family members who have pursued their individual courses. Recent events indicate that FTD and SAF, offspring and parent, are approaching a closer integration of the affairs of both organizations. In January, 1960, a joint meeting of the Boards of Directors of both organizations was held in Detroit.

The meeting was devoted largely to an orientation and explanation of their programs. Those present were enthusiastic over the exchange of information and felt that this close realignment would be helpful in the furtherance of programs of both groups, for the mutual benefit of the entire floral industry.

The Florists' Telegraph Delivery Association approaches its fiftieth birthday with pride and satisfaction of accomplishment. Those who remember it from early years are slightly bewildered but extremely gratified by its present position. From a beginning based more upon fraternity than business, more upon cordial acquaintance than careful commercial practice, FTD has reached a place of pre-eminence among nonprofit corporations.

It has not reached this peak through association alone. More, perhaps, than the impulse of the original idea, the devotion and hard work of its early members account for its climb. Theirs was not an easy task. To nurse the young FTD until it outgrew its early infirmities took the constant attention and dedication of its pioneers. They saw in it the seed of a great idea. But they would marvel that the idea has developed into a reality of such magnitude.

The FTD florist is a member of a proud organization. Fifty years of growth and greatness lie behind him. To take advantage of his membership by toiling manfully in every phase of the Association's multitudinous activities is to bring himself and his future advantages beyond computing. Not to do so is to watch Opportunity march swiftly by.

Today, the individual florist can see the value of his FTD membership. It has been said and repeated that FTD is now a mark of envy and competitive attack by other organizations seeking to use its facilities for their profit. Members are offered plans for transmission of candy, gifts and other merchandise. Credit card schemes and other so-called modern merchandising ideas are daily presented to be included in the florists' operations.

The FTD member is aware that all these schemes include some profit for their promulgators. He knows that his organization, the Florists' Telegraph Delivery Association, is a nonprofit organization; that when the time is ripe for the

inclusion of other merchandising plans in the florist industry, FTD will be the first to suggest them and will offer the
member an arrangement, studied, tested and given to him
at the lowest possible operating cost, and with the highest
profit to him.

The power of FTD as an organization of world scope
has contributed immeasurably to the health and growth and
destiny of the florist industry. It has accomplished for every
individual member, in his private career, what it has done at
large for the whole, globe-encircling operation. And, as
single bricks compose a mighty tower, it is the single florist-
member who, in his legions, creates the strength and firmness
which benefit him so magnificently.

The story is here set down for all to see.

END

Appendix

FTD

OFFICERS AND DIRECTORS

PRESIDENTS

1910-12	J. A. Valentine	*Denver, Colorado*
1912-16	Irwin Bertermann	*Indianapolis, Indiana*
1916-19	William F. Gude	*Washington, D.C.*
1919-22	Philip Breitmeyer	*Detroit, Michigan*
1922-24	Edward Sceery	*Paterson, New Jersey*
1924-26	Charles H. Brown	*New York, New York*
1926-28	William J. Smyth	*Chicago, Illinois*
1928-30	Charles H. Grakelow	*Philadelphia, Pennsylvania*
1930-32	Thomas C. Luke	*Portland, Oregon*
1932-34	Frank J. Baker	*Utica, New York*
1934-36	Otto Lang	*Dallas, Texas*
1936-38	Ernest S. Simmons	*Toronto, Ontario*
1938-40	Willard Crain	*Cincinnati, Ohio*
1940-46	William E. Joy	*Columbus, Georgia*
1946-48	Edward J. McCarthy	*Brooklyn, New York*
1948-50	H. Rollo Mueller	*Columbia, Missouri*
1950-52	Granville Gude	*Washington, D.C.*
1952-54	James Lawrie	*Toronto, Ontario*
1954-55	Ed Ludwig	*Pittsburgh, Pennsylvania*
1955-56	Victor Stein	*San Francisco, California*
1956-57	Mrs. Marion Fisher	*Syracuse, New York*
1957-58	Eugene R. Daudelin	*Chicago, Illinois*
1958-59	Stanley C. Minshall	*St. Petersburg, Florida*
1959-60	Irving Allen	*Bremerton, Washington*

VICE-PRESIDENTS

1910-12	W. J. Palmer	*Buffalo, New York*
1912-16	William F. Gude	*Washington, D.C.*
1916-17	George Asmus	*Chicago, Illinois*
1917-19	Philip Breitmeyer	*Detroit, Michigan*
1919-20	Irwin Bertermann	*Indianapolis, Indiana*
1920-21	H. G. Dillemuth	*Toronto, Ontario*
1921-22	Charles Feast	*Baltimore, Maryland*
1922-23	Fred C. Weber	*St. Louis, Missouri*
1923-24	Charles H. Brown	*New York, New York*
1924-25	Karl P. Baum	*Knoxville, Tennessee*
1925-26	William J. Smyth	*Chicago, Illinois*
1926-27	Herman P. Knoble	*Cleveland, Ohio*
1927-28	Henry Penn	*Boston, Massachusetts*
1928-30	S. A. Anderson	*Buffalo, New York*
1930-31	Alfred T. Bunyard	*New York, New York*
1931-32	Frank J. Baker	*Utica, New York*
1932-33	Arthur Leidiger	*Milwaukee, Wisconsin*
1933-34	Otto Lang	*Dallas, Texas*
1934-35	Herbert Clausen	*Denver, Colorado*
1935-36	Ernest S. Simmons	*Toronto, Ontario*
1936-37	Peter A. Chopin	*New Orleans, Louisiana*
1937-38	Willard Crain	*Cincinnati, Ohio*
1938-39	Ed Ludwig	*Pittsburgh, Pennsylvania*
1939-40	William E. Joy	*Columbus, Georgia*
1940-41	Bruno D. Smoke	*Detroit, Michigan*
1941-46	Alfred H. Serveau	*San Francisco, California*
1946-48	Mrs. Bert Schiller McDonald	*Chicago, Illinois*
1948-49	John H. Claus	*Germantown, Pennsylvania*
1949-50	Allen W. Hixon	*Worcester, Massachusetts*
1950-51	Victor Stein	*San Francisco, California*
1951-52	James Lawrie	*Toronto, Ontario*
1952-54	Ed J. Barnes, Jr.	*Kansas City, Missouri*
1954-55	Mrs. Marion Fisher	*Syracuse, New York*
1955-56	Vern A. Oppenlander	*Denver, Colorado*
1956-57	Carl E. Bohnert	*Charleston, West Virginia*
1957-58	Edward Lutey	*Detroit, Michigan*
1958-59	Steven P. Dalsimer	*Cedarhurst, L.I., New York*
1959-60	P. Joseph Hynes	*Chicago, Illinois*

TREASURER

1910-49	William L. Rock	*Kansas City, Mo.*
	(1949 Treasurer Emeritus)	
1949-52	Julius Pochelon	*Detroit, Michigan*
1952-53	G. Stewart Barnaby	*Brookline, Massachusetts*
1953-54	Clarence E. Muelleman	*Chicago, Illinois*
1954-56	Harald Thompson	*Rochester, Minnesota*
1956-57	Edward Lutey	*Detroit, Michigan*
1957-58	Steven P. Dalsimer	*Cedarhurst, L.I., N. Y.*
1958-59	Mrs. Sylvia M. Valencia	*Westboro, Massachusetts*
1959-60	Andrew H. Strang	*Philadelphia, Pennsylvania*

SECRETARY

1910-11	H. B. Dorner	*Urbana, Illinois*
1911-12	Irwin Bertermann	*Indianapolis, Indiana*
1912-24	Albert Pochelon	*Detroit, Michigan*
1954-55	Harold R. Hewey	*Detroit, Michigan*
(Apr.)(Nov.)		

EXECUTIVE SECRETARY

1924-29	Albert Pochelon	*Detroit, Michigan*
1929-41	Al Barber	*Detroit, Michigan*
(Apr.)		
1953-53	Harold R. Hewey (Acting)	*Detroit, Michigan*
(Jan.-Jun.)		

GENERAL MANAGER

1954-56	Morris R. Liles	*Detroit, Michigan*
(Apr.)		

EXECUTIVE SECRETARY AND GENERAL MANAGER

1941-48	John Besemer	*Detroit, Michigan*
1949-53	Philip W. Jones	*Detroit, Michigan*
1953-54	J. Paul Ostrander	*Detroit, Michigan*
(Jun.)(Apr.)		
1956-	John L. Bodette	*Detroit, Michigan*

DIRECTORS

Allen, Irving	1956-59	*Bremerton, Washington*
Allen, Jack	1932-35	*Glendale, California*
Anderson, Lou N.	1935-38	*Montclair, New Jersey*
Anderson, S. A.	1924-28	*Buffalo, New York*
Anderson, S. A., Jr.	1938-41	*Buffalo, New York*
Asmus, George	1910-15	*Chicago, Illinois*
Bachman, Ralph W.	1957-60	*Minneapolis, Minnesota*
Barnaby, G. Stewart	1949-52	*Brookline, Massachusetts*
Barnes, Ed J.	1949-52	*Kansas City, Missouri*
Baum, Karl P.	1916-25	*Knoxville, Tennessee*
Bertermann, Irwin	1910-13	*Indianapolis, Indiana*
Bertermann, John	1910-16	*Indianapolis, Indiana*
Bohnert, Carl E.	1950-53	*Charleston, West Virginia*
Borden, A. F.	1918-24	*Los Angeles, California*
Boswell, Gordon	1936-39	*Ft. Worth, Texas*
Bradley, Ed, Jr.	1955-58	*Omaha, Nebraska*
Breitmeyer, Philip	1910-15	*Detroit, Michigan*
Broderick, Richard T.	1941-48	*Yonkers, New York*
Bunyard, Alfred T.	1926-29	*New York, New York*
Carey, John M.	1959-	*Detroit, Michigan*
Carroll, Paul M.	1946-49	*Houston, Texas*
Cartledge, A. B.	1910-14	*Philadelphia, Pennsylvania*
Caruthers, J. M.	1949-52	*Orlando, Florida*
Casey, Joseph	1958-	*Melrose, Massachusetts*
Cason, Robert L.	1952-55	*Corsicana, Texas*
Cherry, Robert C.	1959	*Paducah, Kentucky*
Chopin, Peter A.	1933-36	*New Orleans, Louisiana*
Claus, John H.	1940-47	*Germantown, Pennsylvania*
Clausen, Herbert	1930-33	*Denver, Colorado*
Clemensen, Arthur C.	1959-	*Chicago, Illinois*
Clody, Laurent E.	1926-29	*Chicago, Illinois*
Coombs, Joseph F.	1930-33	*New Haven, Connecticut*
Cooper, Charles	1935-38	*Toronto, Ontario*
Crain, Willard	1934-37	*Cincinnati, Ohio*

Dale, James H.	1935-38	*Houghton, Michigan*
Dalsimer, Steven P.	1954-57	*Cedarhurst, L.I., New York*
Darling, H. Reeve	1931-34	*Los Angeles, California*
Daudelin, Eugene R.	1953-56	*Chicago, Illinois*
Defenthaler, G. Wright	1947-50	*Royal Oak, Michigan*
Dillemuth, H. G.	1917-20	*Toronto, Ontario*
DiVito, Lou	1956-59	*East Cleveland, Ohio*
Donn, James	1939-43	*Miami, Florida*
Eubank, Luther	1955-58	*Waxahachie, Texas*
Forth, Arthur M.	1954-57	*Rhinelander, Wisconsin*
Foster, Lon	1939-46	*Oklahoma City, Oklahoma*
Frank, Vernon	1943-46	*Decatur, Georgia*
Fredenhagen, Frank W.	1950-54	*Burbank, California*
Gallivan, Dan	1936-39	*Holyoke, Massachusetts*
Gammage, W. W.	1919-25	*London, Ontario*
Geraghty, George	1924-28	*Toronto, Ontario*
Gifford, Marshall B.	1959-	*Portland, Oregon*
Gorly, Frank	1923-26	*St. Louis, Missouri*
Gould, Edward W.	1937-40	*Chicago, Illinois*
Graham, Robert L., Jr.	1931-34	*Baltimore, Maryland*
Grakelow, Charles H.	1918-24	*Philadelphia, Pennsylvania*
Gude, Granville	1937-40	*Washington, D.C.*
Gude, William F.	1910-14	*Washington, D.C.*
Harris, Vernon	1946-49	*Birmingham, Alabama*
Harrison, Phil M.	1952-55	*Nashville, Tennessee*
Hasselmann, William	1939-40	*Independence, Kansas*
Heck, Otto	1947-50	*Reading, Pennsylvania*
Hixon, Allen W.	1946-49	*Worcester, Massachusetts*
Hoebel, Louis	1948-51	*Fort Lee, New Jersey*
Hoffman, Sidney, Sr.	1929-32	*Boston, Massachusetts*
Holbrow, Willmore F.	1939-46	*Dorchester, Massachusetts*
Hornecker, Henry	1927-30	*East Orange, New Jersey*
Hum, Charles R.	1957-60	*Los Angeles, California*
Hunter, Ralph	1958-	*Charlotte, North Carolina*
Hynes, P. Joseph	1956-59	*Chicago, Illinois*

James, Lew	1954-57	*Galt, Ontario*
Johnston, Donald L.	1931-34	*Canton, Ohio*
Joy, Thomas H.	1925-28	*Nashville, Tennessee*
Joy, William E.	1936-39	*Columbus, Georgia*
Kayton, Harold	1949-52	*San Antonio, Texas*
Kent, Charles I.	1940-47	*Cleveland, Ohio*
Kipp, Carl T.	1934-37	*Spokane, Washington*
Knoble, Herman P.	1917-26	*Cleveland, Ohio*
Lang, Otto	1926-29	*Dallas, Texas*
Lange, August	1915-18	*Chicago, Illinois*
Lange, Homer	1934-37	*Chicago, Illinois*
Lawrie, James	1948-51	*Toronto, Ontario*
Leidiger, Arthur	1929-32	*Milwaukee, Wisconsin*
LeMar, Clarence	1947-50	*Chicago, Illinois*
LeMoult, Adolph, Jr.	1932-35	*New York, New York*
Ludwig, Ed	1934-37	*Pittsburgh, Pennsylvania*
Ludwig, James	1959-	*Pittsburgh, Pennsylvania*
Luepke, Rudy	1953-56	*Vancouver, Washington*
Luke, Thomas	1927-30	*Portland, Oregon*
Lutey, Edward	1953-56	*Detroit, Michigan*
Macklin, Douglas I.	1951-54	*Sarnia, Ontario*
McCarthy, Edward J.	1924-28	*Brooklyn, New York*
McKenna, Frank J.	1924-27	*Montreal, Quebec*
McKenna, Leo J.	1938-41	*Montreal, Quebec*
McMullen, William C.	1953-56	*State College, Pennsylvania*
Meinhardt, Fred W.	1910-14	*St. Louis, Missouri*
Minshall, Stanley C.	1955-58	*St. Petersburg, Florida*
Moore, Dr. Walter A.	1924-27	*Seattle, Washington*
Muellemann, Clarence	1950-53	*Chicago, Illinois*
Mueller, H. Rollo	1936-39	*Columbia, Missouri*
Nelson, Edward K., Jr.	1930-33	*Tampa, Florida*
Niklas, Hans	1937-40	*Portland, Oregon*
O'Brien, John J.	1933-36	*Boston, Massachusetts*
Olson, Olaf J.	1914-17	*St. Paul, Minnesota*
	1924-27	
O'Neill, Jerry	1950-53	*Seattle, Washington*
Oppenlander, Vern A.	1952-55	*Denver, Colorado*

Palmer, W. J.	1918-24	*Buffalo, New York*
Papworth, Harry	1914-17	*New Orleans, Louisiana*
Pelicano, Frank D.	1915-18	*San Francisco, California*
Penn, Henry	1913-16	*Boston, Massachusetts*
	1923-26	
Peters, William F.	1940-47	*Spokane, Washington*
Petit, Alfred K.	1951-54	*Mineola, L I., New York*
Pratt, Mrs. Alma Lou	1957-60	*Hamilton, Ontario*
Remis, Mrs. Doris	1959-	*Schenectady, New York*
Rentschler, George F.	1948-51	*Madison, Wisconsin*
Rock, William L.	1910-16	*Kansas City, Missouri*
	1928-31	
Rosacker, Hans	1938-41	*Minneapolis, Minnesota*
Rosaia, P. F.	1931-34	*Seattle, Washington*
Rossi, Angelo	1928-31	*San Francisco, California*
Saltford, W. A.	1927-30	*Poughkeepsie, New York*
Sanders, O. K.	1933-36	*St. Louis, Missouri*
Scanlan, Phillip E.	1940-47	*Chicago, Illinois*
Sceery, Edward	1917-23	*Paterson, New Jersey*
Schiller, Herman D.	1925-28	*Chicago, Illinois*
Schling, Max	1920-23	*New York, New York*
Schramm, Frank	1929-32	*Toledo, Ohio*
Schroeder, Nick	1947-50	*Portland, Oregon*
Schultheis, Miss Gertrude	1925-28	*Scranton, Pennsylvania*
Scott, James E.	1952-55	*Providence, Rhode Island*
Scott, Victor L.	1941-48	*Winnipeg, Manitoba*
Serveau, Alfred H.	1938-41	*San Francisco, California*
Seulberger, J. Fred, Jr.	1935-38	*Oakland, California*
	1941-48	
Siebrecht, Charles W.	1932-35	*Winona, Minnesota*
Simmons, Ernest S.	1932-35	*Toronto, Ontario*
	1941-48	
Simon, Al	1954-57	*Culver City, California*
Smoke, Bruno D.	1937-40	*Detroit, Michigan*
Smyth, William J.	1917-25	*Chicago, Illinois*
Stein, Victor	1948-50	*San Francisco, California*
Stoll, Victor W.	1950-53	*Hamilton, Ohio*
Strang, Andrew H.	1956-59	*Philadelphia, Pennsylvania*

Stumpp, G. E. M.	1914-17	*New York, New York*
Stuppy, Frank X.	1915-18	*St. Joseph, Missouri*
Swartz, Marty	1958-	*Dallas, Texas*
Swoboda, Herman	1940-46	*Omaha, Nebraska*
Thatcher, Frank A.	1931	*San Francisco, California*
Thompson, Harald	1951-54	*Rochester, Minnesota*
Thomson, Logan D.	1916-17	*Atlanta, Georgia*
Tobler, Earl	1958-	*Kansas City, Missouri*
Tryforos, Peter	1957-60	*New York, New York*
Valencia, Mrs. Sylvia M.	1955-58	*Westboro, Massachusetts*
Wademan, C. E.	1933-36	*Houston, Texas*
Waters, Mrs. Percy	1928-31	*Toronto, Ontario*
Weber, Fred C.	1930-33	*St. Louis, Missouri*
Weiland, John M.	1931-34	*Chicago, Illinois*
Wienhoeber, Ernst	1910-15	*Chicago, Illinois*
Wilson, James S.	1946-49	*Des Moines, Iowa*
Wolfe, T. J.	1916-19	*Waco, Texas*

DIRECTORS-AT-LARGE

1929-30	Henry Penn	*Boston, Massachusetts*
1930-31	H. Reeve Darling	*Los Angeles, California*
1931-32	Ernest S. Simmons	*Toronto, Ontario*
1932-33	Miss Rachel Butterworth	*Framingham, Mass.*
1933-34	Mrs. Bert Schiller McDonald	*Chicago, Illinois*
1934-35	Mrs. Amelia Gude Thomas	*Washington, D.C.*
1935-36	Miss Emily Dunn	*Cleveland, Ohio*
1936-37	Mrs. Irene Hayes	*New York, New York*
1937-38	Mrs. Alice Flick	*Ft. Wayne, Indiana*
1938-39	Mrs. Yvonne Benafel	*Los Angeles, California*
1939-40	Miss Margaret Blackistone	*Washington, D.C.*
1940-41	Mrs. Lauretta Rausch	*Chicago, Illinois*
1941-46	Miss Anabelle Smith	*Pasadena, California*
1946-47	Eugene C. Butler	*Niagara Falls, New York*
1947-48	Ben F. Siebrecht	*Aberdeen, South Dakota*
1948-49	Mrs. Geraldine Hale	*Dallas, Texas*
1949-50	Miss Elizabeth Bertermann	*Indianapolis, Indiana*
1950-51	Mrs. Maude Howard	*Salt Lake City, Utah*
1951-52	Mrs. Marion Fisher	*Syracuse, New York*
1952-53	Miss Emma Louise Pochelon	*Detroit, Michigan*
1953-54	Mrs. Jane Hunt Smith	*Humboldt, Tennessee*
1954-55	Miss Nellie Whitley	*Hamilton, Ontario*
1955-57	Mrs. Cel Scherrer	*San Antonio, Texas*
1957-59	Mrs. Kay Carron	*Biloxi, Mississippi*
1959-60	Mrs. Bessie Pawson	*Santa Ana, California*

CHAIRMEN

of the

FTD ASSOCIATE

MEMBERSHIP DIVISION

1928-29	C. C. Pollworth	*Milwaukee, Wisconsin*
1930	W. Ray Murphy	*Cincinnati, Ohio*
1931-32	William F. Ekas	*Baltimore, Maryland*
1933	N. A. Benson	*Denver, Colorado*
1934-36	Howard J. Hook	*Pittsburgh, Pennsylvania*
1937-38	Herbert M. Sauber	*Washington, D.C.*
1939-40	Ben J. Clarke	*Columbus, Ohio*
1941-45	Samuel S. Pennock, Jr.	*Baltimore, Maryland*
1946-47	James Sykora	*Chicago, Illinois*
1948-49	John Henry Dudley	*Lansing, Michigan*
1950-51	A. J. Grigsby	*Cleveland, Ohio*
1952-53	Oscar G. Carlstedt	*Jacksonville, Florida*
1954-55	Jack B. Kaufman	*Chicago, Illinois*
1956-57	James E. Kelly	*Rochester, New York*
1958-60	O. Ben Haley, Jr.	*Denver, Colorado*

FTD INTERFLORA

OFFICERS and DIRECTORS

PRESIDENTS

1948-49	Willmore F. Holbrow	*Dorchester, Massachusetts*
1951-53	H. Rollo Mueller	*Columbia, Missouri*
1956-57	Ed Ludwig	*Pittsburgh, Pennsylvania*
1959-60	Victor Stein	*San Francisco, California*

VICE-PRESIDENTS

1946-47	Willmore F. Holbrow	*Dorchester, Massachusetts*
1950-51	H. Rollo Mueller	*Columbia, Missouri*
1955-56	Ed Ludwig	*Pittsburgh, Pennsylvania*
1958-59	Victor Stein	*San Francisco, California*

SECRETARY AND TREASURER

1946-49	John Besemer	*Detroit, Michigan*
1949-52	Julius Pochelon	*Detroit, Michigan*
1952-53	Philip W. Jones	*Detroit, Michigan*
1954-55	John P. Beitler (Acting)	*Detroit, Michigan*
1959-	John L. Bodette	*Detroit, Michigan*

ASSISTANT SECRETARY AND TREASURER

1953-54	J. Paul Ostrander	*Detroit, Michigan*
1955-56	Morris R. Liles	*Detroit, Michigan*
1956-58	John L. Bodette	*Detroit, Michigan*

SECRETARY AND ASSISTANT TREASURER

1958-59	John L. Bodette	*Detroit, Michigan*

INTERFLORA DIRECTORS

1946-48	Alfred H. Serveau	*San Francisco, California*
1946-49	Charles I. Kent	*Cleveland, Ohio*
1946-50	Willmore F. Holbrow	*Dorchester, Massachusetts*
1948-51	William E. Joy	*Columbus, Georgia*
1949-50	Laurent E. Clody	*Chicago, Illinois*
1950-52	Leo J. McKenna	*Montreal, Quebec*
1949-56	H. Rollo Mueller	*Columbia, Missouri*
1951-54	Granville Gude	*Washington, D.C.*
1952-55	Henry Forster, Sr.	*Detroit, Michigan*
1954-57	James Lawrie	*Toronto, Ontario*
1955-58	Ed Ludwig	*Pittsburgh, Pennsylvania*
1956	Harald Thompson	*Rochester, Minnesota*
1956-59	Frank Schramm	*Toledo, Ohio*
1957-60	Victor Stein	*San Francisco, California*
1958-	Harold Kayton	*San Antonio, Texas*
1959-	Eugene R. Daudelin	*Chicago, Illinois*
1960-	Lou DiVito	*East Cleveland, Ohio*

FTD NATIONAL CONVENTIONS

YEAR	PLACE	ATTENDANCE	MEMBERSHIP
1910	Rochester, New York	15	15
1911	Baltimore, Maryland	6	40
1912	Chicago, Illinois	16	57
1913	Minneapolis, Minnesota	19	125
1914	Boston, Massachusetts		200
1915	San Francisco, California		250
1916	Chicago, Illinois		315
1917	Detroit, Michigan		469
1918	Cleveland, Ohio	89	589
1919	Buffalo, New York		1,188
1920	Indianapolis, Indiana		1,615
1921	Toronto, Ontario		2,200
1922	Baltimore, Maryland		2,400
1923	St. Louis, Missouri	800	2,917
1924	New York City, New York		2,700
1925	Atlanta, Georgia		2,769
1926	Chicago, Illinois		3,269
1927	Washington, D. C.		3,979
1928	West Baden, Indiana		4,781
1929	Boston, Massachusetts	500	5,361
1930	San Francisco, California		5,917
1931	Atlantic City, New Jersey		6,254
1932	Toronto, Ontario		6,414
1933	New Orleans, Louisiana	1,172	6,363
1934	Denver, Colorado	1,976	6,493
1935	Pittsburgh, Pennsylvania	2,500	6,698
1936	Dallas, Texas	1,700	6,702
1937	Philadelphia, Pennsylvania	3,000	7,151
1938	Portland, Oregon	1,200	7,667
1939	St. Paul, Minnesota	1,500	6,866
1940	Cincinnati, Ohio	2,689	6,975
1941	Los Angeles, California	2,000	6,512
1946	New York City, New York	4,000	6,806
1947	Chicago, Illinois	2,829	7,236

YEAR	PLACE	ATTENDANCE	MEMBERSHIP
1948	Miami Beach, Florida	1,537	7,790
1949	Montreal, Quebec	1,748	8,278
1950	San Francisco, California	1,571	8,650
1951	Washington, D. C.	1,526	9,087
1952	St. Louis, Missouri	1,588	9,343
1953	Houston, Texas	1,524	9,613
1954	Buffalo, New York	1,436	9,874
1955	Seattle, Washington	1,057	10,279
1956	Boston, Massachusetts	1,416	10,489
1957	Chicago, Illinois	1,909	10,731
1958	Miami Beach, Florida	1,482	11,955
1959	Los Angeles, California	1,632	11,317
1960	Detroit, Michigan	—	—